2030499

Richard A. Gaunt is Lecturer in Modern British History at the University of Nottingham and a Fellow of the Royal Historical Society. He has edited the diaries of a major Ultra-Tory politician of the period, *Unhappy Reactionary: The Diaries of the Fourth Duke of Newcastle under Lyne*, and a book of contemporary texts concerning Benjamin Disraeli. He has contributed to the *Oxford Dictionary of National Biography* and is currently writing *Conservative Politics in the Age of Reform: From Pitt the Younger to Sir Robert Peel, 1780–1850* (I.B.Tauris).

LIBRARY OF VICTORIAN STUDIES

Series ISBN: 978 1 84885 247 1

See www.ibtauris.com/LVS for a full list of titles

SIR ROBERT PEEL

The Life and Legacy

RICHARD A. GAUNT

I.B. TAURIS

LONDON · NEW YORK

Published in 2010 by I.B.Tauris & Co Ltd
6 Salem Road, London W2 4BU
175 Fifth Avenue, New York NY 10010
www.ibtauris.com

Distributed in the United States and Canada Exclusively by Palgrave Macmillan
175 Fifth Avenue, New York NY 10010

Library of Victorian Studies: 2

ISBN: 978 1 84885 035 4

A full CIP record for this book is available from the British Library
A full CIP record is available from the Library of Congress

Library of Congress Catalog Card Number: available

Printed and bound in India by Replika Press Pvt. Ltd.
from camera-ready copy, edited and supplied by 4word Ltd, Bristol

For Kevin

CONTENTS

ILLUSTRATIONS

All illustrations are reproduced from originals in the possession of Mr Nigel Morris.

ACKNOWLEDGEMENTS

My principal thanks must be to Dr Lester Crook, who first made me realise how much I wanted to write a book on Sir Robert Peel. I am also grateful to Lester's colleagues at I.B.Tauris (especially Liz Friend-Smith) for their help and assistance with the production process. John Roost and all at 4Word prepared the text for the publishers with their usual efficiency and professionalism.

I am grateful to all those who have helped me out during the process of researching and writing this book – not least Jack (gone but not forgotten) and Eli: 'go well now'. I would also like to thank the University of Nottingham for granting me research leave during the academic session 2007–8 in which to complete the book. Of friends and colleagues at the University, Denise Amos, Alan Booth, Harry Cocks, Roshan Das Nair, Colin Heywood, Caroline Kelly, Jane McVeagh, Philip Riden, Haniel Riviere-Allen and Amanda Samuels deserve special mention. I am particularly grateful to John Beckett and Chris Wrigley for reading and commenting on the book for me. For access to material, I would like to thank Bruce Dolphin and Jon Parry. I am grateful to the anonymous referee who commended the project to the A.H.R.C. Research Leave Scheme and the academic reader who reviewed the text for I.B.Tauris. I am also grateful to Lord Briggs of Lewes for his kind interest in the project. The Tamworth-based Peel Society continue to 'fly the flag' on Peel's behalf – my thanks to Norman, Mavis and David Biggs and Nigel and Jan Morris for their practical help and encouragement. I am particularly grateful to Nigel Morris, who provided the illustrations for the book from originals in his collection. I have been pleased to meet three of the most distinguished of Peel scholars and biographers – Norman Gash, Boyd Hilton and Douglas Hurd – at different times and in different settings. Whilst my portrait of Peel differs from theirs, in important respects, their contributions (individually and collectively) have been essential in helping shape what follows. Any errors or inaccuracies are, of course, entirely my own.

I am grateful to the custodians, archivists and keepers of manuscript collections listed in the bibliography for their help and assistance during my research. Dr Dorothy Johnston (Nottingham University Manuscripts Department), Professor Chris Woolgar (University of Southampton, Hartley Library), Mark Dorrington (Nottinghamshire Archives) and the staff of Sheffield Archives and the Record Offices of Durham,

Flintshire, Glamorgan and Northamptonshire merit special thanks. I am particularly grateful to the owners of privately held collections for permission to consult and quote from them: in particular, the Trustees, Chatsworth House Settlement (by permission of the Duke of Devonshire), the Harrowby Manuscripts Trust (by kind permission of the Earl of Harrowby), Lord Kenyon, Lord Mansfield and the Trustees of the Broadlands Trust. Michael Bosson of Sandon Hall, Staffordshire and Andrew Peppitt of Chatsworth House, Derbyshire were particularly helpful in my research in the Harrowby and Devonshire Collections.

Dr Joan D'Arcy first introduced me to the 'Age of Peel'. Half a lifetime later, I am still pleased to call her a friend. Helen Redhead also nurtured my youthful interest in history and has continued to take an interest in my subsequent teaching and academic career. Of friends and acquaintances who encouraged me during the writing-up process, Janice Avery, Peter Hatter (who took the author photograph: www.peterhatter.com), and Peter Hildebrand are due my thanks. As always, my family provided the bedrock of emotional support – and so much more – which was essential to the completion of this book. Of individual family members who have not previously received specific mention, John and Julie Gaunt and Shirley MacKenzie deserve their due. My mother Margaret and elder brother Patrick contributed more than they realise to the whole process of writing and research. The book is dedicated to Kevin Powell, without whose friendship, support and encouragement it would not have been completed.

Richard A. Gaunt

1

SIR ROBERT PEEL IN HISTORICAL PERSPECTIVE

Remember me when I am gone away,
Gone far away into the silent land...
Yet if you should forget me for a while
And afterwards remember, do not grieve:
For if the darkness and corruption leave
A vestige of the thoughts that once I had,
Better by far you should forget and smile
Than that you should remember and be sad.

Christina Rossetti (1830–94).

* * *

Sir Robert Peel was born on 5 February 1788 at Chamber Hall, near Bury, in Lancashire and died on Tuesday 2 July 1850 at 4 Whitehall Gardens, London, after a fall from his horse on Constitution Hill three days earlier. The contours of Peel's public life thus took him from the heartlands of industrial Lancashire to the centre of metropolitan London, from the crucible of the Industrial Revolution to the nucleus of political power. Peel was one of the most prominent political figures in nineteenth-century Britain. He was also one of the most controversial. In a parliamentary career extending over forty years (1809–50), he served – successively – as Under-Secretary of State for War and Colonies (1810–12), Chief Secretary to the Lord Lieutenant of Ireland (1812–18), Home Secretary (1822–7, 1828–30), Leader of the House of Commons (1828–30), Chancellor of the Exchequer (1834–5) and Prime Minister (1834–5, 1841–6). His historical reputation largely derives from the legislative achievements of his period in office and from being the first acknowledged leader of the Conservative Party (1834–46). As Home Secretary, Peel is remembered for the 'liberalisation' and consolidation of the criminal code, for statutes relating to magistrates, prisons and juries and, pre-eminently, as the founder of the Metropolitan Police Force in 1829. Indeed, this body still defines itself (as 'Bobbies' and 'Peelers') by reference to his name. As Prime Minister, Peel's reputation has been founded upon important 'Free Trade' Budgets of 1842 and 1845, a period of ground breaking legislation relating to Ireland (1843–5), a notable Bank Charter Act (in 1844) but above all for the Repeal of the Corn Laws in 1846. The irony for a man claimed as the 'Founder of Modern Conservatism' for his 'Tamworth Manifesto' (December 1834) is that his legislative record suggests he was the architect of Victorian Liberalism and Free Trade. The most prominent of his political legatees, the 'Peelites', made this connection tangible by joining the newly formed Liberal Party in 1859. William Ewart Gladstone, who emerged as the leading Liberal politician in mid- to late-Victorian England, nevertheless owed much to his political apprenticeship under Peel. This connection was reinforced subsequently by a Gladstonian-inspired historiography which claimed Peel for its own. This ensured that (insofar as his subsequent historical reputation and identity was concerned) Peel achieved a 'good death'. Yet Peel maintained that the acts which twice divided him from his ostensible followers – the concession of political rights to Catholics ('Catholic Emancipation') in 1829 and the Repeal of the Corn Laws in 1846 – were the most conservative of his life.[1]

As such, Peel's historical legacy remains a troubled, contested and at times doubtful one. Whilst Peel remains one of the few political figures to have inspired a group of politicians who claimed his name and mantle after his death, subsequent arguments over his temperament, manner and legacy tell a different story. The things for which Peel is principally remembered are those which, according to an alternative perspective, a Conservative ought never to have passed. Peel's successors as Conservative Party leaders may admire his name (many have not even done that) but are not keen to emulate his example.[2] Putting 'nation' before 'party' – as Peel claimed to have done in 1846 – cost the Conservatives power for nearly thirty years (between 1846 and 1874) and left him with a reputation for espousing causes which he had previously opposed. It is not, perhaps, surprising why Benjamin Disraeli's name and allure has proved the stronger of the two over the past 150 years.[3]

Yet neither image of Peel – the paragon or the pariah – is entirely satisfactory. Only accorded a complete, full-scale scholarly biography as late as 1972, Peel has continued to attract academic controversy ever since.[4] Consequently, his star has waxed and waned relative to those of Disraeli, Gladstone and (to a lesser extent) Palmerston. A perceived lack of warmth of personality has not helped resuscitate him as a personality nor compensated for any of the political deficiencies imputed to him by contemporaries. As William Thomas has noted:

> Peel was a strange mixture of public articulateness and private reserve. Unrivalled at setting out in parliament a piece of complex legislation, he was gauche and awkward in society and unskilled at forming an idea of the mood prevailing among colleagues and associates. His own huge capacity for work … blinded him to the motives … of men who looked on politics as a pastime and parliament as a club [or] those whose leading political views derived from party polemics or high theory … When undecided he preferred silence to consultation, and in the political crises which brought men crowding into the clubs to exchange news, he often held aloof.[5]

For a man who played so dominant a role in the government of his age, there is a remarkable and lingering sense of anonymity surrounding Peel.[6] Contemporaries and biographers have faced considerable problems in trying to locate him securely and satisfactorily in his political and ideological context. Even the opinions of long-standing friends – such as John Wilson Croker, who finally split with him over the Repeal of the Corn Laws – have been compromised by the knowledge that he could be cold and unforgiving towards them too.[7] Peel can hardly be relegated from the historiography of the period but historians are much more sceptical of according him the status which he achieved both immediately after his death and as a result of scholarly rehabilitation from the 1920s (when his papers first became publicly accessible) to the 1970s (when the first major biography based upon them was completed). This in itself provides an illuminating case study of our attitudes to the past.[8]

Whilst Peel occupies a central place in nineteenth-century British history and remains incapable of being ignored by students of political history in the period, his relative dominance over the historiography of his age has been severely challenged of late. In the first place, historians have moved to re-interpret Peel himself by presenting alternative visions of the driving force behind his acts and policies. Peel's political context (as Conservative or proto-Liberal) and his ideological context have thus assumed significance.

The notion that Peel was never a true Tory, but a Liberal wolf in sheep's clothing, has a long and distinguished pedigree. It was fuelled by tantalising – but uncorroborated – nuggets gleaned from the diaries of high-placed political observers like Charles Greville, Clerk to the Privy Council. According to Greville (who had it from Charles Arbuthnot), Peel's political future with the Tories was only secured when his father procured the Chief Secretaryship of Ireland for him in 1812.[9] Whether or not this was true, Peel was a prisoner, thereafter, to the circumstances of his political apprenticeship. As Lord Hatherton subsequently observed:

> Peel's great misfortune was to have been introduced into political life under the auspices of his father, and [Spencer] Perceval [the Prime Minister]. He was thus engaged in all the strife of Catholic Emancipation and reforms of various sorts – on the wrong side. His good sense enabled him gradually to throw off the thraldom of early connection, and when he became his own master, to disavow the false principles he had been made to defend. He thus appeared to forfeit consistency and character, though every man in his situation did the same thing…but we could do it unobserved and earlier than he could, for we had no engagements, and to us our constituents freely granted forgiveness of errors of opinion and the privilege to grow wiser with events. But classes and party attempted to hold him rigidly to the execution of their work, and on his refusal, attempted to brand him with infamy.[10]

Hatherton's observations had much to commend them. The characteristic secrecy in which Peel usually shrouded his political course of action compared markedly (and unfavourably) with the free and unrestrained enthusiasm he displayed when advocating Catholic Emancipation in 1829 and the Repeal of the Corn Laws in 1846. Peel appeared to exult in his liberation from unwelcome political allies by pursuing a course of action which (it was argued) he had intended all along.[11]

During the twentieth century, the dominant interpretations of Peel were those of a body of conservative-minded historians, George Kitson Clark, Robert Blake and Norman Gash, who stressed the pragmatic, expedient, flexible, centrist values of the man. In different ways, each of these historians championed the notion of Peel as an outstanding politician and statesman, wedded to the idea of a structured, rational and practical political system irrespective of party, faction or personal interest. As such, Peel responded to the challenges of his age by adapting his policies in the light of reasoned argument and practical necessity (the fear of political insurrection in Ireland in 1829, of social insurrection in Britain in 1845–6). This was done at the cost of his reputation for consistency but was ultimately to the benefit of the peace and harmony of the nation as a whole.[12] More recently, Boyd Hilton has mounted a successful (but by no means complete) challenge to this interpretation, suggesting that Peel was far from being a value-free pragmatist. Rather, Peel was an inflexible, driven, doctrinaire, 'hard-core' politician, much influenced by the evangelical religious thinking of his age. Hilton's work itself has been challenged and cannot be said to have wholly discarded the mid- to late-twentieth century view of Peel. Hilton's attribution of evangelical motives to Peel (and fellow 'liberal' Tories such as George Canning) has come in for particular criticism as has his argument that Peel was ideologically converted to the Repeal of the Corn Laws from the mid-1820s.[13]

There has also been a relative historiographical decline in Peel's centrality to events *vis-à-vis* other politicians. A notable recent trend has been the move to reassess those figures around Peel who were once thought to have been of secondary status. Significant reappraisals of Lord John Russell, the 14th Earl of Derby and the Duke of Wellington have each done something to 'close the gap' on Peel's pre-eminence and predominance in the period.[14]

The degree of Peel's ideological prominence – of the centrality of his vision of conservatism relative to other conservative identities – has similarly been challenged. In many respects, Peel remains the central figure through whom the dilemma of Conservatives and Conservatism were focused in this period; namely, how to embrace timely, practical and necessary reforms without compromising essentials or opening the floodgates to wider and more far-reaching changes. It was a dilemma which was crystallised by the French Revolution of 1789 and one which a subsequent generation of politicians had to deal with on a daily basis.[15] Lately, the historiography of the period has emphasised the composition, ideology and organisation of the 'massed troops' of Conservatism. No longer regarded as die-hard reactionaries or blinkered bigots, the protectionist politics of the Tory country gentleman have, for example, received corroboration and amplification in studies of Conservative periodicals, writers and intellectuals of the period. Peel emerges as the exponent of one form of response to the pressing social, economic and political issues of the day but by no means the only one which contemporaries thought available.[16]

This study does not offer a new cradle-to-grave biography of Sir Robert Peel. In many respects, as Gash himself has acknowledged, the work of the biographer (at least insofar as Peel is concerned) is done: 'it is now over the more subjective matters of motive, purpose, consequence, justification and significance that discussions and disagreements continue'.[17] Rather, this book offers a reinterpretation of Peel's attitudes to what he was doing in key areas of activity which have subsequently formed the nucleus of his political legacy. Each subsequent chapter addresses a major theme or crisis in Peel's career and analyses his role, his successes and failures and how each affected his career and reputation. This avenue of investigation was opened up by Donald Read in the last significant monograph-length work to be published on Peel. However, this was very much concerned with Peel's reputation at the time of his death, rather than with his own attempts to lay the foundations for his posthumous standing in posterity.[18] In August 1850, the Roman Catholic *Rambler* singled out six areas of achievement with which to associate Peel's name. Each of them has been subjected to lively debate and analysis in succeeding years. These six were: currency reform; reform of the criminal code; formation of the Metropolitan Police; Catholic Emancipation; reform of the Tariff and Repeal of the Corn Laws.[19] Perhaps understandably, the *Rambler* did not mention Peel's claims to have founded the Conservative Party – a central contention of Norman Gash's work. Nor can Peel's own character traits and personality and his unique position in British politics in the final four years of his life be exempted from any consideration of his political career. It is these which form the focus of investigation in this book. In the process, it offers a synthesis of the expanding historiography on Peel, whilst using new or under-utilised material from the extensive range of available printed sources for the period.[20]

By examining Peel's statecraft and political legacy in the areas of achievement with which contemporaries associated his name, it is possible to study the man himself. Peel was an extremely ambitious man both for himself and for his subsequent place in history. To that extent, Peel's statecraft was shaped and undertaken with at least one eye to his long-term reputation at the hands of contemporaries and future historians. This process of 'self-fashioning' had a different focus from that undertaken by his great political rival, Benjamin Disraeli, who was concerned with accommodating his self-acknowledged 'genius' to his own age, rather than to that of posterity.[21] In turn, this raises important questions about the current state of the historiography on Peel. How far are current historical opinions of Sir Robert Peel's political achievements and legacy reflective of his own attempts at 'reputation building' in the areas which he prioritised as significant and which contemporaries subsequently debated? To what extent was Peel's posthumous reputation, as set out by *The Rambler*, consciously fashioned, selected and chosen by Peel himself as an attempt to procure his posthumous fame? How far is it the consequence of his treatment at the hands of subsequent historians and biographers? To what extent did Peel's conceptions of his achievements mirror those of his contemporaries? Peel's stress on notions of honour, consistency, character and posterity, in respect of his public reputation, were frequently remarked upon by contemporaries. In 1848, for example, *Blackwood's Edinburgh Magazine* promised to leave Peel 'to the judgment of that posterity which he is so peculiarly prone to invoke'.[22] Peel's political evolution away from the strict Toryism of his youth towards the liberal-Conservatism of old age, in the manner noted by Hatherton, may be said to have made his posthumous legacy a matter of particular concern to him. Yet, as the next section demonstrates, this was the natural outcome of a highly complex and brittle personality who was always more feared and respected than liked.

* * *

1: 'Black Monday; Or, The Opening Of St. Stephen's Academy', *Punch*, VIII, January–June 1845, 71. Peel is seen leading a parade of political luminaries (including Wellington, Brougham, O'Connell, Disraeli and Russell) in to the Houses of Parliament.

Few politicians exercised a keener self-control over their acts and utterances than Robert Peel. His frequent invocation of posterity and history was remarked upon by more than one commentator as a telling indication of his character:

> Whenever [Peel] can speak, with modest pride, of himself, his origin, his purposes, his hopes; when the higher aim – historical renown – displaces for the hour the smaller, but more immediate stake – temporary opinion and power – upon which the ultimate triumph unfortunately rests; then ... you see that there is fire smouldering beneath – that there is a moral elevation you did not suspect – that his aspirations tend to a kind of greatness, not at all compatible with the popular notions of his character.[23]

At Hipperholme School in Lancashire, Peel is supposed to have displayed his early 'longing after immortality', by inscribing a block of stone with the inscription 'R. Peel. No hostile hands can antedate my doom.'[24] At the same time, Peel's tendency to 'play to the gallery' in the House of Commons by seeking after (and lapping up) their praise, revealed the self-consciousness that he was, socially speaking, an interloper, a cuckoo in the nest of aristocratic dominated politics.[25] For *Blackwood's Edinburgh Magazine*, writing after Peel's death, this was a fact which he (wisely) never tried to conceal. Lord Melbourne's biographer, W.M. Torrens, claimed that Peel's 'inveterate self-consciousness and nervous irritability' led him to weigh everything he said in parliament, to such an extent, 'that it might be said without exaggeration, before he answered a question or made a speech, he had in his mind corrected it for the press'.[26]

The sense that Peel was constantly weighing the effect of what he said on his public reputation was revealing. Throughout his life, Peel was renowned for a highly-strung temperament which he struggled carefully (and not always successfully) to keep in check. Peel always faced a twin dilemma. On the one hand, he was patronised and condescended to (from his youth upwards) as the cleverest boy amongst the rich but seemingly dim aristocratic wits amongst whom he was cast like pearls before swine. Lord Byron, his peer at Harrow, famously recalled that 'I was always in scrapes, and he never.'[27] Peel was the son of a well-to-do Lancashire calico printer and cotton manufacturer who had risen through the economic and social hierarchy to become a baronet, MP for Tamworth and close friend of the Prime Minister, William Pitt the Younger. Like Joseph Kennedy in the twentieth century, the elder Peel cherished political ambitions for his son which he was willing to finance liberally and 'set out, successfully, to found a dynasty'. The apocryphal admonition from father to son, though uncorroborated, has the ring of authenticity about it: 'Bob, you dog, if you are not Prime Minister some day I'll disinherit you.'[28]

The young Peel demonstrated a prodigious intellect but was hampered by what many of his compatriots regarded as an undistinguished social pedigree. He was the first scholar to take a double-first (in Classics and Mathematics) at the University of Oxford in 1808 – a fact of which his father was justifiably proud – having received a semi-private education at the hands of assorted clergymen and tutors before going up to Christ Church (the premier Oxford college).[29] Sir Lawrence Peel noted that, in his youth and schooldays, his cousin had been:

> under a strict discipline, a good boy of gentle manners, by choice rather seeking older than younger companions, shrinking from all rudeness or coarseness, praised by the old, and therefore not over popular with the young. He was quick in feeling, very sensitive, impatient of opposition from his young companions, and dreading ridicule overmuch.

This regime had served to act 'like an overtight ligature on a plant'.[30]

On the other hand, Peel was ostracised as a traitor to his class (both his native 'middle' and adopted 'upper' class) for his subsequent political conduct. One critic argued that Peel's class and upbringing personified 'two tendencies in constant opposition to one another'.[31] As the first ostensibly 'middle class' British Prime Minister (in terms of family origins and wealth), the expanding industrial and merchant classes of early-Victorian Britain expected him to realise their expectations of him.[32] In November 1845, after Peel turned the first clod of the Trent Valley Railway, *The Economist* expressed their disappointment in the following terms:

> We hope that models of the jenny and the dye vat will be placed side by side with the spade and the wheelbarrow; and remain for ever as memorials of the means by which the house of Peel rose into existence, and honoured the arts, by which its wealth and power were created. Then a wondering but not admiring posterity, contrasting these cherished memorials of the origin of the family greatness with Sir Robert Peel, will speak of him not merely as inconsistent and foolish, but as false and treacherous ... that the Prime Minister and labourer, who owed his elevation to industry and professed to govern by maxims of justice and civil wisdom, pretended to honour labour, and encourage the production of food, should have been false to the principles of his own greatness – a traitor to the cause he professed to serve ... in depriving industry of its reward, and the people of bread.

But *The Economist* had been established specifically to campaign for the Repeal of the Corn Laws and before the end of November 1845 it was still a matter of conjecture whether Peel would embrace that particular *volte face*.[33]

Peel's frequent public declarations that he was the son of a cotton spinner made good revealed a barely concealed sense of social self-consciousness which the new-modelled manor house he built himself at Drayton near Tamworth in Staffordshire and the acquisition of a fine collection of Dutch Renaissance masterpieces could never entirely compensate for.[34] As William Thomas has remarked:

> Peel's mastery of public business and his political acumen were legendary, but he had little general culture; or rather, he had cultural aspirations which his precocious political succession had left undernourished, and he kept wanting to abandon politics to pursue them ... Peel repeatedly announced his intention of retiring from politics, and sincerely hankered after the life of a country gentleman, but the only effect of this was to underline the fact that he was politically indispensable.[35]

Peel combined the rigidity of the self-made man (a rigidity which hardened into arrogance and an unwillingness to compromise his opinions) with a sense of high-handedness and autocracy. In 1828, Harriet Arbuthnot observed that Peel's 'low birth & vulgar manners would be not only forgiven but forgotten if he would practise the arts of conciliation'.[36] Peel's propensity to resignation threats (two in 1844 alone), his repeated statements of the unfettered terms on which he would exercise power (in advance of the 1841 General Election), his unwillingness to have the leadership of the Conservatives thrust upon him in 1831–2 (and to resume it after the schism of 1846)

THE PREMIER NAVIGATOR.

2: 'The Premier Navigator'. Peel's turning the first clod of the Trent Valley Railway. The barrow and spade were preserved in commemoration of the occasion.

all bespoke a dissatisfaction and restlessness with politics. Yet his indispensability to
Lord Liverpool and the Duke of Wellington during the Catholic Emancipation crises
of 1825 and 1829, his ability to scupper Wellington's plans to enter office on a
platform of Parliamentary Reform (in May 1832), his triumphant recall to office after
the Whigs disagreed amongst themselves in the autumn of 1845, his role as 'arbiter'
of British politics, keeping Russell's Whig government of 1846–52 afloat, all reflected
an acute self-awareness of his indispensability to the political process.[37]

Peel's consciousness of his own cleverness – a perception that he was the perfect
example of individual intelligence subverting the natural social order[38] – led him into
ill-concealed displays of condescension towards his political followers:

> when he was perfecting an argument which he considered conclusive of the
> question, [he would] turn round to his supporters, with his back to the House,
> his hands under his coat as before, and address his 'point' to them, with a
> delightful chuckling expression, as much as to say 'Is not that a good hit?' I
> cannot say that all this was very dignified, or that it was in accordance with our
> received notions of parliamentary action; but it was nevertheless very effective,
> and far more influential with the members than the most perfect specimens of
> the lofty, declamatory, stiff, automaton style of oratory … The average
> intelligence of the members being practical, they naturally inclined with a
> favourable feeling towards one who would condescend to meet them on their
> own peculiar ground; and, by that law of nature under which the inferior mind
> must submit to the superior, they at once acknowledged in him a *master-spirit*.[39]

For all their recognition of his merits, Peel's relationship with his political followers was
never harmonious. They spent their time complaining about his not wanting to be in
office, and then complaining about him when he was. Any sign of gauche conduct or
behaviour – from his lack of French to his 'vulgar' table habits – was seized upon with
icy disdain by political opponents and aristocratic detractors alike.[40] When Peel
unsuccessfully attempted to cultivate Queen Victoria's good favour, during the
'Bedchamber Crisis' of May 1839, he found an unlikely ally in Lord Melbourne, the
displaced Whig Prime Minister. With a condescension which revealed as much about
Melbourne's world-view as Peel's, he told the Queen:

> 'You must remember that [Peel] is a man who is not accustomed to talk to
> Kings; a man of quite a different calibre; it's not like me; I've been brought up
> with Kings and Princes. I know the whole Family, and know exactly what to say
> to them; now he has not that ease, and probably you were not at your ease'.[41]

From a similar perspective, Greville complained that Peel adopted the 'accustomed
attitude of a dancing master giving a lesson' whenever he was at Court.[42]

By way of compensation, Peel had the satisfaction of a secure and contented family
life, over which no whiff of scandal has ever been cast, and the independence born of
a substantial family fortune founded on his grandfather's migration from farming into

the manufacture of cotton goods.[43] The family's financial fortunes were burnished by his father's steady ascent to the achievement of a hereditary baronetage and an equally hereditary stake in the parliamentary representation of Tamworth in Staffordshire (which became the family's political fiefdom for several generations thereafter). This allowed the younger Peel to combine his father's political aspirations with his own pretensions to social and cultural gentility as a patron of the arts.[44]

According to one hostile polemicist, in 1844, 'there is nothing on which the premier values himself more [highly] than the slight knowledge he has in paintings'.[45] Whilst the artist Benjamin Haydon also thought Peel's knowledge lacking in some important particulars, he nevertheless echoed numerous contemporaries in acclaiming Peel's 'exquisite assemblage of gems'. This included Rubens' *Chapeau de Paille* ('The Straw Hat'), which has frequently been hailed as the acme of Peel's activities as a collector.[46] Peel's colleague Lord Ellenborough found him unusually relaxed and animated whenever he entered on the subject of art – in marked contrast to their usual personal relations – and numerous observers commented on Peel's interest and excitement in showing them his collection.[47] Undoubtedly, these events could become self-consciously political events as well as occasions upon which Peel could show-case his status as a 'self-made' man.[48] As Peel commented, on one occasion, 'I am, as you are well aware, possessed of probably the finest collection of portraits of distinguished Englishmen to be found in my private gallery in the country numbering eleven Prime Ministers of England exclusive of several busts of great men.'[49] When he opened his London home to 500 select visitors, in April 1847, Peel made special efforts to invite reporters and journalists and plied them with fulsome praise – even Thackeray (a writer for the satirical illustrated weekly *Punch*). This 'seeking popularity by fulsome praise' amused traditionalists.[50] Unfortunately for Peel, it did not garner him a more flattering press from *Punch*:

> Several of our contemporaries have been giving very interesting details respecting a portrait gallery which Sir Robert Peel has lately formed with much completeness. Politicians of every shade and every turn are to be found ranged side by side in this remarkable collection. It is not, however, generally known that the room is lighted by a lantern in the centre, which represents on its six sides the portraits of the proprietor in six of his most favourite characters. The lantern is a revolving one, so that Sir Robert Peel is represented in such a manner as to enable him to keep all his friends in countenance. The room is full of all the lights of the age, but the great revolving light of the age most appropriately occupies the centre.[51]

Peel's reputation as a parliamentary orator was second only to his fame as a connoisseur of fine art. Indeed, in many respects, Peel's oratorical reputation was the foundation of his political success and assured his early entry into ministerial office. It was Lord Ashley's contention that Peel was a 'master in the art of talking'. The compliment was clearly double-edged.[52] It was reinforced by Ellenborough's suggestion that, for all Peel's renown as a public speaker, he retained 'great faults as a Speaker. He is too slow in his delivery. He drops his voice frequently, & having once got possession of his audience he sometimes drops them. He has no élan – but he is a powerful reasoner & has great tact.'[53]

A more searching and frequently expressed criticism of Peel was his tendency to assume an air of artificiality and affectation – a charge usually levelled at the young Disraeli. *Punch* thought Peel's speeches 'bore a remarkable resemblance to Turner's pictures. Both of them are admirable, but neither of them understood'.[54] This was the more surprising given that, according to Gladstone, Peel was 'inclined to think that the less preparation a young man makes for his first speech, the better'. However, Peel also advised Gladstone never to be too short, when speaking officially.[55] G.H. Francis considered Peel's over-forced oratorical style denied him true renown as a public speaker – 'the fame of a first-rate orator would never have satisfied Sir Robert Peel's ambition, even if he could have attained it':

> His style is correct, not elegant; elaborate, but not graceful. With great fluency of words he has little power over language … He opens a great speech – as, for instance, in introducing the Income-tax, or his currency plans – with a pompous pretension, an exaggerated solemnity, a half inaudible tone of breathless importance, that is itself almost burlesque. At other times he condescends to an unworthy levity. Though he but seldom perpetrates jokes, he usually chokes them in the utterance, by chuckling over them before hand.[56]

Robert Lowery, visiting the House of Commons for the first time in 1839, was also disappointed at the poor quality of parliamentary eloquence. He was particularly surprised at Peel, who 'would not have commanded the attention of a working man's meeting'.[57]

Nothing was more likely to disturb the habitual self-control which Peel demonstrated in the House of Commons than an indictment of his honour.[58] 'Charge him with any thing, either in his private or public capacity, inconsistent with the character of a man of honour,' the parliamentary sketch-writer James Grant observed in 1836, 'and that moment he demands an explanation, which if not satisfactory … will be followed up … by a challenge to a hostile meeting.' In a political system still animated by a highly-prized sense of the aristocratic ideal, Peel embraced its code of ethics with more than usual vigour.[59] Few high ranking political figures issued more challenges for the 'satisfaction of a gentleman' than Peel. The most famous (in September 1815) involved his inveterate political opponent, Daniel O'Connell, the leader of the campaign for Catholic Emancipation and the Repeal of the Act of Union between Britain and Ireland. Having publicly attacked O'Connell, from his seat in the House of Commons, on more than one occasion, Peel responded to his adversary's claim that he had not the courage to deliver such a charge without the immunity afforded by parliamentary privilege by goading him into a challenge. He pursued his prey thereafter with a determination which was truly remarkable, considering that O'Connell had killed John Norcot D'Esterre, a member of the Guild of Merchants in Dublin, in a duel barely six months before. For a man charged with upholding the civil government of Ireland and England, at different stages in his career, Peel demonstrated an unnerving degree of success in evading the authorities, who were charged with preventing the two men from escaping to the Continent in order to settle their differences in person. In the event, O'Connell's wife ('fearing for her husband's life') facilitated his arrest by the authorities. He was subsequently bound over to remain in England. The dispute between the two men was taken up by their respective seconds, Samuel Brown and George Lidwill, and – as a result of Peel's sensitivity to some subsequent remarks by the latter – by Peel and Lidwill themselves. The initial dispute between O'Connell and Peel endured for a decade, until the Irishman issued an apology in 1825.[60]

Six years later, Peel sent Sir Henry Hardinge to upbraid J.C. Hobhouse for 'using strong language in my speech of April 26 [1831]'; Hardinge informed him that, if the matter were not settled satisfactorily, a 'meeting' would be arranged between them at Dover. Hobhouse denied uttering one of the two sentences which Peel complained of as derogatory to his honour. In the event, the *contretemps* was settled between the two 'seconds', Lord Dacre and Hardinge.[61]

Peel's disputes with O'Connell and Hobhouse were characteristic of his sensitivity to slights and rebukes by political opponents. He felt these to a degree which was quite exceptional in a high-ranking political figure, who served as a Minister of the Crown, Leader of the Opposition and Prime Minister.[62] In 1837, after a dispute arose between Peel and Captain Townshend, his opponent at Tamworth in the General Election, Peel was again on the verge of pursuing his political differences to the point of a gun. John Walter, of *The Times*, considered that Peel's life was 'too valuable to be risked against petty adversaries'. To Croker, he expressed a wish that some 'means could be devised whereby he might avoid incurring those hazards, to which he has been more exposed than any other public man of his day, and to which he will be yet more exposed if he returns to office'.[63] Ruminating on the issue to Peel's prospective biographer (Goldwin Smith), nearly thirty years later, Edward Cardwell regarded the incident as indicative of the prevailing influences of Peel's day:

He came into public life when the vulgar mind of George IV had a great influence upon society: when aristocratic insolence was high: and when the son of a Cotton Spinner could not lead the House of Commons without being exposed to many, mortifying proofs that he was not regarded by those around him as one of themselves. Duelling in those days was not only considered gentlemanlike, but was a touchstone of good breeding ... Railways, Reform Bills, & other salutary influences have taught us better views of life. But I am not surprised at a challenge in 1837 when I recollect the state of feeling in 1841. I had then a bitter contest, and if I had met with any personal insult, I think I should have been considered a coward if I had not resorted to the common mode of vindicating my character – In 1847, it was probably a doubtful point: & in 1852 I should have been regarded as an idiot if I had thought of such a course.[64]

Cardwell struck a different note in talking to Edward Stanley during the same period. Cardwell recalled that Peel had nearly 'called out' Lord George Bentinck for his parliamentary attacks upon him during the Repeal of the Corn Laws. He had only been dissuaded from this course of action by the Earl of Lincoln (his chosen second on the occasion). Cardwell commented that the transaction appeared to him to be 'extraordinary'.[65] It is hard to escape the conclusion that Peel defended the 'common mode of vindicating [his] character' to a more than usual extent – pointedly refusing to legislate against the practice of duelling during his time in office.[66]

Given Peel's constant genuflection to the sanctity of principle and honour, it is hardly surprising to find that he lacked a well-developed sense of the ridiculous or much of a reputation for good humour. According to Hobhouse, 'his genius was too ponderous for a joke'.[67] No facet of Peel's character was more frequently and bitterly remarked upon by contemporaries than his lack of health and temper. For all Peel's undoubted skills as a politician and parliamentarian, friend and foe alike were united in considering him a remarkably ill-tempered and implacable personality with whom to deal. Disraeli knew Peel to be, 'by reputation, the most jealous, frigid and haughty of men' and took any sign to the contrary as a remarkable proof of personal confidence in him.[68] This element of Peel's constitutional make-up was a particular crotchet of Harriet Arbuthnot, the 'microphone of muttered gossip',[69] who acted as Wellington's political confidante and unofficial private secretary. 'As to Peel [she remarked in 1831] he appears to hate every body & every body hates him:'

> he is cross grained, timid, afraid of committing himself, afraid of having followers & a party for fear they should be a clog upon him in any future arrangements ... If any of the young men are anxious to speak, he throws cold water on it because speaking well would give claims; & yet, while he was in office, he never ceased to complain of getting no support. He is supercilious, haughty & arrogant & a most bitter & determined hater.[70]

Her husband was no more enamoured of Peel, four years later, during his first period as Prime Minister. To Wellington, he complained that Peel 'has not what I should call the feelings of a high bred gentleman; but is always actuated by personal and selfish motives ... He keeps all his ill temper for his friends'.[71]

Peel was never considered clubbable. Dining in company with him, Ashley thought himself in 'the neighbourhood of an ice-berg with a slight thaw on its surface'. On another occasion, he described Peel as 'an exaggeration & caricature of his habitual coldness'. The young Edward Stanley also found Peel unwilling to say 'more than politeness required'.[72] When Lionel Tollemache tackled Gladstone (late in life) on the subject of his mentor's unsociability, Gladstone responded that Peel's 'mind was too full of the public interest to be able to occupy itself with smaller matters'. Gladstone regaled Tollemache with 'examples of Peel's communicativeness' which seemed 'conspicuous by their slightness'.[73]

Gladstone's underlying point was not unmerited. Peel set new standards of Prime Ministerial labour, personifying the determination, industry and attention to detail which was the hallmark of his political success. This came at an immense physical and psychological burden upon him. As Asa Briggs shrewdly observed, whilst Lord Ashley was busy campaigning for a restriction on the working hours of industrial operatives during the 1840s, Peel never limited himself (as Prime Minister) to a ten hour day.[74] 'We never had a Minister who was so truly a First Minister as he is [Sir James Graham observed, in 1842] he makes himself felt in every department and is really cognisant of the affairs of each.'[75] At the same time, few politicians carried the burdens of office more self-consciously than Peel. He was self-absorbed by their burdens and animated with a sense of the personal sacrifice he was making in enduring them. On one occasion, Hobhouse went down to the House of Commons to find Peel 'talking, as usual, a great deal of his own purity'.[76] In a much-quoted letter to Charles Arbuthnot (which reflected comments Peel communicated to a range of correspondents), the Prime Minister indicated how severe the toll was becoming, not only upon him personally, but on the good government of the country:

> I defy the Minister of this country to perform properly the duties of his office – to read all that he ought to read, including the whole foreign correspondence, to keep up the constant communication which he must keep up with the Queen and the PRINCE [*sic*] – to see all whom he ought to see – to superintend the grant of honours and the disposal of civil and ecclesiastical patronage – to write with his own hand to every person of note who chooses to write to him – to be prepared for every debate including the most trumpery concerns: to do all these indispensable things – and also sit in the House of Commons eight hours a day for 118 days.[77]

The burdens in attending upon the Court were especially onerous, according to Peel. To Gladstone, he confessed the advantages of being Prime Minister from the House of Lords, 'which would get rid of the very encroaching duty of attendance on and correspondence with the Queen'. Stanley felt that some of the time Peel spent with the royal couple might profitably be surrendered to 'the purpose of paying such attentions' to the younger Conservative MPs as might counteract their 'insubordination'. The Queen herself (responding to the promptings of her constitutional adviser, the King of the Belgians) did what she could to rally the morale of her beleaguered and over-stretched Prime Minister.[78]

Peel's sense of self-sacrifice was almost as great as his sense of ambition and an over-bearing egotism which was more than usually remarked upon.[79] 'Under that placid exterior [Greville commented in 1833] he conceals, I believe, a boundless ambition'. The same point was made two years earlier by Lord Ellenborough – 'His talent is eminently fitted for turning things to his own account ... He thinks only of Sir Robert Peel.'[80] During the state visit of the Emperor of Russia, in 1844, *Punch* sarcastically observed that, in attending the Windsor Review with Queen Victoria and the Emperor, 'Sir Robert Peel, the only individual out of uniform, pranced about considerably ... as much as to say, "Look at me, I take the lead in everything".' Elsewhere, the magazine portrayed him as the political equivalent of Pecksniff,

Dickens' character in *Martin Chuzzlewit* (1843–4), who was never slow to 'puff' his own achievements.[81]

Peel's habitual egotism (which was remarked upon as characteristic of him in private as well as public company)[82] might have come with a better grace had he not been so grudging in the acknowledgement of other people's success. In March 1844, *The Economist* calculated that Peel 'contrived to use the word "myself" ten times, the word "me" twenty-six times, the word "my" forty-two times, and the word "I" three hundred and fifty times' in the course of one parliamentary speech.[83] By contrast, according to Gladstone, Peel 'was the most conscientious man I ever knew in spareness of eulogium' in praising the parliamentary speeches of others.[84]

The issue of Peel's character thus relates directly to his political conduct, his desire for posthumous fame to his political statecraft. Endowed with talents which made him gifted, ambitious and determined, Peel was at the same time aloof, self-contained, impatient, moody and earnest. The two facets of Peel's character merged, even at moments of the highest 'statesmanship'. In July 1850 *The Illustrated London News* reflected upon this in pointed terms:

> It is argued that if conviction, or expediency, or State necessity, or whatever motive had led Sir Robert Peel to see that the time was come for a change of policy, he ought not to have been the Minister to introduce the measures which he had consistently and perseveringly obstructed … An obvious suspicion suggests itself, that ambition and a love of fame may have influenced Sir Robert Peel in seizing on two such great and tempting occasions [as Catholic Emancipation in 1829 and the Repeal of the Corn Laws in 1846] to inscribe his name on the page of history. There may be some truth in the imputation that he was disinclined to forego the dazzling reward.

Although the journal distanced itself from this interpretation of Peel's actions, the fact that they raised it at all is highly suggestive.[85]

As such, given that historians have lately devoted so much collective energy to unravelling 'the Mind of Mr Gladstone', the 'Self-fashioning of Disraeli' and 'Lord Salisbury's World',[86] in order to understand more about their 'springs of action', would it not appear time to delve in to 'the ego of Sir Robert Peel'?[87]

2

'ORANGE PEEL'? CATHOLIC EMANCIPATION AND POLICY TOWARDS IRELAND

... that ludicrous enemy of ours, who has got in jest the name he deserves in good earnest – that of Orange Peel – a raw youth, squeezed out of the workings of I know not what factory in England ... sent over here before he got rid of the foppery of perfumed handkerchiefs and thin shoes, upon the ground, I suppose, that he had given a specimen of his talents for vindication, that might be useful to the present and future administrations of Ireland; in short, that he was a lad ready to vindicate anything – everything.

Daniel O'Connell, Speech to the Catholic Board, 29 May 1813.[1]

* * *

Ireland has been the rock upon which many promising political careers have been forged – or broken. For Robert Peel, it did something of both. Before the Catholic Emancipation crisis of 1829 Ireland was the foundation of Peel's political fortunes. As Chief Secretary to the Lord Lieutenant of Ireland, between 1812 and 1818, Peel established his reputation for administrative competence whilst gathering an intimate (but essentially executive-oriented) knowledge of the problems in 'John Bull's other island'. Long before Macaulay christened Gladstone 'the rising hope of those stern unbending Tories', for his defence of the constitutional connection between the Anglican Church and the State, Peel had attracted high favour for his unyielding defence of the Protestant settlement and the consequent subordination of the Catholic majority in Ireland. However, Ireland was in many respects the tragic thread running through Peel's career and the sources of his success before 1829 came at a heavy price, in terms of his reputation and consistency, thereafter. The defence of the Church of Ireland provided a rallying-point for the Conservative Party, during the 1830s, and a key element in its success in the 1841 General Election. However, Peel's subsequent Irish policy suggested that 'Orange Peel' (the sobriquet applied to him by O'Connell in his youth) had 'ripened' into something else. Indeed, for Gladstone, the crisis of Catholic Emancipation marked the dividing line in Peel's life, separating the aspiring politician from the mature and 'profound statesman'.[2] To what extent contemporaries and historians have shared this judgement is the focus of this chapter.

* * *

Robert Peel's connection with Ireland was established from his first return to Parliament. In April 1809 he entered the House of Commons, with government backing, for the Irish pocket borough of Cashel in Tipperary.[3] In May 1812 he was appointed Chief Secretary to Ireland in Lord Liverpool's administration.[4] This was a post which Peel occupied until August 1818 – longer than all but two of his eighteenth-century predecessors and all of his nineteenth-century successors.[5]

In retrospect, it is tempting to exaggerate the importance of the post of Chief Secretary to being akin to that of 'Prime Minister' of Ireland.[6] It is better to regard it as the necessary administrative conduit between an unpopular Protestant 'Ascendancy' administration at Dublin Castle and the British government in London. Peel was charged with supervising the conduct of Irish policy on both sides of the Irish Sea and travelled to London for six to seven months each year in order to see legislation through parliament and account to MPs for the government's Irish policy. The relatively loose definition of the role, during this period, enabled an ambitious incumbent 'to enlarge their sphere of responsibilities at the expense of central government': an opportunity which Peel seized with relish.[7] Peel was second choice for the post of Chief Secretary (after William Huskisson) but enjoyed the warm support of Liverpool, with whom he had worked at the Department of War and Colonies between 1810 and 1812.[8] After some initial reluctance Peel also gained the confidence of the Irish Viceroy, the Duke of Richmond.[9]

It was these strong personal recommendations, as well as the considerable latitude allowed to the Chief Secretary, which enabled Peel to gain such dominance within the Irish administration during his time in Dublin. In turn, the office served his ambitions well, burnishing his reputation as an administrator and politician in a way which few of his predecessors had sought or achieved. Peel 'possessed qualities of application and analysis which impressed and persuaded his older and more experienced political superiors'. This enabled him 'to increase the visibility of the office and make it the centre of a powerful web of influence and authority'.[10] In turn, this gave him a profile and a reputation which he might otherwise have lacked. As one (sometimes jaundiced) commentator observed, at this period, 'it seems to belong to Mr Peel's character to do well whatever he undertakes'.[11]

However, the corollary of this was a hardening of the habits of self-reliance and arrogance within Peel's governing temperament. These characteristics were already fully matured by the time that he took leave of Ireland, with a mixture of relief, self-satisfaction and contempt, in the autumn of 1818. Two contrasting quotations are, in this respect, revealing. On 23 July 1818 Peel publicly addressed the Corporation of Dublin, expressing the:

hope and belief that the motives of my public conduct will be justly appreciated, with deep gratitude for the kindness and liberality which I have experienced, and with the most heartfelt wish for the welfare and happiness of all classes of the inhabitants of this country, I shall bid adieu to it with stronger and more generous feelings of attachment to Ireland than mere obligations of official duty could have inspired, and with an interest in her fortunes which will not be extinguished or abated when those obligations shall have ceased.[12]

To his close friend, John Wilson Croker, Peel struck a rather different note, during the same period:

A fortnight hence I shall be free as air – free from ten thousand engagements which I cannot fulfil; free from the anxiety of having more to do than it is possible to do well; free from the acknowledgments of that gratitude which consists in a lively sense of future favours … free from Orangemen; free from Ribbonmen … free from the Lord Mayor and Sheriffs … free from Catholics who become Protestants to get into Parliament … free from perpetual converse about the Harbour of Howth and Dublin Bay haddock; and, lastly, free of the Company of Carvers and Gilders which I became this day in reward of my public services.[13]

Peel's unbounded capacity for hard-work and the single-mindedness with which he acquired his knowledge of official business were undoubtedly crucial in compensating for some of the material deficiencies of his office. To Charles Abbot, for example, Peel complained about the inadequacy of the Chief Secretary's working library.[14] As a young, unmarried politician, he was able to occupy himself completely with official business and the social intercourse which accompanied it. 'I have scarcely dined once at home since my arrival [he informed Croker within weeks of his arrival]. I see no great prospect of it for some time to come, excepting with about twenty-five guests.' Peel acquired a reputation for living in splendour which frightened his successors in the post – not least Henry Goulburn, who went to Ireland in 1822.[15] Maintaining a frenzied round of personal entertaining was of apiece with making the Chief Secretary the indispensable source of Irish patronage – a role which Peel attached to the office for the first time and tenaciously held on to thereafter. Although patronage-hunters were a species of humanity Peel always regarded with disdain, the reality of governing Ireland successfully was intimately connected with a succession of jobs and favours. As John Prest argues, Peel 'found the tools with which he was constrained to work, a jobbing aristocracy with a "vortex of local patronage" … distasteful, [but] he had been called upon to govern Ireland "circumstanced as Ireland now is"'.[16] Politically speaking, Peel knew that controlling the flow of patronage was essential in manufacturing an identity of interest between the recipients of government favour and the Union with Britain (which was still barely a decade old).[17] For similar reasons, Peel attempted to rectify what he regarded as irregularities in the Irish newspaper press, a sizable portion of which relied on subsidies from Dublin Castle. From his earliest days in office, Peel identified the press as the major constituent factor in stirring up agrarian disturbance and sectarian disputes in Ireland, targeting John Magee, the editor of the *Dublin Evening Post*, for particular assault. Peel was also careful to encourage a good press for himself, using it to publicise activities and initiatives directly associated with his name.[18]

Peel's efforts to foster a network of patronage and re-assert the Castle's control over the press were only part of his success. Richmond's departure from Ireland in 1813 and his replacement with the inoffensive Lord Whitworth (who remained as Lord Lieutenant until 1817) helped enhance Peel's dominance within the administration. He resisted attempts to combine the post of Chief Secretary with that of Irish Chancellor of the Exchequer, in imitation of his predecessors, successfully pressing his friend Vesey Fitzgerald to continue in office until the Irish and English Treasuries were combined in 1817.[19] Peel also developed genuinely strong working relationships with his closest colleagues – the Under-Secretary for Civil Affairs, William Gregory, and the Irish Attorney General, William Saurin – although neither of them was allowed to forget that he was their political superior. The Home Secretary, Lord Sidmouth, who was Peel's principal link with the government in London, also gave Peel a large amount of discretion. This was the result of Sidmouth's comparative lack of interest in Irish affairs, preoccupation with pressing domestic disturbances in England and growing estimation of Peel's abilities.[20] However, Peel did not extend a similar compliment to either Goulburn or Lord Francis Leveson Gower when he was Home Secretary and they were Chief Secretary. The fact that Irish business was usually debated in the House of Commons at the close of the parliamentary session, when MPs drifted away to more congenial pursuits, both reinforced Peel's self-reliance and mitigated some of the severities of opposition which he might otherwise have encountered.[21]

In subsequent years, the office of Chief Secretary was described as 'the nursery in which the future legislators of England were sent unfledged to develop their powers of mischief'.[22] This charge was borne out by the fact that, of future British Prime Ministers, Wellington, Peel, Melbourne and Stanley all cut their political teeth in the role. According to 'the old woman who lived at the Porter's Lodge of the Chief Secretary's House in Phoenix Park', Melbourne 'was by far the handsomest' of the secretaries since the Union, 'but Mr Wellesley Pole [Peel's predecessor] was by far the best; he kept the place alive; carriages rolling in to dinner every day'.[23] By contrast, Peel's tenure of the office brought him few lasting plaudits. Jean Baptiste Capefigue described Peel's conduct as Chief Secretary as 'deplorable', whilst Sir James Prior (who published a life of the leading Irish parliamentarian and politician, Edmund Burke, in 1824) felt that it contributed nothing to his mature reputation – he was writing in 1827. A decade later, Peel was condemned as 'the stubborn oppressor of Ireland, the foremost champion of the penal laws, the grand enslaver of the Roman Catholics' who had 'called agitation and O'Connell into existence; he was the spawn of your intolerance … a monster of your own nurturing'. By contrast, during the 1840s, Peel was addressed as one whose 'official residence in Ireland' had made him 'conversant with the mode of life and habits of the peasantry, so as to qualify you to appreciate, better than any of your predecessors in office, reasonings founded upon them'.[24] The difference in style and tone amongst contemporaries would appear to vindicate Gladstone's notion of a 'ripened' and 'un-ripened' Peel.

Peel went to Ireland relatively untried and with little of the sense of expectation (personal or political) which attached to his successors. Lady Charleville, on first making his acquaintance, found that he had 'a very sharp countenance & unaffected manner, but nothing very polished or genteel in his address or person'.[25] There was relatively little, at this period which could be attached to Peel, that was on public record. His maiden speech had been notable largely for its unflinching support for the government's military strategy in the Napoleonic Wars (notably, its failed Walcheren expedition). Subsequent speeches had established his opposition to Catholic Relief.[26] Peel's early ministerial experience at the Colonial Office (1810–12) imbued him with the kind of imperialist mentality which befitted a Chief Secretary, given that Ireland continued to be regarded by British policy-makers in colonial terms as exceptional (in the sense of different) because of its geography, culture, economics, society and religion.[27] As Peel reminded the Speaker of the Commons, himself a former Chief Secretary, in 1818, any efforts at legislation on the part of the Protestant executive were always likely to be 'embarrassed' by the overwhelming Catholic majority in the country.[28] This may explain why Daniel O'Connell, the leader of the campaign for Catholic Emancipation, attacked Peel as both an imperialist (for defending Walcheren) and a sectarian (for opposing Catholic Relief) in his famous 'Orange Peel' speech of May 1813, regarding it as symptomatic of Peel's oppressive attitude towards human problems.[29]

Historians have generally concurred in seeing Peel as pre-occupied with an administrative concern for constitutional and political stability (law and order, the defence of the Protestant establishment in Church and State) rather than social and economic amelioration, during his period as Chief Secretary.[30] Peel has also been accused of an inherent lack of sympathy for the Irish people. According to Magdalen Goffin, Peel 'displayed a narrow Protestant provincialism. He had no liking for the Irish – no understanding of their religion, temperament or way of life, least of all their national aspirations'.[31] Theo Hoppen has called Peel 'the most eloquent exponent of coercion', during this period, having once informed Gregory that 'an honest despotic Government [was] by far the fittest government for Ireland'.[32] The extent to which this accurately reflects Peel's personal predilections may be judged by some of his recorded table-talk for the period. This was preoccupied with tales of sectarian outrage, revenge and murder rather than sympathetic renditions of the plight of the Irish peasant labourer. Peel had a 'biting, sardonic wit' in respect of the Irish – whether it concerned disappointed claimants for government patronage or the plaintive cries of those embarked on the long and stormy passage from Holyhead to Dublin.[33] As Hoppen argues, 'a species of jocular insouciance came to mark his utterances'. Whilst Peel sometimes claimed to speak 'as an Irishman', the sentiment was not seriously intended. 'I never yet saw an Irishman ... that had not something Irish about him,' he told Goulburn, 'a statement as coolly tautological as it was wonderfully (and almost certainly deliberately) revealing.'[34] An equally telling indication of Peel's sentiments may be that, after 1818, although Ireland dominated his mature political career (indeed, had helped to make it) he never again attempted to revisit it for pleasure, habitually preferring the Scottish Highlands for that purpose.[35]

* * *

The passage of Catholic Emancipation, in April 1829, was the defining moment in Peel's political career before 1830 – and the one he found it hardest to live down thereafter. In its simplest form, the issue concerned the remaining legal restrictions preventing Roman Catholics from holding civic or political office – notably, as Members of Parliament. But it was interwoven with a complex web of cultural and political attitudes arising from suspicion, fear, bigotry and prejudice: the consequence of three centuries of sectarian dispute between Protestants and Catholics.[36] The question bedevilled British politics from the time of the Act of Union with Ireland (1800), serving to define political relationships and shape individual careers on both sides of the issue. Support for Emancipation materially contributed to the fall of two ministries (Pitt's in 1801 and Grenville's in 1807) whilst opposition to it influenced the terms upon which six others were formed (between 1807 and 1828). In Castlereagh, Canning, Burdett, Brougham, Grattan and Plunkett, Emancipation possessed advocates who were fluent, skilled and practised in terms of parliamentary oratory and political manoeuvre. By contrast, defenders of the Protestant Establishment appeared to be haemorrhaging voting support and gifted orators with each parliamentary session, given the regularity with which the Commons passed Catholic Relief measures only to have them frustrated by the House of Lords and the Crown.[37]

Given the paucity of like-minded ministerial talent in the House of Commons – most of the avowed 'Protestants' (or opponents of Emancipation) being in the House of Lords – Peel's place at the 'head of political Protestantism' after 1812 was almost guaranteed. It was reinforced by the fact that he held, successively, two portfolios (Chief Secretary and Home Secretary) necessitating close connection with Irish affairs. Whilst Peel's administrative capacity and skills in parliamentary debate would have assured him high ministerial office in Liverpool's administration, at any time after 1818, it was his 'self-appointed' role as 'protector of the Protestant cause' which made him indispensable in those very offices. In 1812, Peel and the Irish administration constituted a Protestant 'phalanx' against change after Canning and Wellesley failed in their attempt to form a more 'Catholic' (or pro-Emancipation) ministry.[38] Thirteen years later, when Sir Francis Burdett's Catholic Relief Bill passed the Commons, Peel threatened resignation, being conscious of his exposed position on a front-bench overwhelmingly supportive of Catholic claims.[39] Bathurst and Wellington attempted to dissuade him, knowing that Peel's departure would expose Liverpool who would, in turn, resign himself. Bathurst assured Liverpool that Peel's was an exceptional case, the consequences of which were 'of a very limited nature; your resignation is the dissolution of the Government'. The Prime Minister's reply was pointed:

> Who could replace Peel? It must not be an *ordinary man*. A moment's reflection will convince you that the man cannot be found...The first minister is

necessarily at the head of every department when *important business* is concerned, and I feel with Mr Pitt and Lord Grenville that the Secretary of State for the Home Department ought especially to be a person who agrees in opinion with him.[40]

Liverpool's response was a testament to Peel's indispensability as a minister and as the acknowledged parliamentary champion of the Protestant cause. By this point, the two roles were incapable of being disentangled satisfactorily. The tension between them limited Peel's room for manoeuvre and frustrated him at every turn until he abandoned the attempt and piloted Catholic Emancipation through the House of Commons in 1829.

Peel was clearly aware of his anomalous position and of the advantages to be gained, personally speaking, from surrendering office long enough for his dilemma to be resolved by others. In 1822, Peel ruminated to his colleague C.W. Wynn on 'the advantage which would result from our retiring, and the certainty that we must return to power within three months. Does he think that that period would be sufficient for [the] Opposition to pass the Catholic question?' Similar sentiments were being voiced six years later. J.C. Herries thought Peel wanted to 'quit the Government while this question was being debated, stand aloof & then, when the thing was settled, to step back to his office & his leadership!!' Meanwhile, Lord Bathurst privately questioned the strength of Peel's 'Protestant feelings', thought him 'strangely ashamed of the question, and of the eager Protestants' but mindful of the advantages which accrued to him 'as the head of the Church party'.[41]

Peel was undoubtedly considered, by a large section of anti-Catholic opinion in the country at large, as the head of such a party. The increasingly pro-Catholic sentiments of the House of Commons were at variance with the popular (and often visceral) strains of Protestantism which were prevalent outside Parliament. This constituency would turn upon Peel in a storm of petitions, caricatures and fiery declamations in the spring of 1829 but, until then, embraced him 'as peculiarly the champion of the Church – as the watchful guardian of her ark – the *Manlius* of her sacred Citadel'.[42] The rewards to Peel's political reputation were clear enough:

> Ever maintain those principles that placed the family of your Royal master upon the throne of these realms. Be firm amidst all your opponents … Then will you gain an imperishable name, and the tribute of high veneration from generations yet unborn.[43]

Although Peel was 'repelled' by anti-Catholic fanaticism, he found it 'absolutely vital to his purposes'; not least in the campaign he waged, as Chief Secretary, against the Catholic Board. It was this body which claimed leadership of the Irish campaign for Emancipation – although its querulous nature in fact offended many sympathisers. The Board was technically invalid under the Irish Convention Act of 1793 but was revived in 1810. However, continuing disagreements between older 'respectable' members like John Keogh and Lord Fingal and 'the more assertive members led by

Denis Scully and Daniel O'Connell' deprived it of potential unity and strength. Peel initially regarded the Board as 'a front for a wide-ranging conspiracy' and proscribed it, by proclamation of the Lord Lieutenant, on 8 June 1814.[44]

Simultaneously, Peel was defining himself as the consistent and trusty opponent of Catholic Relief. His arguments were advanced almost entirely 'on the grounds of tradition and expediency'.[45] As G.H. Francis observed, in 1852, Peel 'never opposed the emancipation of the Catholics from antagonism to their religion, but always rested his arguments on political grounds'. Consequently, he refused to bind himself in perpetuity, arguing in 1816 that 'circumstances must finally govern the proceeding'.[46] Peel's official status leant his opposition an authority which was hard to ignore and his first-hand experience of Ireland convinced him that his views were more than the product of a Tory-Anglican education. 'Papal superstition', according to Peel, was 'the cause of one-half the evils of this country' and he seriously doubted whether that half 'would be alleviated by Catholic Emancipation'. Rather, it would be the prelude to 'perpetual contention, till one or other of the antagonist powers, should be overcome and silenced'.[47]

It was Peel's speech opposing Grattan's Relief Bill, on 9 May 1817, which finally established him as the shining hope and adornment of the Protestant cause.[48] Peel's opposition to Grattan's Bill of 1813 had garnered him the epithet 'Orange Peel' from O'Connell; this time, it gained him an honorary doctorate and an offer to come in (uncontested) as the MP for Oxford University.[49] As Edward Copleston commented:

> To have been chosen by above fifteen hundred gentlemen of liberal education as their representative in Parliament, without one dissentient voice, and I believe I may add without one dissentient mind in the whole body, is a distinction which confers no barren honour on its possessor. It must give weight and authority to his opinions: it must extend the sphere of his utility: it must afford grounds of self-confidence and self-respect.[50]

Well might the supporters of George Canning (whose ambitions to represent the University were thereby dashed forever) conclude bitterly that 'there never was a speech that did so much for a man as Peel's speech ... has done for him ... his cause wanted an advocate, the Protestants wanted a leader in the House, and he has established himself in that powerful situation'. Lord Lyttelton concluded that the 'Cock of Cotton' had been 'wonderfully impudent and aspiring', had raised himself 'instantly pegs innumerable' and was now being talked of as a future Prime Minister.[51]

* * *

By the end of his period as Chief Secretary, Peel had acquired extensive executive experience of Ireland, a close (if narrowly conceived) understanding of its problems and a reputation as the champion of the Protestant establishment. In turn, this had gained him the representation of the University of Oxford and advanced him to the front rank of contention for high ministerial office. Yet throughout the 1820s Peel's

A DISTURBER OF THE PUBLIC PEACE.

PEEL.—"There's a Maynooth Grant for you! So you now be quiet, and move on!"
O'CONNELL.—"Grant, indeed! I never moves on under Repale! D'ye think I don't know the value of peace and quietness!"

3: 'A Disturber Of The Public Peace', *Punch*, VIII, January–June 1845, 185.
A satire on relations between Peel and Daniel O'Connell at the time of the Maynooth Grant.

fixity of purpose on the Emancipation issue provided an important dividing line separating him from what many contemporaries regarded as his 'natural' home amongst the 'liberal Tories'. As *Blackwood's Edinburgh Magazine* argued in March 1829, Peel had 'long been only separated from [the liberals] in general creed and policy by the Catholic question'. The fact that he continued to hold out against the liberals precisely because of his hostility to Emancipation correspondingly reinforced expectations of him as indelibly committed on the issue.[52]

A Catholic Relief Bill, backed by the full resources of the executive, was finally introduced into the House of Commons by the Duke of Wellington's government in February 1829. As leader of the Commons, Peel not only supported it but agreed to oversee its passage through the House. Either this represented a superhuman act of moral courage, considering the depth and intensity of Peel's personal association with the issue, or else it symbolised a genuine change of conviction on his part.[53] In one sense, 'circumstances' (as Peel had earlier concluded) had finally 'governed the proceeding'. Daniel O'Connell's successful, if technically invalid, election as MP for County Clare, in the by-election of July 1828, had presented a practical challenge which raised Emancipation from an abstract theoretical proposition into a practical issue of government. As Home Secretary, Peel was duty bound to confront it on such terms without necessarily being intellectually converted. As J. Blanco White observed, 'notwithstanding the political measure he is now supporting: at all events, his conduct does not necessarily imply a change of views on the abstract question itself'.[54] Rather, Peel chose to resolve the dilemma between his twin roles (the committed Protestant, the indispensable minister) in favour of the latter, conscious that he could not ask George IV to make a sacrifice which he was not prepared to make himself.[55] In 1828, Peel had warned the King not to make resistance to Emancipation a matter of personal conscience because the claims of 'necessity' might prove sufficient to overwhelm them.[56] Peel, ever the administrator, preferred to resolve the problem himself – simply, cleanly and quickly – rather than precipitate a further constitutional impasse or devolve responsibility to less able hands. As such, Peel presented the measure 'purely in terms of the existing schism between the Irish executive and the actual administration of justice' and grounded it in terms of 'practical government rather than any change of conviction'.[57]

However, Boyd Hilton has argued that Peel genuinely changed his mind or (in Gladstone's terms) 'ripened' his views on the subject. On this reading, Peel finally accepted that the protected status of the Anglican Church and the Protestant religion could no longer be maintained in Ireland – at least insofar as Catholic Emancipation was concerned. There had been no Protestant Reformation in Ireland and there would be none whilst Emancipation stood unresolved. Culturally and economically, it was essential to liberate every Irishman from the continuing bitterness of the Catholic Question, allowing all faiths to compete equally for adherents (without encroaching further upon the privileges and property of the Established Church of Ireland). It was necessary for the Irish to enjoy 'free trade' in religion in order that they might enjoy free intercourse in other aspects of social and economic life.[58]

Of 'the train of thought and stages of development by which [Peel] arrived at the eventual crossroads' in his thinking on Emancipation 'we do not as yet know enough', although both its genesis and outcome are clear.[59] The turning-point for Peel, as for the political establishment in general, was the summer of 1828 and the immediate stimulus was provided by O'Connell's Catholic Association. The Association had been founded in Ireland in 1823 in order to pursue Emancipation more energetically than the Catholic Board had done. It was modelled on the Anti-Slavery Society's successful campaign to secure the abolition of the Slave Trade in 1807 and supported itself with the innovative 'Catholic Rent' (1d a week) which the Catholic peasantry and priesthood willingly subscribed in order to fund the Association's activities in the press, the courts and at election time. Although banned for three years under Goulburn's Act of 1825, the Association's strong roots amongst the Catholic forty shilling freeholders (who had enjoyed the right to vote, if not to enter Parliament, since 1793)[60] gave it a completely new dimension. Unlike earlier initiatives, the Association harnessed this power, first at the 1826 General Election and more significantly at the County Clare by-election. In turn, it necessitated a materially different response from any that had been required before.[61]

Until this time, Emancipation was debated with theological intensity in parliamentary debates, learned journals and popular polemics, but it was as a constitutional problem of the first order that most front-rank politicians experienced it. After July 1828, the constitutional issue assumed a new and more threatening aspect, given the prospect of civil disturbance which might accompany any attempt to deprive O'Connell of his seat. Such attempts had been made before (most famously, in respect of John Wilkes' Middlesex election of 1768) but never with such explosive potential, considering the additional combustible ingredient provided by the five million Roman Catholics of Ireland.[62]

From his earliest opposition to the measure, Peel had argued that the advocates of Emancipation needed to prove the necessity for repealing the offending statues which prevented Catholics from attaining office rather than admitting that the government had to prove the expediency of continuing them.[63] That proving point had now been reached. In opposing Burdett's motion, in May 1828, Peel had indicated a willingness to suspend his opposition if he could be satisfied of the beneficial consequences which its advocates claimed for it: a sentiment which suggested he was 'open to conviction'.[64] Mrs Arbuthnot concluded that 'a little persuasion & flattery' would be enough to turn Peel in favour of Emancipation, whilst Palmerston saw no reason why such a conversion should necessitate his resignation from office. In March 1828, Peel had raised suspicions, in anti-Catholic circles, by overseeing the Repeal of the Test and Corporation Acts (of 1673 and 1685) which removed the restrictions on Protestant Nonconformists from holding civic and political offices. This raised expectations, in some quarters, that he would proceed to concede Emancipation.[65] The standing impediment to such a *volte face*, as Lord Ellenborough perceptively commented on 31 July, was 'not with Peel's real opinions, but with his position and reputation, which may throw great difficulties in the way. He is so embarrassed by his Oxford connections, and by being the head, in spite of himself, of the anti-Catholics.'[66]

Ellenborough's observation suggested that Peel's sentiments were indeed 'ripening' in this period. Thomas Denman 'long suspected' that this was the case and felt that

Peel had 'done some violence to his own understanding in the long resistance' he had maintained. By December 1828, several commentators were observing the enthusiasm with which Peel supported the government's determination to press ahead with a Catholic Relief Bill – although this predated the point at which he finally committed himself to remain in the ministry and take responsibility for it in the House of Commons.[67]

That he did so only served to inflame the reaction against him when the ministerial intentions were finally unveiled, by Peel himself, on 5 February 1829. It was clearly the King's desire that Peel should remain in his service and see through the course of action that he had recommended to him. However, this was hardly sufficient to rely on as a defence, for George IV's new-found predilection for the measure was far from settled (or steadfast). Within days, Wellington and Peel were complaining at the use made of the King's name and influence (with his tacit encouragement) by the opposition in the Oxford University by-election.[68] Had Peel resigned from government but offered his support from the back-benches, his reputation might have survived, although it would hardly have been unscathed. As Jean Baptiste Capefigue observed, 'when a statesman finds himself in contradiction with the necessities of affairs, he withdraws, and makes room for another man more in harmony with the situation of the public mind'. Conversely, Peel not only supported the measure but took charge of it and refused to resign office, a fatal trinity of indictments against him. As Peel commented to Lord Londonderry, in February 1829, 'would to God your lamented brother [Castlereagh] had been spared to us – and that I were at this moment fighting under his banner, instead of occupying a post which most justly belonged to him'.[69]

As such, contemporaries drew a clear distinction between their attitude towards the measure, and their attitude towards Peel. Some were disposed to give Peel the benefit of the doubt, even whilst regretting the fact of his support. Croker considered that Peel had been 'cordially converted' to Emancipation whilst W.H. Clinton (a junior minister in the government) doubted that ambition had 'any shade in the part he is taking. But I think that he is mistaken & I am disappointed in my expectation of a superior mind – which I thought him to possess.' 'I will not charge you, Sir, with any thing approaching to political apostasy, in the recent change which has taken place in your conduct upon this important subject', another commentator observed, 'The motives I believe to be good; the policy I believe to be mistaken.'[70]

Peel's own attempt at self-vindication, in his speech of 5 February 1829, was widely condemned (by friend and foe alike) as 'lame' and 'pitiful'. Peel himself seems to have heeded Lord Ellenborough's privately offered advice to take a 'high tone' and refrain from apology.[71] Commentators felt Peel was trying to make out a case with which he did not agree, being 'impelled, by the posture of Public affairs and the force of circumstances, into a measure which your understanding did not approve, to avoid other acts, at which your responsibility staggered'.[72] Conversely, Peel's speech of 5 March 1829 outlining the terms of the government's scheme in more depth, was widely praised as Peel's finest parliamentary oration to date, not least in the passage leading up to its peroration:

I have not the slightest hesitation in saying, that I fully believe that the adjustment of this question, in the manner proposed, will give better and stronger securities to the Protestant interest and the Protestant establishment, than any that the present state of things admits of; and will avert evils and dangers impending and immediate … In the course I have taken, I have been mainly influenced by the anxious desire to provide for the maintenance of Protestant interests; and for the security of Protestant establishments. This is my defence – this is my consolation – this shall be my revenge.[73]

Peel's defiant claim to have conserved the Protestant establishment in Ireland through conceding Emancipation revealed much about his handling of the issue once he had become practically committed to it. In June 1828 Palmerston observed that Peel took the 'most sensible view' of Emancipation by arguing against accompanying it with any of those 'wings' or securities which its supporters had advanced in order to make the measure more palatable to its Protestant opponents. Peel had strenuously opposed such securities as a veto (in the appointment of Catholic Bishops), the State payment of the Catholic clergy and the restoration of full diplomatic relations with the Vatican. Variations of these had been integral to Grattan's and Burdett's Relief Bills in 1813, 1817 and 1825.[74]

Consequently, it was Peel's tactics which prevailed in the final legislative form which Emancipation assumed. The Roman Catholic Relief Act of 1829 (*10 Geo. IV c.7*) maintained the existing penal statutes prohibiting Catholics from civic and political office but provided exceptions to them under specified conditions. Catholics who were elected to Parliament had to subscribe to a special oath in order to be exempted from the existing legal disabilities, which remained on the statute book. Anyone refusing to subscribe the oath – which abjured 'any intention to subvert the present church establishment as settled by law … or weaken the Protestant religion or Protestant government in the United Kingdom' – was debarred. Similarly, the Crown and the Regency, the Lord Lieutenancy of Ireland, the Lord Chancellorships of Britain and Ireland and offices or places in schools and universities were reserved to Protestants whilst Catholic office holders were limited in their power to advise the Crown on the distribution of patronage in the Established Church and in respect of licensing Catholic religious orders. Peel successfully inserted clauses requiring the registration of male religious orders (notably the Jesuits) 'the clear legal intention [of which] was to suppress such orders'. The Act affected none of the existing restrictions on Catholic worship, church buildings, tithes, marriages, bequests, charities and ecclesiastical titles, much of which remained the subject of severe political conflict over the next two generations.[75]

Equally important were the two bills accompanying Catholic Relief, the first of which banned the Catholic Association, the second (more pointedly) disenfranchising the 40s freeholders, in an attempt to subvert undue influence – whether exerted by Catholic priest or aristocratic landlord – and raising the voting qualification to £10. In turn, this necessitated that O'Connell re-fight his election for Clare: a swingeing and petty technicality which Peel was not above pressing in deference to his own views and those of the King. As one commentator bitterly observed, this was a policy of 'divide and rule'; the Relief Act was widely supported by liberals, the adjusted franchise by their opponents and yet the effects of the former would be mitigated by the consequences of the latter.[76] Nevertheless, when the legislation as a whole was considered, Peel might justifiably argue that he had attempted 'to maintain intact and inviolate the integrity of the Protestant Established Church, its discipline and government, and also to maintain the essential Protestant character of the Constitution'. However, none of this appeared credible to his contemporary detractors, who reasoned that the measure was 'the major milestone on the road leading to complete legal and constitutional equality between Catholics and Protestants'.[77]

In the course of a few short months, Peel's reputation was transformed from that of 'Orange Peel', the oppressor of the Catholics of Ireland and the 'Coryphaeus' of the Church, to 'Peel emancipated', their unlikely benefactor. A contemporary squib announced a new Catholic feast-day, 'The Conversion of Saint Peel' and the freedom of the City of London was voted to Peel in recognition of his conduct.[78] The artist Haydon hailed Peel's actions as 'a Roman sacrifice of feeling' and Croker thought that Peel's reputation would survive the shock which had been administered to it, for 'all minor difficulties and personal considerations [would] be lost in the magnitude of the question itself'. But Croker was a friend and acolyte on the issue. Years later, Lord George Bentinck accused him of an over-optimistic appraisal of Peel's actions, concluding that Wellington and Peel had decided on Emancipation in the summer of 1828, antecedent 'to Peel's triumphant Protestant progress through Lancashire to Liverpool and Manchester, when he planted the celebrated "Protestant oak" with great ceremony and parade upon the occasion of a grand public breakfast given him as the champion of Protestant ascendancy'. For Bentinck, the salient point was Peel's hypocrisy in publicly supporting a measure which he had privately convinced himself could no longer be defended (a course of action which set the pattern for the Repeal of the Corn Laws).[79] Likewise, Palmerston publicly defended Peel's 'direct, manly, & honourable' proceedings in Parliament, denying they would impact seriously on his mature political reputation: 'he will fix upon his conduct on this question as the greatest and most glorious portion of his career'. However, privately, he felt that Peel's was a 'false position' because 'he has always concealed his opinions more or less'.[80] It was this charge, more bluntly stated ('Popery, Faction, & *Deceit*, which three words being combined, produce Wellington's & Peel's Administration') which was to pursue Peel furthest and hardest through his subsequent political life.[81]

The immediate effect on Peel was to deny him the representation of Oxford University. In acknowledgement of the fact that his occupancy of the seat owed everything to his Protestant reputation, both in 1817 and subsequently, Peel offered his resignation to the University – an act which Croker felt to be a dangerous 'democratical' precedent and a course of action which Peel afterwards condemned in others.[82] Critics thought it a hollow gesture: 'It is easy for Mr Peel *now* to give back to the University that mark of distinction which originally created opportunity and advantage to his very moderate talents: it is easy to make a merit of laying down the ladder which has long since raised him to his present eminence.'[83]

The Oxford University by-election of February 1829 raised all the internecine rivalries of academic life with the dangerous additional ingredient provided by sectarian animosity. Although Peel was a genuinely popular MP for the University, no political sin was greater in that constituency, at that period, than a change of sentiments on the Catholic Question. In spite of a vigorous campaign on his behalf, Peel lost the election decisively to the Ultra Protestant Sir Robert Henry Inglis.[84] Worse was to follow. To ensure Peel was able to carry Emancipation through Parliament, the government resorted to purchasing the electoral influence held by the Jewish borough-monger Sir Manasseh Lopes, thereby allowing Peel to be returned to Parliament for Westbury in Devon. Peel held this seat until inheriting his family's electoral influence at Tamworth (and the baronetcy), on his father's death, in May 1830. In retrospect, it is not surprising why many Ultra Tories argued that Emancipation would never have passed through a reformed parliament nor why Peel's position gave rise to such naked religious and racial virulence as that epitomised in the political doggerel of the day. This was paraded before the public in a mass of broadsheets and printed publications and was carefully preserved long afterwards, a standing indictment of Peel's infamy, in the papers of numerous Ultra Protestant parliamentarians:

> Once Peel the Rat for Oxford sat
> Of Christian men the choice
> But now he sits for Westbury
> Without one Christian voice
> By Christians spurned
> Where'er he turned
> He bribed an old Hebrew
> He bought his vote
> For many a groat
> And represents *a Jew*.[85]

As the Reverend Charles Girdlestone commented bitterly, if Peel had kept his place, he had 'at least *sacrificed* his *reputation*. Without it much good may he do the cause he has espoused! A statesman who has lost his reputation, has lost all that can in a free country give effect or value to his services ... he has LOST HIS POLITICAL EXISTENCE.'[86]

In the desire to justify himself, Peel could not refrain from what Charles Greville described as 'his never-failing fault, egotism ... Too great a noise is made about Peel and his sacrifices'. Twenty years later, Greville's mature conclusion was little revised: 'Historical justice' demanded 'that a large deduction should be made from Peel's reputation as a statesman and a patriot' given his role in resisting Emancipation from 1817–29, for 'whatever his motives may have been, it is indisputable that he was the principal instrument in maintaining this contest, which terminated in a manner so discreditable to the character, and so injurious to the interests, of the country'.[87]

'Why, then', another exasperated critic exclaimed, 'will Mr Peel so eternally refer to himself?' Peel's characteristic tendency to elevate the moral superiority of his own position and the infallibility of his own arguments served, by extension, to lower the estimation of those upon whom he had once relied for political support:

> [Peel] has never been remiss in paying a proper tribute of respect to his own moral worth, to his talents, to his consistency; and he may now, therefore, be permitted, without exciting any surprise, to talk about 'his heart and his conscience' ... [but] who can pass without indignation, the gratuitous insults poured forth upon the Protestant party? Raised by the misplaced affection of that party, who, more from respect to his principles than his talents, chose him as their leader, the Right Honourable Gentleman turns round, and with unexampled ingratitude, reviles them for this very act.[88]

Time and again, in subsequent years, Peel was forced to retrace the part he had played in 1829. Consequently, he developed a not unsurprising sensitivity on the issue.[89] Events in some quarters served to restore him to good favour. In May 1832 Wellington attempted to form an administration committed to a measure of parliamentary reform, in opposition to his previously declared sentiments on the subject. Peel refused to play the part of 1829 over again by agreeing to serve alongside him – a fact which restored him to good favour in the eyes of two of his more zealous Protestant critics. Both the Duke of Newcastle and Lord Mansfield concluded that Peel's actions in 1832 proved that he had been actuated by selfless motives, not love of office, in 1829.[90] Others maintained a Machiavellian view of Peel's conduct. For Lord Ashley, writing during the political crisis occasioned by the Repeal of the Corn Laws, Peel had 'acquired consequence, distinction, power, & a party, by heading the resistance to [Emancipation]. When resistance had become troublesome, and raised impediments in his way, he changed his front, developed his opinions, seduced some of his followers, & browbeat the others'.[91]

* * *

For all the political drama occasioned by the Catholic Emancipation crisis of 1829, and the consequent fall-out Peel suffered in terms of his character and reputation, he remained intellectually committed to the supremacy of the Protestant establishment in Ireland and to the political and economic foundations upon which the Act of Union was based. Robert Shipkey has argued that nothing in Peel's Irish policy between 1812 and 1844 suggests that he was other than a committed 'Protestant' throughout the period – in the sense that he envisaged no fundamental alteration in the basic distribution of political, social or economic power in Ireland or the assumptions that underpinned it.[92] There is little, in the surviving evidence, to contradict this view. Certainly, the trinity of Irish measures pursued by the Whig Ministries of the 1830s – Irish tithe, Municipal Corporation and poor law reform – helped Peel to overcome some of the bitterness of 1829 by once more assuming the Conservatives' natural mantle as defenders of the Protestant establishment. Conservatives were willing to excuse (if not forget) Peel's role in Emancipation, hoping that he would regard it as a misjudged experiment with ill-attended consequences.[93]

THE MAN WOT PLAYS SEVERAL INSTRUMENTS
AT ONCE.

4: 'The Man Wot Plays Several Instruments At Once', *Punch*, IX, July–December 1845, 17.
Peel attempts to deal with Maynooth, Income Tax and Tariff Duties at the same time (1845),
watched by an incredulous Russell. An artistic tribute to 'The Man Wot' series, pioneered by
the caricaturist William Heath in the 1820s.

The problem, for the opponents of Emancipation, was that it had been argued to be a 'healing measure', the resolution of which would settle the antagonistic state of relations between Britain and Ireland. The continuing status of the Church of Ireland as the established Church of the country, representing the interests of only one tenth of the population whilst being simultaneously supported by the tithes of the remainder, made this an elusive hope. Nevertheless, Ireland proved to be as serious a problem for the Whig governments of Grey (November 1830–July 1834) and Melbourne (July–November 1834, April 1835–September 1841) as it had for their Tory predecessors. In particular, Melbourne's government of 1835–41 found itself yoked in uneasy alliance to O'Connell's Irish parliamentary following through the 'Lichfield House Compact' of 1835. The arrangement had been concluded during Peel's 'Hundred Days Ministry' of 1834–5 and was directed solely to the ministry's downfall. It persisted, thereafter, as a means of preventing the 'Protestant' Peel from returning to power (a clear enough indication that Peel had not been 'emancipated' from his former opinions by the events of 1828–9). In the short term the Compact succeeded. However, for a longer tenure in office the Whigs reaped a severe Protestant backlash against its measures. This came, in part, from within the Church of England, elements of which had decried the 'National Apostacy' of the government's measures since the Irish Church Temporalities Act of 1833 abolished bishoprics in the Church of Ireland. Opposition also came from the Protestant Evangelical movement of the 1830s. The Whigs' particular commitment to a policy of 'appropriating' what it regarded as the surplus financial revenues of the Church of Ireland in order to apply them, without religious bias, to projects of social and economic amelioration, offered Peel a ground-work of strength – defending the institutional, constitutional and propertied basis of the Irish Church and Corporations.[94]

Consequently, Peel's resumption of office in 1841 was accompanied by the resumption of O'Connell's extra-parliamentary agitation for the Repeal of the Act of Union. This process reached its zenith with the projected 'monster meeting' at Clontarf in October 1843. The government interceded to ban this, at the eleventh hour, on public safety grounds. However, Clontarf crystallised (as County Clare had done fifteen years before) a materially different response in Peel. The years 1844–6 represent the true 'ripening' of Robert Peel, insofar as his Irish policy is concerned. They were hallmarked by the government's determination to investigate, constructively, Irish socio-economic problems – notably through Lord Devon's landmark 1844 Commission on landownership. This policy, and the legislation to which it gave rise, was designed to 'kill O'Connellism with kindness' by depriving him of his natural constituency of support amongst the Catholic priesthood and peasantry. It was accompanied by secret (and ultimately frustrated) negotiations to engage with the Papal Curia at Rome – formal diplomatic relations having been suspended since the Reformation – in an attempt to deprive O'Connell of legitimacy in the eyes of the Catholic Church.[95]

According to David Eastwood, the purpose of Peel's Irish policy after 1844 was to provide for 'a moderate Catholic clergy, appeased by modest State support and an expanded, more culturally cosmopolitan Irish middle class'. This represented 'a reforming vision of considerable social ambition'.[96] Peel's ministry successfully passed a Charitable Bequests Act (1844), allowing for legacies to non-Protestant institutions, and an enhanced and fiercely controversial financial grant to the Catholic training seminary of Maynooth (1845). Though the grant had been instituted fifty years earlier by the government of Pitt the Younger, Eastwood regards its enhancement by Peel as the corollary of Catholic Emancipation.[97] By tripling the grant from £9,000 to £26,000, making it a permanent charge on the Consolidated Fund (rather than subject to an annual vote by the House of Commons) and providing a one-off maintenance grant of £30,000, Peel not only provoked an open and deeply damaging breach with his own followers, but – as Lord Aberdeen, the Foreign Secretary observed – effectively endowed the Catholic Church in Ireland. Lord Ashley thought that, in the long term, Maynooth would prove to be the downfall of Peel's government. Had it not been for the intervening struggle over the Corn Laws, this may well have proved to be the case.[98]

Equally controversial was the establishment of the Queen's Colleges at Cork, Galway and Belfast (1845) in order to provide higher education on a non-sectarian or (as critics maintained) 'Godless' foundation. The Whigs had already had their fingers burned with a system of non-denominational 'National Education' for Ireland, during the 1830s, but Peel's ministry pressed on regardless.

Unsurprisingly, Peel's new more 'conciliatory' attitude towards Irish affairs revived old memories of Protestant betrayal. In 1844, Peel's fellow Lancastrian, Reverend W.K. Tatam, urged him to consider 'that judgment at which you must account for your immense responsibilities' and argued that, by his part in Catholic Emancipation:

> the enemy was let in like a flood – the high places of the State were deluged by his influence, directly or indirectly exerted – and many, partly in despair of ever again confiding in political leaders, partly from disgust and disappointment, sat down in mute submission to the worst of consequences, judging that the struggle was utterly hopeless where the master-spirits gave way, and the standard-bearers fainted.[99]

Maynooth gave rise to the sort of petitioning campaign which had not been witnessed since the anti-Catholic agitation of the late-1820s; a campaign which encompassed Nonconformist ministers, lay divines and country gentlemen as well as Protestant zealots and paranoid pamphleteers.[100] Nor were the last, fatal months of Peel's second ministry without significance insofar as Ireland was concerned. The Repeal of the Corn Laws in 1846 was predicated in essence as a prophylactic against the potato famine which had already occurred and the much more serious general famine which was prophesied in consequence of it. The ministry got its measure through but resigned after being defeated on a 'Coercion Bill', designed to reinforce the executive power in maintaining law and order in Ireland. *The Freeman's Journal* received the news with rapture:

> Having succeeded in carrying the greatest social reform that a British minister ever conceived, in enjoying a popularity with the middle classes in England such

as no minister ever enjoyed, Sir Robert falls an unlamented victim to his insane
desire to forge fetters for Ireland.[101]

The *Journal's* triumphal tone was uncharitable, given Peel's recent policy towards
Ireland. In any case, context was everything. In other circumstances, the latest in a long
line of 'Coercion Bills' would have raised little controversy, having been (in different
forms) the habitual resort of governments of all political complexions since the time
of the Union. In some respects, Peel himself had set the tone for this policy during his
time as Chief Secretary. In 1814, he had renewed the terms of the Irish Insurrection
Act (of 1796) for three years and when the Act lapsed in 1817 renewed it again for a
further year. Amongst other things, the Act imposed a night-time curfew, arms
searches and martial law in proclaimed districts. Each of these measures, to different
degrees, found their way into subsequent Coercion Acts. It was one of the more
symmetrical ironies of history that a measure which helped to make Peel's name at the
start of his political career should play a supplementary role in helping to end it.[102]

* * *

Although historians have followed Gladstone in detecting a 'ripening' in Peel's
sentiments towards Ireland, neither of the prevalent images of Peel (as 'Orange Peel'
before 1829 and 'Peel emancipated' thereafter) accurately reflects his position. From
his first foray into Irish politics, Peel maintained an abiding dedication to the
Protestant establishment. Circumstances in 1829 and 1844–6 required that he make
such concessions to the Catholic community as could safely be offered as a means of
destabilising O'Connell's campaign to Repeal the Act of Union. This aim was always
implicit in the struggle for Catholic Emancipation before 1829 and was explicitly
stated (for example, in O'Connell's Loyal National Repeal Association) thereafter.
Constitutional issues took primacy in Peel's thinking because it was these which –
epitomised in the Lord Lieutenancy, the Municipal Corporations, the Castle executive
and the established Church of Ireland – gave the Union focus and integrity. For David
Eastwood, the intention of Peel's mature Irish policy 'was to accommodate diverse
religious and economic interests to a still conservative Parliament, a limited monarchy,
and an enduring legislative union'. Only latterly, and in a strictly 'limited sense', did
Peel come 'to recognise that he might uphold the Union by working with rather than
against the grain of Irishness'. This did not entail the abandonment of Peel's
Anglicanism but a rejection of anti-Catholicism 'as a necessary corollary of that
Anglicanism'.[103] As such, it was the strength of Peel's 'Protestant' reputation before
1829, and the corresponding strength of reaction to his perceived abandonment of
that position after 1829, which made the change in his policy seem sharper than was
the case, at least before the mid-1840s.

However, a populace overwhelmingly distanced from Britain by its religious and
socio-economic situation required moderate government intervention in areas beyond
those of law and order. It was this reality which Peel belatedly came to recognise after
1844. Wholesale government intervention to solve the problems of Ireland was never

the answer, in Peel's view, for this would be inadequate compensation for the difficulties created by absentee landlords and unresponsive churchmen. As he informed Lord Charleville (somewhat imperiously), on one occasion:

> *Aide-toi et le ciel t'aidera* [help yourself and the sky will help you] should be the motto and ruling principle in these matters of every Irish Proprietor – The great cause of the backwardness of Ireland as to improvement – is the unwise interference of the Government and reliance on the Government instead of individual exertion.[104]

Nor was Peel enamoured of indiscriminate charitable relief to the Irish as a substitute for individual exertion. These sentiments were evident in Peel's final parliamentary speeches on Ireland, on 14 and 30 March 1849. In the period following his fall from office, in June 1846, events conspired to keep Ireland at the centre of political debate. In particular, the Irish potato famine (1845–7), the death of O'Connell (in 1847) and a failed attempt, on the part of 'Young Ireland', to raise an Irish Rebellion in 1848 (fifty years after the troubles of 1798) suggested, for the third time in Peel's lifetime, the necessity of a different response on the government's part. Privately, Peel 'professed the most earnest desire to do anything in his power to co-operate with Clarendon [the Lord Lieutenant] in doing good to Ireland'.[105] Publicly, he attacked the uncontrolled distribution of charity by Lord John Russell's government. Peel thought this amounted to little more than the creation of a dependency culture in Ireland. Rather, as a means of establishing an economically viable Irish peasantry in one of the most distressed provinces (Connaught, in the west of Ireland), Peel proposed that a government commission should be formed in order to assume responsibility for the many Irish estates 'encumbered' with debt. The commission would co-operate with the government in encouraging the re-plantation of the province by English capitalists and superintend the work of the Irish poor law unions. Peel subsequently outlined the benefits of such a policy in a letter to Thomas Campbell Foster on 16 April 1849:

> an extensive change in the tenure of landed property in the West of Ireland would have a direct tendency to improve the relations between the landlord and the priest ... the new proprietor would consider those relations and the policy of cultivating them with much less of prejudice than the old one and ... any loss which the priest might suffer from the introduction of a few Protestants or the emigration of a certain portion of his own flock would be more than compensated.[106]

Argued in this way, Peel's 'plantation' policy would have brought economic benefits to Ireland as well as neutralising the connection between the Catholic priesthood and the dispossessed and dispirited Catholic tenant. In its combination of 'paternalism ... empire ... English superiority, industriousness, and self-reliance', Peel's policy attracted high favour from Thomas Carlyle, who lauded it in *The Spectator*.[107]

The Times described Peel's intervention as 'a thunder-clap', the Irish *Evening Mail* estimated it an 'open bid for place and popularity' and *The Cork Examiner* augured that 'the man who said "let Catholic Emancipation be" and it became a fact: that is the man, and this is the hour, to revolutionize the land'.[108] 'The project is now the all-engrossing theme of Irish journalism,' *The Economist* noted in April, and 'lauded in strains of rapture of which Irish eloquence can alone convey the idea of intensity.' In the year before his death, Peel's public reputation had metamorphosed from 'Orange Peel' into the new Saint Patrick.[109]

However, in spite of the expectations to which his policy and pronouncements gave rise in the years 1844–50, Peel's policies were always constructed with an eye towards the maintenance of the Protestant establishment in Ireland. Likewise, he consistently refused to assume more responsibilities for the state than it could reasonably be expected to bear.[110] As Chief Secretary, he had responded to the threat of famine in 1816–17 with a strictly limited (and temporary) programme of public works, outdoor relief and incentives to encourage emigration. At the height of the crisis, he had resorted to a special commission in order to oversee them.[111] What had changed between then and the late-1840s was not so much Peel's convictions or strategies for Ireland (although there had been some 'ripening' there, notably after 1844) as the context in which his changing reputation had placed them. As 'Orange Peel' nothing more had been expected of him than a resort to such short-term practicalities. Out of office, after 1846, Peel's prescriptions were coloured by the expectations he had raised through his association with Emancipation and the policies he had pursued in his final years in power. As *Punch* sardonically observed, Peel's plan to 'fertilise waste lands, to reclaim bogs, send bog-trotters literally trotting, and elevate the Sons of Erin' no longer made him the Judas or the Julian but the 'Caesar' of the modern age.[112]

However, in essence, Peel remained the personification of the Conservative statesman, yielding in the face of necessity in order to retain and secure the fundamentals:

> No other man of your party is considered capable of yielding to the exigency of the times, while adhering to your own great principle of *conservatism*, taken in its proper sense [it was observed in 1846]. You have abandoned most of those positions, which your old colleagues still rely upon; and you are wise enough to see that by pleading necessity as an excuse for change of sentiments on the Catholic question, you taught the people of Ireland a lesson not to be forgotten, namely – that nothing can ever be obtained from England except by agitation and threatened violence.[113]

Yet Peel's defence was also his indictment. He was the statesman who had risen to greatness on his reputation as 'Orange Peel' – he had 'abandoned' it. At the severest moment of contest between Protestants and Catholics, in 1828–9, he had pleaded 'necessity *as an excuse* for change of sentiments'. Most dangerously of all, Peel had consistently yielded to force (to 'agitation and threatened violence') what he had continually denied to argument.

5: 'The New St. Patrick; Or, Sir Robert Turning The Reptiles Out Of Ireland',
Punch, XVI, January–June 1849.
A response to Peel's 'plantation' policy for Ireland.

There can be little doubt that Peel felt the need to justify his part in Catholic Emancipation above all the political acts of his life, because so many consequences for his reputation flowed from it. In many ways, he was the prisoner of his own circumstances – as 'Orange Peel' before 1829 and 'Peel [seemingly] emancipated' thereafter. In 1847, J.W. Croker, the trusted intimate of Peel's Protestant youth and the advocate of Catholic Emancipation, cast these sentiments aside in condemning him as a 'turncoat' who had exchanged 'the *orange* exterior … for the *green* lining'.[114]

The charge was hardly proven. Nevertheless, it is unsurprising that Emancipation constituted the first and lengthiest of the *Memoirs* which Peel bequeathed to posterity for publication by his literary executors, Mahon and Cardwell. Its appearance in 1856 gave rise to renewed historical re-examination of Peel's statesmanship in general and his role in 1829 in particular, much of which remained highly critical. For Jelinger Cookson Symons, Peel's self-defence remained unconvincing to those 'whose ambition extends beyond the tenure of office, to posthumous reputation':

> [His] Memoirs were written as a vindication of his own pretensions to a very high order of political integrity; and in fact to a degree of magnanimity as a Statesman almost chivalrous. And he himself challenges scrutiny into the validity of claims to a reputation for disinterested devotion, and single hearted integrity…Posterity will be well able to judge how far such a politician deserves the reputation to which he lays claim.[115]

More famously, Walter Bagehot, the journalist and essayist of *The Economist*, believed Peel would:

> have to answer to posterity not for having passed Catholic Emancipation when he did, but for having opposed it before; not for having been precipitate, but for having been slow; not for having taken 'insufficient securities' for the Irish Protestant Church, but for having endeavoured to take security for an institution too unjust to be secured by laws or lawgivers.[116]

In spite of Peel's later Irish policy – which Gladstone commended as that of a 'profound statesman' whose views had ripened from error into truth – these sentiments proved irredeemable insofar as his posthumous political reputation was concerned.

3

'PEEL'S ACT':
ROBERT PEEL AND CURRENCY
REFORM

Although I have no intention of discussing the Question of the Currency, and no wish to continue a correspondence on a subject on which my opinions are fixed, I am not willing to permit your letter to remain altogether unnoticed. I attach about the same importance to the imputations upon my honour and integrity on account of the part I took in the bill of 1819 that I do to the reasoning of the Chairman of your association, in favour of a paper-currency, representing the National Debt. Perhaps I am the more indifferent to such imputations inasmuch as I inherited from my father the whole of his landed property – the whole of that very description of property, the value of which is supposed to have been so ruinously affected by the Bill of 1819, and as I had a much greater personal interest in maintaining the value of land than of funded property. What the Whigs may do with regard to the Currency I know not, but with my opinions on that subject if I were to take the course you suggest, I should then indeed be justifying some of those imputations on my integrity from which you have been good enough to defend me, and which I hope will be preferred, where I can have the opportunity of meeting them.

Sir Robert Peel, in correspondence, 29 December 1835.[1]

* * *

On 24 May 1819 Robert Peel performed the first of the three political conversions which defined his parliamentary career. Having given a silent and (by his own admission) unthinking vote against the restoration of cash payments and a return to the gold standard in 1811, Peel now presided over their resumption by chairing a committee, writing a report and overseeing an Act – *59 Geo. III c.49*, popularly known as 'Peel's Act' – motivated to that end. By comparison with Catholic Emancipation in 1829, and the Repeal of the Corn Laws in 1846, it was a conversion which was comparatively little remarked by contemporaries.[2] Nor did Peel himself feel compelled to extensive self-justification on the issue: none of the three *Memoirs* he bequeathed to posterity explicitly discussed it.[3] Yet the impact of Peel's decision in 1819, and the tenacity with which he upheld it thereafter, was in many ways more important than the fall-out from either of the two later issues, for it went to the heart of Peel's political character. Above all, as Boyd Hilton has argued, Peel's views on currency reform – as enunciated in 1819 and reinforced in the Bank Charter Act of 1844 – in many ways defy later impressions of him as a careful, progressive, moderate pragmatist. Rather, Peel's 'defence of the gold standard ... became perhaps the main keynote of his career'. In turn, this suggests that Peel was capable of a dogmatic and doctrinaire inflexibility which put him at odds with large numbers of his putative political followers.[4] This chapter considers the importance of the issue, in terms of Peel's political character and statecraft, in order to test Hilton's argument.

* * *

To start requires some attention to the history of the currency question. On 26 February 1797, in response to an appeal from the directors of the Bank of England, the government of William Pitt the Younger issued an Order-in-Council suspending cash payments. This meant that holders of bank notes with the traditional inscription promising 'to pay the bearer upon demand the sum of x pounds' were unable to convert them into their equivalent weight and value in sterling (gold bullion). The 'gold standard' was the basis of the English currency system, paper notes having established themselves as a convenient circulating medium in order to transact business, purchase goods and extend credit. The acceptability of bank notes as a medium of exchange reflected a trust (on the part of giver and receiver) that the Bank of England would be willing and able to convert them at will into their equivalent value in bullion.[5] The order was followed up by the Bank Restriction Act (*37 Geo. III c.45*) of 3 May 1797, preventing the conversion of notes at will into 'a coin which is exportable' and giving bankers discretion to issue paper money. The measure reflected the growing financial burden being borne by the nation as a result of the wars with Revolutionary France, which had begun in 1793. It also reflected the fear – which had become increasingly discernible in the demands being placed on the Bank's gold stock – of a diminution in specie and its export abroad. As such, the Bank's directors were acting in their capacity as custodians of the nation's gold reserve by petitioning the government for relief from these transactions. Although the Act was originally due to expire on 24 June, its terms were progressively extended and inconvertibility became the defining characteristic of Britain's economic policy for the next twenty-two years.[6]

Before 1797, Bank of England notes, typically with face values of £10 and upwards, had circulated to the extent of about £12m, with a further 200 joint-stock, private or 'country' banks (i.e. banks with fewer than six partners) circulating notes of £5 and upwards to a similar extent. Britain's gold stock stood at some £20–30m. However, by the Act of *37 Geo. III c.32* (30 April 1797), bank notes of £1 and £2 were allowed to circulate as legal tender. This contingency – the necessary corollary of the restriction of cash payments – was to cease (by law) within two years of the resumption of the gold standard.[7]

In subsequent years, the increasingly high price of gold in the currency market and the adverse state of the foreign exchanges suggested a growing divergence between the value of the bank notes which were being advanced (seemingly without restriction) and the bullion in which they would (eventually) have to be repaid.[8] On 1 February 1810, Francis Horner moved for a Commons committee of inquiry, which was granted eighteen days later. Horner was appointed chairman, with William Huskisson and Henry Thornton establishing themselves as the most influential of the committee's members. Together, the three men produced the committee's report which was published on 8 June 1810. Its principal significance was in positing a connection between the price of gold (which was at a premium) and the state of the exchanges (which were falling) in regulating the issue of bank notes. In short, paper notes were being depreciated through over-issue and insufficient restriction: 'when a paper currency originally founded on & convertible into coin has become inconvertible [the committee concluded], it can only be kept up to its proper value by a limitation of its quantity based on observation of the price of bullion and the foreign exchanges'. In other words, the notional value of the paper notes issued by the bank must keep pace of their actual, convertible value in gold bullion.[9]

Horner's committee put forward sixteen resolutions on 6 May 1811, recommending the restoration of the gold standard within two years as a means of re-asserting control and endorsing the 'Bullionist' theory that the foreign exchanges and the price of bullion were key to regulating a paper currency. The argument was phrased in terms of restoring the 'soundness' of England's credit, gold being considered an impartial measure of value which provided a natural, self-correcting mechanism for an economy founded upon its standard (silver having been dismissed as too variable and unreliable a marker). 'Paper money is a convenience [*The Economist* argued, years later] but in order to be really so, it must ever be convertible into gold, as gold, being a mercantile commodity, is the representative of value, whereas paper money is a representative of credit.' The theory of the Gold Standard foreshadowed the modern 'monetarist' doctrine that a nation's money supply depends on its economic performance relative to other countries, as measured by the state of the foreign exchanges (its imports and exports).[10] However, the report raised severe opposition from a range of leading politicians and ex-ministers. Vansittart, Castlereagh, Perceval, Rose and Herries argued that inconvertibility was too valuable a system for raising funds (through the unrestricted issue of paper notes) to abandon it at the height of the Napoleonic Wars. Lord Redesdale, commenting on the report to another sceptic, Lord Harrowby, observed:

> They do not immediately reflect that if there were less of paper money there would be less of circulating medium of any kind, especially in the present circumstances of Europe; and if this should be suggested to them, they persist in one opinion [–] that if there were less of circulating medium of any kind things would be cheaper ... but then the circulating medium would be so much more valuable, and consequently dearer ... As long, therefore, as paper will answer the purposes of circulation as well as gold and silver coin, it seems

advantageous to the country to have a cheap instead of a dear circulation; to transact their business at a small expense instead of a large expense.[11]

Those who opposed what came to be known as the 'Bullionist' theory were convinced that a restoration of cash payments, at their 1797 values, would be tantamount to deflation – such was the divergence between the market and the mint price of gold. It would strangle 'sound and useful' enterprise by establishing an over-restrained currency, adversely affect the price of produce (by halving it) and increase the burden of individual debt (by doubling it) – for debts contracted in the depreciated currency would be payable (together with dividends and interest) in the enhanced currency. These arguments remained at the heart of the anti-Bullionist case for decades. In 1842, the artist Haydon, speaking from personal experience, complained that Peel had 'ruined more families, blasted more fortunes, & broken more hearts than any minister that ever ruled a great nation', through his restoration of cash payments. 'Was not all *our* embarrassment owing to incurring debts in paper & being called to pay them in gold, 27 shillings in the pound?'[12] Two years later, another polemicist opined:

No language can, adequately, describe the distress and ruin and misery caused by your Bill. The fall, owing to the difference occasioned by this Bill in the value of money, in the prices of all commodities, the violation of contracts, the want of employment, insolvencies, bankruptcies, the destruction of families, in some instances madness, in more suicide; such were some of the effects of your Bill ... [the Act of 1819] was wholly unsuited to the then existing rate of prices; to the relations which had been formed, for nearly a quarter of a century, between property and money. It was unsuited to the large mass of private debts; and still worse, to the stupendous amount of the national debt.[13]

But this was for the future. In the short term, arguments like these secured the defeat of Horner's resolutions on 10 May 1811 and the passage of seventeen counter-resolutions, proposed by Vansittart three days later. Thereafter, restoration was put off on an annual basis. Whilst the Bank of England undertook a partial resumption after 1816 by 'calling-in' some of the notes issued in the intervening period, the straitened political and economic circumstances in which the country found itself after Waterloo, and the House of Commons' decision to discontinue the Income Tax, provided ministers with a continuing justification for maintaining an inconvertible paper currency.[14]

In 1819, Liverpool's ministry attempted a final settlement of the issue by appointing secret committees of inquiry of both Houses of Parliament, to 'consider the state of the Bank of England with reference to the expediency of the resumption of cash payments at the period fixed by law'. Of the twenty-one members of the Commons committee (chaired by Peel), one-third was made up of opposition MPs; Lord Harrowby chaired the Lords Committee.[15] Boyd Hilton has presented the operation as a triumph for 'Liberal Toryism' and for Huskisson, who had lobbied the Prime Minister to institute a programme of economic retrenchment and debt repayment to replace that of deficit financing and short-term borrowing pursued by Vansittart as Chancellor of the Exchequer.

Peel would seem to have been an apt choice as chairman of the Commons committee. His voting record in 1811 suggested his opposition to resumption, yet he was less committed on the subject than Harrowby, Vansittart and Huskisson and his reputation as Chief Secretary suggested he would tackle the role assiduously. Peel was said to be 'open to conviction' on the issue, but aligned himself (in favour of resumption) with Huskisson and Canning on 3 April, a full month before the committee's report (6 May) was issued. By contrast, 'High Tories' like Sidmouth, Eldon and Herries remained unyielding opponents of Bullionism.[16]

Peel's role in these proceedings is a mixed one. In one respect, as he freely admitted to the Commons on 24 May 1819, in introducing the committee's report, he was executing a policy that had already been laid down by Huskisson and Horner. More importantly (for him), it was a policy founded on an irreducible basis of theory incapable of being broken down by the existence of troublesome 'facts'.[17] As Peel told his former Oxford tutor, Charles Lloyd, in a flourish of intellectual bumptiousness, he had convinced himself as clearly as he was convinced of an undergraduate mathematical proposition, that the Bullionist case made out by Horner's committee in 1810 was impervious to such inconveniences:[18]

> Still, there are facts apparently at variance with the [Bullionist] theory. If the demonstration is complete, this can only be so apparently. They are like the triangles that I used to bring to Bridge [my mathematics tutor], and declare that the angles of those particular triangles amounted to more than two right angles. The answer in each case is the same. There is some error in the fact, and in the triangle, not in the proof, which was as applicable to that fact, and to that triangle, as to any other.[19]

As one observer had remarked, at the time of Horner's Report, this represented 'the most audacious assumption of superior judgement derived from theory in opposition to opinions founded on experience ever offered to the world'. It was one to which Peel remained implacably wedded for the rest of his life.[20]

* * *

Whilst Peel's attachment to Bullionism forms the central tenet in Hilton's revisionist reading of his life and character, contemporaries were well aware of his fixity of purpose (and opinion) on the subject.[21] 'Dr Arnold used to say that the currency question was the only one of the principles of which Peel had rendered himself complete master, and that on this alone his consistency could be safely depended on.'[22] Similarly, Richard Cobden observed that Peel's mind had:

> a natural leaning toward politico-economical truths. The man who could make it his hobby so early to work out the dry problem of the currency question, and

arrive at such sound conclusions, could not fail to be equally able and willing to put in practice the other theories of Adam Smith.[23]

This made the currency issue (and its consequences for Peel's statecraft and reputation) of a materially different nature from, for example, his thinking on Ireland. Whereas Peel's declared hostility to Catholic Emancipation turned out to be provisional and capable of being revised in the light of changing practical circumstances, his views on the currency question were rooted in an unshakeable foundation of theory which was incapable of being affected by subsequent economic crises. Both positions made Peel controversial (and hence problematic) in his own day, though for different reasons.

From the outset, Peel had fixed his political star to the currency question. He openly requested a place on the Commons committee through Charles Arbuthnot; the subsequent decision to appoint him its chairman ensured his name and reputation were attached to the report (and the Act arising from it) at a time when his semi-detached status from the ministry, allied to his growing popularity and ambition, were becoming a subject of remark. As Arbuthnot observed to Castlereagh, in March 1819, Peel was being spoken of as a potential replacement for Vansittart:

> It is in human nature to be pleased with the sort of following which he must observe is now attaching to him. He has dinners without end, & this he is enabled to have throughout the week, not only by his own great means, but also by his never being tied to the House when we are obliged to be attending to the debates … I should think he showed better taste if he would let it be seen that he was still closely connected with the Government to which he so recently belonged.[24]

Peel's speech of 24 May 1819, introducing the resumption of convertibility, was thus important personally as well as politically. Above all, it was remembered by Wellington for its 'ability'. This is a judgement which subsequent historians have endorsed. John Prest argues that the speech set 'the tone for an era that relished plain facts … in thus rounding up the theoretical complexities of an issue, and giving effect to the solution he favoured … Peel was to have no equal'.[25]

By 'Peel's Act', the Bank of England was required to return to the gold standard in progressive stages, which were designed to afford a degree of economic re-adjustment. From 1 February 1820, the Bank would redeem its notes (on demand) for gold ingots. Thereafter, the amount of gold paid in exchange for paper was to be increased periodically as the amount of paper currency in circulation decreased. This would be accompanied by a gradual return to the 1797 gold standard. The Bank's exchange rate would decrease in stages from £4 1s 0d (1 February 1820) to £3 19s 6d (1 October 1820) before attaining the 1797 mint value (£3 17s 10½d per ounce) by 1 May 1821. Full convertibility of notes into cash was to be completed by 1 May 1823 – although this was achieved in practice by 1821 – and all bank notes with a face value under £5 were to be withdrawn two years after that. The wartime restrictions on the melting and exportation of gold were also removed.[26]

'Peel's Act' was, in the words of the contemporary economist Robert Torrens, 'strenuously opposed by a numerous and not un-influential section of the commercial community'.[27] The most telling political divergence was between Peel and his father, which the younger Peel paraded before the House of Commons on 24 May 1819:

> Many other difficulties presented themselves to him on discussing this question; among them was one which it pained him to observe, and that was the necessity he felt of opposing himself to an authority [his father] to which he always had bowed, and he hoped always should bow with deference; but here he had a great public duty imposed upon him, and from that duty he would not shrink, whatever might be his private feelings ... he felt himself called upon to state, candidly and honestly, that he was a convert to the doctrines regarding our currency which he had once opposed.[28]

Peel's father remained as devoted to the financial system introduced by Pitt the Younger in 1797 as his son was to its dismemberment.[29] In 1826, he reiterated his support for this system in an open letter to both Houses of Parliament. Lord George Bentinck later stated that it had helped to shape his own views on the subject.[30] As such, the elder Peel was an obvious choice to present the petition of the merchants, bankers and traders of London to the House of Commons. The petitioners argued that the restoration of cash payments would:

> tend to a forced, precipitate, and highly injurious contraction of the circulating medium of the country ... lower the value of all landed and commercial property ... [seriously] affect both public and private credit ... embarrass and reduce all the operations of agriculture, manufactures, and commerce [and] throw out of employment a great proportion of the industrious and labouring classes of the community.

The directors of the Bank of England (the original midwives of the system) also expressed their dissatisfaction with 'a measure calculated to compromise the universal interests of the empire in all the relations of agriculture, commerce, and revenue'.[31]

In 1822, the government conceded to the growing discontent voiced by the financial, business and merchant community (as well as from the increasing number of agricultural anti-Bullionists) by passing a Small Note Regulation Act (3 Geo. IV c.70). This allowed the circulation of £1 and £2 notes to continue until 1 January 1833, in the hope of stemming the precipitate 'calling-in' of notes in exchange for specie. The ensuing feverish period of speculation (fuelled, amongst other things, by Britain's involvement in, and recognition of, the new Latin American republics) led to the founding of some 600 joint-stock companies. The end of this speculative 'bubble' had severe consequences. Gold began to drain from the Bank of England from October 1824, as the run to exchange bank notes for gold began. By the following autumn, the Bank's cash reserves dropped to £18,000 and some seventy country banks collapsed in the space of six weeks. For the most part, these events were attributed to the continued circulation of small notes, although contemporaries were divided as to whether the fault lay with the government's legislation of 1822 or a lack of foresight (and control) on the part of country bankers.[32] J.C. Symons later laid the blame with Peel:

> in 1825 the crisis came, and the country narrowly escaped universal bankruptcy. The evil was undoubtedly somewhat aggravated by the immediate increase of the burden of the national debt and of all other debts ... Against such an obvious injustice and disaster, Mr Peel ought surely to have guarded. That he did not do so, certainly impairs his character as a financier.[33]

The cabinet was also divided between 'High Tory' interventionists and 'Liberal Tory' Bullionists: the latter prevailed in resisting pressure to issue Exchequer Bills to distressed firms. Instead, by an Act of 1826 (*7 Geo. IV c.6*), the government brought forward the deadline for withdrawing notes under the value of £5 from circulating in England, facilitating a complete return to the gold standard by 1830.[34]

* * *

Rather than challenging Peel's faith in Bullionism, events in 1825 seem to have hardened them – a fact reflected in the somewhat unfeeling tone he adopted in correspondence with Edward Littleton at this time: 'Ultimate good, after some suffering, will result.' This phrase has given rise to a good deal of historiographical discussion. Boyd Hilton regards it as symptomatic of the somewhat stern evangelical precepts under which Peel was actuated on the currency issue. Norman Gash has dismissed this as a slight and partial use of evidence.[35] However, Peel was equally unyielding five years later. With Wellington, he maintained that the economic distress of the period was partial in scope and localised in nature rather than systematic and general (i.e. linked to the currency issue). Peel's attitude entrenched Ultra Tory opposition against him – already enflamed by his retreat on Catholic Emancipation – and converted some Ultras to the advantages of parliamentary reform. To Goulburn, Peel reflected that he would not yield an iota of his beliefs in the hope of conciliating Ultra Tory support. For different political reasons, the well-known currency reformer, Thomas Attwood, began his Birmingham Political Union in January 1830 in order to campaign for parliamentary (and, by extension, currency) reform. The currency issue was fast becoming a lightning rod of discontent for the government's opponents and one on which Peel was fatally implicated. Although much of the blame for the fall of Wellington's ministry in November 1830 has been attributed to the Duke's hostility towards parliamentary reform, Peel must be held equally culpable for his stridency on the currency issue.[36]

Peel's attachment to Bullionism – what the Chartist James Bronterre O'Brien called the 'Procustean bed of [his] monetary system' – provided a fixed point in Ultra Tory and Radical critiques of him during this period.[37] In 1828, the Ultra Tory Lord Kenyon told his fellow sympathiser, Lord Stanhope, that Peel's Act of 1819 was 'mischievous in the extreme ... it is self evident that it can be maintained on no sound principle of science as to the interests of trade or commerce as existing under the circumstances of this country'. Two years earlier, Kenyon had argued that:

> the simplest way of lessening the evil would be by altering the standard of value, & making the ounce of gold pass for what was its price during the period of an exclusively paper currency, namely at about £4-10s instead of £3-17-6 its present assigned value. As about 2/3rds of our Debt was contracted under such a state of things … it would only be returning by a different but more simple course to the state of things which existed before the alteration produced by Mr Peel's mischievous & unjust Bill.[38]

However, whilst it was often pointed out that 'Peel's Act' had incidentally caused the doubling of his family's already significant financial fortune (from £1m to £2m), no one (not even the markedly sensitive John Wade, whose *Black Book* regaled the personal self-interest practised by monopolists and sinecurists in loving detail) believed that Peel had willingly acted from self-interested motives in passing the measure.[39]

Nevertheless, the prospect of a combined Radical/Ultra Tory assault on the currency question remained far from implausible, when the 'Reformed' House of Commons met for the first time in January 1833.[40] To Goulburn, Peel reiterated his unwillingness 'to make any *concessions of opinion* in order to gain support or increase our strength in the House. He mentions the *currency* as one of the topics to which this observation applies.' Two months later, news reached Wellington that 'a considerable number of Members of Parliament attributed the present depression of business … in a great measure to the state of our monetary system, and were desirous of obtaining a parliamentary committee of inquiry into that subject'. Peel was 'too much pledged by the Act which bears his name, to originate any such inquiry'. In these circumstances, Viscount Mahon (later to become Peel's literary executor) appealed to the Duke to intercede in the matter:

> I take up the question only from a deep and thorough conviction that it is not a party question but one of immense national importance – that nearly all parties equally concurred in the Acts of 1819 and 1826, and that the advantage of our subsequent experience may therefore with equal justice and consistency modify the views of all. I entreat your Grace … not positively to pledge yourself against any future reconsideration of this momentous question, and to remember that the force of circumstances – a force to which all other forces in politics must sometimes yield – will irresistibly press the question forward against any Government, combine men of all parties for its promotion, and loudly call upon your Grace's wisdom and public spirit to effect some safe and satisfactory settlement.

Wellington (who had given way to 'the force of circumstances' in respect of Catholic Emancipation in 1829 and Parliamentary Reform in 1832) replied that he could 'give no opinion upon the subject'.[41]

By contrast, Peel united with the Whig ministry in opposition to Attwood's motion for an inquiry into the financial system. More pointedly (and more personally), he repelled William Cobbett's proposal to have him removed from the Privy Council for having introduced the Act of 1819. Cobbett was a veteran Radical, lately returned to Parliament as MP for Oldham, who had long identified himself in opposition to the resumption of cash payments. In Cobbett's estimation, resumption had 'doubled, if not tripled, the real amount of the taxes, and violated all contracts for time; given triple gains to every lender, and placed every borrower in jeopardy'.[42] From the start, he maintained that a return to the gold standard was impossible without repudiating the national debt. In November 1819 he had publicly given Castlereagh leave 'to lay me on a gridiron, and broil me alive, while Sidmouth may stir the coals, and Canning stand by and laugh at my groans', should the measure be successfully executed. Thereafter, Cobbett and the gridiron were indelibly associated together and the symbol formed the masthead to his *Weekly Political Register*.[43]

Peel's defence of himself in his speech of 16 May 1833 was widely praised by contemporaries. However, the Ultra Tory Lord Mansfield noted that the 'fear of inconsistency' was Peel's principal motivation on the subject: 'it is doubtful whether his successful attack upon Cobbett added much to his fame, it was not a worthy triumph'. More pointedly, Gladstone recalled that Peel's show of emotion on the occasion was out of all proportion to the significance of Cobbett's attack:

> what struck me at the time as singular was this, that notwithstanding the state of feeling [in the Commons against Cobbett], Sir Robert Peel was greatly excited in dealing with one who at the time was little more than a contemptible antagonist. At that period, shirt collars were made with 'gills', which came up upon the cheeks: and Peel's gills were so soaked with perspiration, that they actually lay down upon his neck cloth.[44]

* * *

The sense that Peel was psychologically committed to Bullionism in a manner impervious to counter-argument was reinforced by his subsequent role, as Prime Minister, in passing the Bank Charter Act of 1844 (*7 & 8 Vic. c.32*). Boyd Hilton regards it as 'a good example of how Peel could combine political pragmatism with doctrinal rigidity' and 'the high point of Peel's evangelical, hair-shirt economics'.[45] The legislation was understood at the time (and subsequently) as the corollary of 'Peel's Act' of 1819 and leant a neat symmetry to Peel's public identification with the issue, which he reinforced in introducing the measure to the House of Commons on 6 May 1844:

> Considering the part which I took in the year 1819 in terminating the system of inconvertible paper currency, and in re-establishing the ancient standard of value, it will no doubt be a source of great personal satisfaction to me, if I shall

now succeed, after the lapse of a quarter of a century since those measures were adopted, in obtaining the assent of the House to proposals which are, in fact, the complement of them, and which are calculated to guarantee their permanence, and to facilitate their practical operation.[46]

As Gladstone later observed, with evident admiration, everyone who knew Peel knew that his Bank Charter Act 'was a kind of Baptismal Creed with him'.[47] Peel himself regarded it as the 'complement and defence of the Act of 1819' and was heartened by the international praise it garnered him. In 1846, in response to a memorial from the inhabitants of the town of Elbing in Prussia, Peel commented that the Act had 'been the means of checking abuse in times of great critical importance to the commercial interests of the country, as well as of unusual speculation. This bill has given to paper money a settled value in making it always exchangeable with specie.'[48]

The Bank Charter Act addressed the anomalous position of the 400 or so remaining joint-stock and country banks, which had failed to exercise the necessary degree of monetary discipline (in respect of note-issue) intended by the return to cash payments in 1819. 'Peel's Act' had left the issue of bank notes unregulated and unlimited and this allowed the Bank of England and country banks to 'compete' for business. As the latter were responsible for about one-quarter of the notes in circulation, their policy was not insignificant. The currency crises of 1832, 1835–6 and 1838–9 convinced Peel (once more) that it was the unrestricted issue of bank notes on the part of country bankers, rather than any fallibility in Bullionist theory, which was to blame. Because the country banks had not contracted their note-issue soon enough, they had prevented the Bank of England, when the state of the foreign exchanges turned against them, from decreasing the amount of paper currency in circulation quickly enough to protect against speculation, instability and price fluctuation. The subject exercised successive select committees of the House of Commons in 1836–8 and 1840–1. Peel, who was a leading member of the latter, used the 'get-out' clause in the 1833 Bank Charter Act – allowing the terms of the Bank of England's charter to be considered by Parliament halfway through its 21-year period – in order to legislate on the issue.[49]

In the same way that the currency issue in 1819 had divided commentators into Bullionist and anti-Bullionist camps, so that of banking gave rise to a 'currency school', roughly approximating to Peel's views on the subject, and a 'banking school'. The most famous advocates of the currency school were Samuel Jones Loyd (afterwards Lord Overstone), Colonel Robert Torrens and George Warde Norman (of the Bank of England). Their principal argument was that note-issues should be strictly determined by reference to the gold bullion in reserve at the Bank of England: in turn, this suggested the need for a strong degree of central control and Parliament's regulation of the banking sector. As such, the principle upon which Peel operated in the Bank Charter Act reflected their view that note circulation should expand and contract with the amount of bullion in reserve. When the bullion reserve declined, a restriction of the note-issue would help to raise the value of money and lower the price of British goods, thereby attracting foreign buyers and bringing bullion back into the country. Conversely, when the bullion reserve increased, an enlarged note-issue would lower the value of money and raise prices, thereby facilitating the export of bullion from the country to pay for more competitively priced foreign goods. Gold bullion would help to maintain the equilibrium between these two economic processes. It would automatically regulate the state of the currency and prices and determine the appropriate level for the issue of bank notes.[50]

By contrast, leading advocates of the banking school were John Fullarton, Thomas Tooke, J.W. Gilbart and James Wilson, the editor of *The Economist*. The latter, which was established as an avowedly 'Free Trade' publication in 1843, maintained a particularly long and animated campaign on the subject.[51] Peel himself seems to have concluded, erroneously, that his banking school critics were all anti-Bullionists. Significantly, he absented himself from attending the hearings of the 1840 select committee when Tooke gave evidence.[52] In fact, the banking school were Bullionists who felt that the amount of bank notes in circulation should be left to the discretion of bankers. As *The Economist* put it, in May 1845:

> It is because we feel strongly that the interference of Parliament, under the pretext of supplying prudence, and regulating the interests and responsibilities of commerce in any way, has always proved a serious failure, and a miserable substitution for that individual caution which it is so well calculated to supplant, that we feel bound to oppose such legislation generally. And particularly so in the present instance, because we believe that the means proposed are calculated to have an opposite tendency; to endanger more the solvency of banks, and very materially and unnecessarily to aggravate the evils arising from commercial revulsions and adverse exchanges, to which a great commercial country must ever be less or more subject.[53]

Rather than exalting the bullion reserve as the barometer of economic pressure, the banking school pointed out the importance of prices and interest rates: to them, the amount of bank notes in circulation depended on prices and wages. In addition, they argued the 'real bills doctrine' that there were more forms of credit than just bank notes and that these 'negotiable instruments' (cheques, deposits and bills of exchange) had a crucial impact in determining prices. This was a line of argument which Peel and the currency school were apt to underestimate, dismiss or ignore.

By the terms of the Bank Charter Act, which came into operation on 5 September 1844 (the sesquicentenary of the Bank of England's foundation), the Bank's operations were divided between two separate departments, one concerned with 'issue' and one with 'banking'. On the one hand, the Act gave the bank the (eventual) monopoly of the issue and circulation of bank notes by centralising note-issue under its authority. There were to be no new banks of issue and the Bank of England would gradually absorb all lapsed or defunct country banks. The current note-issue of the existing country banks (some £8m) was set as its maximum note-issue thereafter: the right of issue would be surrendered when a country bank lapsed, went into bankruptcy or had more than six partners. As such, when all private banks had been phased out, the Bank of England would stand unchallenged as the single bank of note-issue and exchange.

The corollary to this was a tightly controlled and restricted regulation of the amount of notes the Bank of England could issue in its own right. The Act, working to the principles enunciated by the currency school, laid down that the Bank could only issue some £14m of notes unsupported by bullion (its fiduciary limit) – for the rest, its circulation would be strictly regulated by the amount of bullion in its vaults. When the Bank's bullion reserves declined, it would have to contract its note-issue to the same extent. In order to ensure better scrutiny, the Bank's accounts (and the state of the reserves) would be published on a weekly basis. By contrast, the banking department, concerned with the discount and deposit business of putting money on deposit and lending it as bills of exchange or convertible securities, was to be free of all regulation, leaving the Bank of England to compete on open terms with other lenders. As such, the Act was designed to secure a single, strong and regulated note-issue, maintain the system of convertibility from paper to gold and, through dampening speculation, prevent the ill-effects attributed to an unrestricted paper currency.[54]

In introducing these measures to Parliament, on 6 and 20 May 1844, Peel demonstrated a 'marvellous command of an abstruse subject'. As one commentator later observed, 'the new currency Law of 1844, regulating the paper circulation by the Foreign Exchanges, was declared to be a self-acting principle, a panacea for all monetary disorders. Speculations, fluctuations, panics, were to be no more.'[55] Particularly memorable was the 'What is a pound?' section in the speech of 6 May, in which Peel attempted to establish the history and definition of the pound sterling as a contract between the bank and the note-bearer to pay in gold bullion of a standard weight and value:

> Now, the whole foundation of the proposal I am about to make rests upon the assumption that ... that which is implied by the word 'pound' is a certain definite quantity of gold with a mark upon it to determine its weight and fineness, and that the engagement to pay a pound means nothing, and can mean nothing else, than the promise to pay to the holder, when he demands it, that definite quantity of gold.[56]

The Aberdeen Herald, commenting on the widespread support advanced for the measure, complained that the 'real effect' of Peel's proposal was 'to give government the virtual control of the whole issues of the country – a power which few ministries ought to be invested with'. However, the *Herald's* view of a banking consensus in favour of the Bill was misplaced. On 11 June 1844 some 44 of the principal banking houses in London memorialised Peel against the proposals, arguing that the fiduciary limit of £14m was dangerously restrictive.[57] This was a line of argument which was well represented in subsequent discussions of the legislation. The writer William Leckie argued that £20m was a far more reasonable threshold and, from within the government, Lord Stanley maintained that he had never understood the basis upon which Peel calculated the issue at £14m. The Nottingham banker Ichabod Wright was more blunt, describing the limit as 'suicidal'.[58] In particular, it was maintained that such a restrictive circulation would tend to stimulate, rather than prevent, an economic crisis. To the essayist Thomas Joplin, the panic of 1825 had demonstrated 'that the idea of compelling the Bank to contract its issues to the full extent of the gold exported, with a view to prevent pressures and panics, is a great mistake. If contractions so small have produced such disasters, larger will only increase them.' A similar point was made by Lord George Bentinck in 1847.[59]

Unsurprisingly, given Peel's long and close identification with the issue (and with memories of 'Peel's Act' undimmed) a number of critics attacked the Bank Charter Act by reference to the Prime Minister's own record on the subject. Within weeks of the Bill's introduction, 'An ex-MP' argued that Peel's 'overweening self-complacency', as a currency reformer, was unmerited. John Taylor also prophesied a quick and painful vindication of Peel's critics:

> Your success now is but the prelude to your defeat hereafter. Your measure carries with it the elements of its own destruction. Your triumph will be your overthrow … when this great measure of yours, on which you so much pride yourself, will be swept away for ever.[60]

The most serious challenge to the principles and practice of the Bank Charter Act, and the whole thrust of Peel's currency policy since 1819, came within three years of its passage. It was a crisis precipitated by the profusion of 'cheap money' (registered as cheques, deposits and bills of exchange rather than as bank notes) and the railway mania of the mid-1840s.[61] As bullion began to leave the country, the issue department of the Bank of England contracted its note-issue, in conformity with the operation of the Bank Charter Act. However, the banking department of the Bank of England found itself increasingly unable to meet the claims of its depositors in notes. The thrust of Peel's thinking on the subject, reinforced by the arguments of the currency school, had been to underestimate the significance of 'real bills' doctrine and to focus completely on meeting the demands of holders of bank notes to convert them into specie. The incongruity of the situation was reinforced by the physical separation of the two departments within the same institution. It was well known that the issue department held a large bullion reserve next door to the banking department, which was in serious need of relief. However, the issue department was prevented from extending relief to the banking department by the terms of the Bank Charter Act, which treated them (to all intents and purposes) as two separate institutions.[62]

On 25 October 1847, Lord John Russell's Whig government was forced to advise the Bank of England to increase its unsupported note-issue beyond the £14m fiduciary limit laid down by the Bank Charter Act and indemnified the Bank against liability for infringing it. It was an unfortunate reversal of the position fifty years earlier, when the Bank had petitioned the government for relief from its burdens. Much controversy arose from the fact that, under the original terms of the Bank Charter Bill, provision had been made for the Bank to exceed its fiduciary limit on the authority of the First Lord of the Treasury, the Chancellor of the Exchequer and the Master of the Mint. This contingency had been removed (on Peel's insistence) by the time the Bill went

THE POLITICAL "ROBIN" DRIVEN BY THE SEVERITY OF THE
TIMES TO SEEK FOR GRAIN.

6: 'The Political "Robin" Driven By The Severity Of The Times To Seek For Grain',
Punch, IX, July–December 1845, 223.
Lord John Russell offers a 'crumb' of comfort to 'Robin' Peel. Note the inversion in the usual
physical contrast between Peel and Russell (signifying Peel's subservience to events following
the 'Edinburgh Letter').

into its committee stage; indeed, it was the loss of this security which stimulated the protest of the 44 leading banking houses of London.[63]

The government's intervention amounted to the suspension of the Bank Charter Act. This was never realised in practice on this occasion because the Bank's bullion reserves began to increase from the end of the month and the crisis abated. The Act of 1844 had clearly failed (in the short term) to prevent a severe financial crisis.[64] Parliament instituted a commission of inquiry, but in spite of an attempt (on the part of its Protectionist and Radical members) to have the Act repealed, the legislation emerged unscathed. Had it succeeded, it would have been (as Bentinck commented), 'a tremendous blow to [Peel's] Financial Reputation'.[65] The fiduciary limit remained at £14m – a level which was too low for subsequent economic crises and one which meant that the Act had to be suspended twice (1857 and 1866) in subsequent years. However, it remained the bedrock of British financial policy down to the First World War when special measures had to be enforced and the Gold Standard was suspended again until 1925.[66]

* * *

In the long run, Peel's judgement on the operation of Bullionist theory was vindicated. However, although the Acts of 1819 and 1844 became the mechanism through which the mid-Victorian boom was (in part) engineered, Hilton maintains that this was at variance with Peel's intentions, which were static and stationary (in economic terms) rather than expansive and energetic.[67] It may be the case that the 'ultimate good' which Peel felt would 'result' after 'some suffering' was indeed a carefully controlled, rather than unbridled, economy, but Hilton would seem to be in danger of condemning Peel at every turn. That the Bank Charter Act helped to avert the periodic banking crises which afflicted the USA and other parts of Europe, because of the confidence engendered by the strict requirements of notes backed by gold above the fiduciary limit, is a judgement borne out by the later history of the nineteenth century.[68] Unlike Ireland – where Peel was accused of not coming to an enlightened understanding of the situation until it was too late – he had come, early on, to fasten on the economic theory which drove his entire political career. That he stuck to it dogmatically (almost doctrinally) thereafter, and that it prevailed, would seem to be a cause for praise rather than censure. In political terms, it engendered a lifetime of hostility from Radicals and Ultra Tories and subjected many more to severe economic consequences. To Peel's contemporary critics, the Bank Charter Act was a piece of legislation held in almost equal contempt with the Repeal of the Corn Laws. Croker told Lord George Bentinck that he had 'always suspected that it was a piece of machinery of no great use in fair weather, and which would and must break down under any serious pressure' whilst the financier Adam Hodgson argued that the country had 'had a hair-breadth escape from national confusion' in 1847. According to Hodgson, 'the commercial energies of the country have been prostrated in a degree to which, in an experience of thirty years, I have seen no parallel'.[69]

As such, it has been forgotten that, in the same period that Peel was being lauded for having repealed the Corn Laws, his mature political reputation was coming under serious assault for having legislated the Bank Charter Act. Peel was consulted at the height of the financial crisis of 1847, by the Whig Chancellor of the Exchequer Charles Wood. This was a course of action which Lord Ashley (for one) thought 'quite right – & yet rather mean' considering that the Whigs had helped to eject him from office the previous year.[70] At the same time, by continuing to identify Peel with the operational difficulties of the Bank Charter Act, the Whigs may have helped to indemnify themselves (as well as the Bank of England) from some of the hostile publicity generated by the crisis. To Peel's critics, the financial crisis of October 1847 seemed to be of a piece with his life-long commitment to Bullionism; as such, he continued to be the lightning-rod for criticism of the measure. The downside of having been the author of 'Peel's Act' of 1819 and its complement, the Bank Charter Act of 1844, was that Peel was regarded as the author of the financial crises of the autumn of 1825 and the autumn of 1847. In retrospect, it is less surprising that Hilton should have re-discovered Peel's dogmatism on the currency issue (which was abundantly clear to contemporaries) than that it should have remained neglected by historians and biographers for so long.[71]

4

MR HOME SECRETARY PEEL:
AN ILLIBERAL 'LIBERAL TORY'?

I may be a Tory – I may be an illiberal – but the fact is undeniable, that when I first entered upon the duties of the Home Department, there were laws in existence which imposed upon the subjects of this realm unusual and extraordinary restrictions: the fact is undeniable, that those laws have been effaced. Tory as I am, I have the further satisfaction of knowing, that there is not a single law connected with my name, which has not had for its object some mitigation of the severity of the criminal law; some prevention of abuse in the exercise of it; or some security for its impartial administration.

Peel, Speech on resigning office, 1 May 1827.[1]

* * *

The 1820s represent a crucial decade in Peel's political evolution and self-presentation. They were dominated by his two periods as Home Secretary; first, between January 1822 and his resignation from the ministry in April 1827 and secondly (after a nine month absence) from January 1828 until the fall of the Tory government in November 1830. During this period, Peel was pre-occupied with reforms to the criminal law, to juries and to policing, some of which he inherited from his predecessor (Sidmouth), some of which were the necessary response to humanitarian campaigns and parliamentary recommendations but others (like the Metropolitan Police) were the product of Peel's experience in Ireland and his own thinking on the subject. The result was that, in marked contrast with Peel's contemporary reputation on the currency issue, he was universally held in high regard for his work as Home Secretary. Similarly, in May 1830 *Blackwood's Edinburgh Magazine* noted the contrasting positions afforded by Peel's negative association with Catholic Emancipation, on the one hand, and his positive association with criminal law reform on the other.[2] This position was faithfully adhered to by historians for much of the next century-and-a-half, reaching its apogee in the work of Norman Gash. In *Mr Secretary Peel*, first published in 1961, Gash lauded Peel's record as Home Secretary in terms which would have befitted an

Elizabethan first minister like Walsingham or Cecil.[3] However, within the past generation, historians have subjected Peel's once unimpeachable credentials as a reforming Home Secretary to almost continual assault. Why has this occurred? This chapter re-considers Peel's record as Home Secretary, relating it to developments in his evolving political persona. Two facets assume prominence: Peel's increasingly personal association with his ministerial success and his growing reputation as a 'liberal Tory' in the governments of Liverpool and Wellington.

* * *

Peel's promotion to high office had been the cause of frequent speculation since he left Ireland with a reputation, the representation of Oxford University and a parliamentary following, in August 1818. Events in the intervening period made Peel's ministerial future a subject of political speculation and real significance, given the severe downturn in the fortunes of Lord Liverpool's ministry.[4] On 16 August 1819 the Manchester magistracy dispersed a meeting convened at St Peter's Fields to hear Henry 'Orator' Hunt deliver a speech in favour of parliamentary reform. The severity of that dispersal – which resulted in over 400 injuries and a dozen fatalities – immortalised those proceedings forever as the 'Peterloo Massacre' in mock homage to the Battle of Waterloo.[5] Following George IV's accession in January 1820, the government was forced to institute steps denying his wife (Caroline) her rights as Queen. Given that the couple had been divorced in all but name for over a decade, a Bill of Pains and Penalties was subsequently introduced into the House of Lords. However, the government's majority was so small that it was withdrawn before going to the Commons. The protracted divorce proceedings shed unwelcome light on the personal predilections of both royal parties and generated negative publicity against an administration which did not lack potential successors. The widespread popular acclaim which attached to the Queen's cause was one indication of the growing importance of public opinion – registered in petitions, newspapers and political squibs – a constituency which was beginning to assume growing significance with a rising generation of politicians like Peel.[6] In a justly famous letter of 23 March 1820, Peel told his close friend and colleague Croker:

> Do not you think that the tone of England – of that great compound of folly, weakness, prejudice, wrong feeling, right feeling, obstinacy, and newspaper paragraphs, which is called public opinion – is more liberal – to use an odious but intelligible phrase – than the policy of the Government? Do not you think that there is a feeling, becoming daily more general and more confirmed … in favour of some undefined change in the mode of governing the country? … Can we resist – I mean, not next session or the session after that – but can we resist for seven years Reform in Parliament?[7]

In marked contrast with the government's fortunes, Peel appeared to be carrying all before him. Frances Shelley met 'the celebrated Mr Peel' for the first time in 1819, having been apprised of his 'superior talents' by the 'enthusiasm' of her friends. Being predisposed 'to criticise, rather than to admire him' (on account of his social background) Lady Shelley afterwards concluded that he was 'undoubtedly the English Metternich': 'Mr Peel's talents have placed him in the front rank of statesmen. He has great oratorical gifts; but they say that he is not a good debater ... Will he rise to superiority, or will he give up public life? *Nous verrons* [we will see]'.[8]

As such, ministers quickly realised the advantage of securing Peel's administrative talents and political following. Peel 'certainly has many partizans', Mrs Arbuthnot observed in 1820.[9] Admittedly, Peel's semi-detached status did not imply any lack of real support for ministers at this period. His defence of the Manchester magistracy was such that one commentator feared he would repent his 'honesty' should he ever become Home Secretary.[10] However, Peel did refuse to become President of the Board of Control in 1820 because of the government's handling of the Queen Caroline affair, regarding it as one element in the 'cauldron which has been bubbling a long time, and upon which, as it always seemed to me, the Government never could discern the least simmering'. Under these circumstances, Peel refused an offer which – as Lord Bathurst observed – would not be 'advantageous to us or creditable to himself'.[11]

Managing a mutually advantageous transaction between Peel and the government was to prove especially difficult, given that the claims of several existing – and many more aspiring – members of the cabinet had to be met without causing undue offence. In the aftermath of the King's divorce bill, Liverpool attempted some political courtship of his own – not least with the followers of Lord Grenville (who had broken away from the Whigs following Peterloo) and George Canning, who had resigned as President of the Board of Control because of his close association with the Queen. Canning was too valuable (and potentially dangerous) a political asset to leave outside the pale of government but he was unwilling to return to the Board of Control when the immediate crisis passed. Peel was also exhibiting signs of increasing political independence, 'but whether it is because he likes to live retired with his pretty [new] wife, or that he thinks the Ministry will not stand', no one was sure.[12] In the spring of 1821, an attempt to replace Vansittart (the Chancellor of the Exchequer) with Peel foundered on the opposition of Castlereagh, the Leader of the Commons, who feared that Peel would rival his own position (and dominance) on the government front bench. The Exchequer would have been a natural position for Peel, given his role on the Currency Committee, and both Canning and Vansittart supported the arrangement. Mrs Arbuthnot was less impressed:

> Peel has scarcely ever given us a vote this session, and his relations & friends have constantly voted against us, besides which Mr Peel has never shown any financial talents & is decidedly a bad debater. He can make good speeches when he can prepare them beforehand, very classical and fine language, but he never can answer.

Peel's perceived deficiency in debate (which was observed by both Lady Shelley and Harriet Arbuthnot) was something he freely admitted, although it was not a view which was widely shared in all quarters.[13]

Liverpool approached Peel again in the summer of 1821. He did so in such 'strange, shuffling, hesitating' terms that Peel's rejection was almost guaranteed. According to report, Peel declared himself 'well-disposed towards the Government' and willing to hear 'what changes were to be made & what office offered to him before he made a more decisive answer'. Peel offered the state of his health (his eyes in particular) as a reason why 'office was not a matter of much anxiety or importance to him' – a sentiment he repeated to his friend Croker: 'He seems generally disinclined to official life, but *haud credo* [I do not think so].'[14]

It was far more likely, as Mrs Arbuthnot concluded after Peel finally rejected the government's overtures, that he did not think the Board of Control was 'good enough'.[15] Croker had already suggested to ministers (through Lord Melville) that Peel would only accept an 'office of business', such as the Exchequer or the Home Office, although he agreed with Colchester in thinking that Peel was 'looking a little too high at first'. The Exchequer was impossible (given Castlereagh's sentiments) and the Home Office (to which Sidmouth was amenable) presented difficulties in respect of Canning. 'In short', Croker concluded, Liverpool 'keeps Peel open to have him at hand to put into any gap which he may not be otherwise able to fill up, in the Admiralty if Canning should refuse, or in the Home Department, if that should be more convenient'.[16] It is not surprising why Peel, who placed a high value on himself, held out until he was offered the Home Office (without conditions) at the end of 1821. The appointment was considered as some consolation for Sidmouth's retirement by Ultra Tories like Lord Kenyon: 'Thank God, Peel succeeds him.' For himself, Peel made a characteristic self-reference to the 'very painful sacrifices' he was making in accepting office and 'the fear that I have undertaken what is beyond my strength'.[17]

* * *

In 1822, a government-sponsored pamphlet described the work of the Home Office as 'the maintenance and supervision of the public peace and the due execution of the laws for the support of an internal order and tranquillity'.[18] These constituted the primary functions of an office whose extension into the realms of factory working-hours, public health and the poor laws was still a decade away. The popular memory accords Peel's significance as Home Secretary to his founding of the Metropolitan Police Force in September 1829 – as exemplified in the continuing currency given in some quarters to the terms 'Bobbies' and 'Peelers'.[19] Though the groundwork for this was laid during Peel's first period at the Home Office, it was not realised until the second. To contemporaries, Peel was more closely associated with the attempt to mitigate the severities of the criminal law, especially that part of it which imposed the death penalty on a range of offences (many of them petty by modern standards).[20] This took the form of abolishing obsolete or inefficient legal statutes and bringing together – with necessary revisions – those which remained useful. During Peel's time in office, the majority of legal statutes imposing capital punishment in cases of larceny (i.e. theft), criminal damage, offences against the person and forgery were revised.[21] Peel also sought to make the empanelling of juries more efficient and legislated for the better administration of gaols.[22]

These were causes which had been the subject of frequent campaigning on the part of Samuel Whitbread, James Mackintosh, Samuel Romilly, Thomas Fowell Buxton, Stephen Lushington, John Howard and Elizabeth Fry in the preceding decade, and had stimulated an 'avalanche of reform petitions' to the House of Commons. A select committee on criminal law was established in 1819, the report of which called 'for a mixture of substantive reform, consolidation and removal of capital punishment for a broad range of offences'. The same conclusion, more forcefully expressed, emerged from another select committee report five years later.[23] Sidmouth had begun work in this area before leaving office but had been pre-occupied with the severe domestic disturbances which had occurred in the aftermath of the return to peace, 'Peterloo' chief amongst them. As such, it was Peel who (in John Prest's words) 'distinguished himself from other contemporary reformers by his ability to see the process whole and to attend to all aspects, from the formulation of the criminal law and the mechanics of policing, through indictment, trial, and sentencing, to punishment on the scaffold, in prison, and in penal colonies'. Moreover, for Prest, Peel's consolidation of the criminal law was the 'most striking achievement ... perhaps of his whole career'.[24] In March 1825, Richard Rush, the American ambassador to London, noticed how Peel was able 'to look at the law, as a science, through the lights of his general reading in that and other fields; and therefore qualified to take hold of it with a reforming hand, though no professional man'.[25]

What one commentator called Peel's 'great task of simplifying & consolidating the criminal code' reached its apogee on 9 March 1826. Peel introduced measures to consolidate the laws relating to property and theft and improve the administration of justice in a speech which Canning commended to the King as a specimen of 'rare ability, temper, & information'.[26] A year later, Peel embodied these proposals in four separate bills, consolidating and amending the laws on larceny, malicious injury to property and remedies against the administrative district or Hundred. 'The manner in which [Peel] has proceeded' was commended by the Ultra Tory Duke of Newcastle as 'most sound & judicious – he has not sought to innovate, or alter, merely to prune & clear away the lumber & dead branches & leave the tree in a healthy state'.[27]

The Duke's sentiments, with their organic conception of reform as a safe and gradual process, were conservative in tone and symbolism. Newcastle's satisfaction with Peel's reforms revealed much about the conceptions behind them and the ability with which he gathered support from such guardedly traditional sectors of public opinion as that represented by the Duke. Desmond Brown has described Peel's speech of 9 March 1826 as 'a virtuoso performance. It was cogent, logical, beautifully phrased, and well calculated to appeal to the deep-rooted conservatism of the Members'. As such, it was designed to appease his intended audience. In many important respects, Peel was still the 'illiberal Tory' he presented himself as to parliament (half-seriously, half-mockingly) in May 1827, for he was unwilling to pursue the process to what legal reformers like Anthony Hammond and Jeremy Bentham regarded as its 'logical' conclusion – the codification of the English law.[28]

Bentham was the pre-eminent political philosopher of the day, whose belief in the utilitarian principle – that all human endeavour should provide for 'the greatest happiness of the greatest number' (the utilitarian or felicific calculus) – extended most pointedly to the criminal justice system.[29] Throughout his life, Bentham was devoted to establishing a constitutional code, after the fashion of the *Code Civil* (or *Code Napoleon*) in France, which would set out (with scientific certainty) the scale of punishments attached to any individual crime and the scope and operation of the different functions of the law. This would replace the uncertainties and, in Bentham's estimate, corruption which the present legal system perpetuated. The English legal system was primarily based on unwritten, un-codified common law and the interpretations to which it gave rise in successive generations (which were embodied as case law or precedents). Like other legal reformers of the period (such as Henry Brougham, who delivered a six-hour speech to Parliament on the subject in May 1828) Bentham attacked the impenetrable legal formularies in which lawyers worked,[30] the closed, self-governing professional oligarchies through which their monopolies were perpetuated (the Inns of Court and barristers' chambers) and the system of fees by which they maintained themselves. This made them self-interested parties in the (in Bentham's eyes, unnecessary) prolongation of legal cases.[31]

Moreover, the fact that the legal system was shot through with judicial discretion and mercy in determining guilt and punishment meant that two different individuals charged with the same crime would not necessarily meet with the same treatment at the hands of the law: a blatant anomaly in Bentham's eyes.[32] The discretionary nature of English criminal justice during this period has been interpreted by historians in two particular ways. On the one hand, Douglas Hay argues that it represents a system of 'gross and capricious terror', forming the basis of a 'ruling class conspiracy'. On this reading, the law was used to subjugate the population and enforce deference to the ruling classes, through dangling the threat of the gallows before society, but then only applying that power selectively. About half of all capital convictions were commuted in eighteenth-century England by the judiciary or the crown. The gratitude felt by acquitted felons towards their patriarchal superiors made it a powerful method of reinforcing the existing social and political order which could be manipulated for self-serving ends. Consequently, there was substantial resistance to legal reform amongst the Tory squirearchy and the professional legal establishment.[33]

On the other hand, discretionary justice could be seen as a vital and nuanced thread running through the whole criminal justice system to the extent that it was impossible for any one party to control it. As Peter King has demonstrated, discretion of this sort motivated every stage of the judicial process and was crucial to its working and success – from deciding whether or not to bring charges, to what charges to bring, how to try the case and what punishment to enforce. It allowed the circumstances of any given crime (such as its context, place, timing, severity and motivation) to be taken into consideration, in determining the outcome, thereby mitigating the severities that might otherwise have ensued under a more scientific and more certain system.[34]

Consequently, the difference between consolidation and codification (between Peel's position and Bentham's) was not immaterial, for it symbolised everything about their respective attitudes towards legal reform, its advisability and extent. As Bentham informed Peel, in August 1826:

> *consolidation* and consolidation only, is your as yet declared design … By that *word*, resistance was obviated, support bespoken and obtained. Against this *consolidation* plan, no official or professional voice has … been lifted up: why? Because, to the lawyers, and to them alone, if the design *stopped there*, could it be of any use … by alleviating their labours: leaving the rule of action throughout as incomprehensible to non-lawyers, as before; especially if the lengthy and involved phraseology in the established style, in which the consolidation plan has commenced, be *persevered* in.

However, there was also a degree of political opportunism in Peel's strategy. Given the formidable intellectual assault which faced him from within the legal and political establishment, Peel had to combine what K.J.M. Smith has described as his 'gradualist inclinations' towards legal reform with substantive measures which would 'regulate the content and pace of reform'.[35] Politically, Peel had to retain the support of his traditional Tory supporters and satisfy powerful vested interests in the legal profession whilst also mollifying public opinion. As Peel informed Liverpool in October 1822, 'it was in vain to attempt to defend what is established, merely because it is established … [The] best policy [is] to take to ourselves the credit of the reform, and that by being the author of it we should have the best chance of presenting limits to the innovation.' The means of achieving this was through a process of incremental and piecemeal consolidation, which would publicly expose the existing system to scrutiny and allow ministers to defend what was retained whilst reforming what could be mitigated.[36] John Prest describes Peel's approach to consolidation as:

> the collection 'of dispersed statutes under one head' followed by the rejection of what was 'superfluous', the clearing up of what was 'obscure', the weighing of 'the precise force of each expression', and 'ascertaining the doubts that have arisen in practice and the solution which may have been given to those doubts by decisions of the courts of law'. Where he found any gap 'through which notorious guilt escapes' … he would remedy it. In Peel's hands, then, a consolidating act was a reforming act which incorporated case law and supplied omissions.[37]

In his lifetime, Peel's criminal law reforms gained him a wide range of plaudits. These sentiments continued long after his death, even where other aspects of his life and political legacy remained contested. In 1827 Peel was described as 'the ablest Home Secretary we ever perhaps had' and two years later, on being presented with the freedom of the City of London, he was hailed 'as the Justinian of the British empire'. Similarly, *Blackwood's Edinburgh Magazine* eulogised Peel's industriousness and administrative competence as Home Secretary: 'constantly to be found at his post; conscientious and scrupulous, he devoted the powers of an active and vigorous mind to the discharge of [his] momentous duties'.[38]

However, a number of commentators were as perceptive as Peel had been in perceiving the advantages (for the government's reputation as well as his own) which accrued from this carefully calibrated policy of reform. After hearing Peel's celebrated speech on criminal reform, on 9 March 1826, the young Whig politician, J.E. Denison, observed:

> The House showed him extreme favour, committed the charge to his hands with unbounded confidence, & the highest praise & thanks for his undertaking – What a change of times – Here is the Secretary of State proposing a great revision & amendment of the statute law of the land – & a House of Commons cheering him to the task – a very few years ago – the same ministry opposed all attempts at any unhallowed meddling with our sacred & venerable laws, & the House of Commons essentially the same turned a deaf ear to every entreaty.

Edward Littleton also criticised Peel's new-found status as a 'liberal': having 'opposed all Romilly's and Mackintosh's attempts to soften our criminal law, [Peel] only took up the work when the public mind was prepared by them to demand it'.[39]

That Peel was being talked of in a different vein from his cabinet colleagues, as a result of his legal reforms, became abundantly clear in April 1827 when he resigned from the government on Canning's appointment as Prime Minister. The veteran Radical, Francis Place, observed that:

> Those who have resigned, with the exception of Mr Peel whom on account of the part he has taken in digesting the Laws every body wishes may consent to remain in office, are a set of men the least fit of any to govern such a nation as this in its present circumstances. They are all of the old stupid illiberal school, too ignorant of the state of mankind to be able to conduct themselves with even seeming propriety, and having therefore no hold on the wishes, or sympathies of the people.[40]

The same month, James Loch (the commissioner of the Marquess of Stafford's Scottish estates, who had recently entered Parliament on the Whig interest) told the Earl of Carlisle that all his fellow countrymen regretted 'the loss of Mr Peel's liberal system of administration' at the Home Office. Lord Binning (a close associate of Canning) conceded that Loch's sentiments were 'entertained by many, many of my countrymen'. Likewise, J.C. Hobhouse was criticised by his fellow Whigs for an 'encomiastic' appreciation of Peel's legal reforms, a fact about which he remained unrepentant: 'I only said what I felt and what was true. Peel is a good man, and he has gained a great and – if he goes on – a lasting reputation.'[41]

* * *

Peel's first period as Home Secretary had gained him a glowing reputation as one of the more 'liberal' members of the administration. It was accompanied by a strengthening of the egotistical vein within him. The highly personal strain in which he associated himself with his legislative acts as Home Secretary and the defiance with which he defended them from assault represent important staging-posts in this process. For example, on 9 March 1826, Peel declared that he could have:

> no motive, but the desire to improve the opportunities which have been placed within my reach, and to exert, to useful ends, the influence and authority, which constitute, if rightly applied, the real value of high official station. And, sir, if there be mixed with that desire any latent feeling of a more personal nature, why should I disavow the legitimate ambition, to leave behind me some record of the trust I have held, which may outlive the fleeting discharge of the mere duties of ordinary routine, and that may, perhaps, confer some distinction on my name, by connecting it with permanent improvements in the judicial institutions of the country?[42]

Sir James Prior observed these developments with a mixture of cynicism and disdain. 'As a Tory, I flatter myself I have some claim to your notice [he observed after Peel's resignation speech of 1 May 1827], as a *liberal* Tory, I trust that all confidence will not be withdrawn from the opinion of a class, from which I would fain hope you are for a time separated, less by differences in substance and principle, than in form.' Prior's complaint was that Peel had proved himself a 'useful' rather than a 'brilliant' Home Secretary. He had seized upon 'the popular topic of criminal law' as a means of 'securing a reputation' and given the government the 'semblance ... of youth and vigour'.[43]

Peel's newly acquired reputation was also accompanied by a hardening in his attitude towards criticism and an unwillingness to compromise his opinions. In 1827 Peel responded to Bentham's proposals for a revision of the Jury Act of 1825 with a curt negative. He was equally dismissive five years later, when the Duke of Richmond proposed amendments to Peel's Act of 1827, granting remedies in case of outrage against the Hundred: 'I thought Peel seemed very unwilling to allow that *his* Act was not *perfect* [Ellenborough observed] – & that that was the true ground of his objections.'[44] Likewise, whilst Peel had worked harmoniously with one Under-Secretary, Henry Hobhouse (who had been in the Home Office since Sidmouth's day), his relations with another, Samuel March Phillips (himself a writer on the English law), were reported to be brusque and condescending. After returning to the Home Office in January 1828, Peel is supposed to have sent for Phillips:

> and receiving him standing, said, 'I think it right, Mr Phillipps [*sic*], that I should offer the Under-Secretaryship you hold to the gentleman to whom I gave it before' [Peel's brother-in-law, George Dawson]. To which Phillipps replied that when Lord Lansdowne appointed him, he told him it was a permanent appointment, on which Peel, looking him steadfastly in the face, after a pause said, "Oh! I see!", and never added another word. But Peel treated him ever after with great coldness and distance, always keeping him standing in his presence, and never once throughout his official connexion with him asking

him to take a chair…but I believe that all Peel's subordinates would make the same complaint of him.[45]

At the end of Peel's first period as Home Secretary, Peel's political complexion as 'liberal', 'Tory' or 'liberal Tory' was still a matter of keen debate. During his second period in office (1828–30), Peel's political attitudes (relative to those of his cabinet colleagues) increasingly marked him out as a 'liberal'. This provoked consternation amongst some high-placed political observers. In the space of a few short months during 1830, Peel was castigated for being 'liberal in principle in order to catch votes', *over liberal*, and proposing 'the most absurdly liberal measures in order to please our enemies'. However, the same inclinations meant that, as Peel's stock fell progressively with Mrs Arbuthnot, so it rose with Jeremy Bentham.[46]

However, in the same period that Peel's liberalism was generating (sometimes adverse) political comment, his establishment of the Metropolitan Police Force was suggesting, in some quarters at least, a contrary political temperament. Few issues were more likely to raise a sense of outraged English constitutionalism than that of a police force.[47] The prevailing suspicions against the establishment of such a force – that it was expensive, absolutist and 'un-English' in nature – had dogged legislative experimentation in the field since it became a leading topic of debate in the late-eighteenth century. The same suspicions ensured that what Radicals and Ultra Tories alike thought of as an English *gendarmerie* (a military body entrusted with policing the civilian population) remained a staple part in its diet of criticism down to the time of Chartism.[48]

According to Stanley Palmer, it is 'impossible to speculate how long substantial police reform would have been delayed in England had Peel not been in office in the 1820s'. In 1822, a select committee of the House of Commons famously commented that it was 'difficult to reconcile an effective system of police with that perfect freedom of action and exemption from interference, which are the great blessings and privileges of this country'. This viewpoint continued to prevail over the course of Peel's next half-decade in office. However, within a month of his return, on 28 February 1828, Peel delivered a 'performance of lachrymose hand wringing' to Parliament. In it, he highlighted the growth in the rate of recorded crime in London since the publication of the 1822 report and decried the 'imperfect, inadequate and wretched' means of remedying it through the existing system – the parish watch.[49] This voluntary and unsalaried mechanism for maintaining law and order was instigated in the time of Charles II (giving rise to the popular description of watchmen as 'Charleys'): it was comprehensively remodelled within eighteen months of the speech. Peel secured the appointment of a new select committee, the report from which (July 1828) provided him with the necessary parliamentary sanction to press ahead with reform. Further weight was leant to Peel's arguments by the increasing amount of public comment in newspapers on the 'lawless' state of the metropolis and the need for police reform.[50] The veteran Radical, Francis Place, felt that Peel had secured an unfair ascendancy over his opponents by exaggerating the extent of metropolitan crime:

Mr Peel having most unwisely in his speech declared a great increase of crime, will no doubt do all he can to prove his case, and it is very probable that the Report will contain assertions of the increase of crime directly at variance with the facts, and that from not having had the proper witnesses ... and from not putting the proper questions ... the assertions in the Report may be borne out, and thus a false showing be made, which will be hereafter quoted by historians, as a proof of the demoralization of the population of London, when in fact no place on the earth has improved so much in morals.[51]

The Metropolitan Police Bill was introduced by Peel on 15 April 1829 and passed through all its stages within two months: the first policemen appeared on the streets of London on 29 September 1829. The final Act (*10 Geo. IV c.44*) amalgamated all government-controlled parish day and night watches into a single, salaried constabulary. To point up the contrast with the regular army, the new police wore blue (as opposed to scarlet) uniforms and carried truncheons or batons rather than incisive weapons like swords and sabres. Promotion was based on merit, as opposed to purchase or aristocratic connection, and the whole constabulary was answerable to the Home Secretary by way of two salaried Commissioners of Metropolitan Police based at 4 Whitehall Place. This was the site, before the Act of Union with England in 1707, of the Scottish embassy and was more familiarly known as Scotland Yard. The new police operated within strictly defined metropolitan boundaries – the 'square mile' of the City of London was excluded from their remit in deference to its fiercely defended jurisdictional autonomy. However, existing smaller-scale police operations (notably, the Bow Street Horse Patrol, the Foot Patrol and the Thames Police) were gradually absorbed into the Metropolitan Police Force within a decade, as was the Bow Street police office from which the famous 'Runners' had operated since 1749. A decade later, Lord John Russell began to legislate for the voluntary extension of police functions into counties, although this remained a highly controversial and long drawn-out process.[52]

Peel's reform of the Metropolitan Police 'used to be presented by historians as the replacement of an inefficient, wretched, corrupt & undermanned system of overlapping local jurisdictions by a rational, modern efficient force'. However, historians have increasingly pointed out the continuities in the police system, either side of 1829. In particular, it is clear that the watch system initiated its own reformation, long before Peel, by moving from a system of unpaid local constables to paid watchmen. As such, a system which reformers criticised as old-fashioned and out-of-touch now appears to have been more popular and 'responsive to local needs' than was once thought to be the case.[53]

Peel's commitment to the establishment of the Metropolitan Police is habitually explained by reference to his experience in Ireland. As Chief Secretary, Peel's 'first major essay in legislation' had been the Peace Preservation Act (*54 Geo. III c.131*) which became law on 25 July 1814. Along with the two amending Acts of December 1814 and March 1817 (*55 Geo. III c.13, 57 Geo. III c.22*), this provided the basis for the establishment of the Royal Irish Constabulary between 1822 and 1836.[54]

However, the nature and extent of the Irish law and order problem was markedly different from the English context and its solution by resort to a police force was correspondingly more difficult.

On arriving in Ireland, in September 1812, Peel was faced with a situation in which undue reliance was placed on the 25,000 or so regular troops stationed there. This constituted the first line of defence for the 2,000 voluntary magistrates upon whom responsibility for law and order rested. Given the end of the wars with France (1814–15), and the necessity of reducing the peacetime establishment to more manageable (and economical) levels, something more constructive and effective was required in order to police Ireland. Informed opinion was generally agreed that the existing system of parish constables (whose jurisdiction was limited to the parish boundary) and the baronial constables (or 'old barnies'), who lacked uniforms, discipline and training and who undertook their duties in their spare time, were insufficient replacements. Nor were the alternatives more inviting. The militia was 3,000 strong but its socially diverse composition made its allegiance to the side of law and order uncertain. By contrast, the more socially and religiously exclusive yeomanry, although ten times larger, was characterised by its Orange zeal – reflecting its overwhelming geographical concentration in the north. Any deployment of the yeomanry further south was regarded as an act of religious and political provocation against the majority Catholic population. Conversely, many of the most serious outrages committed by ribandmen (or ribbon men) and similar agrarian-based combinations occurred in exactly that area. It was the upsurge in these disturbances, especially during Peel's first year in Ireland, which necessitated action.[55]

In a 'dispassionate' speech to Parliament on 23 June 1814 Peel introduced his Peace Preservation measures. He justified them on the basis that the ordinary powers of the government (in this case, the magistracy) were insufficient to the maintenance of civil order – the line upon which much of Peel's subsequent Irish legislation, including Catholic Emancipation, was proposed.[56] The Act empowered the Lord Lieutenant to appoint supplementary, paid magistrates in counties which had been proclaimed to be in a state of disturbance. These stipendiary (or salaried) magistrates would be responsible to the government. However, once appointed, they could only be removed when they were satisfied that the district had been restored to order. The supplementary magistracy enjoyed superior authority over the ordinary (unpaid) magistracy and were able to appoint special, salaried constables, drawn from the ranks of respectable farmers. Most importantly of all, the costs of the magistracy and constabulary were to be borne by the district, in order – as Peel informed Lord Colchester – that it might 'pay for the luxury of disturbance'.[57]

This was a new way of disciplining the magistrates to their duty and of making them restore order as quickly and cheaply as possible. Francis Horner complained that it would 'tend rather to exasperate the people, and considerably exaggerate the mischief it proposed to remedy, than to produce any salutary consequences'.[58] One might see it as the genesis of the Peelite method of government – uniting administrative efficiency and economic prudence in order to stabilise the existing social and political order. However, its rational simplicity was also its failing: 'it tried to be cheap, it tried to avoid the stigma of central control, and it tried to spare both the pride and the pocket of the local gentlemen. Small wonder it had no very large measure of success.' Within its first three years of operation, the Act was invoked only three times (primarily in Tipperary) and until 1822 was 'almost a dead-letter'.[59] The principal problem lay in residing superior authority – and superior salaries – in the stipendiary magistrates and constables. The latter could make up to £50 per annum compared with an 'old barney' who might achieve £4 a year. Professional and private jealousies were one explanation for the limited application of Peel's legislation. Another was the fact that the Peace Preservation Act was accompanied by the renewal of the Insurrection Act. This meant that a district was provided with a legislative alternative to the expensive encroachment of the 'Peelers'. By waiting long enough, a region might justify a resort to that Act, thereby providing magistrates with their preferred solution of martial law and the presence of regular troops.[60]

Both the Peace Preservation Act of 1817 and the Metropolitan Police Force of 1829 were designed as immediate, localised, practical solutions to a specific problem and not as the genesis of a wider and more comprehensive police system, Nevertheless, Peel's efforts to convince the Irish of the necessity of an efficient police, paid for locally and with officers appointed by the government, continued in his period as Home Secretary.[61] Peel's amending Act of 1817 conceded the depth of the financial obstacle, in the wider application of the Peace Preservation Act, by dividing the costs between the district and the government. However, Peel's faith in a preventative solution to crime rather than one which targeted its underlying causes never wavered. As Tadhg Ó Ceallaigh observes, 'perhaps in the circumstances of the time there was little else he could do. He certainly tried to do little else.'[62]

For reasons which are only partially explained by his police measures, Peel had 'the good fortune of arriving in Ireland when it was disturbed and of leaving it tranquil. Peel's successors would not be so fortunate.' His reforms had brought 'recognition to himself and [pointed] the direction for a new approach to the problem of "pacifying" a recalcitrant populace'. As Peel informed the House of Commons, in 'a slightly smug piece of self-congratulation', during 1817 Ireland had required neither the suspension of *Habeas Corpus* nor a resort to the regulation of 'Seditious Meetings', as had been the case in England.[63] The suspicion of Peel's reactionary-Tory tendencies revived a decade later when he introduced his policemen (or 'citizen soldiery') into the heart of the nation's capital. Having 'ratted' on Emancipation and successfully 'Peeled the Charleys', it is unsurprising why, far from being seen as a champion of liberal virtues, Peel came to be represented in political caricatures of the period as little better than the Duke of Wellington, in combining political guile with military proclivities. In one of the more memorable satirical images of the year 1829, Peel was portrayed as the 'cad' (or conductor) to Wellington, 'the Man Wot drives the Sovereign'.[64]

* * *

If the originality and extent of Peel's police reforms has formed one aspect of historical scrutiny over the past three decades, then his policy in respect of the execution of criminals has proved to be another. In 1974, in one of the more influential review essays to have been published in recent years, Derek Beales took issue with Norman Gash's portrayal of Peel as a great and reforming Home Secretary. In particular, Beales demonstrated that there was no decline in the number of people being executed for capital crimes in the period immediately after Peel's criminal law reforms. Real reform, as measured in terms of a decline in the number of executions, had to await Lord John Russell's tenure at the Home Office (1835–9).[65] The impression that Peel was, at heart, a Tory disciplinarian, unmoved by the sort of humanitarian impulses which occasionally actuated High Tories like Sidmouth and Castlereagh, was subsequently reinforced in the work of Vic Gatrell:

> Peel's interest in criminal law reform had less to do with repudiating the barbarism of past times than with his interest … in restoring the law's credibility against public attack, and … in making it more efficient, even more punitive … This was a man who was embarking on a holding operation … Peel, hailed as a great penal reformer, was the most committed protagonist of the old order … the man's reputation in this context begins to look tattered.[66]

In their different ways, Beales and Gatrell were challenging the emphasis which Peel's contemporaries (as much as subsequent historians) had placed on his 'liberalism' as Home Secretary, offering instead a more conservative reading of his attitudes, intentions and achievements. Gatrell focused on one particular element of Peel's duties as Home Secretary: his responsibility to present, before the King in Council, senior cabinet ministers, members of the judicial bench and the Recorder (the chief sentencing officer of the Old Bailey), the report listing the calendar of capital offences which had been tried at the Old Bailey in order to review those which had resulted in the death penalty. Lord Ellenborough, for one, did not like the 'Recorder's report':

> I am shocked by the inequality of punishment. At one time a man is hanged for a crime which may be as two; because there are few to be hanged, and it is some time since an example has been made of capital punishment for his particular offence. At another time a man escapes for the same crime, having the proportion of five to two to the other, because it is a heavy calendar, and there are many to be executed. The actual delinquency of the individual is comparatively little taken into consideration. Extraneous circumstances determine his fate.[67]

It was within Peel's remit to present pleas for clemency and in the power of the King to grant them. George IV (frequently acted upon by his mistress Lady Conyngham and his own desire to act as the 'father of his people') was occasionally moved to intervene in particular cases on the side of leniency, thereby resulting in a battle of wills between the monarch and the Home Secretary. Peel threatened resignation, on at least one occasion, whilst the intervention of Wellington, Eldon and Liverpool was required to resolve other disagreements.[68] Gatrell, observing the frequency with which Peel rejected pleas with the ominous phrase 'the law to take its course' concluded that Peel was 'a great hangman' who was 'determined to hang men even-handedly and as numerously as good order required, and not to make exceptions where distinctions were narrow'.[69]

Gatrell's work has been criticised (for different reasons) by Boyd Hilton and Simon Devereaux. Hilton upbraids Gatrell for assuming that there was a 'simple spectrum of opinion [on legal reform] ranging from advocates of harsh discretionary justice' on the one hand to 'those who believed in more lenient and relatively fixed penalties' on the other. It did not automatically follow from Peel's more 'liberal' approach to legal reform (in terms of consolidation of the criminal code) that he would also be more 'lenient' in respect of pleas for clemency. Rather, Peel favoured 'harsh fixed penalties'. He took particular care to define culpability in respect of crimes to which secondary (or non-capital) punishments attached. The stealing of vegetable matter from orchards and gardens was a case in point. By clarifying distinctions in the nature of the crime ('between the type and value of property; between stealing, destroying, and damaging; and between a first and subsequent offence') Peel maintained, under carefully circumscribed conditions, the element of discretion. At the same time, he provided for a more certain outcome, by specifying 'an appropriate range of punishments such as transportation, solitary confinement, the treadmill, and whipping' in respect of each gradation of offence. As such, Peel's criminal law reforms were not designed to result in less punishment but in its more precise and efficient application.[70] It follows from this that there would be no immediate down-turn in capital executions (as Beales found) because that was neither the intention nor the practical outcome of Peel's reforms. Consequently, rather than providing Gatrell's 'holding operation' against change, the reforms actually constituted the groundwork for further developments during the 1830s.

In arguing thus, Hilton is keen to place Peel's record as Home Secretary within his wider conception of 'liberal Toryism'. For many years historians have debated the extent to which liberal Toryism supplanted the more authoritarian, reactionary policy of Liverpool's ministry and considered its motivation, timing and significance. Traditionally, the reconstruction of the government between 1821–3 and the promotion of Peel, Canning, Huskisson and Robinson to leading cabinet positions has assumed a crucial role. Older accounts (such as that by W.G. Brock) suggested that liberal Toryism represented a battle between different sectional interests based on agriculture (on the one hand) and merchant, trading and industrial wealth (on the other).[71] This line of argument was superseded by Hilton, who stressed contrasting religious and intellectual outlooks. These separated High Tories like Castlereagh, Eldon and Sidmouth (who dominated the ministry before 1823) from liberal Tories like Canning and Peel (who did so thereafter). For Hilton, liberal Tories shared a 'pre-millenarian Evangelical' desire to make the world fit for the Millennium (the second coming of Jesus Christ) through stripping it of all those impediments, outworks and interventions which stood between mankind and what Peel was apt to call 'the dispensations of Providence'. To liberal Tories, society was a self-acting mechanism and it was the aim of all 'good men' (quite literally) to ensure its unobstructed operation. 'High Tories believed that all government functions, whether local or central, required constant management, interference, and discretion … whereas liberal Tories wanted the State to operate neutrally according to rule'. For this reason, Peel discontinued Sidmouth's use of spies, informers and *agents provocateurs* as Home Secretary and maintained his campaign in support of a *visible*, uniformed police force: 'It was his conviction that the State should be visible as well as small, rather than any misattributed *humanity*, that made Peel a liberal.'[72]

Though it is undoubtedly attractive in theory, Hilton's case would appear to be unproven at least in respect of motivation. Few of the leading liberal Tories – least of all Peel and Canning – can be classified as 'evangelicals' on their own terms. It might also be fair to observe that the level of threat which faced Peel, as Home Secretary, was of a correspondingly different order from that which confronted the 'High Tory' Sidmouth, considering that his tenure at the Home Office (1812–22) encompassed everything from Luddism to the Cato Street Conspiracy.[73]

Admittedly, execution levels had reached 'appalling new high-points' during Sidmouth's final two years in office but, as Simon Devereaux has recently argued, the conduct of the Recorder's Report, thereafter, 'was more restrained and more closely-considered' than Gatrell has allowed for. Like Hilton, Devereaux does not look for misplaced evidence of 'humanitarianism' in Peel (although he finds it in that notoriously High Tory figure, Lord Chancellor Eldon). Neither Peel nor his colleagues, including the sceptical Ellenborough, 'questioned their right to impose death on a wide range of criminal activities'. However, there were changes in the extent and workings of the death penalty, during Peel's period as Home Secretary, an increasing sense 'that most of the capital convicts would not face the noose' and a corresponding emphasis on reviewing 'in detail a handful of more problematic cases' during the presentation of the Recorder's Report. After a generation of detailed scholarly criticism it would appear that the new historiography on Peel's time at the Home Office does not 'so much reveal a new figure as cast light into some of the darker corners of the long-established portrait'. Peel may not have been a 'great hangman', the state's executioner-in-chief. But he was not (at least in this respect) a great humanitarian either.[74]

* * *

The disagreement between historians over the extent of Peel's 'liberalism', as Home Secretary, is indicative of the conditional nature of that term during this period. Peel's place on the spectrum of political opinion between 'High' and 'liberal' Toryism, during the 1820s was variable, negotiable and, above all, relative. By comparison with the likes of Eldon, Castlereagh and Sidmouth, Peel appeared to be more liberal. But relative to Canning, Huskisson and Robinson, he appeared more Tory or 'illiberal' – a position he himself claimed to occupy in his resignation speech on 1 May 1827. However, Peel's experience as Home Secretary reveals the dangers of too rigid a classification along these lines. Considered a 'liberal' in his willingness to undertake reform of the criminal law, he was 'not liberal enough' to consider codifying it. Equally, as the progenitor of the Metropolitan Police force, Peel appeared (to many sections of opinion) nothing better than a reactionary Tory – although some of the keenest opponents of that measure were themselves designated as 'Ultra Tories'.[75]

The comparative increase in Peel's 'liberal' reputation during this period was assisted by his record as Home Secretary, on the one hand, and the achievement of Catholic Emancipation on the other. Before 1829 it was an individual's attitude towards the Catholic Question which decided, for many commentators, whether they were regarded as a liberal or not.[76] Peel's reputation also advanced because his closest competitors for pre-eminence amongst the liberal Tories – Canning, Huskisson and Robinson – had died, defected or been defeated during the period 1827–30. Their successors, Melbourne, Palmerston, Grant and Dudley, had more contested claims to leadership. Their political pasts (as Tories) and their political futures (as Whigs who ended up in Lord Grey's ministry of 1830) pointed in contrary directions.[77]

Consequently, for most of the 1820s, Peel was perceived as a 'liberal' in terms of his ministerial portfolio and a Tory by reference to his Protestant constitutionalism. In no respect were the consequences of this more apparent than in Peel's relationship with George Canning. Throughout this period, Peel and Canning were widely regarded as the respective leaders of the 'Protestant' and 'Catholic' camps in the government. They were also seen as competitors for the leadership of liberal Toryism, the succession to Lord Liverpool and the soul of the ministerial party. Each of them came from non-aristocratic backgrounds and each was driven by an overarching sense of ambition. This gave their relationship points of similarity but also a potentially fractious edge: the diarist Thomas Creevey called them 'the Merry Andrew' and 'the Spinning Jenny'.[78] The perception that Peel and Canning were political rivals proved to be enduring. When in 1875 the Ministry of Works considered the most appropriate location for Matthew Noble's statue of Peel, 'within the precincts of the Houses of Parliament', reference was made to an unexpected difficulty:

> [In light of the] political rancour which existed between Peel & Canning, it would be in the worst taste, to oppose to each other, the statues of those statesmen ... more particularly, as the Peel statue, would have the pre-eminence by 3 feet in the height of the pedestal – Such an allocation of the Peel statue would be likely to give rise to a political demonstration, of perhaps a virulent character; in which, it might perhaps be said that, whilst Peel was received within the precincts of the New Palace, Canning was excluded from them.[79]

Thirty-four years earlier, on Peel's assumption of the premiership, *Punch* imagined a conversation between Canning's statue in Palace Yard and the new Prime Minister in which the cynicism and unreliability of both men was emphasised. 'By the bye, Bob, [Canning's statue was made to say], I don't at all like my situation here ... I want to get into [Westminster] Abbey, St. Paul's [Cathedral], or Drury Lane, anywhere out of the open air': to this, Peel turned a deaf ear. Meanwhile, *Blackwood's Edinburgh Magazine* dismissed any similarity between the two men, during the same period, concluding that Canning was an 'adventurer' who had compromised his principles in order to achieve power. Even worse, he had given the impression of wishing to rule without the aristocracy. At the start of Peel's second ministry, *Blackwood's* was inclined to hope that he was cast in a different mould.[80]

Though there is a suggestive hint that Peel, on first entering Parliament, was willing to mast himself under Canning's standard as part of his 'Little Senate' of political followers, both men's futures were set in place by the end of 1812. After Canning's failed attempt to become Prime Minister, Peel's course was set fair as the Protestant bedrock of Lord Liverpool's government whilst Canning was seen (not least by the Prince Regent) as too open an advocate of the Catholic claims, as well as his own.[81] Over the next decade Canning joined (1816) and resigned (1820) from Liverpool's cabinet, whilst Peel established himself as his nearest rival for political pre-eminence – in the process achieving Canning's prize ambition of the representation of Oxford University.

Castlereagh's death in August 1822 transformed the situation.[82] In 1821, Peel's political future had depended on gratifying Canning's unrequited ambitions. With their failure (and Peel's consequent elevation to the Cabinet as Home Secretary) Canning had accepted the Governor-Generalship of India. However, Castlereagh's suicide vacated the posts of Leader of the Commons and Foreign Secretary which Canning most desired. Whether he would accept any, either, both or neither of them was a subject of prolonged political speculation. In the negotiations by which Liverpool, Eldon and Wellington convinced George IV to accept Canning, Peel's thoughts and sentiments proved to be of some importance.[83] Although he had only been Home Secretary for seven months, by the time of Castlereagh's death the leadership of the Commons was widely felt to be within his grasp. 'Fresh as Peel is to the task (Palmerston observed) no man who has seen him do his work can doubt that in discretion, in personal following, in high mindedness he is superior to Canning & though not so eloquent an orator yet speaks quite up to the situation of Leader.'[84] Though an incorrect report circulated that Canning would forego his claims in favour of Peel, Croker (a close friend of both) reported Canning's real sentiments on the matter: 'he had been five-and-twenty years before you in the House, [and] you would probably not have long to wait before he himself ... would leave you the career open; that he thought he could not with honour take an inferior station in the House, and if *that* were the alternative he must go to India'. Peel maintained a posture of ambivalence with the Prime Minister and George IV, although Croker thought he could 'guess what he would wish'.[85] To Liverpool and the King, Peel disclaimed 'all ambitious views' and stated 'his indifference to office ... declaring a preference for the enjoyment which he is able to derive from his fortune, his domestic connexions, and his fondness for field sports, all of which are impaired by office'.[86] Lord Bathurst also noted that Peel had taken occasion to speak 'of his ill-health; which I do not think was without design'. At the beginning of September 1822, Wellington was assured of Peel's willingness to serve under Canning in the House of Commons, and the appointment was confirmed later that month.[87]

Over the next five years, Peel and Canning established themselves as the moving forces in two of the great offices of state – Peel at the Home Office, Canning in Foreign Affairs. *The Illustrated London News* later described Peel's criminal law reform speech of 9 March 1826 as a tacit re-assertion of strength in the face of Canning's challenge.[88] Certainly, after 1822 political commentators were sensitive to any sign of competition between the two men, although a more significant development may have been the emergence of 'Prosperity' Robinson (the Chancellor of the Exchequer) as a Commons performer who could outshine them both on occasion.[89] Canning had his own defining political moment in December 1826, when he told the Commons that, as Foreign Secretary, he had 'called the New World into existence in order to redress the balance of the Old'. Two months later, Liverpool suffered the stroke which ended his political career. Eight weeks after that, Canning succeeded him as Prime Minister.[90]

Historians have tended to over-stress the differences between Canning and Peel on the Catholic Question, the immediate cause of Peel's resignation as Home Secretary in April 1827. The under-stressed corollary, which Peel himself maintained, was that the two men were united on almost everything else.[91] Peel's Tory (Protestant) and liberal selves were in tension throughout the 1820s. There was some doubt amongst contemporaries whether the former would win out over the latter. This suspicion was reinforced by the fact that Peel kept his own counsel in the weeks leading up to Canning's appointment.[92] Canning himself was reported to be 'surprised' at Peel's ultimate decision to resign from the government. Commentators generally united in praising Peel for the manner and cause of his departure, concluding that he had acted honourably in reference to his 'peculiar situation' on the Emancipation issue.[93] Even a dyed-in-the-wool Whig like the Duke of Devonshire was upset: 'I die for him to join Canning.' Membership of Canning's government was felt to be the 'natural' outcome for Peel's political sentiments. It was not a question of frustrated ambition, for Peel's claims to the succession were widely regarded as subordinate to those of Canning and, increasingly, Wellington.[94] Moreover, Peel strictly circumscribed the extent of his opposition to Canning's ministry. Though he enjoyed a renewed sense of esteem in the provincial Pitt Clubs (which were increasingly outspoken in their opposition to Catholic Emancipation) and was thought to have some 200 followers at his disposal in the House of Commons, Peel refused to capitalise on his situation – to the evident frustration of his more zealous political supporters.[95]

However, Peel did offer some hostile overtures to the new administration.[96] On 3 May 1827 (two days after the resignation speech in which he described himself as an 'illiberal Tory') Peel delivered a short but incisive attack on the government. The speech was mentioned in Canning's daily despatch to the King and was described by George Agar Ellis as 'violent and inflammatory'. Evelyn Denison thought that, by it, Peel had 'pulled off his mask' and revealed his true intentions. Denison later surmised that, by his resignation, Peel had hoped to 'become the martyr of the Protestant cause'. This plan had been frustrated by finding himself 'one of a pact' of ministerial defectors, including half a dozen cabinet colleagues and some forty junior ministers.[97]

Sir James Prior made a similar point, in an extended consideration of Peel's position, published before Canning's death in August 1827. 'Permit me, with the freedom of a friend, to hint, that your political reputation is yet but young ... [and barely] five years old; not a very long period of probation to ascertain the capabilities of one who sets up for the leader of a party.' For Prior, it was unbecoming of Peel to set up 'the race of popularity you have attempted to run against the first statesman and orator of the age', because it suggested that he possessed 'that species of ambition, which, because it cannot obtain all its desires, will accept of nothing':

> If anything, therefore, in the nature of reproach escape me, it will be, because you did not continue to retain an office and to pursue a career so advantageous to your fame; rather than to become the ringleader of a species of civil mutiny in which it remains to be settled, whether mere indiscretion, petulance, resentment, personal hostility, or simple folly, chiefly predominated.[98]

Canning's death frustrated Prior's hopes for a prolonged premiership under liberal leadership. Commentators concluded that Peel would look to return to office 'by conciliatory rather than fertile measures', after Lord Goderich (the former Frederick Robinson) succeeded Canning as Prime Minister.[99] However, Goderich proved to be an abject failure as Premier – in the process, removing one of Peel's closest competitors from future contention. Wellington was appointed as Prime Minister in January 1828 with Peel in a leading position to advise him on cabinet positions in the House of Commons. Significantly, it was Peel who insisted on the inclusion of the leading Canningites (led by Huskisson) in the ministry. This was as much the result of fellow-feeling on policy as it was an aid to Peel in his newly combined role as Home Secretary and Leader of the Commons.[100] The friction between Wellington and Huskisson made the arrangement a temporary one; after the collective resignation of the Canningites in May 1828, Peel became the last significant liberal in a cabinet where he felt increasingly exposed. As William Thomas has noted, contemporaries thought Peel 'a liberal yoked against his better judgement with illiberal associates. He himself probably did not see the matter in such an ideological light.' After all, he had dismissed liberalism as an 'odious but intelligible' phrase in 1820. Nevertheless, Peel's former tutor, Charles Lloyd (now Bishop of Oxford), counselled his *protégé*:

> There is a liberality consistent with a mixed form of Government: there is another consistent only with a Democracy, I wish it to be known that you have the former, & only want the latter: and I feel exceedingly anxious that the young men of promise should know this & remain with you, so that they may be content to serve under you at a future time.[101]

The resignation of the Canningites from Wellington's ministry frustrated Peel's hopes of a wide-ranging liberal Tory alliance. More seriously, it left the government dangerously exposed in the House of Commons. This must go some way to explain the repeated expressions of disgust, petulance and irritation recorded by Peel (and noted by his colleagues) as he performed his duties as Leader of the House in the months preceding the ministry's fall. It might also explain the exultation he felt at being released from these labours in November 1830.[102]

The standing impediment of the Catholic Question prevented Peel from assuming the leadership of liberal Toryism until after 1830 when the old political equation between Toryism and hostility to Emancipation had been rendered irrelevant.[103] In its place, a new political terminology and new political leadership was required and it was this which Peel and the newly-christened 'Conservative' party attempted to provide. As such, it is unsurprising that it was Croker (the friend of both Canning and Peel) who helped to publicise the name in the *Quarterly Review*. Similarly, Charles Canning (the Prime Minister's heir) received his first ministerial appointment from Peel in 1835 and became a leading political supporter thereafter, assuming his father's intended place as Governor-General of India in 1855.[104]

What David Eastwood has called the 'hard-edged certainties' of Peel's Toryism began to abate during the 1830s and 1840s. In the process, Peel increasingly came to identify himself with the language of 'liberal Conservatism'. This change of terminology reflected Peel's 'formal attempt to distance himself from what he now regarded as the factional fundamentalism of the Ultra Tories'. By the time of his second ministry (1841–6), 'Peel was increasingly disposed towards the language not so much of liberalism but of liberality'.[105] As such, his administration might plausibly be represented as the 'second phase' of Liberal Toryism.[106]

Consequently, it was Peel (rather than the Canningite ministers of the 1830s) who proved to be Canning's natural successor. Stephen Lee has recently reminded historians of the 'Tory' element in Canning, pointing out that (like Peel) he was opposed to both the Repeal of the Test and Corporation Acts and Parliamentary Reform. Contemporaries also thought the two men in the strict line of political succession. In 1865, Lord John Russell remarked that Canning and Peel had both attempted to exercise power 'with liberal ideas and conservative allies' – a fate which he recognised, rather than recommended.[107]

Given the repeatedly recorded doubts about their personal relationship, it is unsurprising why Peel became a Canningite in all but name. Certainly, Peel's subsequent *volte face* on Emancipation, and the perception that he had engaged in a virulent campaign of hostility, during Canning's premiership, made Peel's relations with him a matter of controversy in his lifetime. In 1829, 'Brutus' in *The Times* asked how Peel could refuse office in 1827, on the grounds of contrary views on Emancipation, and yet legislate for it two years later.[108] The charge was felt seriously by Canning's family. In 1831, Thomas Babington Macaulay encountered Canning's daughter (Lady Clanricarde) at dinner:

> The daughter of a statesman who was a martyr to the rage of faction may be pardoned for speaking sharply of the enemies of her parent: and she did speak sharply. With knitted brows, and flashing eyes, and a look of feminine vengeance about her beautiful mouth, she gave me such a character of Peel as he would certainly have had no pleasure in hearing.[109]

During the Repeal of the Corn Laws, in 1846, the accusation that Peel had secretly changed his mind on Emancipation (in 1825 or 1827) and yet chased and 'hunted Canning to death' for supporting Catholic Relief became a form of posthumous vengeance from beyond the grave. The charge was led by Canning's residuary legatee,

Lord George Bentinck (his nephew by marriage), in close collaboration with Benjamin Disraeli.[110] The political classes generally condemned their tactics on the occasion and the diarist Greville, who was no friend of Bentinck, felt that Peel's vindication of himself 'shed something of lustre over his last days' in office.[111] Nevertheless, Peel had little reason to complain of his treatment by the two men. In the hands of the 'Peelites', his own political legacy would be defended with a depth and intensity which made it pale in comparison.[112]

5

'THE FOUNDER OF MODERN CONSERVATISM'? PEEL AND THE CONSERVATIVE PARTY

To that class which is much less interested in the contentions of party, than in the maintenance of order and the cause of good government [I say that] ... if the spirit of the Reform Bill implies merely a careful review of institutions, civil and ecclesiastical, undertaken in a friendly temper, combining, with the firm maintenance of established rights, the correction of proved abuses and the redress of real grievances, – in that case, I can for myself and colleagues undertake to act in such a spirit and with such intentions.

'The Tamworth Manifesto', 18 December 1834.[1]

* * *

Of all the posthumous claims to greatness made on Peel's behalf, none has proved more controversial than Norman Gash's contention that he was the 'Founder of Modern Conservatism'. Gash first made this claim in 1970, at a time when the Disraelian orthodoxy in the Conservative Party was at its height and followed it up in the second volume of his biography of Peel two years later.[2] In reviewing the party's history, Gash discovered an apparent contradiction: 'though its practice has almost invariably been Peelite, its myth has been largely Disraelian'.[3] By it, Gash meant that whilst Disraeli had been amongst the fiercest of Peel's contemporary critics insofar as his relations with the Conservative Party were concerned, in due course he came to adopt exactly the same course of action. In March 1845, a disgruntled backbencher Disraeli had proclaimed that 'a Conservative Government is an organised hypocrisy' because of its willingness to adopt the views and policies of its Whig Liberal opponents. Fourteen years later, as the party's leader in opposition, he had concluded: 'we shall have to keep together a great party, as Peel had in 1835, whose strength will really increase in proportion to their inaction. But a party does not like to be inert; and to combine repose with a high tone of feeling in the troops is difficult.'[4]

Gash's views on 'Peel and the party system' had evolved over the years in an increasingly favourable direction.[5] His mature reflections on the subject became 'well established' in academic circles, although they 'never struck any political root'.[6] Gash's perspective exhibited itself in 'a veritable forest of articles on the organizational side of the party, its funding, whipping and structural development' and in a robust defence against alternative readings of the party's evolution.[7] The intervening period of Thatcherism threatened to render constructions of the party's history along the Peel-Disraeli dichotomy 'obsolete'. However, Gash reiterated his point in 1989, claiming that Thatcher and Peel, alone amongst Conservative leaders, stood out in terms of their achievements, their willpower and the radical nature of their Conservatism.[8] This analogy between Thatcher and Peel – strong-willed and determined Prime Ministers who were opposed from within the ranks of their own party – had a particular resonance in this period, and was echoed by Robert Blake in his valedictory assessment of 'the Iron Lady' in November 1990.[9]

In October 2000 Gash conceded that, whilst Disraeli 'so long the oracle of the Conservatives, is now perhaps less invoked, it is unlikely that Peel will ever replace him in the eyes of party pietists'.[10] As such, the argument would seem to revolve more around the use of Peel's legacy by the modern Conservative Party than the significance attached to it by contemporaries. To that extent, it may be less important whether Peel was the 'Founder of Modern Conservatism' as whether he understood the new political realities created by the 1832 Reform Act, in terms of creating and leading a political party. It is this which provides the focus of this chapter.

* * *

By the turn of the twenty-first century, Gash's conception of British politics after the Reform Act had been under assault for some time. In particular, his stress on Peel's successful adaptation and modernisation of Toryism into a pragmatic, reforming, Conservative Party, and the development of a distinctive two-party system during this period,[11] was shown to ignore not only the pressures exerted by different blocs or groups of opinion within those parties,[12] and the distinctive political contribution made by the Whigs[13] (the governing party until 1841), but to under-estimate the continuing scope and strength of Ultra-Toryism within the Conservative Party. The 1841 General Election victory is now seen less as the personal triumph of Peel and of the principles enshrined in the Tamworth Manifesto – which Gash saw as an appeal to the new urban, Dissenter electorate created by the Reform Act[14] – than as a confirmation of the party's revived Protestant and Protectionist instincts in its traditional strongholds (the counties and small market towns of England) and on a markedly defensive electoral platform.[15] Jon Parry has stressed the limited impact Peel exercised upon these events: 'what Peel did or did not do mattered very little in 1841'.[16] This makes less surprising the strained relationship between Peel and his followers for much of his 1841–6 ministry[17] and the consequent fissure in the party after 1846. As David Eastwood has commented, 'the seeds of the great crisis of 1845–6 were sown in the election triumph of 1841'.[18]

A number of historians have also testified to the continuing significance of the House of Lords in British politics after 1832, in spite of the loss of much of its influence over the composition of the House of Commons.[19] Despite threats of reform or mass peerage creations, the Lords' inbuilt Conservative majority retained its potential to harass ministerial legislation. Indeed, the persistent Ultra Tory presence amongst the Conservative peers made it difficult to synchronise their conduct with that of the party in the House of Commons. Peel himself confessed that it was 'impossible to prevail on the House of Lords and the House of Commons to take the same views of many important public measures'.[20] The most serious divergence arose over the English Municipal Corporations Bill of 1835, when Peel resolutely stuck to the amendments he had helped to shape, in committee of the House of Commons, in the face of the House of Lords' subsequent blocking tactics. Peel absented himself from London during this period, unmoved by the Ultra Tory peers' efforts to derail the Bill: a course of action which gained him few friends amongst his followers but the ungrudging thanks of the government and the King.[21] To Wharncliffe, Peel justified his absence on the grounds of pressing 'local matters ... not unconnected with Conservative interests':

> Suppose the Government were to decide upon acquiescing in the course to be taken by the Lords – then probably my presence would not be necessary ... I left the Duke of Rutland's the other day and came to town not for the purpose of maintaining my own views on parts of the Corporation Bill – but under the impression that the Bill would be insolently rejected or some proceeding adopted derogatory from the honor of the Lords. I came to oppose such proceeding. Being in town I had no alternative but to act upon this very strong impression which I feel that the settlement of this question ought to be effected – if it can be consistently with the honour of the Lords.[22]

Given the often fraught personal relations between Peel and the Ultra Tory grandees, an understanding of Wellington's role (as leader of the Conservative Party in the Lords from 1828–46) in the management and stabilisation of the upper chamber appears to be a more crucial element than was once allowed for. Wellington's importance was emphasised by a crucial difference of temperament. For all the rigidity suggested by the epithet 'the Iron Duke', Wellington 'put a comparatively low value on his own opinions and consistency – in marked contrast to Peel. That is because he put the highest value on what he called necessity, which can roughly be translated as the national good.'[23] This dimension casts new light on Peel's strategy of 'governing in opposition' during the 1830s; working to restrain incidents of factious opposition on the part of the Conservative Party in the House of Commons in order to prevent a corresponding reaction on the part of the Whigs' more radical supporters. According to Ian Newbould, Peel worked with mainstream Whig opinion (between 1833 and 1839) to affect a *via media* by which to skirt the extremes of Ultra-Toryism, on the one hand, and Whig Radicalism on the other.[24]

* * *

7: 'Young Gulliver, And The Brobdignag Minister', *Punch*, VIII, January–June 1845, 155.
A famous representation of relations between Sir Robert Peel and Benjamin Disraeli, cast in
the form of *Gulliver's Travels*.

The scale of the Conservative revival in the period 1832–41 is not in doubt. From an
electoral nadir of 150 MPs, following the first post-Reform Act General Election
(of December 1832), the Conservatives advanced, at successive contests in January
1835 and July 1837, until they achieved a Commons majority approaching 80 in
September 1841.[25] The frequency of election contests in this period had less to do with
any turbulence in the post-Reform Act electorate as such, than with the political
manoeuvres of its leading actors (notably King William IV). For the Conservatives,
this proved to be an unintended benefit of the politics of the 1830s. Moreover, the
requirement that all post-1832 electors be identified on an electoral register provided
the Conservatives with a key to future success. As Philip Salmon has demonstrated, the
Conservative revival was achieved as much through the activities of the party's agents
in the revising courts of provincial England as it was in the environs of Westminster.[26]

As such, it seems unhelpful to exaggerate the role which Peel played in this process –
although there were clear personal political benefits, at the time, in doing so. 'The more
Peel is credited with the Tory revival, the harder it is to understand his role in the split
of 1846' – unless he is to be held equally culpable for both.[27] 'The late Dr Kitson Clark
in his *Peel and the Conservative Party* (1929) committed himself so fully to the first side,
that he never completed an explanation of the second.'[28] Nor does a stress on 'the
Foundation of the Conservative Party' as an end in itself accord with Peel's explicitly

stated priority for the period.[29] This, as he stated to Lord Harrowby (amongst innumerable others) was the maintenance of a stable executive authority and the constitutional integrity of the leading institutions of the state. The Whig Government was, in Peel's view, increasingly likely to be held hostage by its more Radical political supporters, having encouraged a popular clamour in order to pass the 1832 Reform Act:

> Why have we been struggling against the Reform Bill? Not in the hope of resisting its final success in the House of Commons – but because we look beyond this bill – because we know the nature of popular concessions – their tendency to propagate the necessity for further and more extensive compliances … to teach young inexperienced men charged with the trust of government, that though they may be backed by popular clamour they shall not override on the first spring tide of excitement every barrier and breakwater raised against popular impulses.[30]

In these circumstances it was necessary for the Conservatives to save 'the authors of the evil from the consequences of their own work'.[31] Admittedly, in his Merchant Taylor's Hall speech of 1838 and in addressing his Tamworth constituents in June 1841, Peel stated that he 'foresaw the good that might result from laying the foundation of a great Conservative party in the state, attached to the fundamental institutions of the country'. However, this was at the peak of Conservative Party fortunes and Peel was clearly 'willing to accept the credit. But the idea that he deliberately built the party up to achieve a victory at the polls is the invention of historians who have assumed that a two-party system was an inevitable development of the 1830s'.[32] Peel's perceptions remained entirely focused on the achievement of that 'governmental ethic' which Gash perceived in his earliest work on 'Peel and the party system' and which, in spite of half a century's historical revisionism, remains the best description of his attitudes and priorities in the period.[33] The Conservative Party was a means of achieving Peel's own, individually determined, political ends and not an end in itself. His success between 1832 and the autumn of 1845 was in making this utilitarian and functional view of party correspond with the more enlarged and, in some respects, romantic conceptions of his followers. As Peel frequently told the Conservative backbenchers in the House of Commons, before assuming the premiership for the second time (in September 1841), his own (implicitly superior) judgement was to be the monitor of his political actions:

> If I exercise power, it shall be upon my conception – perhaps imperfect – perhaps mistaken – but – my sincere conception of public duty. That power I will not hold, unless I can hold it consistently with the maintenance of my own opinions; and that power I will relinquish, the moment I am satisfied that I am not supported in the maintenance of them by the confidence of this House, and of the people of this country![34]

The diarist Greville approved this 'manly and direct' admission: 'there can be no doubt that it was wise and bold thus … to put forth a manifesto which leaves no doubt of his future conduct, and from which there is no retreat for him, and by which all his adherents must be equally bound'.[35]

* * *

Consequently, attaining high political office was about securing the stability Peel craved after the Reform Act changed the terms upon which ministers exercised control of the House of Commons. Peel had not been totally averse to the concept of some parliamentary reform before leaving office in November 1830, and seems to have been willing (at least initially) to keep the Whigs in power long enough for them to deal with it.[36] As a keen student of the French Revolution, Peel frequently called to mind the analogous situation between the state of France in the later years of Louis XVI and the end of George IV's reign in England.[37] However, the scope and scale of the government's scheme seems to have put him off balance when it was unveiled on 1 March 1831. As Peter Ghosh has noted, Peel perceived that the Whig measure would enact a '"revolution" … which among many changes annihilated the power of the executive to manage elections'. Peel's interpretation is at odds with that of his biographer. Norman Gash famously argued that (whatever the intentions of its authors) the Reform Act 'made no essential difference to "the political scene"'. He never subsequently explained the discrepancy between them.[38]

The Whig Reform Bill proposed the disenfranchisement of over 140 parliamentary seats. Many of these had, by way of the influence enjoyed by leading property owners, returned aristocratic nominees and government supporters to the House of Commons. It proposed the redistribution of those seats, on the grounds of population size, to hitherto unrepresented or under-represented constituencies. Finally, it proposed the institution of a uniform borough franchise based on the ownership of property rated at £10 per annum. As such, it eroded many of the political foundations upon which governments had relied for the maintenance of their executive authority before 1830 – a system which Peel knew only too well.[39] The Whig Lord Chancellor, Brougham, exulted in the fact that Peel failed to move the immediate postponement of the Bill: he had 'allowed the opportunity to pass, and now will never recover it'. Lord Ellenborough agreed:

> The astonishment – nay the shock produced by the sweeping provisions of the Bill, would I think have given Peel a large majority had he chosen to divide at this critical moment … No one, however, was less himself than Peel. He sat pale and forlorn, utterly at a loss how to act. His countenance at times looked convulsed. The workings within him were evidently beyond his controul [sic].

The Leader of the Commons, Lord Althorp, also observed Peel's increasingly despondent nature as the terms of the Bill were unveiled: 'At last he put his hands before his face and appeared quite overcome. He felt that the knell of the Tories had rung.' Peel's subsequent speech, accepting the need for some measure of reform, was commended by Greville as 'brilliant, imposing, but not much in it'. Such displays led the Ultra Tories to make their own arrangements for opposing the Bill. Several years later, Peel 'expressed distinctly his conviction that the course taken on the introduction of the Reform Bill in 1831 was a *very bad* one. (Seven nights' debate and no division).'[40]

Commentators were divided in their estimation of Peel's leadership during the struggle for the Reform Bill (1831–2). In September 1850, *Blackwood's Edinburgh Magazine* was moved to suggest that there was 'no part of his career upon which his biographer will dwell with such unmixed satisfaction as this, because there is none on which *all* parties are now so entirely agreed'. However, this was extending the benefit of hindsight to an Act which, for different reasons, was subsequently felt to be inadequate. A few months earlier, in ruminating on Peel's career, Charles Greville found it difficult to 'discern any proofs of sound judgement and foresight in Peel's conduct ... [his] deficiency in sagacity and foresight [during this period] must be accounted one of the blemishes of his political career'.[41]

Greville had not been so unfeeling at the time, but his wider point – subsequently echoed by historians – was well made. Peel's reputation was still suffering from the blow which it had sustained at the time of Catholic Emancipation for him to act credibly as the opponent of parliamentary reform. In Peter Ghosh's words, the political fall-out from Emancipation 'disabled' him from exercising effective leadership.[42] He had yet to atone sufficiently, in the eyes of his Ultra Tory colleagues, for 'the fatal measure' of 1829. At the same time, his tacit acknowledgement of the case for reform threatened to render his position inconsistent for a second time – something from which his political character and ambition could never have recovered. Political sensitivities (and memories) on Emancipation remained raw – not least with Peel himself. In December 1831, Thomas Babington Macaulay attacked Peel on his weakest ground by charging him with inconsistency for having conceded Catholic Emancipation after previously opposing it. Peel responded with a lengthy self-justification which Greville (for one) condemned: besides 'savouring of the egotism with which he is so much and justly reproached', it was 'uncalled for and out of place' in a discussion on the Reform Bill.[43]

A similar point was made by such diverse political spirits as Lord Holland and William Gladstone in May 1832, after Peel refused to join Wellington's still-born attempt at a Tory administration committed to a measure of parliamentary reform. To Holland, it 'was shrewdly suspected from the beginning that Sir Robert Peel's timidity or principle would prevent him from joining. He saw the impossibility of crushing reform and shrunk from the shameless inconsistency and profligacy of carrying it.' Likewise, Gladstone maintained that Peel 'seemed to be perpetually thinking and to have exclusively thought of what other people would say of him instead of driving right at the question'.[44]

* * *

The Reform Act was finally passed in June 1832. Although Peel quickly (and explicitly)[45] accepted that, as a piece of legislation, it was incapable of being reversed, it affected a change in the nature and composition of governments which he perceived but did not feel compelled to accept. As William Thomas observes, 'the time had gone by when cabinets had had to include owners of parliamentary boroughs, but that of governments returned by parliamentary majorities held together by party discipline had not yet dawned'.[46] Peel had never represented a genuinely large or populous constituency himself and had been bred in a political environment where a government enjoying the confidence of the crown and the patronage of the Treasury was almost guaranteed a working majority in the House of Commons. The Reform Act accelerated a process which had already begun, in terms of dismantling that influence and that patronage – in due course, disciplined political parties would fill the vacuum thereby created.[47] Almost alone, of the leading pre-1830 Tory ministers in the House of Commons, Peel remained a survivor of that earlier age. It was unreasonable and unlikely to expect that, with a widely known reputation for high-handedness and self-belief, Peel would willingly compromise his entire political existence to date and reinvent himself in the guise of a committed party politician. That argument 'seems to depend on more modern and exacting criteria than circumstances then permitted'.[48]

Conversely, the terms upon which Peel would accept office had to satisfy his own over-scrupulous standards of political rectitude and conscience. This took precedence, in his mind, over the construction of a government founded on parties, factions or temporary coalitions of political interest. This, in his view, was the abiding weakness of the ministries of Lord Grey and Lord Melbourne. The Conservatives, by contrast, would offer disciplined moderation and a policy of reform tempered by prudence and discretion:

> I have done more in the cause of substantial and permanent improvement than nine-tenths of those who call themselves Reformers [Peel boasted in 1835 ...] My judgement of what constitutes an abuse may, and probably will, differ from that of many who require alterations in the law and institutions of this country. I may sometimes doubt whether the evil of the remedy is not greater than that of the disease ... I shall approach the consideration of an alleged abuse with a firm belief, that, if the allegation be true, a government gains ten times more strength by correcting an admitted evil, than they could by maintaining it.[49]

As such, although it was increasingly necessary (after 1832) to build a constituency of interest out of the materials supplied by party, rather than 'the influence of the crown', the Tamworth Manifesto was not – as has so often been claimed – the dawn of a new political movement. It was an exercise in rational politics as much as an exercise in political ideas. Indeed, it only appeared because of Peel's unexpected summons to become Prime Minister in November 1834. The significance of the Manifesto (emulated as such to this day) was in offering 'the party leader's own statement of policies' to the country at large. It became a collective statement of the new Conservative cabinet by virtue of having been approved at a meeting at the Lord Chancellor (Lord Lyndhurst's) house the day before it was sent out for publication in *The Times*, *The Morning Herald* and *The Morning Post*.[50]

Peel thought it expedient to make 'some early declaration of the principles of the Government' within days of assuming the premiership. In one sense, the Manifesto was necessary to steady the country's nerves. Peel was the head of a minority Conservative government placed in power by the will of the King. Greville feared that if Peel was to make 'a High Tory Government and [hold] High Tory language', in these circumstances, it would exacerbate a collision between Parliament and the Crown: 'My mind, I own, misgives me about Peel; I hope everything from his capacity and dread everything from his character.'[51] William IV had dismissed his Whig ministers in fright at their perceived threat to the Established Church. In its place, he had sought a coalition government including the most conservative of Whigs and the most liberal of Tories. This was politically impossible for Peel because it was exactly the sort of temporary political coalition which he abhorred and which had led the Whigs into their present impasse.[52] In the weeks preceding Peel's return from Italy, where he had received the King's summons to form an administration, Wellington had combined the leading offices of state in a caretaker administration. 'It is strange to remember that [it took Peel] as long to get from Rome to London when summoned to form a government as it had taken a high functionary of the Roman empire seventeen centuries earlier.'[53] It is not surprising why the lengthy interregnum generated an air of crisis, expectation and foreboding. Wellington's interim premiership gained the new government an Ultra Tory reputation – an impression which remained stubbornly resilient, in spite of all Peel's efforts to counteract it.[54]

The Tamworth Manifesto was Peel's attempt to do so. He may also have been conscious that the talented 'Rupert of Debate', Lord Stanley, was gathering a small but influential party of conservative Whig MPs to his standard. Stanley (who was heir to the Earl of Derby, Lancashire's premier aristocratic grandee) had resigned from Lord Grey's government over the issue of Church appropriation. One of the more interesting consequences of the Manifesto's appearance, on 19 December 1834, was to spike Stanley's guns. The 'Knowsley Creed' – named after Stanley's ancestral family home in Lancashire – was delivered at his inauguration as Rector of Glasgow University on 21 December. Its timing made it appear an imitation, rather than a progenitor, of Peel's moderate-conservative message.[55] Peel hammered home his advantage in a speech at the Mansion House before Christmas. Whilst Lord Ashley felt that this was not religious enough for the occasion and Lord Wharncliffe thought it would read better than it was spoken (Peel having delivered it 'rather below the mark'), Ellenborough praised his performance.[56] In turn, this frustrated Stanley's hopes of capturing the centre ground in British politics. It must have been galling for Stanley, who had a high sense of self-entitlement, to be upstaged by the grandson of a Lancashire yeoman farmer.[57] An element of rancour subsisted between the two men thereafter.[58] Stanley refused Peel's immediate offer to bring him into the government – a course of action which Lord Wilton thought he would have cause to regret, considering the sentiments of the Tamworth Manifesto.[59] However, the eventual absorption of Stanley's followers (the so-called 'Derby Dilly' which included Sir James Graham, the Duke of Richmond, Lord Ripon and Lord George Bentinck), within the ranks of the Conservative Party after 1835 was almost guaranteed. As Peel told Croker:

I should have thought, having been one of the main causes of the King's embarrassment, [Stanley] might, on the highest and most courageous principles, have assisted in the King's defence. Mind what I now say to you. If he really entertains the principles he professes, he *shall* not be able to maintain them and oppose me.[60]

* * *

The more one views the pronouncements of politicians in this period, the more the Manifesto looks, in Russ Foster's words, 'like an echo than a voice'. Rather than innovating, it amplified a tone and sentiment which was widely prevalent in the political discourse of the period.[61] In November 1834, Ellenborough had written an address on behalf of the King, expressing a wish 'to correct abuses and to improve the condition of the country'. Three months later, Melbourne was to be found advising his colleagues 'to work out the necessary reforms which the state of our institutions may require, upon safe and moderate principles, in accordance with the constitution of our mixed government and with the spirit of the age'. More surprisingly, as Wellington confessed to Peel, was the attitude of the Tory peers, who were 'well disposed to go all reasonable lengths in the way of reform of institutions. I have their letters to shew [sic] you. I have been astonished at their being so docile.'[62]

The Ultra Tories paid due obeisance to Peel in the autumn of 1834 but their acceptance was not unconditional. As Newcastle, 'the very pontiff of High Toryism', put it several months later (in a rather back-handed compliment to Peel), his 'satisfaction at seeing Peel at the head of affairs was not pure and unmixed'.[63] In fact, in spite of the claims of some historians, the 'Hundred Days' of Peel's first ministry (10 December 1834–18 April 1835) did not mark the end of the Ultra Tories.[64] As Lord Holland perceptively observed on 6 February 1835:

> The great danger of Ministers will arise from divisions among their own friends. To keep their places they must reform the Church; but if they propose extensive reforms … the real Tories will separate from them as they did before on the Catholic question. I see no reason to think there will be a complete victory on either side. Questions will be alternately won and lost till some compromise or arrangement is effected by which a mixed Government will be formed under the guidance of either Peel or Stanley, the extremes on both sides being laid aside. How long it will take to bring about this result depends on the measures of Reform brought forward by the Ministers. If they be such as to alarm the real Tories Peel will be abandoned by those who constitute the real strength of his party.[65]

Holland's fellow-Whig, Edward Ellice, also felt that Peel's fate depended 'rather upon the incapacity and unpopularity of his colleagues and supporters than upon any union and energetic action on the part of his opponents':

He fights his battle well; pleads his duty to the King as a justification for submission to the personal mortifications which his position necessarily exposes him to; takes a bolder and better line in the measures he brings forward than Lord Grey's Government did, and hopes to escape attack on the points on which he is prepared to make no concession.[66]

The Tamworth Manifesto addressed itself to a non-partisan audience which prized stability and sound government above sectional interests. It expressed a willingness to take into consideration the claims of the Dissenters to have their marriage and baptismal rites recognised in law and to address the questions of tithe, church rate and Municipal Corporation reform, all of which were already under political consideration. It was an open (and, in motivation, extremely traditional) bid to secure sufficient MPs for Peel to manage the House of Commons. It was delivered in the novel form of a Manifesto because of the exigencies of the political situation. It had to perform a delicate balancing act, poised 'between the retro-active tendencies of the majority of [Peel's] own supporters, and the mad passion for change with which the events ... of the last four years had inspired the people'.[67] It was acclaimed by *The Times* as 'creditable' to Peel 'and satisfactory to the public' and by Greville as 'well written and ingenious' but Ellenborough subsequently confessed that it had 'produced no movement in the public mind in our favor'.[68] More famously, Disraeli called it 'an attempt to construct a party without principles'.[69] Unfortunate comparisons were drawn, by the more zealous of Peel's supporters, between his situation in 1834 and that of the Younger Pitt half a century earlier. Pitt had been installed in power by George III in 1783 and went on to achieve a working majority at the General Election of 1784. Lord Clarendon told Peel that:

It was not a powerful party, it was not the hereditary splendour of his great name, nor his surprising talents & spotless character, nor even (to use your own beautiful expression) the <u>magic</u> of his eloquence, nor was it the well deserved respect & popularity which for so many subsequent years the King enjoyed ... which gave Mr Pitt this victory – It was <u>the cause</u> in which he contended – It was <u>that</u> in which he was confident, & not in himself, & the people at once justified his confidence.

Peel continually dismissed the analogy. Indeed, he found it 'implausible and embarrassing'. It may even have stiffened a counter-reaction against him in the country.[70]

Although the number of Conservative MPs increased, the General Election of 1835 did not provide Peel with the working majority he required to strengthen his control of the House of Commons. Rather, (as Croker observed to Lord Hertford) his executive authority had 'no solid basis to enable it to stand against a shift of wind'. It left him dangerously – and in light of his experience as Leader of the Commons in 1830 – uncomfortably dependent on his backbenchers. When they failed to materialise he upbraided them for their lack of seriousness. To Lord Haddington, Peel complained of being reliant on the support of gentlemen 'who have engagements in society which they are not willing to relinquish for House of Commons attendance, whereas the evening pursuits of a great body of our opponents do not connect them with the refinements of the fashionable world'. It was reported, subsequently, that the party's managers divided London 'into districts with a superintendent over each, who is to summon the absent from Balls, dinner parties, Clubhouses &c wherever they are to be found'.[71]

Peel habitually spoke in terms of being 'determined to do his duty' in this period. In December 1834, Lord Ashley found his manner 'unusually urgent & emphatic – he talked of duties, necessities, dangers, sacrifices' – and expected others to feel equally strongly.[72] As such, Peel felt the embarrassment of his situation more keenly than any of his cabinet colleagues; he was correspondingly quicker and more insistent in his determination to resign as decently as circumstances would permit. Ellenborough complained that 'Peel rather assumed the necessity of resigning' – a sentiment he castigated as a weakness of character:

> If he had the spirit of Pitt, or of the Duke [of Wellington], or that of Sir Robert Walpole or indeed of any one great Minister we have ever had Peel would succeed; but he is essentially selfish – & although thoroughly honest he has no nobleness in his nature – and none of that manner which attaches & leads men.[73]

Other commentators, ever conscious that Peel set his sights on a more lasting and permanent sense of vindication for his actions, addressed him with a naked appeal to posterity:

> There yet remains, even looking only as far as this world is concerned, one thing more which a noble mind may well aspire after; and that is, a high and honourable fame – a page in history's volume, of bright and enduring splendour. *This* you have yet to gain! True, you have already secured to yourself immunity from oblivion. While the annals of England are preserved, your name cannot be wholly forgotten. But the higher prize of a leading rank among your country's greatest sons yet remains to be achieved![74]

However, even these heady appeals proved unavailing in the face of political circumstances and continued reverses, at the hands of the Opposition, in the House of Commons. As the Ministry limped towards its inevitable dissolution, Greville (on 5 April) perceived an end to the temporary truce between Peel and his Tory followers:

> The fact is that they cannot forgive him for his Liberal principles and Liberal measures, and probably they never believed that he was sincere in the professions he made, or that he really intended to introduce such measures as he had done … Peel sees and knows all this, and cannot fail to perceive that he is not the Minister for them and they no longer the party for him.[75]

* * *

Peel himself never sought to exaggerate the significance of the Tamworth Manifesto (as a party document) or attempt to trace its genesis to the political requirements made necessary by the Reform Act. As he was at pains to point out to Croker, his first ministry was called into existence by the actions of William IV and was not due to any precipitate action on the part of the Conservatives. As such, it is surprising that the Manifesto should 'by a curious lack of curiosity [have] acquired the status of a founding document of modern conservatism'.[76] Conversely, Gash was right to claim that William IV brought the Conservative Party into existence in November 1834, as George III had 'unwittingly' done the same for the Whigs fifty years earlier.[77] However, the corollary was that it was Wellington who installed Peel as its leader. In counselling the King of the necessity (post-1832) for the Prime Minister to sit in the House of Commons, Wellington did what no one else (Peel included) had managed to do since they had gone into opposition. It may also have eased the somewhat icy frondeur between the two men, exacerbated by Wellington's recent succession – in preference to Peel – as Chancellor of the University of Oxford.[78] As William Thomas observes, 'Peel did not seek a party to lead. It would be more accurate to say that, while enjoying his release from old political ties after November 1830, he found one thrust upon him.' Nevertheless, whilst the 'Hundred Days' advanced Peel to the leadership of the Conservative Party, they did not alter his essentially executive outlook:

> He knew he had won a great reputation for tenacity and courage and that respectable men deplored the way he had been brought down…But he seems to have seen this less as a party defeat than as a symptom of the sort of politics he deplored and refused to imitate.[79]

This was a stance which was bound to raise dissension. Before the autumn of 1834, relations between Peel and his nominal followers were far from harmonious. The diaries and correspondence of leading Conservatives of the period (as indeed for some time afterwards) are full of complaints at his unwillingness to offer leadership and direction or to seize the opportunity provided by failures on the part of the government. Wellington privately vented his frustration at Peel's 'woeful want of spirit' and doubted his willingness to undertaken the government.[80] 'A party more and more united, with a strong support in the press, a growing organization in the constituencies, and a higher morale and *esprit de corps* through its clubs, was apparently being held back by a leader who made a parade of his indifference to office'.[81] Conversely, after the 'Hundred Days', commentators perceived Peel's growing ascendancy over his followers. In 1836, James Grant concluded that 'never had the leader of a party a more complete ascendancy over that party than has this Tory Coryphaeus over the Conservatives in the House of Commons'.[82] The same year, Wellington concluded that Peel appeared 'more disposed than heretofore to put himself at the head of the Party'.

However, in doing so, Peel retained his latitude of action. According to G.H. Francis, Peel:

> gradually disembarrassed himself of every tie that could render him dependent on his own party, while at the same time he steadily declined to compromise himself with the democratic section of his opponents…The result of this combination of abstinence and adroit assault was…he stood perfectly unpledged to any specific principle or measure, but had enveloped his plans in such vague generalities as to leave him comparatively a free agent.[83]

For Peel's Ultra Tory critics, this development was ominous. 'The only difference between Sir Robert Peel & Lord John Russell, [the Duke of Newcastle complained] is that one would only give a handful where the other would give bushels'.[84] A decade later, Disraeli put the same point in famous fictional terms: "'a sound Conservative government" [Taper mused]. "I understand: Tory men and Whig measures"'. In it lay the kernel of Disraeli's complaint against Peel – that he would neither form the opinion of his political friends nor, in turn, be guided by them but used the masthead of his political opponents instead.[85] Nor, as Disraeli complained to his sister Sarah, after reading Peel's inaugural speech as Rector of Glasgow University in January 1837, was Peel capable of rousing his followers with inspiring rhetoric:

> he cannot soar, and his attempts to be imaginative and sentimental must be offensive to every man of taste and refined feeling. But fortunately the Radicals are not versed in *belles lettres* and have the respect of ignorance for a scholar…and the Tories who see the weak points or are capable of doing so, are either blinded by party, or too subtle to bewray [sic] their own nest.[86]

Peel's installation at Glasgow occasioned two speeches. These provided him with the opportunity to outline his vision of Conservatism and advertise his personal credentials to the nation at large. The more academic of the two orations was hailed by Queen Victoria as 'a very clever speech'. The Duke of Hamilton, an arch-Whig, also esteemed it highly:[87]

> I must allow, that Peel made a most brilliant display here: I could not have conceived that a Conservative (with all my prepositions in their favour) could have shewn [sic] himself to such advantage, & I think his accademical [sic] discourse was the better of the two – He had many difficulties to encounter at his dinner, but his ability, & his subdued cultivated mind carried him through with <u>honor</u>.[88]

The most famous passage in Peel's Glasgow speeches was his analogy between the progress of society and the movement of a great machine 'progressing in the discharge of its important action, beating with healthful and regular pulses, animating industry, encouraging production, rewarding toil, and purifying wherever there is stagnation':

Gladstone thought the speech 'explicit and bold'.[89] Nevertheless, in spite of the wide coverage accorded them in the newspapers, the political part of the proceedings failed to have the intended effect, at least when measured against the celebrations which had attended the Duke of Wellington's installation as Chancellor of Oxford in the summer of 1834. As Lord Holland observed, 'the election of Peel to the Rectorship of Glasgow gave him an opportunity of a display, of which however he did not avail himself so largely or so ably as his partisans expected'.[90]

This ambivalence towards the claims of party suited Peel's temperament precisely. A devotee of field-sports and hunting game, Peel habitually looked upon his followers as a recalcitrant pack of hounds that needed bringing to heel: not for nothing was his favourite metaphor, in respect of leading the party, 'heads see but tails follow'.[91] In April 1839, just before Peel attempted to assume the government once more, *The Times* defended his strategy:

> Never was there a political leader who more dissatisfied his opponents than Sir Robert Peel does. With a rigidity which they find altogether unpardonable, he positively declines to shape his course to their views. When they choose a ground, and, putting themselves into an attitude, call on him to strike a blow, he churlishly rejects their invitation to the offensive, and refuses to accommodate them with a commencement of quarrel. When they retreat, in hopes of seducing him to follow, he unaccountably adheres to his own steadfast position. In short, he seems always, by some cross purpose or other, to do just the thing which they find most inconvenient.[92]

However, these comments were as applicable to the Conservative backbenchers as they were to the government. Melbourne resigned as Prime Minister in May 1839, after an adverse parliamentary vote on the government of Jamaica. On this occasion Peel was frustrated in his attempts to become Prime Minister by the open partiality of the monarch towards the Whigs. Queen Victoria declared her unwillingness to bestow a mark of confidence on the new administration (which lacked a Commons majority) by consenting to change *some* of her Ladies of the Bedchamber. The constitutional point was undoubtedly on Peel's side, the Queen having wilfully misinterpreted his request as a demand to replace *all* her female attendants. Peel did not press the issue. Given events five years earlier, he could hardly complain of being defeated at the hands of petticoat influence at Court, although his own 'cold, odd' manner towards the Queen was clearly a contributory factor in his failure on this occasion.[93]

* * *

In terms of Peel's reputation, the most significant event of the 1830s was undoubtedly his 'Hundred Days' ministry. Not only did this elevate him to the premiership and the (effectively undisputed) leadership of the Conservative Party, but his own conduct in office and the timing of his departure were well tuned to garner him substantial plaudits.[94] Having earlier criticised Peel's determination to resign, Ellenborough

8: 'The Letter Of Introduction', *Punch*, I, July–December 1841, 91.
An early *Punch* cartoon illustrating the tensions between Sir Robert Peel
and Queen Victoria.

concluded that, when it finally occurred (on Wednesday 8 April 1835), it was to the general satisfaction of the ministry's followers. 'Had our resignation been offered on Friday they would not have been so – Had it been delayed longer there would have been an unpleasant intimation from Lord Stanley.'[95] Both *Blackwood's Edinburgh Magazine* and Greville, in their posthumous reflections on Peel, judged this to be amongst the most glorious portions of his career.[96] For once, Greville's mature assessment tallied with his immediate response to events:

> I believe it to be impossible that anything can prevent Peel's speedy return to office [he concluded on 3 April 1835]; he has raised his reputation to such a height during this session, he has established such a conviction of his great capacity and of his liberal, enlarged, and at the same time safe views and opinions, that even the Radicals ... join in the general chorus of admiration which is raised to his merits; he stands so proudly eminent, and there is such a general lack of talent, that he must be recalled by the voice of the nation and by the universal admission that he is indispensable to the country.[97]

A sense of Peel's enhanced public reputation was demonstrated in the addresses of public support which followed his resignation as Prime Minister as well as in the poetic tributes which it occasioned: [98]

> PRIDE of our country, terror of our foes,
> Source of our honor, solace of our woes,
> Welcome, Sir Robert Peel, a reckless band
> Conspire to wrest the sceptre from thy hand –
> Their selfish plot may prosper – but the throne
> Of public confidence is thine alone –
> Thy private virtue – and thy public fame –
> Thy moral influence is still the same.
> Theirs be the victory – but let none repine –
> Theirs be the victory – but the triumph thine.[99]

Peel himself was characteristically sensitive to the judgement of posterity. On 7 April 1835, in a refrain which became typical of his thoughts on recent events, Peel responded to an address from the City of London by observing that he looked forward to:

> that judgment which will ultimately be formed upon the motives and actions of public men, when the events that are now passing shall be viewed from a greater distance, and through a medium unobscured by the passions and interests which at the period of their occurrence they naturally excite.

He drew up the materials for such a judgement, from his own papers and correspondence for the period, and this was published (in due course) as the second of his three posthumous *Memoirs*.[100]

In legislative terms, the most significant outcome of Peel's first ministry was the establishment of the Ecclesiastical Commission in January 1835. George Kitson Clark considered that it was this, 'more than any other one reform, [which] made possible the renewed usefulness of the Church of England in the nineteenth century'.[101] To Lord Harrowby (who accepted Peel's invitation to join it) Peel outlined his hopes for the Commission:

> in the encouraging and (where possible) the compulsion of residence – the prevention of improper pluralities [and] the gradual extirpation of sinecures in the Church. The immediate course I propose to pursue for the purpose of laying the safe foundations at least, of progressive reform in the Church, is the appointment of a commission, to which I should <u>confidentially</u> refer, on the avoidance of any great preferment, the consideration of those arrangements in detail, which might best promote the object I have in view – and which commission might also consider prospectively – the arrangements which it might be advisable to adopt, either with the consent of those who have at present existing interests, or, if this consent cannot be had, on the occurrence of a vacancy.[102]

Given the central role which the Church of England's fate had played in the removal of Melbourne's government in November 1834, some response on the part of Peel's ministry was required. Peel was able to find a key ally in Charles James Blomfield, the reform-minded Bishop of London. However, like Peel, Blomfield had to deal with a hard core of 'Ultras' from amongst the Anglican bishops.[103] Nor was the Commission universally popular amongst Peel's political friends. Croker thought it 'a bad precedent from good hands' whilst (more predictably) Ultra Tories like Newcastle condemned it as an unwarranted interference with Anglican property. Nevertheless, the Commission usefully subdued political passions on the subject and left the Church of England's fate, to a large extent, in its own hands.[104] The Commission's reports provided the basis for future legislation and its permanence was guaranteed by its acceptance – with a revised political membership – after the Whigs returned to office in April 1835. During the 1840s the Commission became the mechanism through which Peel promoted 'not so much … free trade in religion as liberality in the State's attitude towards the religious plurality of British society'.[105]

* * *

Following Peel's resignation, a meeting of merchants, traders and bankers was arranged at the Merchant Taylor's Hall (on 11 May 1835) to pay homage to his services in the Conservative cause.[106] Gladstone recorded the reception as 'enthusiastic' and the speech was described by *Blackwood's Edinburgh Magazine* as 'a practical and useful direction to the general burst of public feeling which had broken forth in the country'.[107] Ten days later, an anonymous West Country pamphleteer published a scurrilous response to these proceedings:

Quoth the Duke, 'He's a low cotton spinner,
But still the plain truth we must tell;
From the speech he had made at this dinner,
For a tool he will do very well'.[108]

The company each then departed,
Though some of them looked very BLUE,
Declaring it made them faint-hearted,
As they feared Bobby Peel wasn't true.

The TIMES and the STANDARD pronounced
Peel's speech of all speeches the best,
And in high sounding language announced
This kind and consoling behest.

'That thousands – nay, millions – should be
Placarded on house and on wall;
And the price, they did wisely decree,
If a FARTHING, would not be too small'.[109]

For all its crude political cynicism, the doggerel raised an under-emphasised point in the historiography of this period: Peel was as much a 'tool' of the Conservative Party, in their quest to regain power, as they were a 'tool' of his. In December 1845, Lord Hatherton ruminated on a 'positively murderous' article in *The Times*, which observed that, if the Conservative Party had been deceived, 'it is they who have compelled the deception, and helped to make the deceiver'. Hatherton agreed with this sentiment – 'that [Peel] used the Agricultural Party as a stepping stone to power, is quite true. But it is equally true that they used him, and they did it knowing his sentiments. Verily they have both met their reward.'[110]

That Peel's ostensible supporters were always a minority within the broader Conservative Party is well attested. Norman Gash always maintained that the avowed number of Peelites in the party never exceeded a quarter to one third of the whole – a figure borne out by the divisions over the Repeal of the Corn Laws in 1846. In the face of this, Ian Newbould's argument that the 1830s constituted the 'failure' of Peel's 'New Conservatism' (because of the continuing prevalence of Protestant and Protectionist tendencies within the party) could be countered by a resort to the realities of political power. As Gash subsequently argued, 'Failure is a relative term. Most political leaders would gladly compound for a "failure", which gave them a majority of eighty in the Commons and made possible five years of epoch-making legislation.'[111] Yet, by extension, the same argument reinforces the perception that, for Peel at least, the Conservative Party served a utilitarian function which could ultimately be dispensed with, should the circumstances demand it. This, of course, is precisely what happened in 1846. As Peel told Lord Aberdeen after the event, he 'had no hesitation in sacrificing the subordinate object [the keeping together of the Conservative Party] and with it my own political interests'.[112]

The extent to which Peel and the Conservative Party were locked in a mutually restrictive embrace was revealed by a small but significant issue on the eve of his return to power. In January 1841 Peel delivered a speech at the opening of the Tamworth Library and Reading Room. In it he extolled the virtues of extending the benefits of a scientific and secular education, arguing that knowledge made a man more moral. The leading Anglican divine, John Henry Newman, writing under the pseudonym 'Catholicus', published seven letters in *The Times*, in which he condemned this (on philosophical and practical grounds) as a denial of the importance of faith. Most famously of all, Newman concluded that 'man is not a reasoning animal'.[113] *The Times* had increasingly aligned itself with the Conservative Party, over the course of the 1830s. The appearance of the 'Catholicus' letters in its columns was interpreted as a tacit disavowal of Peel. John Walter III, the editor of *The Times*, put the matter plainly in a letter to Newman:

> unfortunately we are so situated with reference to the political world, that [it] is thought dangerous to raise a question about the principles of the leader whose party we are supporting, even on the most independent subject, and people cannot be persuaded that the condemnation of certain principles when adopted by such a person does not imply an attack on his character, and a desertion of his cause ... all here whose opinions I am bound to respect are perfectly satisfied themselves with the opinions you have expressed on Sir Robert Peel's conduct, but yet think it would hardly be *discreet* to pursue the subject at present, when a change in the Government is contemplated as likely, and Conservatives, however much they may disapprove of Sir Robert Peel for this and many reasons, have yet no one else to look to as a leader.[114]

An editorial comment was inserted as a preface to Newman's fourth letter, two days later, denying the charge that they represented a political attack on Peel.[115]

The caution exhibited by *The Times* was justified. Ian Newbould has dated the end of Peel's effective co-operation with the Whigs to 1839. Over the next two years, Peel's gradualist policy (in respect of his followers and the electorate) began to mature as events moved inexorably in his favour. The severe economic downturn, which began in 1837 and set in after 1839, forced the Whigs to propose drastic reductions in the protective duties on sugar, timber and corn. This was designed to offset the budget deficit and counter the rise of extra-parliamentary political agitation in the shape of Chartism and the Anti-Corn Law League (both of which came to prominence after 1838).[116] This rallied the Conservatives behind Peel and quelled any residual doubts the party entertained about his leadership. 'The whole town is astounded and disgusted at what took place last night,' Lord Lincoln informed his father, the Duke of Newcastle, after the proposals were revealed:

> We went to the House expecting resignation or ... dissolution, and instead we had a budget with repeal of the Corn Laws and other less obnoxious crudities ... Our party is so completely up at what has taken place and Peel & Co. are so

thoroughly indignant that I think we shall go at them ... [The Whigs] have now indeed filled up the measure of their wickedness and though it is an atrocious scheme for the purpose of maintaining power I do not despair of seeing it become the final grave of the whole accursed crew.[117]

The defeat of the government's proposals, on a motion of no-confidence (by a margin of one vote), precipitated the General Election of 1841.[118] The Whigs campaigned on a fixed duty for sugar and corn whilst the Conservatives pledged themselves (ominously, in light of subsequent events) to the maintenance of the Corn Laws. Peel dexterously avoided a specific personal pledge on the issue. *The Illustrated London News* later observed that his conspicuous lack of utterances on the subject 'carried *finesse* almost to the point of deliberate deception and ... left himself many loopholes of escape from the charge of intentional tergiversation'.[119] Instead, Peel assumed the easier ground (at least in Parliament) of mocking the government's financial ineptitude:

> Can there be a more lamentable picture than that of a Chancellor of the Exchequer seated on an empty chest – by the pool of bottomless deficiency – fishing for a budget? I won't bite; the right honourable gentlemen shall return home with his pannier as empty as his chest.[120]

Peel's policy of timely delay and cautious progress also paid off at Court. The Queen's marriage to her cousin, Albert of Saxe-Coburg in 1840, and the moderating influence of his adviser, Baron Stockmar, eroded some of the reliance she had hitherto placed on Melbourne as her political and personal counsellor. Peel became to Albert what Melbourne had been to Victoria – and no one stood higher in Victoria's estimation than Albert. By a process of conciliation at Court and proven electoral strength, in Parliament and the nation, Sir Robert Peel came to kiss hands as the Queen's first Conservative Prime Minister on 30 August 1841.[121]

* * *

Whilst Peel's personal chemistry with Prince Albert undoubtedly facilitated his re-introduction at Court, it was political circumstances which proved decisive in determining his return to office. In August 1841 Queen Victoria was reluctantly forced to yield to the logic of political circumstances, as her uncle William IV had done in parting with Peel six years earlier. Melbourne's Whig government was the first to be replaced, in defiance of the known wishes of the monarch, by virtue of a defeat in the House of Commons as the result of a General Election. Peel had finally obtained the means by which to govern and maintain his executive authority in Parliament. He had done so through the mechanism of party; a fact which necessitated that he conform, subsequently, to the political platform upon which that party had been returned and nurture the support of his parliamentary followers, rather than (as in the pre-Reform days) rely upon 'the influence of the crown' and a judicious application of patronage. However, Peel did not perceive party, and its attendant claims, to be the basis of his success. Flushed with electoral gains, it was easy for Peel to regard his victory in 1841 as a triumph in the face of the Reform Act, rather than a telling example of its operation. Restored to power, Peel argued that he 'owed his position to his superior experience and judgement (aided of course by the fact that in office he had access to the best information). If his supporters could not accept that, he would resign, and they must take the consequences of their want of faith.'[122] The reverse, in fact, was true. The political failure of the Whigs, after 1839, showed that government by party had replaced government by executive (and royal) fiat, for it was no longer possible for a ministry to survive merely upon the tolerance of a supportive monarch. The working out of this lesson during the 1830s resulted in the installation in office of the first, unashamedly Conservative, administration in modern British history – a fact which is still, justly, celebrated.[123] However, Peel's unwillingness to perceive the consequences of this, in terms of his relationship with the party, worked themselves out (with disastrous consequences) during the 1840s. Viewed in this light, it is hardly surprising why Peel continues to occupy an ambivalent status amongst modern Conservatives.[124]

6

'RE-PEEL': REFORM OF THE TARIFF AND REPEAL OF THE CORN LAWS

In relinquishing power ... I shall leave a name execrated by every monopolist who, from less honourable motives, clamours for protection because it conduces to his own individual benefit; but it may be that I shall leave a name sometimes remembered with expressions of good will in the abodes of those whose lot it is to labour, and to earn their daily bread by the sweat of their brow, when they shall recruit their exhausted strength with abundant and untaxed food, the sweeter because it is no longer leavened by a sense of injustice.

Peel, Speech on Resignation as Prime Minister, 29 June 1846.[1]

* * *

The significance of Peel's second administration has been the subject of historical controversy ever since Peel delivered a valedictory assessment of his achievements on resigning office. Historians of the 1841–6 government have continually been caught between the magnetic impulses of two polar opposites. On the one hand, the government is seen through the prism of Peel and the evolving teleology leading from the election victory of 1841 (at which the Conservative Party achieved a majority of 76 seats) to the Repeal of the Corn Laws in 1846 (which preceded the ministry's defeat, on the Irish Coercion Bill, by a majority of 73 votes). This line of argument – which began with Peel's resignation speech – stresses the greater good emanating from Repeal, leading inexorably towards W.L. Burn's *Age of Equipoise*, in establishing Britain's mid-Victorian prosperity and frustrating the efforts of Chartists and radical proponents of further constitutional change alike. As Peel himself commented to John Hope, 'I am a Conservative – the most Conservative act of my life was that which has caused the sacrifice of power.'[2] What George Kitson Clark called *The Making of Victorian England* was thus symbolised by Britain's relative insulation (in a period of intense social, political and economic disorder) from the impact of the European Revolutions of 1848. It bore fruit three years later in the 'Great' Exhibition of 1851, housed in Joseph Paxton's Crystal

Palace in London's Hyde Park. This event above all others appeared to reinforce the sense of 'Great' Britain's exceptional standing in Europe. It represented Peel's posthumous legacy to the nation, given form and structure in metal and glass.[3]

On the other hand, the ministry is seen through the prism of its most vocal (and memorable) opponents. This line of argument emphasises Peel's betrayal of his erstwhile Conservative followers, of the platform upon which he won the 1841 General Election and the extent to which he defied the necessity for party in the political environment created by the 1832 Reform Act. This was essentially the position of Benjamin Disraeli, Lord George Bentinck, Lord Stanley and the 'Protectionists', who formed the majority of the party that broke away from Peel in 1846. To some extents, the fact that they constituted the broad mass of Conservative backbenchers amplified the sentiment (reinforced by subsequent liberal historiography) that the 1846 split was a front-bench/back-bench division rather than an urban/rural one.[4] By extension, Peel's opponents were dismissed as inevitably retrograde, self-interested and myopic blockheads as opposed to the liberal, progressive and enlightened 'Peelite' front-bench ministers. In December 1845 *The Economist* designated the struggle over Repeal as a contest 'between prejudice and intolerance on the one hand, and intelligent progress on the other'. This remarkably tenacious reading of events has only lately begun to be revised.[5]

More recently, Boyd Hilton has suggested that, far from engineering the mid-Victorian boom through his budgets of 1842 and 1845 and by the Repeal of the Corn Laws, Peel's economics (like Huskisson's before him) were dominated by issues of food supply and monetary stability. According to this interpretation of events, Peel was interested in reviving commerce rather than concerned with expanding the economy to inexhaustible limits. His over-arching concern was to help foster the economic climate in which the country might escape the 'horrors of a stationary or even retrogressive state'.[6] These goals were infused with an evangelical eschatology which was obsessed with the deleterious effects of famine, hunger and an unrestricted currency on the wider population. Peel gave vent to these feelings during the Repeal of the Corn Laws with his repeated and increasingly emotionally-charged references to 'the exhortations of a suffering people', 'the dispensations of Providence' (i.e. calamitous and unseen events like plague and tempest) and the fear that these were being artificially 'aggravated by laws of man restricting in the hour of scarcity the supply of food'.[7] Moreover, according to Hilton, Peel:

> had undoubtedly been complicit in Huskisson's project for free trade in grain, at least so long as population continued to rocket upwards, and though it cannot be proved that his own determination went back as far as the 1820s, it certainly went back a long way. He could hardly have come clean about his intentions before the 1841 election, but his speeches were sufficiently equivocal to leave the door open.[8]

Consequently, whilst sharing Norman Gash's belief in the continuity of Peel's economic thinking between the 1820s and 1840s, Hilton argues for Peel's long-term and pre-meditated commitment to the Repeal of the Corn Laws, rather than seeing it as the outcome of immediate stimuli such as the failure of the Irish potato crop in the autumn of 1845.[9]

This chapter considers how Peel's retrospective interpretation of his premiership, from the time of his resignation speech onwards, gave colour to the idea that Repeal was the inevitable (and to that extent pre-meditated) outcome of his economic policy as Prime Minister. However, the re-introduction of Income Tax (in 1842) and the revision of duties on imports and exports (in the Budgets of 1842 and 1845) were – as Peel had declared at the time – 'great experiments', the success of which provided the government with a higher revenue stream than had been anticipated. This gave Peel the necessary economic leeway to enable him to undertake the great political gamble of Repeal when events in Ireland forced his hand.

* * *

Few Prime Ministers have written a more effective political epitaph for themselves than Sir Robert Peel did, in resigning office after the Repeal of the Corn Laws, on Monday 29 June 1846. In his closing peroration, Peel arraigned his fiercest political adversaries as 'selfish monopolists', aligned himself with those 'whose lot it is to labour and earn their daily bread by the sweat of their brow' and openly bid for the suffrages of their popular memory in making a bold and explicit claim to the judgement of posterity. The *Quarterly Review* sardonically observed that the passage had subsequently been printed in gold letters on blue card, ornamented with allegorical decorations, and given away *gratis*.[10] As Boyd Hilton observes, Peel 'revelled in his martyrdom' and 'floated on waves of righteous self-esteem'.[11] 'There can be little doubt that Peel sought this apotheosis,' David Eastwood has observed, 'and cherished a public status which owed nothing to party and everything to national acclamation.'[12] As such, his resignation speech – with its 'wilful wounding' of former political colleagues – represents 'a truly heroic parliamentary moment ... quite uncharacteristically populist in tone and almost aggressively demagogic in idiom':

> Nothing did so much to establish [Peel's] political reputation than the manner of his political dying. He seemed to sacrifice all in the great and indispensable gesture of Repeal ... There could be no clearer bid for posthumous recognition and moral high ground than this. Peel quite explicitly and quite deliberately placed himself above party, and demanded to be remembered and to be judged, not by the conventional standards of parliamentary politics, but by the much less exacting (or less well-defined) standards of the *statesman* ... Peel had quite deliberately isolated himself, and in so doing he had destroyed his party, or at any rate driven an immovable wedge between Peelism and Toryism. The destruction of the Party was not an unfortunate, unintended consequence of the Corn Law crisis – it was, rather, quite deliberately engineered by Peel.[13]

Although Peel told Queen Victoria that his speech had been 'very well received', there is little doubt that it caused general offence to his followers and was regarded as a calculated snub to those who, as Lady Burghersh observed, had '*eat dirt* for him'. Although he was accompanied between Parliament and his London home by the 'immense' cheers of 'the mob (chiefly consisting of well dressed respectable persons)', amidst what Greville called 'a sort of halo of popularity',[14] reactions amongst Peel's colleagues and opponents were remarkably adverse.[15] One anonymous pamphleteer was in no doubt that Peel's conscious tilt at an enduring popularity would be unavailing:

> The labourer is generally a shrewd man, with a good share of honest common sense ... He is perfectly capable of discriminating between those who consistently advocate a cause, and those who, having profitably opposed it in the hour of its weakness, when they might have aided it, embrace it at the eleventh hour, in the time of its triumph, when it is capable of aiding them. It is not on time-serving patriots, such as these, that posterity confers her gratitude. Posterity gives her gratitude to the upright and sincere, not to the crafty, servile, and deceitful. Posterity admires those who convert their fellows to truth by persuasion, she scorns those who can only convert them to dishonour by government influence.[16]

These sentiments were echoed by informed political commentators. 'Peel spoke about an hour, which was at least half too long [Hobhouse observed], and a bad speech in every sense of the word ... egotistical in the highest degree.'[17] The Bishop of Oxford also left a vivid impression of the scene:

> Peel came, in, walked up the House: colder, dryer, more introverted than ever, yet to a close gaze showing the fullest working of a smothered volcano of emotions ... By-and-by he rose, amidst a breathless silence, and made the speech you will have read long ere this. It was very fine: very effective: really almost solemn: to fall at such a moment. He spoke as if it was his last political scene: as if he felt that between alienated friends and unwon foes he could have no party again; and could only as a shrewd bystander observe and advise others. There was but one point in the Speech which I thought doubtful: the apostrophe to 'Richard Cobden'.[18]

It was Peel's open avowal that the 'name which ought to be, and which will be, associated with the success of these measures ... is the name of Richard Cobden', the leader of the Anti-Corn Law League and MP (since 1841) for Stockport, that was received as a deliberate and provocative offence to the sensibilities of the Conservative Party and a breach of parliamentary etiquette. Disraeli called it a display of 'glorification and pique' whilst Cobden himself seems to have been embarrassed by it, feeling it paid insufficient justice to Charles Pelham Villiers, who had proposed Repeal annually since 1838.[19] Even Queen Victoria, who expressed her 'great admiration' for the speech to Peel, privately commented that she regretted it and did not know why '(though we *can* guess)' he had paid him such a conspicuous honour.[20]

The Chartist *Northern Star* regarded Peel's anointing of Cobden as 'a great revolution in our political and social system. The twin rival sections [of Whigs and Tories] who used to play at the game of "outs" and "ins", and toss the nation between them like a shuttlecock are henceforth political nullities.' 'Peel has raised the League higher than the Parliament [Richard Oastler observed] – he has enthroned Richard Cobden in the seat of higher power!'[21]

Peel's political supporters were less enamoured of the speech. Lord Ashley, incredulous that Peel might now be, as Francis Bonham maintained, 'the most popular man in England' thought the encomium on Cobden's merits particularly hard on the 112 'Peelites' who had 'made every sacrifice to support him, bore many insults, and surrendered some principles' by voting for Repeal in the House of Commons. Peel had been 'a powerless creature without them; yet not a word of compliment or thanks for their friendship & services; not a syllable of respect to his late colleagues! I, I, I, runs throughout; "I shall leave a name &c &c" – alas, alas, what an immersion into himself!'[22]

Gladstone also felt 'the declaration about Cobden' to have been unjust; in particular, Peel's attribution of pure and disinterested motives to him: 'if his power of discussion has been great & his end good, his tone has been most harsh, & his imputation of bad & vile motives to honourable men incessant'. Delivering such a eulogium reflected something unworthy in Peel's mind, because it suggested he was 'very sensible of the sweetness of the cheers of opponents'. To Sir James Graham (Home Secretary between 1841 and 1846), Gladstone 'admitted the truth of every word that Peel had uttered – but complained of its omissions, of its spirit towards his own friends, of its false moral effect, as well as and much more than of its mere impolicy'. Gladstone found Aberdeen, Sidney Herbert and Graham all agreed in thinking the Cobden panegyric unfortunate. It had upset everybody (including the Whigs) and conciliated nobody. The tone of the resignation speech suggested an unmovable determination on Peel's part to mediate an apolitical future for himself, above party, within Parliament. Graham thought the passage 'preconceived and for the purpose'. Herbert felt that Peel's 'natural temper, which he said is very violent though usually under thorough discipline, broke out and coloured that part of the speech' which dealt with Cobden. Peel himself had, 'not long ago' put his hand up to the side of his head and exclaimed, 'Ah you do not know what I suffer here.'[23]

* * *

That Peel was, in many respects, the first historian of his administration, should hardly be surprising. Most Prime Ministers have been concerned with delineating the terms upon which (as they hoped) subsequent historians would judge them. However, Peel was the first and most prominent of nineteenth century premiers to do so. In the final part of his *Memoirs*, published posthumously in 1857, he laid down in close detail the stages by which he had come to Repeal the Corn Laws. A decade earlier, in his 'Tamworth Letter', an address to his Staffordshire constituents at the General Election of 1847, he had defended himself from the charge of inconsistency:

Between the maintenance of the corn law inviolate, and a measure involving their ultimate repeal, I saw no middle course satisfactory or advantageous to any interest: I saw still less of satisfaction or advantage in indecision and irrational delay: I could not admit the incompetency of the present parliament to deal with this as with every other question of public concern: there appeared to me, upon the whole, much less of public evil in the resolution finally to adjust the question of the corn law than in any other that could be then adopted, and that being my deliberate conviction, I felt it to be my duty to incur the painful sacrifices which the acting upon that conviction must inevitably entail.[24]

Peel's critics were unmoved by the attempt to explain away his conversion on these terms. Even *The Economist* (which, as an acknowledged supporter of the Anti-Corn Law League, was generally commendatory towards Peel at this time) recommended his opponents to study 'that speciousness in making out a case' which so 'distinguished' him as a politician.[25] Richard Cobden also felt that there was 'much that is difficult to reconcile in his conduct in this question, after everything is said and confessed that he can urge in his defence'.[26]

In retrospect, it was easier to trace a line of inevitability, in Peel's actions, than to consider them within the context of prevailing circumstances. In 1846, *The Economist* observed that the whole tenor of Peel's policy as Prime Minister, between 1842 and the autumn of 1845, had been consistently oriented towards 'Free Trade': equally consistent was the support registered for that policy by Tory Agriculturist backbenchers, even though it was apparent that the Corn Laws would eventually be swept up within its orbit.[27] In this respect, there were marked similarities between Peel's conduct on the Corn Laws and his earlier 'conversion' to Catholic Emancipation. Peel's publicly stated sentiments on the subject of agricultural protection, from at least 1839, had included the sort of habitual reference to 'circumstances' and 'considerations' which had been the hallmark of his pronouncements on Emancipation:

I have no hesitation in saying, that unless the existence of the Corn-law can be shown to be consistent, not only with the prosperity of agriculture and the maintenance of the landlord's interest, but also with the protection, and the maintenance of the general interests of the country, and especially with the improvement of the condition of the labouring class, the Corn-law is practically at an end.[28]

This led hard-bitten Tories like the Duke of Newcastle to record their continuing sense of unease about Peel: 'He appears to have contracted a habit of late years of suiting himself to the times, whilst his proper line would be boldly & nobly to lead public opinion – to moralise & reclaim the nation.'[29]

Peel subsequently gave colour to these suspicions by his retrospective interpretation of his ministry's economic policy before Repeal. This was most clearly demonstrated in the so-called 'Elbing letter' of August 1846 (a response to a memorial from the

PEEL'S BANE AND ANTIDOTE.

9: 'Peel's Bane And Antidote', *Punch*, VIII, January–June 1845, 103.
'Dame' Peel offers a continued dose of Income Tax to the infant Russell in return for a
promise of relief on the sugar duties.

inhabitants of the town of Elbing in Prussia), in respect of the re-introduction of the Income Tax.[30] Peel had re-introduced the tax, in 1842, at the rate of seven pence in the pound (or 3 per cent) on incomes over £150. At the time, this was justified on the basis of the extraordinary financial deficit (some £8m) which the ministry had inherited from the Whigs and the continuing economic depression through which the country was passing. It was also necessary to provide the government with a stable and guaranteed flow of income to offset the 'great experiment' of reducing protective duties on a wide range of raw materials and manufactured goods, in furtherance of the work of Liverpool, Huskisson and Robinson in the 1820s and in conformity with the recommendations of Joseph Hume's Select Committee on Import Duties (1840).[31] Pitt had first introduced Income Tax in 1799 as an emergency measure, made necessary by the exigencies of war. It had lapsed in 1802 and been re-introduced at the seven pence rate from 1806–16, at which time Liverpool's government had been forced to accept a parliamentary revolt against its continuation. In spite of occasional declarations of opposition, during the 1830s, Peel had been intellectually committed to the re-introduction of the Income Tax from at least 1830 – a position which J.C. Symons thought 'sound, and serviceable' because it was in 'the very best interests of the country'.[32] The re-introduction of Income Tax was presented as a short-term expedient, the means of waging war on the internal enemies of poverty, famine and under-consumption and the necessary analogue to Peel's 1842 Budget. In Martin Daunton's estimation:

> an income tax for three years [would] cover the immediate deficiency and … provide sufficient revenue to revise duties, with the hope of stimulating commerce and industry, and reduc[e] the cost of living. The income tax was therefore intended to provide a *temporary* source of income to cover the transition from a regime of high duties and low yields to a dynamic economy based on low duties and high yields.[33]

As Gladstone later recalled, the tax was 'a powerful tool for a temporary purpose, namely the reform of our system of commercial legislation'. Peel admitted it was 'an impost, unusual, and, under ordinary circumstances, unpopular' but expressed the 'sanguine expectation' that the country would 'cheerfully submit' to it 'rather than incur the evil and disgrace of continued and increasing deficiency in the public revenue after 25 years of general peace in Europe'. Throughout, the Income Tax was presented as a short-term augmentation of revenue rather than its substitution by other means.[34]

Peel also justified it on the grounds of political stability, telling Croker that 'the property of the country must submit to taxation, in order to release industry and the millions from it; that the doing so voluntarily and with a good grace, will be a cheap purchase of future security'. This is why Queen Victoria was not exempted from paying the tax whilst, in a significant gesture of intent, the Irish were exempted.[35] Peel was particularly moved by the example of Paisley, where 10,000 people had been subsisting on charity for some time. Croker took the hint, publicly echoing (through the pages of *The Quarterly Review*) Peel's privately stated sentiment that 'our lot', as a manufacturing economy, 'is cast':

> If you had to constitute new societies, you might on moral and social grounds prefer corn fields to cotton factories; an agricultural to a manufacturing population. But our lot is cast; we cannot change it and we cannot recede ... We must make this country a *cheap* country for living, and thus induce parties to remain and settle here – enable them to consume more, by having more to spend.[36]

The priority was to make this new economic reality work. Together with many other sceptics, *The Quarterly Review* put aside any doubts it entertained about the justice of re-introducing the tax on the grounds that it 'was simply a socially equitable means of covering expenditure in the interim before economic growth in a free market led to higher tax revenues'.[37]

These sentiments were sufficient to still some, but by no means all, general sentiments on the subject:

> Sir Robert Peel has proposed to carry into effect such alterations as it is believed not any other statesman would have dared to suggest, and it must be highly satisfactory to him and his friends that Parliament and the country generally are disposed to approve the outline of his plans. It is however to be feared that many who are now in comparatively easy circumstances will be ruined by the adoption of measures which are deemed to be requisite for the general good; and it is presumed that the relief of such, by not carrying the proposed system too far is specially worthy of consideration; or the Agricultural Interest will probably suffer so materially that in a few years a special legislative enactment will become requisite for upholding it.[38]

The first inklings that the Income Tax constituted something more permanent – 'a yoke set upon the neck of the people and tacitly accepted by them' – came when it was renewed, for a further three years, in Peel's second 'Free Trade' budget of 1845.[39] *Punch* observed that the relevant legislation should, in fairness, 'have at the end the same notice as is attached to serial articles in magazines, viz: – (*To be Continued*)'.[40] As with the 1842 Budget, the measure was introduced by Peel himself. This rendered Goulburn, his Chancellor of the Exchequer, little more than a cipher, relegated to the conduct of less important business.[41] Peel had privately conceded the need to extend the Income Tax to five years and raise it to 5 per cent in August 1843.[42] An exhilarated Peel, who revelled in gaining the ascendancy over his own followers (many of whom never reconciled themselves to the tax)[43] told Hardinge that he had 'repeated the coup d'etat of 1842, renewed the income tax for three years, simplified and improved the tariff, and made a great reduction on indirect taxation'. More tellingly, he commented, 'the fact is, people like a certain degree of obstinacy and presumption in a minister. They abuse him for dictation and arrogance, but they like being governed'.[44]

The process of making the Income Tax permanent by stages led Peel to suggest, in his Elbing letter, that this had *always* been intended, as the means of laying 'the foundation of a more just system of taxation'. This policy marked a significant shift away from the indirect taxation of consumer goods, raw materials and manufactured articles to the direct taxation of property and income.[45] Re-adjusting the tax burden from indirect to direct means could reasonably be seen as a concerted effort to conciliate the economic interests of (what Peel called) 'that class of the people with whom we are brought into no direct relationship by the exercise of the elective franchise'.[46] By demonstrating the essential 'disinterestedness' of Conservative rule – in the sense of equalising the treatment of all sections of the community (regardless of whether or not they possessed the vote) – and in helping to make the country a '*cheap* country for living', Peel would give the labouring population no reason to contest the fact that they were still denied political power. As David Eastwood observes:

> Peelism was a heroic attempt to reconcile the constitutional instincts of Toryism with the realities of having become a manufacturing nation. In this contest it is striking that Peel shared, or came to share, High Tories sense of the importance of conciliating economically, whilst excluding politically, the interests of labour.

Whereas High Tories favoured paternalistic state intervention in the realms of poor laws, public health and factory regulation, Peel privileged an approach centred on tax yields and economics. That is why he countered so many of Lord Ashley's initiatives for the relief (through state intervention) of the factory operatives.[47] That Peel succeeded in his purpose may be indicated by the comments of the leading Chartist, Feargus O'Connor, in 1846, that Peel's proposals represented 'the wisest, the most statesman-like, the most comprehensive and patriotic measure ever proposed by a British minister'.[48] A positive reading of this policy would be that Peel genuinely under-cut the ground upon which the Chartist movement relied for its support (thereby neutralising its effective threat to the state and preserving Britain from prospective revolutionary turmoil in 1848). A more Machiavellian reading would be that it provided a mechanism for ensuring the continuing 'social control' of the lower orders.[49]

However, the notion that the end always justified the means was scant compensation for those who had suspended their abiding suspicions about the Income Tax in the belief that it was a strictly limited imposition made necessary by extraordinary social and economic circumstances. As such, Peel's original justification of the tax as a temporary impost came in for severe criticism when Russell's government proposed a further extension in 1848.[50] The Nottinghamshire Whig, Evelyn Denison, declared himself 'by no means friendly to adopting direct taxation as an important part of our fixed principle of finance. 5 per cent for ever is a very serious affair.'[51] The notion that Income Tax and Free Trade were 'complementary props of the liberal, free trade, economy' became the orthodox argument in their favour, in mid to late-nineteenth century Britain, but this correlation was by no means so clear during Peel's lifetime.[52]

Consequently, the Elbing letter generated a good deal of adverse comment – not least amongst Peel's former cabinet colleagues. *The Quarterly Review* called it the '*Magna Charta* of confiscation' and saw it as a continuation of Peel's '*Revolutionary Speech*' on resigning office.[53] Sir Edward Knatchbull interpreted the letter as a declaration that Income Tax was 'preparatory to and intended to lead to [the] measure of 1845' (i.e. Repeal of the Corn Laws), whereas his own recollection – as well as that of Stanley, Lyndhurst, Wellington and Hardinge, whom he subsequently canvassed – suggested otherwise. The letter, Knatchbull concluded, was 'entirely inconsistent with the truth … How he can live under such a delusion is to me and to very many others a cause of unutterable surprise'. J.G. Lockhart, ruminating on the subject to Croker, suggested that the letter had been sent '*furieusement l'apoplexie*' [in furious apoplexy] as the result of a serious accident which Peel had sustained to his foot whilst bathing.[54] *The Times* was equally censorious, when Peel argued in favour of the further extension of the Income Tax, eighteen months later:

> It is a little curious that Sir Robert Peel should so often be under the necessity of stripping to show how clean his linen is. Other men get on without proving every five years that their professions had all along been in consonance with their practice. Upon the Ex-Premier's tomb should be engraved words to signify to posterity that under that slab lies the great victim of misconstruction.[55]

* * *

If Peel's re-introduction of the Income Tax represented (what Gladstone called) 'the cardinal act of the really great financial scheme, the tariff was in bulk and detail the main matter' of his budgets of 1842 and 1845.[56] Peel revised the duties on some 750 articles in his first budget and introduced a graduated scale comprising 5 per cent on imported raw materials, 12½ per cent on semi-manufactured goods and 20 per cent on manufactured imports. Three years later, Peel abolished the remaining export duties and only reprieved those on the import of luxury goods like wine. In total, duties on some 430 articles were entirely repealed. *The Quarterly Review* lauded the measures as so 'cautiously selected, so carefully balanced, so judiciously combined, that no sudden shock or injury will be felt by any one of the various interests concerned'.[57] Lord Kenyon considered the measures 'very statesmanlike' and Greville thought they augured well for Peel's lasting claim to fame: the measures were 'lofty in conception, right in direction, and able in execution …There can be no doubt that he is now a very great man, and it depends on himself to establish a great and lasting reputation.'[58] 'The Government have proposed nothing that they cannot carry, nothing that they will not carry, nothing that they ought not to carry,' *The Times* concluded.[59]

By contrast, Ultra Tory malcontents like Sir Richard Vyvyan and Anti-Corn Law Leaguers like Richard Cobden remained unmoved. Cobden thought Peel's 1842 Budget an attempt 'to govern for a class, under the pretence of governing for the people' and believed it had been 'artfully dished up', because corn and sugar (the two principal points of contention in the 1841 General Election) remained untouched.

Considering Peel a 'politico-economic, and not a Protectionist, intellect', Cobden had little doubt that the budget was essentially a compromise between his own 'Free Trade' proclivities on the one hand, and the bulk of his Conservative followers on the other, with the Duke of Wellington acting as a breakwater between them:

> Peel was called in, not to save the trade of the country but the great monopolies, & he has done so for a while, but only to render their eventual fall the more certain …What Catholic Emancipation did for the boroughmongers, Peels tariff has effected for the 'landed interest'.[60]

By contrast, Vyvyan complained that Peel had used every ounce of executive power to legislate against the fundamental interests of his agricultural followers, barely six months after having been returned on a Protectionist mandate. Peel's newly-stated maxim that the ruling principle of economic policy, hereafter, should be to 'buy in the cheapest and sell in the dearest market' came in for particular notice:

> Persons presuming to differ from [Peel] and his colleagues, have been stigmatised as *ultras* and prejudiced supporters of existing abuses. The *consumer* has been the object of their great sympathy; and the *producer*, whether he be engaged in raising the raw material for manufacture, or in manufacturing it, has been sacrificed to the doctrine that it must be the great object of a nation to obtain articles at the lowest possible price.[61]

The political sensitivities involved in legislating on corn and sugar remained apparent in succeeding years – first in respect of Lord Stanley's Canadian Corn Bill of 1843 and, a year later, on the government's revised Sugar Duties. In both cases, competing interests (between colonial and native producers in the former instance and 'free' and 'slave-grown' produce in the latter) served to complicate the issues involved.[62] The conflict over the Sugar Duties came fast on the heels of a bruising encounter with Lord Ashley over his campaign for a ten hour working day for factory operatives. Within the space of one parliamentary session, Peel became embroiled in two destabilising (if not fatal) disagreements with his backbenchers.[63] His handling of the Conservative Party, during 1844, revealed all of his propensities to arrogance and dictation. It was observed by Wellington, Stanley and Gladstone with unease and regret. This undoubtedly influenced Stanley's decision to go up to the House of Lords, in his father's lifetime, as Lord Bickerstaffe – a fateful decision in light of subsequent events.[64]

* * *

The events of 1844 – and the renewed sense of arrogance, impatience and intemperance which they occasioned in Peel – were indicative of the deeper processes at work within the Prime Minister's mind. In the same period that Peel's views were 'ripening', in respect of his Irish policy, the consequence of his successful experiments in Free Trade economics (insofar as the Corn Laws were concerned) were starting to

THE AGRICULTURAL QUESTION SETTLED.

10: 'The Agricultural Question Settled', *Punch*, VIII, January–June 1845, 39.
A satire on Peel's perceived hard-heartedness during the 'Hungry Forties'.

become clear. This was the more significant because Peel was an active landowner and farmer whose own interests were intimately connected with agriculture.

On 24 December 1849, three-and-a-half years after leaving office, Peel addressed a letter to the tenant farmers on his Staffordshire estates. In it he described the Repeal of the Corn Laws as 'irrevocable' and advised them:

> to dismiss altogether from your calculations the prospect of renewed protection. It is my firm persuasion that neither the present nor any future Parliament will consent to re-impose duties upon the main articles of human food, either for the purpose of protection or revenue.[65]

For Peel to have made such a statement five years earlier would have been politically unthinkable. However, by the late 1840s, English agriculture was entering an era of low prices and open competition, inaugurated (in part) by the Repeal of the Corn Laws. Sustaining agricultural profits, in this climate, remained a subject of intense political controversy. Benjamin Disraeli, newly-installed as leader of the Conservative Party in the House of Commons, had recently proposed a complicated system of tax relief for agriculture in response to the efforts of Richard Cobden's Financial Reform Association.[66] In these heightened political circumstances, Peel publicly declared himself opposed to an abatement of rent. Instead, he offered his tenants an amount equivalent to 20 per cent of their annual rental 'in such improvements as may be most beneficial' to them – with preference given to schemes for improving drainage, the removal of unnecessary fences and the means of preventing the wastage of manure.[67] According to Disraeli, Peel's letter was:

> not, I think, very happy: at the same time, pompous & trite. He has succeeded in conveying an impression, that his estate is in very bad condition ... Though he really says nothing, which might not have been said if the Corn Laws had not been repealed, he nevertheless writes with an awkward consciousness of having led his friends into a hopeless scrape.[68]

However, whilst the political context had changed, after Repeal, Peel's prescription for his tenant farmers was entirely consistent with his long-term (and openly declared) commitment to the principles of 'practical and scientific husbandry'. 'High Farming' of this sort was regarded as the means of infusing traditional farming practices with some of the enterprise, efficiency and competitiveness usually associated with capitalist enterprises in manufacturing, trade and industry.[69] In opening the Tamworth Reading Room, in 1841, Peel had sympathised with the farming community in their suspicions of abstract speculative theory, observing that it was 'much easier to talk of farming than to farm'.[70] Two years later, his speeches to the Lichfield and Tamworth Agricultural Shows had attracted national attention. At the former, Peel:

> advised farmers to travel, said he would give leases to his tenants, if they asked for them ... favored the allotment system (in this he was right) & expressed his

opinion that a flourishing state of agriculture was beneficial to the strength & glory of England – of this there can be no doubt – it may be called a truism.

The Duke of Newcastle thought the speech 'shallow, speculative [and] falsely theoretical … Sir Robert is not a very knowing agriculturalist … what he knows he has gained as a lawyer, by his brief'.[71] At Tamworth, on 24 October 1843, Peel promised to procure a prize bull for his tenants, in order to improve the breeding of livestock, and declared a willingness to sacrifice the rabbits on his estates in the interests of improved and efficient farming. However, the hares were to be spared to a moderate extent, in order that he might continue to go coursing. 'I do not like it (Newcastle observed) much is foolish, some injurious & very little practically good … I shall keep the speech by me, & watch him closely.'[72] Peel's sporting assistance to agriculture formed the subject of jocular representation at the hands of more than one pamphleteer:

Reader! Sir Robert's now upon his legs,
And your polite attention therefore begs;
All he requests is of your *ears* the loan,
Of *I's* he has a plenty of his own.[73]

… But to return. – You see I freely yield,
Solely for you, the pleasures of the field;
For as a landlord – owner of the ground –
I am, as I conceive, in duty bound,
And am prepared, I say in short, I'm '*game*'
(And other landlords doubtless are the same,)

At once a personal sacrifice to make,
If you declare your interests are at stake.
So kill the rabbits off without remorse –
The hares though, as a matter quite '*of course*',
Must only subject be to such destruction
As will insure their *moderate* reduction;
Just such a one, in short, as you might call
My Scale and Tariff – that is – *none at all.*[74]

On his estates at Tamworth and Oswaldtwistle, Farmer Peel attempted to practice the principles of High Farming which he believed to be the farmers' best means of salvation. He frequently entertained parties of tenant farmers at Drayton Manor to hear about the latest practical solutions to the problems of manure and drainage from geologists and chemists like Patrick Buckland and Leon Playfair.[75] When Alexander Somerville – 'The Whistler at the Plough' – visited Peel's Drayton estate, in November 1846, he found an 'extensive system of farm drainage' under way. Peel had laid out the capital himself but charged 4 per cent to each of his occupying tenants.[76] A month later, Peel endorsed Lord Londonderry's methods to relieve his tenants: 'you are quite right in declining to make indiscriminate reductions of Rent – and in endeavouring to encourage the employment of Labour on the permanent improvement of the Land'. Peel pursued exactly the same policy with his Staffordshire tenants during the depressed winter of 1849–50.[77]

* * *

Peel's credentials as both a landowner and head of a party committed to upholding the peculiar social and economic privileges of the land had frequently been argued in his favour before the great crisis of Repeal. 'There has not been, in our memory, any Cabinet so largely and so exclusively connected with the landed interest ... possessing so great a landed stake in the country, and possessing nothing else,' *The Quarterly Review* observed in September 1843.[78] Three months earlier, Peel had described his 1842 Corn Law (*5 & 6 Vic. c.14*) as a 'compromise assented to by the Agricultural Interest & as such ought to be maintained'. This statement represented a material declaration of intent, in the eyes of his Protectionist backbenchers. Lord George Bentinck later declared that Peel should be forced to uphold it – if necessary 'with a musket at his head' – on penalty of being 'shot or hanged'.[79]

However, if Gladstone's recollection of events is to be believed (and there is little reason to doubt them), Peel had already declared himself incapable of defending the Corn Laws, on principle, in the course of the same year (1843).[80] This was a full two years before Peel is supposed to have turned to Sidney Herbert, during a parliamentary discussion on the Corn Laws, and remarked, 'You must answer this, for I cannot'. A presentiment of this position had been offered on 9 February 1842 when Peel unveiled his revisions to the Corn Law of 1828 (*9 Geo. IV c.60*). In the course of his speech, Peel specifically distanced himself from the idea that he was maintaining protective duties on corn as a means of providing a premium to agriculture. Rather, a sliding scale of import duties on corn, of the sort he proposed, was conducive to the general welfare of the nation. Whilst acknowledging the 'special burdens' which the landed gentry and aristocracy traditionally had to bear, as leaders of their rural communities, in the payment of the land tax, the highway and poor rates and in the maintenance of law and order, Peel explicitly countered the rhetoric of the Anti-Corn Law League and his own backbenchers by steering a middle course. As such, he publicly maintained the need for a Corn Law but also legislated to make it work more efficiently and productively by bringing it within the general scheme of his tariff and taxation reforms.[81]

In doing so, Peel introduced a scale which was (as the joint secretary to the Board of Trade, James MacGregor, subsequently admitted to Cobden) equivalent to an 8 shilling fixed duty on corn: the same amount proposed by the Whigs in 1841.[82] The profitable price for corn had been the subject of periodic investigation over the preceding three decades. The highest average prices, in recent memory, had been achieved at the height of the Napoleonic Wars, during the period that English agriculture was insulated from international competition. Many landowners had pursued the artificially high profits to be had by expanding the amount of acreage under cultivation. Consequently, the return to peacetime conditions had necessitated that the 1815 Corn Law legislate for a profitable price of 80 shillings. Succeeding years (and economic conditions) had gradually depressed average prices, so that the 1828 Corn Law legislated for a profitable price of 73 shillings, and that of 1842 for a profitable price of 56 shillings a quarter. Such calculations were always subject to dispute by those who argued that agriculture required a higher level of protection. In 1813, a Commons Select Committee (chaired by Henry Parnell) maintained that 105 shillings was the required minimum and between 1819 and 1822 Liverpool's government faced concerted pressure for relief from George Webb Hall's Agricultural Association.[83]

Peel faced a similar problem twenty years later. The Duke of Buckingham and Chandos, who resigned from the Cabinet over the issue, maintained that 64 shillings was the profitable price and that the scale should be turned to this higher protection. However, the effect of Buckingham's resignation as Lord Privy Seal was nullified by his acceptance of the Order of the Garter, which made him look more of an opportunist than a 'Farmer's Friend'. Peel also succeeded in quelling some of Edward Knatchbull's unease at the measure.[84] To Ripon and Gladstone (President and Vice-President of the Board of Trade), Peel confessed that:

> if I had not had to look to other than abstract considerations I would have proposed a lower protection. But it would have done no good to push the matter so far as to drive Knatchbull out of the Cabinet after the Duke of Buckingham; nor could I hope to pass a measure with greater reductions through the House of Lords.[85]

The 1842 Corn Law substantially reduced the existing sliding scale of duties without, as Peel told Croker, pushing the argument 'to its logical consequences, namely, that wheat should be at thirty-five shillings instead of fifty or fifty-four'. When corn reached the price of 59 shillings a quarter, a duty of 13 shillings (rather than 27 shillings 8 pence) was paid, a duty of 16 shillings (instead of 30 shillings 8 pence) at 56 shillings a quarter and 9 shillings (instead of 23 shillings 8 pence) at 63 shillings a quarter. The scale revised the duties within the crucial price range – 50 to 70 shillings a quarter – with upper and lower limits of duty of 20 shillings (instead of 36 shillings 8 pence) and 5 shillings (instead of 10 shillings 8 pence) respectively.[86]

Peel's measure was received with a mixture of 'coldness and indifference by his own people and derision by the Opposition'. Greville felt that 'eventually repeal, either total or with a fixed duty, must come, but in how many years must depend upon a chapter of accidents, the course of events and the temper of the people'. Lord Ashley thought Peel's speech, introducing the legislation, 'a chef d'amour of self-confidence'.[87] Whilst *Blackwood's Edinburgh Magazine* thought it was unfortunate that Peel had felt the necessity of yielding to the spirit of agitation stoked up by the Anti-Corn Law League, it recognised that expectations had been raised by the Whigs. On balance, it regarded Peel's measure as a necessary tranquilliser, muting further contention on the issue.[88] In subsequent years, both *Blackwood's Edinburgh Magazine* and *The Quarterly*

PAPA COBDEN TAKING MASTER ROBERT A FREE TRADE WALK.

11: 'Papa Cobden Taking Master Robert A Free Trade Walk', *Punch*, VIII,
January–June 1845, 197.
A famous *Punch* cartoon illustrating the perceived relationship between Richard Cobden and
Sir Robert Peel. This perception was subsequently given colour by Peel's resignation speech.

Review praised the 1842 Corn Law for having provided efficient protection to agriculture. The 1828 Act was believed to have encouraged excessive hoarding and speculation, given the steep differences in the duties paid depending on minor changes in the price of corn. Peel's Corn Law was designed to correct these damaging price fluctuations, protect the home producer by encouraging domestic farming and prevent undue reliance on foreign supplies of corn. Peel's aims had been met to a degree which exceeded his own 'sagacious expectations'.[89]

* * *

What happened in the months between October 1845 and July 1846 'was so central to the development of Victorian politics and political culture that the motivations for, and meanings of, Corn Law Repeal have become obscured beneath myths and misunderstandings of quite epic proportions'.[90] Historians have, in general, been pre-occupied by the 'whys' and the 'whens' of Corn Law Repeal – was it Ireland, the Anti-Corn Law League or the success of Peel's own Free Trade policy which finally tilted the balance in favour of Repeal? Did this movement in thought occur in the 1820s, sometime before the 1841 General Election, sometime between 1842 and the autumn of 1845 or in the months preceding Repeal?[91] Hobhouse thought Peel's conversion to Repeal:

> more miraculous than any that has happened since the days of St. Paul … All his interests, all his connections, must have been against it; nothing but sincere conviction could have produced it. The grave charge against him is, I think, that he could not have been sincere when he supported Protection, but did so for mere party purposes and a love of power.[92]

J.C. Symons also thought that Repeal occupied a unique place in Peel's career. Unlike Emancipation, his conversion 'on the Corn Laws was produced less by altered emergencies and unforeseen events than by a deliberately avowed change of principles, whether real or not'.[93]

For Peel's critics, the crisis was entirely of his own making. It was the belief that the 1842 Corn Law had legislated as much as the agricultural interest could reasonably be expected to bear, as well as the argument that Peel was politically (and morally) committed to the maintenance of the Corn Laws, which helps to explain the ferocity of the reaction against him when he proceeded to Repeal them in 1846.[94] The 1842 Corn Law was regarded as sufficient for the purpose of withstanding the Irish potato famine (news of which began to reach England in the autumn of 1845) and for maintaining the Corn Laws intact. As Sir Edward Knatchbull observed, whilst 'no one supposed [the 1842 Corn Law] was to last for ever, certainly no one contemplated any change or anticipated any reason why any alteration should be made – this law was considered by the Cabinet to be as permanent as any law on this subject could be'.[95] *The Quarterly Review* complained that Peel had decided to tear up his own Corn Law upon the first occasion 'for testing its merits'.[96] Critics did not regard the Irish situation as a sufficient excuse, as it seemed no more pressing than many earlier (temporary) crises of comparable moment. For them, there was little correlation between the failure of the principal Irish root crop and the future of English arable production.[97] As Lord Combermere observed:

> Why Peel should wish to disturb the Corn Laws (his favourite sliding scale) I can't imagine! – why not let well alone? Every thing was prosperous agriculture & commerce, rents well paid, 'Famine' greatly exaggerated O'Connell & Repeal etc [at a] discount – Revenue flourishing; – for the last year wheat has been at a low, & steady price! then why change?[98]

This was the sentiment behind Wellington's famous aphorism that 'Rotten Potatoes have done it all; they put Peel in his d-d fright.' Wellington always maintained that it was the initial (unconfirmed) reports of the potato crop's failure, stoked by the fears of the Home Secretary, Sir James Graham, which made Peel a 'warm-hearted Enthusiast' of Repeal.[99] Lord George Bentinck was in no doubt that the Irish context was a convenient pretext for Peel's conversion:

> The fact is the entire reputation of Sir Robert Peel & his Government depends upon his being able to persuade Parliament & the Country that there is or has been a fearful danger of a real famine in Ireland. Up to this moment certainly the people never were so well off.[100]

Matters were made worse by the political equivalent of the 'boy who cried wolf'. Initial reports of the failure of the potato crop proved contradictory, yet the government maintained they were serious enough to demand Repeal. When the reports were subsequently confirmed they were dismissed as politically motivated.

Peel took a different view of the situation. In his mind, it was not the adequacy or inadequacy of the 1842 Corn Law, but his understanding of the economic impact of the Corn Laws, and the impossibility of pursuing political principles against their logic, which transformed the situation in much the same way as O'Connell's election for County Clare had transformed his understanding of Catholic Emancipation. His 'ripening', in respect of Ireland, the success of his tariff reform policy and the ready availability of the Income Tax as a means of generating a secure stream of government revenue, were the necessary precursors to this change of heart. Consequently, the change in Peel's thinking can be dated, in the medium term, to 1843. As Charles Greville subsequently argued:

> what [Peel] hoped and intended probably was to bring round the minds of his party by degrees to the doctrines of Free Trade, and to conquer their repugnance to a great alteration of the Corn Laws …That, I believe, was his secret desire, hope, and expectation; and if the Irish famine had not deranged his plans and precipitated his measures, if more time had been afforded him, it is not impossible that his projects might have been realised.[101]

Richard Cobden had argued for a remarkably similar line of conduct, in May 1845:

> If I was in Peel's shoes I would go on preparing the public mind during the present parliament for greater changes in the next, & then when the time comes for the dissolution I would announce my opinion ... *the whole of the north of England would rally for him as one man* ... 'Peel & Free Trade' would be the sole rallying cry, & the Whigs would be compelled to join the shout, or be trodden into the dust as a party.[102]

The same interpretation was echoed emphatically by Gladstone (in later life) and reflected Peel's own sentiments; first, as expressed to Prince Albert at the end of 1845 and second, in introducing Repeal to Parliament, in January 1846. On both occasions, Peel 'confined the events which had caused the change [in his thinking] to the three last years'.[103]

It was the Irish potato famine of 1845 that frustrated Peel's plans and led, in the short term, to the Repeal of the Corn Laws. That is why it became as much a matter of Peel's Irish, as his economic, policy. It was impossible to prove the good faith of the British government to the Irish Catholic majority, whilst quietly allowing them to starve.[104] As Peel informed Charles Arbuthnot, 'the worst ground on which we can fight the battle of true Conservatism is on a question of *food*' – especially one relating to Ireland.[105]

Moreover, Peel had already helped to create the economic circumstances in which Repeal could occur, through his tariff reforms and re-introduction of the Income Tax. Before the 1840s, the necessary economic pre-requisites for Repeal did not exist but, after 1843, it was becoming increasingly clear that they would. However much Peel may have been *intellectually* pre-disposed towards Repeal, over the long term, 'the direct evidence for such a conversion is slender'.[106] As J.C. Symons observed, in one of the earliest biographies of Peel, 'neither the terrors of incendiarism in the winter of 1830, the crash of 1836–37, the short crops of 1838 and 1839, nor the collapse of 1840, procured from Sir Robert Peel any effective effort to enlarge the supply of food for the people'.[107] It was the events of the 1840s which proved crucial in his conversion to Repeal.

* * *

Consequently, Repeal was very much Peel's personal policy – a fact which was to be both its strength and (in political terms) its weakness, thereafter. After reports of the potato blight began to arrive, during October–November 1845, Peel recommended a suspension of the Corn Laws and the opening of the ports by Order-in-Council. This was a course of executive action which could have been affected without recourse to Parliament. Even those who opposed the Corn Laws, like the Earl of Lincoln, resisted it as an unconstitutional method for extinguishing them.[108] In an attempt to convert his sceptical cabinet, Peel then proposed a gradual diminution in the protective duties on corn, over an eight year period; a kind of

Repeal by euthanasia. However, after failing to carry his cabinet with him unanimously, Peel resigned on 6 December 1845. Lord John Russell had already come out in favour of Repeal in a letter to his Edinburgh constituents on 22 November 1845. This had taken the opportunity of likening Peel's position on the Corn Laws to that preceding the achievement of both Catholic Emancipation and the 1832 Reform Act. Russell's 'Edinburgh Letter' pre-empted Peel in much the same way as the Tamworth Manifesto had out-manoeuvred Stanley in 1834.[109] Peel told Prince Albert that, 'as soon as I saw [it] I felt that the ground was slipping away from under me, and that whatever I might now propose would appear as dictated by the Opposition'.[110]

Nevertheless, Russell's opportunistic intervention offered Peel a reasonable alternative to his own position – one he willingly took by offering his support (out of office) to any Whig-led attempt at Repeal. Such a course of action ensured the continued fury of the massed ranks of Tory Protectionists. Their anger had been wound up to fever pitch by the revelation of *The Times*, in the days preceding Peel's resignation, that he was attempting to gather Cabinet support for Repeal:

> Sir Robert Peel, at length, resorts –
> To what? – the opening of the ports
> The *Times* has publicly reveal'd
> That corn laws soon will be repeal'd –
> But stop, we must not say too much,
> On politics we never touch ...[111]

Although the consequences might have been less serious, had Russell proved able to form an administration, the impact of delivering a second betrayal (in or out of office) would have been sufficient to end Peel's association with the Conservative Party. As 'Impransus' (or 'Dinnerless') observed:

> I am a Tory; and this much I will venture to tell you – You think of taking Lord John Russell into your counsels, you may think you will be able to keep your party and form another Cabinet, you deceive yourself; you will not, you must go out; but before you do you will put the finishing stroke to your political apostasy and become not only in heart, but in profession, a Whig. You have been gradually going down the sliding scale of political tergiversation for a long time, at the lowest is Whiggery; and as you approach the termination of your political career, the more rapid is your descent; would that I could lend a helping hand to increase your facilities of descent![112]

The situation was transformed by Russell's inability to form a government. This led him, in Disraeli's immortal phrase, to 'pass the poisoned chalice' back to Peel. As Lord Ashley commented, with uncharacteristic sympathy, Peel's position was 'truly distressing. He cannot desert the Queen; he must reconstruct his Cabinet; he must prepare his corn-law scheme; he must face all these responsibilities and vexations; and he must after all perish (for he will never be, in fact, forgiven) by the distrust of the country and the resentment of his party.'[113]

Whilst *The Quarterly Review* and Lady Shelley were willing, even at this stage, to suspend their disbelief in the hope that Peel would step back from conceding Repeal, their worst fears were confirmed after he returned to power as Prime Minister on 20 December 1845.[114] Five weeks later, Peel announced the graduated Repeal of the Corn Laws (over a period of three years), at a rate equivalent to a 4 shillings fixed duty on corn.[115] By way of compensation to agriculture, Peel proposed a package of subsidiary measures which included 'public loans for the improvement of agriculture and a modification of the settlement laws to stem the flow of paupers from town to countryside'.[116] *Punch* exhausted the flow of visual allegories in its attempt to illustrate the scale of Peel's conversion. He was the 'Political Whittington' ('Turn again Bobby, Three Times Prime Minister'), as well as a chameleon, an acrobat and a man who had ridden two horses (Free Trade and Protection) at the same time.[117] The Chartist *Northern Star* greeted the package with ill-concealed delight:

> PEEL has earned for himself a glorious immortality, by his bold and manly bearing; and if little JOHN and the Whiglings should attempt to oust him upon a promise of a more speedy settlement of the question … let the nation rise as one man; and with the voice of thunder and finger of scorn, motion the ghost back to that tomb which it prepared for Chartism, but in which we have enshrined the remains of Whiggery.[118]

The extent to which Peel was 'forced' into Repeal by the efforts of the Anti-Corn Law League provided another keynote of contemporary discussion. After 1844 the League began to proselytise the English agricultural districts and purchase urban freehold property in order to qualify (through the forty shilling freeholder franchise) as electors in county constituencies.[119] As such, the potential existed for a notable electoral challenge (in the manner of O'Connell's Catholic Association) at the next General Election. *The Quarterly Review* concluded that, as in 1828–9, Peel had taken fright in the face of a concerted application of external pressure:

> Sir Robert Peel saw the League audacious, and thought it formidable – he heard it loud, and fancied it was powerful: with that propensity which conscientious men will often have of under-valuing friends and over-rating enemies, he viewed the League with serious apprehensions, and believing (a complete mistake) that it had a strong hold on the sympathies of the working classes, and that it threatened a kind of *servile war* against all landed property and all eminence of station, he thought … that the best course he could take for these menaced interests was to make an early and judicious retreat.[120]

However, it was the League's potential as a focus for national agitation, not its threat as an electoral machine, that most concerned Peel.[121] In December 1845, Peel told Prince Albert that 'the league had made immense progress, and had enormous means at their disposal. If he had resigned in November, Lord Stanley and the Protectionists would have been prepared to form a Government, and a Revolution might have been the consequence of it. Now they felt that it was too late.' By legislating the extinction of the Corn Laws, Peel hoped to prevent other interests, such as 'the system of promotion in the Army, the Game Laws [and] the Church', being challenged with the aid of the League.[122]

Nor, for all the sentiments of amity between them suggested by Peel's resignation speech, had his relationship with Richard Cobden been an agreeable one. In many respects it was no better than that with Daniel O'Connell in the run-up to Emancipation. In 1843, Cobden had personally charged Peel with responsibility for the distressed condition of the country, and for the widespread popular disturbances it had occasioned in the industrial districts during the summer of 1842. Shaken by the recent assassination of his private secretary, Edward Drummond,[123] Peel had responded by implying that Cobden was inciting another attempt upon his life. Peel allowed his habitual self-control to slip in the altercation, memories of which continued to plague personal relations between the two men until a few months before Repeal was conceded and Peel paid his handsome parting acknowledgement to Cobden.[124]

In the process, Peel not only destroyed the Conservative Party but undermined his own carefully crafted policy of legislating on an equitable, national basis. To that extent, there were two Peel administrations during the years 1841–6. The first, predicated on just such a basis (and triumphantly borne out by the manner in which Peel framed his 1842 Corn Law) persisted until Peel's resignation over Repeal on 6 December 1845. The second, characterised by Peel's single-minded obsession with the achievement of Repeal, succeeded it two weeks later. Far from healing social divisions, the politics of Corn Law Repeal actually served to open up a social cleavage between the interests of agriculture and the interests of manufacturing. It is not surprising why Lord George Bentinck, who so resented being 'sold' by Peel, should have enjoyed high favour with the farming community: 'My having failed to win the battle for them does not appear to touch them at all [he observed subsequently]. I have avenged them upon Peel & that seems to be what they most care for.'[125] Another critic maintained that Peel 'ought not to die a natural death' for his betrayal of the Conservative Party. Later, *Blackwood's Edinburgh Magazine* described Repeal as the natural outcome of Peel's entire career. It had been necessary to lower the cost of bread in order to lower the wages of labour in order to offset the severe reduction in prices which had followed the return to the Gold Standard after 'Peel's Act' of 1819.[126] Peel's entire political statecraft was at the centre of a dangerously divisive rupture in English society which was still apparent when he counselled his Staffordshire tenantry to caution at the end of 1849. In attempting to rise above parties, factions and special interests, through the Repeal of the Corn Laws, Peel may actually have served to sharpen the divisions between them.[127]

* * *

The political consequences were no less painful and divisive. Whilst Gladstone, Hardinge and Queen Victoria were united in praising Peel's immense 'moral courage' in advancing a measure with which he had been habitually associated as an opponent, Gladstone (for one) thought Peel lacked 'sagacity in foresight' in expecting that the Conservative Party as a whole would yield to their leader's change of conviction.[128] Peel expected an easy victory over his party and the doubts of his followers, purely because experience taught him that this had always been the case before. 'We are not quite sure that Sir Robert Peel may not have experienced more opposition from his friends than he anticipated,' *The Economist* argued, with admirable under-statement, in March 1846. Lord Ashley summed up Peel's likely calculations on the matter more pithily, two months later: 'A small band of dissidents, a large band of turncoats, a week's debate, a large majority, triumph & commendation, and then total oblivion of the whole matter!'[129]

The crucial turning point in Peel's thinking came with his return to office in December. In some respects, Peel's recall to power not only emboldened him personally but liberated him politically (at least in his own mind) from the trammels of party. 'Peel, thinking that Russell's failure to form a ministry gave him a free hand to choose total repeal, acted as if the Crown's choice raised him above the party battle and provided him with as strong a mandate as he needed to carry it through parliament.'[130] He had resigned office in December 1845 in conformity with the platform upon which the party had been returned to power in 1841 and in face of dissensions amongst his Cabinet colleagues. He could reasonably claim to have fulfilled his obligations to govern on the mandate on which he had been returned to power. Conversely, the political circumstances after Russell failed to construct a Whig administration extinguished all subsidiary considerations and encouraged him to think that he – and his followers – had a free hand to start afresh.[131] Edward Cardwell later informed Peel's prospective biographer (Goldwin Smith) that 'the power of [the] Cabinet was then limited to one single object, the repeal of the Corn Laws. To that single object, every thing was subordinate, & when it was necessary to do so, every thing was sacrificed.'[132] Nevertheless, one anonymous commentator wondered whether Peel's:

> first, most loyal, and least egotistical duty, was not to impress upon the mind of a gracious and most constitutional mistress, that it was impossible that it *could* be for her Majesty's ultimate service ... that he should inflict upon those natural devotees and props of her person and throne, the harsh and difficult alternative, of either abandoning the leader and the friends with whom they had so long hoped themselves identified, and the support of the immediate government of that crown which is peculiarly the object of their wisely-prejudiced affection.[133]

In December 1845, Peel was (as Prince Albert frequently remarked) infused with a spirit of emotional animation or 'warmth' quite unlike any with which he had been seized before. In the days following his resumption of office, he was 'most kind, nay fatherly' towards Gladstone, who assumed the Cabinet post of Colonial Secretary vacated by Stanley: 'we *held* hands instinctively & I could not but reciprocate with emphasis his "God bless you"'.[134] However, towards his Cabinet as a whole, Peel acted in a manner of peremptory assumption, telling the Queen that he had 'informed' them:

> that he had not summoned them for the purpose of deliberating on what was to be done, but for the purpose of announcing to them that he was your Majesty's Minister, and whether supported or not, was fairly resolved to meet Parliament as your Majesty's Minister, and to propose such measures as the public exigencies required.[135]

This *cri de coeur* awakened Wellington's martial virtues and brought the Cabinet dissidents to heel (Stanley alone having held out against Repeal). Wellington declared that the 'Corn Law was a subordinate consideration', in the face of the threat to the Queen's government, and rallied to Peel's standard. In turn, this ensured that the Conservative peers in the House of Lords would fall in behind their leader on the traditional grounds that the interests of good government were superior to all other considerations. In spite of frequently expressed fears to the contrary, the cock-pit of debate and dissension on the Repeal of the Corn Laws proved to be in the House of Commons, rather than the Lords, and Wellington was almost solely responsible for this turn of events.[136]

Wellington was also responsible for ensuring that the transition from his leadership of the party in the upper chamber, to that of Lord Stanley (the anointed heir apparent), was accompanied with as little acrimony and bitterness as possible. Peel felt no such compunction with respect to his opponents in the Commons. To Gladstone, in December 1845, Peel had spoken 'with a kind of glee and complacency in his tone' when intimating 'his belief that he would be able to carry his measure and at the same time hold his party together'. From the vantage point of the mid-1850s, Gladstone thought it a minor 'but not unimportant' question whether Peel could have 'fought the battle as to rouse less anger at the time and leave less resentment afterwards'.[137] Charles Arbuthnot felt similarly, 'I am no Protectionist; but had Sir Robert been more conciliatory to his supporters, & more confidential towards them, none of the evil would have occurred.'[138] Peel's growing inflexibility towards his Conservative opponents was a justifiable emotional response, considering the vitriolic abuse he suffered, as the Repeal legislation made its progress through Parliament, over the next six months. Peel's stance towards his former colleagues became 'noticeably sharper and more uncompromising',[139] during his later speeches on Repeal, although there was little enough of comfort in them from the start. Contemporaries were increasingly mindful of the fact. For Hobhouse, the peroration of Peel's first speech on Repeal was notable for being:

> a personal defence, a proof of his being a true Conservative Minister, by reference to all he had done ... about his having served four Sovereigns and having sought for no reward but their approbation of his services, and of his

being under no obligations to his or any party, but being free and resolved to act solely upon the strength of his own honest [convictions] for the benefit of the country. It seemed clear that he was resolved to go all lengths in regard to the Corn Laws.[140]

For Ashley, Peel was:

> more eloquent than I have ever heard him before … but arrogance, egotism, and temper ruled his heart, & furnished his tongue – the sum and substance of his declaration amounted to this that he was ready to be Minister, provided he were absolute; he demanded unthinking adhesion … joyous & reverential repose in his wisdom whether steady and consistent, or chopping and changing; in black & in white, in white & in black.[141]

There is little doubt that Peel was enveloped in a sense of his own historic destiny in (what should properly be regarded as) his third and final tenure as Prime Minister. He told Princess Lieven that he 'felt like a man restored to life after his funeral service had been preached'.[142] The comment was significant. The consequence of Peel's 'resurrection' was to be his re-birth as the individualistic and egotistical politician which many contemporaries had always suspected him to be. 'He is so vain', Disraeli complained to Lord John Manners, 'that he wants to figure in history as the settler of all the great questions, but a parliamentary constitution is not favourable to such ambitions.'[143] This element of Peel's character was expressed in the Cobden panegyric, the Elbing letter and the *Memoirs*. Together, these constructed a vision of the 1841–6 ministry which rendered its policies (up to and including the Repeal of the Corn Laws) intellectually coherent, consistent and, above all, inevitable. To that extent it relegated the lived experience of the Peel government with its gradualist, experimental approach to policies and its careful balancing of interests in favour of a more expansive (almost predestined) vision. This served to unite, retrospectively, the different trajectories in the policies of the Peel government of 1841–6 but it correspondingly served to colour subsequent views of the ministry, both as to the basis upon which it had been elected (for that now appeared like a deception, deliberate or otherwise) and the outcome to which it had been oriented. In short, it made Income Tax look like it had always been intended as permanent and the Repeal of the Corn Laws appear like it had always been inevitable, both as to form and consequence.[144]

The exaggeration in Peel's status was seen – and admired – by Thomas Carlyle, who was inspired by the Premier's new 'heroic' stature to address him as the saviour of the nation. Carlyle saw in Peel a latter-day Oliver Cromwell and sent the Prime Minister a copy of his account of the 'Lord Protector', during the final stages of the Repeal crisis (allowing Peel to draw his own conclusions). He also compiled a separate account in which he lauded Peel, above Cobden, for having single-handedly achieved Repeal.[145] Similar sentiments were echoed by 'M.P., a supporter hitherto of the League,' who argued that Peel was uniquely fitted to occupy an office 'to which, through the whole course of your long political life, you have seemed to aspire'.[146]

Perhaps more pertinently, in light of Peel's resignation speech, Richard Cobden also viewed his erstwhile opponent in the light of a middle class saviour. Historians have frequently remarked on the remarkable exchange of letters between the two men, in the final stages of the Repeal debates, in which Cobden urged Peel to use his new-found power to dissolve Parliament and lead a new coalition of opinion oriented to the interests of the middle class:

> You represent the IDEA of the age, and it has no other representative amongst statesmen ... Do you shrink from the post of governing through the *bona fide* representatives of the middle class? ... There must be an end of the juggle of parties, the mere representatives of traditions, and some man must of necessity rule the State through its governing class. The Reform Bill decreed it; the passing of the Corn Bill has realized it.

In response, Peel declared himself to have been impelled by nothing but 'a sense of public duty to undertake what I have undertaken in this session' and observed that 'being the organ and representative of a prevailing and magnificent conception of the public mind', it was especially necessary that he should 'not sully that which I represent by warranting the suspicion even, that I am using the power it confers for any personal object'.[147]

It is easy to dismiss this as an appeal stimulated by the heady aura of success attending the activities of the League, muted by Peel's usual sense of statesmanlike modesty and constitutional caution. However, it was the culmination of a long chain of deductive reasoning, on Cobden's part, which played to a strain of public opinion which claimed him and Carlyle for its twin (if somewhat unorthodox) fellow prophets. As John Morrow has argued, 'For Carlyle, Peel's growing popularity with a broad cross section of the population reflected an awareness of his capacity to grasp the realities of the situation. Like other heroes, Peel's actions struck a chord with the population because they discerned that he could articulate the needs of contemporary society.'[148] In May 1845 Cobden had observed that 'Peel has the finest career open to him that ever tempted the honest ambition of a public man. He may appropriate to himself all the glory of liberating the commerce of the world – "Adam Smith wrote, Peel practiced" – would be the award of history.' Nine months later, at the height of the parliamentary battle over Repeal, he told a fellow campaigner in the cause that Peel had:

> secured an immortality by appropriating to himself the triumph of a principle which his less powerful rivals have hardly had the mental capacity to comprehend, still less the vigor to carry into practice ... and I am much mistaken if we shall not live to hear Peel declare that the League alone enabled him to do the good work.

But for the crucial qualification that Peel went on to assign him the individual merit for the achievement of Repeal, Cobden's prophecy turned out to be uncannily accurate.[149]

7

THE RISE (AND FALL)
OF SIR ROBERT PEEL

Then towards the close of day, the bolt, but in mercy, fell: a swerving horse, a heavy fall, a racking pain, a moaning voice, a fainting, a slow transport home, a rally at his own door; again a fainting fit, a suffering body, impatience of the pain, a few hours of trouble, and then came the calm: the solemn offices of religion, the inward prayer, the gentle murmured blessing on wife and children; and all was over in that once happy home, from which the shadow never afterwards quite passed away.

Sir Lawrence Peel, describing Peel's final days, 29 June–2 July 1850.[1]

* * *

The final four years of Peel's life have not, generally speaking, proved problematic for his biographers. The earliest of them passed effortlessly – and without much sense of demur – from his rise to popular acclaim after 1846 to his fall from a horse in the summer of 1850, with barely a hesitation. As J.R. Thursfield put it in 1891, 'There is not much more to tell.'[2] It suited the late Victorian location of Peel within the Liberal political tradition that this should be the case. With an unparalleled public reputation, for his part in having secured Repeal, Peel enjoyed unprecedented popular support during this period. This made him the repository of widespread hope and expectation. Peel's consistently declared intention not to resume political office, or to capitalise upon this democratic constituency, was thought to reflect the same dislike of factious opposition that he had demonstrated, on innumerable occasions, during the 1830s. As Peel himself commented, in defending his support of Russell's Whig government during 1849, 'I have thought that it was for the public interest, that the energy and power of the executive government of this country, during such a crisis of combined dangers, should not be impaired by factious or captious opposition.'[3] Peel's continual disavowal of political ambitions (either present or prospective), and the careful qualification with which he phrased his public speeches during these years, suggests he was conscious of the position he occupied. Nevertheless, however much Peel may have wished to play the part of 'Sir Roger de Coveley', the depth of extra-parliamentary interest in his pronouncements meant that any intervention he did make during these years was subjected to more than usual scrutiny.[4]

The irony was that many of the biographers responsible for this view of Peel's 'Indian Summer' had consulted Gladstone, the late nineteenth-century embodiment of Peel's popular liberalism. Gladstone's contemporary reservations about Peel's political line of conduct make it apparent that the accepted picture overlooks some of the contradictions it contained. Far from subscribing to a positive appraisal of Peel at this time, Gladstone was in fact his fiercest critic. This is particularly significant given that Gladstone reaped the benefit of Peel's mature political reputation.[5] However, Gladstone's reservations were far from singular. As this chapter demonstrates, many of the more telling criticisms of Peel's position during this period came not from his political enemies but from his political acolytes.

* * *

On 28 June 1849, a public dinner was given to Sir Robert Peel at the Mansion House in London. It was the third anniversary of the passing of the Repeal of the Corn Laws. That act had allowed for a gradual diminution of the scale of protective duties on corn until a remaining, nominal, registration duty of a shilling remained. That legislative milestone had been reached four months earlier.[6] It seemed an opportune moment to commemorate Peel's services in the cause of Free Trade and to maintain popular support for its continuance in the face of unabated Protectionist opposition. Peel's speech at the dinner was markedly deferential towards Wellington, with whom relations had not always been easy or harmonious.[7] The Foreign Secretary, Lord Palmerston, thought it 'in bad taste and very injudicious':

> Peel is not by any means so really prudent a man as people think him. He is impelled strongly by sudden and violent impulses, and his reserved and apparently cold manner is, I really believe, not only the result of proud shyness, but is also purposely assumed to assist him in that self-control which he feels to be so constantly necessary.[8]

Disraeli also felt that Peel's public speeches, in the years after 1846, were characterised by an 'earnestness' and 'heat' which marked them out from those before the disruption of the Conservative Party. Before then, yoked with supporters with whom he was in fundamental disagreement, Peel had been forced to maintain an 'affectation of plausibility'. As such, Repeal had liberated Peel, allowing his real political sentiments to shine through.[9]

The Mansion House dinner was, in many respects, the culmination of a process which had been ongoing over the course of the previous three years. Peel was periodically subjected to commemoration, as the architect of Free Trade, during his political 'retirement'. In the autumn of 1847, he made something of an Elizabethan progress through Northern England which drew appreciative crowds in Darlington, Newcastle, Durham and Liverpool.[10] Two years later, Peel was invested with the freedom of the City of Aberdeen.[11] Not for the first time, *Punch* was moved to observe the marked change in Peel's political fortunes (and favour) out of office, contrasting it with the hostility to which he had been subjected as Prime Minister:

> Don't you find, dear SIR ROBERT, the contrast quite charming –
> Beyond shooting, or speaking, or feasting, or farming –
> To escape from the squalls and the storms of the session,
> And thus 'go to the country' in joyous procession?
> To exchange, for the flatteries of mouth and of pen,
> The bullying of BENTINCK, the buzzing of BEN;
> To have freedoms now given where once freedoms were taken;
> To find yourself *féted* instead of forsaken;
> To hear crowds and Town-Councils quite hoarse with huzzaing,
> For irate country gentlemen, howling and braying;
> To meet, when the train sets you down at a station,
> Mayors and maces, to thank you for saving the nation,[12]
> Instead of a mob, in top-boots and long-gaiters,
> With minds made up to swear you're the blackest of traitors? –
> Like Magellan, in short, round a Cape Horn terrific
> To glide on a smooth and sunshiny Pacific![13]

Exactly a year after the Mansion House dinner, on Friday 28 June 1850, Peel delivered his final parliamentary speech in the House of Commons. Ostensibly a critique of Palmerston's conduct of foreign policy in respect of the 'Don Pacifico affair' (a dispute with Greece over a case of English citizenship), it expanded into a soliloquy on the virtues of peace, retrenchment and Free Trade.[14] For Norman Gash, 'it was the speech of an elder statesman … quiet, reflective, unpartisan, not designed to win votes but the more impressive because of its restraint'. It was also significant politically, for the Peelites and Protectionists were as one in voting against Russell's Whig government on the occasion. As Gash observes, 'It was an irony of history that Peel's last act in the House of Commons was to go into the lobby with a united Conservative opposition.'[15] The following day – the fourth anniversary of his resignation as Prime Minister – Peel was returning home from a meeting of the commissioners to the Great Exhibition when his horse reared, threw its rider and fell on him on Constitution Hill. Three days later, on Tuesday 2 July 1850, as a result of the injuries sustained in the accident, Peel was dead.[16]

* * *

Never has the death-watch ticked louder upon the public ear, than on the melancholy bereavement which the country has sustained in the loss of its greatest statesman. In the noon-time of his fame, in the vigour of his intellect, Sir Robert Peel has been snatched from his countrymen by a sudden and shocking death. His loss is regarded by all as a national, and by many thousands as a private and personal calamity.[17]

Thus wrote W.T. Haly in the immediate aftermath of Peel's death. It was a sentiment which was widely shared in the summer of 1850.[18] 'I never recalled so profound an impression on the public mind produced by any event,' Sidney Herbert observed to Lord Lincoln, whilst Aberdeen told Princess Lieven that it had united all classes of society in universal sorrow.[19] According to Carlyle, this was more than natural human sympathy for a tragic accident but represented 'an affectionate appreciation' of Peel 'which he himself was far from being sure of, or aware of, while he lived'.[20] The Duke of Rutland expressed himself unsurprised 'at the interest taken in the case, not by those who know him only, but by all classes of the community'.[21]

Although it was a personal tragedy, Peel died at precisely the right moment for the maturation of his public reputation: 'though his death was so sudden and premature, and he was cut off in the vigour of life [Greville observed], he could not have died at a moment and in circumstances more opportune for his own fame; for time and political events might perhaps have diminished, but could not have increased, his great reputation.'[22] The same point was made by Hobhouse on the one hand ('a longer career could hardly have added to, and might have diminished, his reputation') and Lord Lincoln on the other:

> Thank God he was spared for the speech and vote of the day before his fatal accident! It has saved his reputation which must be dear to all of us from aspersions which his political position of the last 2 or 3 years <u>might</u> otherwise have exposed him to. His honor is untarnished, his patriotism above cavil, his high renown as a beacon light in his Country's history, and he has left a world which will now begin to be grateful to him & to mourn him for another where I feel it is not presumption to say he will receive the rewards of a life such as few Statesman, if any, have spent on earth.[23]

Edward Stanley also felt the timing of Peel's death was 'fortunate for his fame', whilst his father considered Peel's vote in the Don Pacifico debate to have 'elated' him, because he had 'spoken and voted according to his conscience, without thereby producing the result which he had apprehended – that of upsetting the ministry'.[24]

Peel's death coincided with the beginnings of an economic boom and an aura of national well-being which 'combined to invest his memory with a warm glow'. To Boyd Hilton, 'the rash of statues erected in [Peel's] memory, the parks named after him, and the cheap mugs thrown in his image' represent an 'incongruous' outpouring of enthusiasm for 'the People's Robert' because he 'had always opposed popular causes, and had never previously been accorded an ounce of acclaim by working people'.[25] To end up the object of popular adoration (funded by the subscription of working class pennies) was an interesting irony for the grandson of a man who had relocated his textile business from Lancashire to Staffordshire because of incidents of popular machine-breaking.[26] It was equally unexpected because Peel was not a man whose misfortunes had hitherto raised much sense of empathy in the hearts of his countrymen.[27] 'I little thought that I should have cried for his death,' Macaulay confessed, whilst Croker recalled that for over thirty years he had 'loved [Peel] as a brother'. That is what made his subsequent 'betrayal' so hard to take.[28] The national mood of political mourning was amplified two years later, on the death of the Duke of Wellington. The combined loss of the greatest military figure of his age and (in some respects) his political equivalent, at the meridian of Britain's nineteenth-century power, left a hole in the collective psyche of the nation and (one might add) of Conservatism which their successors struggled to fill.[29] Reflecting upon the public statuary springing up in homage to Peel across the county of his birth, *The Manchester Guardian* drew a comparison with Lancashire's other most famous Conservative son: 'Lord Derby has a seat in the House of Lords, and may, for all we know, have a tomb in Westminster Abbey; but when will he get a corner in the market place of a dozen English towns, or a niche in the households of the people?'.[30] In one respect, it was a propitious moment. When a Peelite-Whig administration under Lord Aberdeen was formed in July 1852, *The Times* was moved to its famous and often-quoted comment: 'In one sense, we are all Peelites'. However, its under-quoted coda was equally significant: 'We all reverence the memory of the departed Statesman, but a political party cannot be held together upon sympathies and regrets.'[31]

In a political sense, Peel's death was liberating.[32] 'As long as Sir Robert Peel exists, a strong Government cannot be formed,' the Duke of Wellington observed in August 1846. A month later, Charles Arbuthnot made a similar conclusion in respect of the Conservative Party – 'The schism is as great as ever; & I see no chance unless Peel should withdraw, which he will not do. If he were quite away there might be reunion; but the Party will never forgive him, or act with him.'[33] Whilst dedicating copious obituary columns to the circumstance of Peel's death, *The Northern Star* nevertheless took time out to acclaim 'the breaking up of that dreary political stagnation to which we look forward as a consequence of the death of Sir Robert Peel'.[34]

Similar sentiments were the prevailing consideration of those traditional Tory gadflies, Lords Londonderry and Lyndhurst, at the hour of Peel's death. According to Disraeli, Londonderry 'foresaw the revolution which the death of Peel might occasion in parties' whilst Edward Stanley found Lyndhurst 'cheerful & conversable' in the days after Peel's demise. For his part, Disraeli 'seemed bewildered by the suddenness of the event, and the prospect which it offered of new combinations'.[35] The irony of the situation struck Greville: 'no man who in life was so hated and reviled was ever so lamented and honoured at his death'. However, considering the unusual and unsustainable position which Peel had carved out for himself during the final four years of his life, it is perhaps not altogether surprising why the Protectionists should prove generous towards Peel in death, showing him 'more regret ... and appreciation ... than from their late language could have been expected'.[36]

* * *

There was a clear contrast between Peel's own views on his political situation in the final four years of his life and the outlook of his contemporaries. Personally speaking, this was undoubtedly amongst the happiest periods of Peel's life. To Lord Londonderry, Peel observed that he was 'heartily glad to be released from such

PEEL'S DIRTY LITTLE BOY.

12: 'Peel's Dirty Little Boy', *Punch*, January–June 1845, 145.
A portrayal of Peel in the (by then) characteristic guise of an elderly dame or matron.

obligations as those which appear now to be imposed upon a Conservative Minister – In what a position would the landed aristocracy have been at this moment – if the policy which some of them recommended – a determined opposition to any relaxation of the duties on the import of food – had prevailed?'.[37]

However, this attitude was hardly consoling to his closest political colleagues. Francis Bonham, who had played so important a part in the Conservative Party's electoral and political organization and remained one of Peel's abiding friends, was horrified to find his old political master in unabashed high spirits, after receiving a letter from Drayton Manor in October 1849:

> [Lady Peel] says that she never saw Sir Robert 'So happy'. I trust this is an exaggerated statement as even granting the wisdom or necessity of his support to the Whigs it cannot be a source of <u>happiness</u> that they should govern the country without any check, or that the party which it cost him and his friends such extraordinary exertions to revive and ... render omnipotent <u>as they were in 1841</u> should be now scattered to the winds. This indeed must be a source of sorrow rather than of happiness, even to those who like myself are not disposed to blame the feeling on the simple ground of necessity the tyrant's plea.[38]

It is understandable why Bonham should feel so aggrieved by Peel's levity of spirits. It was Bonham who, in the immediate aftermath of Repeal, had foreseen a short period of disruption in the Conservative Party before 'the great mass' reunited under Peel. Charles Arbuthnot had treated such sanguine expectations with incredulity – 'I can't think that Sir Robert Peel will ever be able to collect the Party again under him ... I feel confident that as the leader of our Party there is an end of him, for nobody will ever trust him again.'[39]

Nor, if Peel's frequently expressed sentiments on the matter are to be believed, is this the outcome he was seeking. He scrupulously avoided giving any external sign of being the head of a political party (such as holding a dinner for supporters before the start of the parliamentary session or issuing a circular to encourage attendance) whilst remaining self-consciously aware that he remained the repository of the hopes (and promotion prospects) of his talented band of political supporters.[40] When the Peelites began to show signs of independence from their eponymous chief, by detaching themselves from his leadership, Graham muttered darkly about 'letting them see the consequences of their insubordination'. As Greville observed, 'It was the *tone* in which it was said that struck me.'[41] Lord Stanley told Croker that Peel was 'bent on keeping together a party whose bond of union shall be personal subservience to Sir Robert Peel'. In turn, Croker informed Brougham that whilst Peel 'disclaims party & sets his people free – nominally ... in fact he only disclaims <u>his own</u> obligation to party & not that of party to him'.[42] Thomas Carlyle, who publicly maintained Peel's pre-eminent ability to lead public affairs through his *Latter Day Pamphlets* (1850), privately observed that 'there might certainly be some valuable reform work still in Peel, though the look of all things, his own strict conservatism and even officiality of view, and still more the *cohue* of objects and persons his life was cast amidst, did not increase my hopes of a great result'.[43] Writing in the same period, one critic maintained that it was the 'darling wish of [Peel's] heart, to be borne triumphantly into power by the masses as leader of the popular movement ... a sort of perpetual Grand Vizier' and this lay 'at length almost within his grasp'.[44] An American writer, Robert Russell, also felt that Peel's return to power on an advanced reformist platform was not unlikely:

> [Sir Robert Peel's party] is not distinguishable from the Whigs, but serves at present to keep up the conservative tendency of the Whig government. The Peel party, however, may be considered as erratic; and it is not improbable that they will at some future period advocate some comprehensive plan of parliamentary reform, under the belief that, a great change being inevitable, they may as well assist in bringing it about.

Lord Ashley concurred. A revived Peel administration would 'do all the mischief that Russell will do, and only a small portion of the good'.[45]

However, according to Aberdeen and Hardinge, Peel was resolutely determined never to resume an official situation. At the same time, they left open the possibility that an emergency or national crisis might (justifiably) over-rule this sentiment.[46] They based their conclusion upon the report – widely retailed and believed – that Peel had personally requested the Queen, at his final audience as Prime Minister, 'never again at any time or under any circumstances [to] ask him to enter her service'. This was, as Greville commented, 'rather inconsistent' given that Peel continued to sit in the House of Commons as a Member of Parliament: 'if such is his determination ... the best thing he could have done would have been to go to the House of Peers; that would have been a dignified retirement from political power'.[47]

Peel himself told Aberdeen that he had retained his seat in Parliament out of deference to the Queen's wishes (a sentiment which suggested she might overcome his other scruples, if the need arose). The analogy which Peel had in mind for his political position, after 1846, was Earl Spencer: 'rare appearances for serious purposes and without compromise generally to the independence of his personal habits'. In many respects, this was the position Peel had been aiming at, throughout his political career. As Lord Althorp, Spencer had been a prominent political operator in the Commons until 1834, when his father's death had enforced his removal to the upper chamber (an act which precipitated the fall of Melbourne's government and the start of Peel's 'Hundred Days' ministry). However, as Gladstone unhelpfully pointed out, Spencer was a peer and this placed him in an entirely different political situation. Peel told Sidney Herbert that Lord Grenville – who had enjoyed a long political retirement in the House of Lords after retiring as Prime Minister in 1807 – was another good example for him to emulate. To Gladstone, this showed that Peel's 'mind had been at work upon the subject' for some time. However, it was the consequences of Peel's thinking which, as Gladstone subsequently told Graham, was at fault:

Do you conceive that men who have played a great part, who have swayed the great moving forces of the State, who have led the House of Commons and given the tone to public policy, can at their will say they will remain there but renounce the consequences of their remaining and refuse to fulfil what must fall to them in some contingency of public affairs [?] – the country will demand that they who are the ablest shall not stand by inactive … it [was] impracticable to remain in the House of Commons as an isolated and independent member of it: though such an intention might be fulfilled in the House of Lords.[48]

Graham himself admitted the argument in respect of Peel. He told Greville later that Peel would (in his view) have resumed office if there was a serious prospect that agricultural Protection might be restored; in those circumstances, Peel would have risked every hazard to prevent it.[49]

Wellington maintained that Peel wanted to be an independent 'umpire' between the different political parties: a position reflected in *Punch's* sardonic observation that 'there ought to be a PEEL Bench, which would enable the occupant to sit on both sides of the House at once'.[50] Another polemicist observed that Peel should be suspended in the centre of the Commons above the two parties in a basket:

There is certainly something grand in thus soaring 'far above all parties'; nevertheless, he should take care not to rise *too* far above them, otherwise they would probably cease, ere long, to strain their eyes in looking after him, and would pursue their sublunary disputes among themselves, leaving him unregarded and alone in his glory. Nay, it is even to be feared that in soaring too high, he might some day vanish bodily with a flash of light, and an odorous smell, through the ventilator, discharged to heaven …[51]

The Quarterly Review, which from the start of 1846 to the end of Peel's life maintained its personal and political opposition to its former idol with unalloyed severity,[52] was equally scornful of the proposition:

We find in well-informed quarters a conviction that [Peel] means to attend regularly, taking a leading part in most great questions, and acting (with a small body of implicit adherents) the part of an arbiter between the Government and the Conservatives – a position anomalous in itself, and productive of the greatest embarrassment to all parties, and which would, we fear, perpetuate, and even exasperate, animosities, and not only render the reconstruction of the Conservative party more difficult, but smooth the way for those measures of gradual, or perhaps rapid, downward progress which Lord John Russell will in those circumstances be constrained … to introduce; but which he will probably introduce as gradually as he can.[53]

There was no favourable analogy for the position which Peel was seeking to occupy in British politics at this time. Gladstone felt it to be 'false and in the abstract almost immoral' that Peel 'and still more Graham, sit on the opposition side of the House professing thereby to be independent … but in every critical vote are governed by the intention to keep ministers in office and sacrifice every thing to that intention'.[54] It was unrealistic for Peel to refuse to head a political party (even one committed to him personally) and yet stand in readiness as a potential head of government – at least not in the political circumstances of mid-Victorian England.[55] Between 1801 and 1804, Pitt the Younger had stood as unofficial guarantor to his successor's administration, but the logic of circumstances had finally brought his (decisive) influence into play and Addington's administration was defeated, and subsequently replaced, as a result of Pitt's personal standing in the House of Commons.[56] When Disraeli, increasingly disaffected by his poor treatment at the hands of the Conservative Party, proposed withdrawing to a position akin to that of Peel, Lord Stanley rebuffed him in decisive terms:

> This, supposing him to be sincere in his professions, is the difficulty, or rather the impossibility, of Peel's position at the present moment. He must be a Leader in spite of himself; & the course which he took in 1845 alone prevents him from being the Leader, hence the disruption which we have all seen & regretted, of the great Conservative party; & what I now anticipate with anxiety, & am desirous, if possible, to avoid, is a similar disruption, into minute sections, of that portion of the party, who, as Protectionists, adhered to their original principles.[57]

In the immediate aftermath of Repeal, Lords Ellenborough and Lyndhurst (abetted by Brougham) had sought to reunite the Conservative Party without Peel and Graham – the most divisive figures in the 1841–6 government who were considered, politically speaking, as 'man and wife'. Ellenborough told Lord Clare that the Protectionists had 'a sort of an army but no staff, & Peel has a staff, but a very small army with which he can undertake nothing'.[58] In fact, as a result of the General Election of 1847, Peel's committed supporters in the House of Commons stood at some 90 MPs. This was sufficient to provide a Praetorian Guard against the formation of a Protectionist government.[59] It was an uncomfortable situation for many of the Peelites and one to which some – notably Gladstone – were never truly reconciled on personal or political grounds. Yet it was a course of action almost entirely influenced by 'the exclusiveness of [Peel's] regard to preventing the Protectionists from obtaining office'.[60] Peel was undoubtedly disposed to treat Russell's government generously (without himself absorbing himself into the Whig Party). In 1862, Lord Hatherton recalled that on a visit to Drayton in 1850 Peel spoke 'in kind terms' of Russell and expressed 'his intention to support his Government … distinctly, and that I took the trouble of memorising it'.[61] At the same time, much of this sentiment was the product of Peel's equally strong aversion to 'Conservative Reunion'. Gladstone always maintained that the 'false position' in which the Peelites found themselves during this period was entirely 'due to Peel himself' and the line he had 'walked with such a set purpose', in supporting Russell's ministry to the exclusion of all potential political alternatives.[62] In April 1847 Peel observed that, insofar as the Protectionists were concerned, some of the Peelites had 'a confidence which I have not in the force of mutual attraction'.

Although Bonham detected some change in Peel's sentiments, on visiting him at Drayton in the autumn of 1848, this was a temporary disposition borne of the unexpected death of Lord George Bentinck.[63]

Gladstone believed that Bentinck's death in September 1848 signalled (for all practical political purposes) the end of the Protectionists – at least insofar as the formation of a government committed to the restoration of the Corn Laws was concerned. In any case, he thought it better for such a ministry to try (and fail) in such an endeavour than allow the groundswell of Protectionist opinion in the country to continue to grow to dangerous levels. Gladstone was prescient in foreseeing that when the time came (as it did in 1852), the Protectionists would find it impossible to re-trace their steps and Repeal the Corn Laws. It was Gladstone himself who issued the *coup de grace* through his demolition of Disraeli's 1852 Budget. But whilst Peel lived, this proved impossible. It was the 'intensity' of Peel's 'anxiety' to keep Russell's government in place which was most notable.[64] Indeed, he pursued it with a resoluteness which stands comparison with his fixity of purpose in relation to the currency question and his final handling of the Repeal of the Corn Laws. As on those occasions, Peel was impervious to any counter-arguments – not least, Gladstone's contention that, in striving so hard to prevent the circumstances in which he might be recalled to power, Peel was in fact stoking up the potential for a crisis in which exactly that contingency might arise. 'He does not seem to allow himself to realise his position [Gladstone noted in February 1848]: but power is surely coming near him, & likely to be forced upon him.'[65]

Whilst Edward Stanley observed an abatement in Protectionist invective against Peel, in the months preceding his death, it was equally notable how adverse Peel was to any hint of political reconciliation with the Protectionists.[66] Though the Peelites were frequently represented as a moderating influence between the Whigs and Protectionists, during these years, the reality suggested otherwise. In fact, as Gladstone shrewdly observed, Peel's latitude for action was remarkably constrained:

> of all Members of Parliament [Peel] has the smallest degree of free judgment in regard to the announced measures of the government. He dare not vote against any of them in any point of importance, and this on account of the weakness of the administration, because through their weakness their existence might be endangered by an hostile vote even though not intended to carry want of confidence, and if he were a party to such a vote he would stand before the world – whatever he might be in his own mind – as a bidder for office, the character he is determined not to bear.[67]

This incongruous situation had been revealed in Peel's first month out of office when he had supported a government measure to remove the distinction between 'free' and 'slave-grown' sugar, in point of the duties they paid. This was the issue on which Peel's own government had nearly foundered in 1844, yet the new political circumstances created by the Repeal of the Corn Laws led him to support the measure from an awareness of the need to shore up support for Russell's government. Lord Ellenborough was in no doubt of its significance:

[Peel] baffles all calculation as to the course he will adopt upon any measure, unless indeed that calculation be founded on the assumption that he will do anything to keep out the Protectionists. He evidently pursues them with a degree of aversion equal to that they entertain for him, & to this he adds disdain & contempt. I am satisfied that he would have broken up his own government rather than have consented to prepare any part of the measure he now adopts as a whole.[68]

The Times was equally unimpressed. 'Sir Robert still tries to say too much, and be too much. He has a face for all.' Like a Paul Potter portrait of three cows, in which 'Two of them stand, lovingly enough, head to tail and tail to head, while a third looks as much as possible in a different direction from either,' so Peel was attempting to embrace three mutually contradictory political positions in the course of one action.[69]

* * *

Peel's vote on the revised Sugar duties raised, in stark form, the essential dilemma which he faced in the final four years of his life – a dilemma which subsequent biographers were too circumspect (or cautious) to address. Whilst he undoubtedly rose in popular estimation, on the back of the reputation he had forged through the Repeal of the Corn Laws, Peel was increasingly confounded by the logic of the political situation which this action had helped to create, in terms of the dissolution of parties. During the 1830s he had papered-over the difference between his own executive-oriented view of government and that of his followers, which was founded on the basis of party. This contradiction became increasingly difficult to resolve after 1846. Although in one sense Peel was increasingly 'unmuzzled' from political connections, he was still confounded by their practical operation. He was too conservative a politician to have considered a popular appeal out-of-doors, in the manner that Cobden and Carlyle suggested in 1846 and Gladstone began to perfect after 1850. Caught between a Protectionist hard-core with whom he remained in instinctive disagreement and a Whig government which it was increasingly difficult to hold in check, Peel's practical political options were few – and uncongenial. It is hard to see how Peel's reputation could have survived the 1850s intact or how he could have positioned himself in such a way as to prove an acceptable choice for Prime Minister. Conversely, his death removed a standing obstacle to Conservative Reunion and to the relative free movement of a host of political heavyweights, whose realm of action (so long as Peel lived) remained circumscribed and protracted. As *Blackwood's Edinburgh Magazine* commented in August 1846, 'their political walk cannot extend a yard beyond the limit of Sir Robert's sufferance'.[70] At the same time as Peel's political stock with the nation rose – on the basis of his reputation for placing country before party – so his political capital (and options) narrowed for precisely the same reasons. Although it cannot be more than a matter of conjecture, it is likely that this process would have continued had a wayward horse not decided the issue in the summer of 1850.[71]

8

PEEL, DEATH AND POSTERITY

This is probably not the occasion on which the public will be disposed to linger long over a resuscitation of the controversy raised by the public life of Sir Robert Peel. Such as he was, in his strength and in his weakness, in his greatness and in his littleness, in the honesty of his ends and the questionable nature of his conduct, this eminent person has been fully discussed by friends and enemies, has met with the usual share of unbounded praise and exaggerated vituperation, and has finally settled down, as we should imagine, pretty much into that position of public opinion in which an enlightened posterity will be disposed to place him.

The Times, 1855.[1]

* * *

Death palliates almost all political sins. The timing, nature and unexpectedness of Peel's death gave rise to a vein of popular mourning and commemoration unlike any hitherto inspired, in peacetime, by the passing of a civilian political leader.[2] As such, it impacted significantly upon his subsequent reputation. 'His sudden death has cast a halo of tenderness round his life,' *The Economist* commented in July 1850, 'and invested his character with the admiration which belongs to greatness and the respect due to misfortune.'[3] The forms which this commemoration assumed sometimes displayed an unconscious lack of insensitivity. Of the ten Staffordshire figures devoted to Peel (a tribute from the potters of his adopted county), the most iconic was the one of him astride a horse. To thus remind people of the means of Peel's death might be thought a strain of irony for which the Victorians are not usually remembered.[4] The tribute of the popular working class periodical, Chambers' *Papers for the People*, was equally capable of double interpretation. 'He fell from official power,' it remarked, 'into the arms of the people' – this on the man who had died as the result of a fall from a horse.[5]

Mawkishness and over-sentimentality was an attribute of the Victorians, above all in relation to human mortality and the mourning process to which it gave rise.[6] After the death of Prince Albert, in December 1861, Queen Victoria would come to epitomise (and champion) it in a manner which has no historic parallel, thereafter, until the autumn of 1997.[7] However, in many respects, this process of posthumous judgement – the passage from life to death to afterlife, from the judgement of contemporaries to that of posterity – was precisely what Peel had sought for himself. According to Horace Twiss in November 1831, Peel was 'always thinking of his reputation and his outward character', whilst fifteen years later, George Henry Francis observed that 'a page in history more fascinates his imagination than the glitter of a coronet'.[8] To that extent, as Francis was able to comment in the revised version of his biography of Peel six years later, 'Sir Robert Peel had the reward while he lived of a satisfied conscience, and at his death, the universal approval of his contemporaries, anticipating with confidence the verdict of posterity.'[9] This chapter considers how a man who was not always much rated in his lifetime, and then by his contemporaries, who lived beyond him, came to be known and remembered as a great statesman.

* * *

There is little doubt that the circumstances of Peel's death gave him an unduly favourable press. Donald Read has helped to chart this process through his consideration of the newspaper coverage which it occasioned.[10] However, the wider significance of this in terms of Peel's reputation has generally been underestimated. As *Blackwood's Edinburgh Magazine* commented in September 1850:

> The death of Sir Robert Peel was an event so sudden, so unexpected, and so distressing, that it excited a universal feeling of sympathy in the British heart, and stilled for a season every voice but that of melancholy among the immense multitudes to whom his public career had made him known. It stifled, during the first paroxysm of grief, even the loud wail of national distress: it obliterated the deep lines of party distinction: it caused to be forgotten the most painful feelings of extinguished confidence. All classes hastened to pay tribute to the eminent statesman who lay extended on the bed of premature death ... But there is a time for all things. There is a time for sorrow, and there is a time for justice. There is a season for sympathy with the agonised hearts of mourning relatives, and there is a season for calm reflection on the acts of public men. Death at once renders them the province of history.[11]

It is an interesting reflection on this process that Peel's tenure as Chief Secretary of Ireland (which had not, generally speaking, been regarded by contemporaries as one of the more glorious portions of his career) was skirted over in obituaries, on the basis that it possessed 'at this distance of time, but few features of interest to readers who live in the year 1850'.[12] Peel's good standing in posterity was subsequently invoked by those who came after him, not merely as the vindication which he had sought, but that to which he was fully entitled as a result of the sacrifices he had made in life.[13] 'Rely upon it', Lord Hardinge informed his son Walter in July 1846, 'posterity, age, & in

our time will do this great and honest man justice'. As Hardinge had foreseen, it was
the Peel of 1846 (and the Repeal of the Corn Laws) who came to be memorialised,
rather than his earlier incarnation as a Protestant and Protectionist Tory. In 1850,
Punch's 'Monument to Peel' played up his connection with the achievement of Free
Trade by inscribing his name above a pyramid of cheap loaves. Nine years later Richard
Cobden invoked 'the fame of Sir Robert Peel, and the veneration in which his memory
was held, as stimulants for [the] honourable ambition' of Emperor Louis Napoleon
of France, during negotiations for an Anglo-French commercial treaty committed to
extending the policy of Free Trade.[14]

In no respect was the attempt to utilise Peel's memory for contemporary political
purposes more apparent than in the movement to commemorate him in some tangible
and permanent form. This process began within days of his death:

> SIR ROBERT! oh! what feelings rise
> At his thrice honoured name;
> Let heroes seek for deeds of arms,
> And conquerors for fame!
> But where's the fame like he acquired,
> By *moral* force, not *steel*;
> A nation's sighs – a nation's tears,
> Fell for the patriot *Peel*!
>
> The poor man's friend, the rich man's trust
> E'en from his earliest youth,
> His attributes – his splendid gifts,
> Were sanctified by truth!
> 'Gone to that bourne whence none return',
> Yet still with joy we feel,
> The slightest token man can give
> Commemorating *Peel*![15]

Commemorating Peel was to take a particularly characteristic form through the
erection of statues funded by public subscription in the industrial towns of Northern
England.[16] It was one of the first outpourings of that civic pride which so transformed
the urban spaces, civic architecture and central meeting places of towns like
Manchester, Leeds and Liverpool in the mid-nineteenth century.[17] The fact that this
process was overwhelmingly urban, metropolitan and middle class and suffused with
the celebration of Free Trade and the Repeal of the Corn Laws may be considered
indicative of the stimulus and motivation behind the endeavour.[18] Boyd Hilton
maintains that it owes everything to Peel's posthumous elevation into the Liberal
pantheon.[19] Nor was the symbolism of the statues erected in Peel's memory lost on
some of the civic worthies who promoted them. At Bury – the town of Peel's birth –
one participant observed that a statue of him atop a plinth with sheaves of wheat at
his feet raised unfortunate connotations of 'Peel trampling upon agriculture'.[20]

Although the patronage and leadership of the governing elite was sought (and received), for this enterprise, the moving force behind the initiative came largely from outside the aristocratic political class. Many of the organising committees were headed by merchants, tradesmen and manufacturers whilst the commissions themselves were open to competition. The process evoked the solidly middle class virtues (initiative, enterprise, efficiency and merit) which were increasingly coming to be associated with Peel's life and career.[21] Likewise, the sanctity of Peel's domestic circle and the manner of his death became a model of family respectability and piety, quite unlike any which had previously been claimed for a politician. The tone was struck perfectly by Sir Lawrence Peel's reference 'to that once happy home, from which the shadow never afterwards quite passed away'.[22]

Nowhere were Peel's 'democratic' credentials more clearly displayed than in the Working Men's National Monument to Sir Robert Peel, which was promoted under the chairmanship of Joseph Hume. Lord Ashley criticised the enterprise as an open bid to appropriate Peel's memory for political purposes. The mood of solemnity attending Peel's death had been 'distorted into an exhibition of party', through the enterprise, 'and free trade against protection is to be fought over his grave!'. This suspicion was reinforced when Cobden 'perfected the party-spirit of the Poor Man's Memorial to Sir Robert Peel' by advising that the peroration of Peel's resignation speech should 'be engraven [sic] on the plate or marble'.[23] However, in a suitably populist touch the memorial committee subsequently committed itself to the provision of a working man's library rather than the erection of a statue.[24]

Aside from the National Memorial to Peel in Westminster Abbey (the work of Benjamin Gibson),[25] commemoration of this sort was considered an appropriate alternative, given that Peel himself had specifically forbidden his widow and children from accepting a pension, peerage or state funeral on his behalf in the manner of his predecessors.[26] This interdict from beyond the grave was regarded by a large number of commentators as a characteristically cynical and pre-meditated gesture on Peel's part.[27] Edward Stanley attributed it to pique and that 'habitual plausibility (I can find no other word) which had become part of his nature. He liked to show forth to the world the disinterestedness of his public services.'[28] Ashley suspected that it reflected the same sentiment 'which predominated in so many actions & speeches, I, I, I'. It also distinguished him from Canning, whose wife and family had received both peerage and pension after his death.[29]

It was (appropriately enough) Lancashire – the ancestral home of the Peel family and the Anti-Corn Law League – which took the pre-eminent part in the process of raising civic sarcophagi to Peel. Whilst Stockport and Ashton-under-Lyne were both unsuccessful in their bids to raise a public subscription for the purpose, the larger towns of north-west England each successfully raised the funds necessary to raise permanent memorials to Peel.[30] At Salford, which claimed the honour of being the first to inaugurate their statue (in May 1852),[31] the commission went to Matthew Noble – who also completed statues of Peel at Tamworth and St George's Hall, Liverpool (both unveiled in 1852) as well as the prestigious commission for Peel's statue in Parliament Square, London.[32] The Salford Peel was located in 'Peel Park' –

a public space for urban promenading and leisure to which the deceased statesman had given both moral and material encouragement.[33] In September 1844 Peel's gift of £1,000 for the purpose of providing public walks in Manchester and its environs had attracted favourable press attention. Lord Ashley was characteristically unimpressed by the gesture: 'Peel gives £1,000 for public walks in Manchester and stakes his ministerial existence on the perpetual refusal, to the people, of time to enjoy them!!'[34]

There was a clear sense of internal county rivalry between the major Lancashire towns – Manchester, Bury and Salford – in their efforts to outpace one another in their memorials to Peel. The fund-raising activities of all three were linked together in the public mind, but each sought to distinguish themselves from the other by the novelty of the outcome or the grandeur of the public display with which the inauguration was attended. The sums raised by public subscription were impressive: £1,200 at Salford, £2,700 at Bury and £5,000 at Manchester (Leeds raised £1,800).[35] Bury produced not one but two prominent memorials to Peel. Edward Hodges Baily's statue was unveiled in Bury Market Place, with appropriate celebrity, on 8 September 1852. The following day festivities adjourned to the newly-erected Peel Memorial Tower on nearby Holcombe Hill. Aside from the unfortunate fact that the inscription on the Tower misdated Peel's resignation speech (the peroration of which habitually adorned the plinth of these constructions) it became a popular magnet for tourists in subsequent years. However, a condition in the grant of land laid down that the Tower was not to be used for 'contentious public meetings'.[36] At Oldham, the funds raised for a statue (some £1,000) were committed instead to the erection of public baths at Union Street. The town's citizens satisfied themselves with a bust of Peel in the entrance hall (unveiled on 25 September 1854 and subsequently transferred to the town's new sports centre in 1975). The sculptor, Alexander Munro, produced what Gladstone described as 'the *best* head & face of [Peel] that I have seen'.[37]

Manchester's monument to Peel (by William Calder Marshall) was the first outdoor statue to be located in the town. It was unveiled on Manchester's Piccadilly, outside the Royal Infirmary, on 12 October 1853, by Gladstone: 'before a great assemblage – of *men* almost exclusively, & working men. There I spoke, to the cracking of my voice.'[38] The design was not to everyone's liking – Calder Marshall's commission had carried the day in the organising committee by 11 votes to 9 (largely in deference to the views of the Bishop of Manchester), but Absalom Watkin felt it represented an 'emasculated' Peel which made him laugh.[39]

Statues of Peel were controversial sites of veneration and commemoration. The fate of Peel's statue in Parliament Square was the most extreme example of the continuing political difficulties to which such endeavours could be subjected. Indeed, the protracted history of the statue bears comparison with other famous architectural *cause célèbres* of the period – such as the Wellington Monument.[40] Shortly after Peel's death, Baron Marochetti (who had unsuccessfully competed for the Manchester Peel) was commissioned to construct a colossal bronze statue by a fund raising committee headed by Lord Aberdeen. Marochetti's statue – some 12 feet high with a 16 foot pedestal – was ready for erection in March 1853 at the height of Aberdeen's ministry. The First Commissioner of Works was approached with a view to providing a site for it (some ten feet square) 'within the precincts of the Houses of Parliament'. The committee's suggestion that Peel should be placed opposite the statue of Canning was rebuffed by the Commissioner (Molesworth) as 'ill advised and, in consequence of their antagonistic political feelings, in bad taste'. Moreover, as he subsequently informed Cardwell (who was part of the fund raising committee), the statue:

> is in fact a private testimonial to the merits of a Public Man, differing but little from many other Statues which have been erected to his honour in various parts of the Country, except in the skill which has been employed in its production, and the rank and political importance of those at whose instance the work has been accomplished. I cannot, however, find in these circumstances any diminution of the difficulty of my position [in being asked to accommodate it]: it is, on the contrary, much increased by the fact of the leading members of the Committee being also Members of the Government.

All Molesworth could suggest was that Parliament be asked to petition the Queen for an appropriate venue. By 1855, having dismissed New Palace Yard, it was decided to site Marochetti's Peel in Privy Gardens, opposite the Treasury. However, the lessees of Gwydyr House raised objections to the alterations required in the garden to facilitate it. Matters lay dormant for six years until Cardwell revived the subject with the First Commissioner (William Cowper). A site was granted at the entrance to (rather than within) New Palace Yard, in front of the railings and between the two gateways. Marochetti agreed to execute another, less colossal, statue and this was erected on the site in 1866.

It was not to be left at peace for long. In 1868, the House of Commons voted for its removal from New Palace Yard. The committee, which had been re-constituted in 1863 under Cardwell's leadership, met to discuss the situation on site.[41] Cardwell subsequently informed the new Commissioner of Works, Lord John Manners (who had been one of Peel's 'Young England' opponents, during the 1840s), that the committee 'unanimously and strongly desire to be permitted to remove the statue from the site which it now occupies to the alternative site proposed' in St Margaret's Square, Westminster. Consequently, the statue and pedestal were removed from New Palace Yard and placed in storage under Whitehall Chapel in December 1868.[42]

On 8 August 1871 the Peel Committee was informed that the statue would be placed at its preferred site, Parliament Square, on an appropriate pedestal to complement the statues of Palmerston (who had died in 1865) and Derby (who had died in 1869). Gladstone – a member of the re-constituted committee – took time out of his Prime Ministerial day to discuss the placing of the statues of Peel, Palmerston and Derby in March 1871 and made the inscriptions on them a subject of cabinet discussion the following January.[43] To compensate the committee for the government's temporising, it was proposed that if the committee felt a new statue was more appropriate for its new surroundings (and neighbours), the First Commissioner would recommend to the Treasury that the cost of the new pedestal should be defrayed at public expense. In the event, Parliament voted the necessary funds (£650) for a granite pedestal. In 1874, the Marochetti statue was delivered to the Peel Committee for melting down and Matthew Noble, the veteran Peel sculptor, was employed to mould its successor. The new statue was finally unveiled in 1877 and, at the request of the committee and by Treasury Authority (dated 23 May 1877), responsibility for the statue was adopted by the Department of Works under *17 & 18 Vic. c.33 sect.7*.[44]

* * *

The history of the Peel statue – with its interminable delays, political in-fighting, administrative wrangling and financial hand-wringing – is emblematic of the wider difficulties attending the 'siting' of Peel in the popular and historical memory. 'The strangulation of discourse about Peel is observable in a number of contexts' in late-Victorian Britain – not least the failure of his literary executors, Cardwell and Stanhope, to 'produce any acceptable portrait of the man for later consumption'.[45] A process of casting, erecting, melting down and re-sculpting may be said to have been performed on Peel by historians, biographers and memorialists ever since his death, in an attempt to mould a satisfactory literary statue to him. In many respects this is a striking outcome, considering the steps which Peel took to amass the materials upon which posterity would work its contending visions of him – whether that of the heroic statesman, cast in bronze astride a granite pedestal, or else composed of base metals and feet of clay.[46]

'No prime minister before Peel had made such minute provision for the transmission to posterity of the records of his political life.'[47] He reportedly told an acolyte that 'no public man who values his character, ever destroys a letter or a paper' – an injunction which he conspicuously abrogated in respect of his father's papers, which he burned after his death, thereby depriving historians of much valuable information about a formative influence in his life.[48] Nevertheless, Peel seems to have compiled well in excess of 100,000 individual documents himself and, as Chief Secretary to Ireland, took especial pains to have his correspondence and state papers collected together and bound in a magnificent livery. Gash considers this to be 'misleading if it is taken to denote any special degree of self-interest'.[49] It was certainly not unique and probably said as much about the paucity of official record-keeping in some quarters as it revealed anything of Peel's deeper psychology. Nevertheless, it was hardly unexampled in his life. At the height of the Repeal crisis, Peel was unsettled by the discovery that Prince Albert had kept a memorandum relating his stated views and sentiments on political subjects:

> He was visibly uneasy, and added, if he knew that what he said should be committed to paper, he would speak differently, and give his opinion with all the circumspection and reserve which a Minister ought to employ when he gave responsible advice; but he had in this instance spoken quite unreservedly, like an advocate defending a point in debate, and then he had taken another and tried to carry this as far as it would go, in order to give me an opportunity of judging of the different bearings of the question. He did so often in the Cabinet, when they discussed important questions, and was often asked: 'Well, then, you

are quite against this measure?': 'Not at all, but I want that the counter argument should be gone into to the fullest extent, in order that the Cabinet should not take a one-sided view.'

When Albert offered to destroy the offending memorandum, Peel said nothing to dissuade him from the proceeding – indeed, he could see that it 'relieved Sir Robert'. However, it was characteristic of Peel that he allowed the Prince to execute a course of action upon which he had already decided, rather than explicitly requesting him to do so. It was even more revealing that Albert recorded the episode in another memorandum.[50]

Peel's own priority was clearly to shape the subsequent historical record to his own account. 'The letters addressed to me, & written by me, were written frequently on the spur of the moment' he wrote in the statement prefacing the papers bequeathed to Mahon and Cardwell:

> for the pressure of official business rarely leaves sufficient time for the mature consideration of the various important matters on which a decision must be taken. It leaves none for the choice of words & the careful construction of sentences. I think I can safely say that there is not a single letter which was written with a view to subsequent publication.[51]

Nevertheless, in spite of the fear of going down to history for crimes against the English language,[52] Peel regarded his Prime Ministerial correspondence as 'probably the best history of the domestic political events of the time which they embrace' and one from which it would be possible to infer 'the degree of controul [sic] which I personally exercised over the general course of the government'.[53] As George Kitson Clark has written:

> these are the letters of a working politician dealing courageously with the problems that the current of affairs have brought to him, or the arguments which have been forced on him by public debate; they are not perhaps the letters of a prophet whose eyes can often pierce the murk ahead and see something of the shape of things to come.[54]

Under the terms of Peel's will, Mahon and Cardwell were entrusted with the care and oversight of Peel's literary remains, which he presumed 'to be of great value, as showing the character of great men of his age' and with an assurance that they would not warrant their 'premature' or 'indiscreet' publication.[55] Under an initial agreement between them, dated 11 December 1850, the two men agreed to work together on all occasions, except if one or other of them was ill or abroad 'at a time when there appeared some attack upon the memory of Sir Robert Peel, such as in the judgement of the other to require some immediate answer'. Under these circumstances, the publication or communication of any papers required to rebut such an assault was to be 'strictly limited to the absolute necessity of the case'.[56]

Throughout the history of Peel's papers, Mahon and Cardwell acted with 'an earnest desire to do the most effectual justice in our power to that high trust, so honourable to us, with which we found ourselves so unexpectedly invested'. Wellington commended Peel's choice, remarking to Mahon that 'he knew that you would make no improper use of them – that you would use them only for the use of history'.[57]

In one respect, the two men may have hoped that the passage of time would be sufficient for their purposes. 'Already you may observe a most marked difference in the tone in general adopted towards the memory of Sir Robert Peel,' Mahon informed Cardwell in October 1851. 'His policy both in 1829 & in 1846 is still questioned by very many, but his personal honor & uprightness, & his zeal for the good & glory of his country, are now denied by few if indeed by any at all.'[58] However, the over-scrupulous regard which they brought to their trust, and the careful husbanding of the resources bequeathed to them, actually proved counter-productive.[59] The marked exception to this deliberately cautious (not to say conservative) line of policy was in respect of the *Memoirs* – one on Catholic Emancipation, one on the Repeal of the Corn Laws – which Peel compiled in the later years of his life, together with a separately compiled account of the circumstances attending his 'Hundred Days' Ministry.

For his part, Mahon had little doubt of the advisability of publishing Peel's *Memoirs* separately and in advance of an edition of the generality of Peel's papers. 'I could make it plain to you from several indications, that such was in all probability the desire of Sir Robert Peel himself,' Mahon informed Cardwell:

> It also seems to me that the Correspondence & the Memoirs would address themselves to different classes of readers; the Correspondence interesting chiefly the politician or historian, but the Memoirs, from the great religious & commercial questions to which they relate, being likely to find an immense popularity. If we suppose each Memoir published separately in a small size & at a moderate price – from four to seven shillings perhaps according to the size of the little volume – I consider it probable that tens & tens of thousands would be sold, & a large sum acquired for those charitable & benevolent objects which we are empowered to pursue.

Whilst there were political objections to 'giving forth the Corn Law Memoir at present' (considering the possibility of a revived political battle over the Corn Laws), there were none in respect of the volume concerned with Catholic Emancipation, which Aberdeen considered 'greatly superior to the other as a composition & an argument'. This could be published immediately, subject to the approval of Wellington and Anglesey (the Lord Lieutenant of Ireland at the time), whose correspondence formed an integral part of it. Otherwise, it would have to 'await the period which in the course of nature cannot I fear be very many years delayed, of the termination of [Wellington's] glorious career'. Likewise, the timing of the Repeal Memoir would be determined when 'the hopes of re-enacting the Corn Law' had 'faded in the distance'.[60]

Gladstone had also read the two principal *Memoirs* (on Emancipation and Repeal) in manuscript form during this period, finding them 'deeply interesting: & infinitely suggestive'.[61] 'For the vindication of his fame both memoirs are needless: yet the writer has by them done in a masterly manner for posterity what posterity would have done only later and more circuitously for itself.'[62]

Peel's *Memoirs* appeared in two volumes over successive years, in 1856–7. In some respects, both their timing and format were unfortunate. This had everything to do with what appeared, how they appeared and when they appeared. In the first place, Peel had selected precisely those things which he thought needed recording, explaining and justifying. As such, he saw himself as critics tended to see him. By dwelling on the two key moments in his political life (in 1829 and 1846) for which critics had assailed him, he refrained from placing those episodes within the broader canvas of his life. By seeing himself as others saw him, Peel hoped to repel them by being taken at his own word (quite literally). This was also Macaulay's judgement, after reading the first volume:

> It contains some interesting details which are new; but it leaves Peel where he was. I always noticed while he was alive, and I observe again in this his posthumous defence, an obstinate determination not to understand what the charge was which I, and others who agreed with me, brought against him ... He is a debater even in this book.[63]

That Peel constructed his *Memoirs* as a series of justifications – to himself and posterity – might be thought unsurprising. They were certainly a compilation with marked historical utility. *The Economist* considered the first volume 'one of the most simple, faithful, and valuable materials ever contributed to history ... a collection of illustrative and explanatory documents'. But of the inner man there was very little.[64] The dry, administrative tone of the volumes did little to humanise Peel's reputation for frigid aloofness. These were the bureaucratic records of a supreme executive administrator, with none of the introspection and colour which emerges from the literary remains of some of his Prime Ministerial colleagues.

The timing of the *Memoirs* – in spite of Mahon's careful calculations – was also unfortunate. In part, this was because the actors in the Repeal drama were still active players on the contemporary political scene. Consequently, certain passages had been excised or edited. 'We learn little more of the back-scenes of the political drama than we might easily deduce from a careful consideration of the general plot,' *The Economist* observed of the second volume:

> One reason for this paucity of unexpected disclosures is probably the discretion which has been very properly exercised by the editors as to the publication of documents and passages of Sir Robert's own Memoir having allusion to living political celebrities. Perhaps the necessity for such omissions might have justified the postponement of the history ... until time had rendered a more complete exposition of the real facts feasible and proper. The editors however, have preferred publishing an imperfect defence of their leader's policy to leaving his character any longer to the mercy of political adversaries.[65]

However, there was a wider problem with the timing of the *Memoirs*. They appeared at a period when the Peelites' purchase was at a political discount due to their role in the Crimean War (1854–6) and in face of the growing ascendancy of Palmerston, who succeeded Aberdeen as Prime Minister in 1855. The obloquy might have fallen on the Peelites rather than on Peel but the Peelites increasingly found that, if Peel had not been able to play the role of arbiter by keeping governments afloat through his presence and toleration during his lifetime, then they could not do so through a perpetual resort to his memory. This must go some way to explaining Gladstone's mood of despondency and irritation with what he called the 'declining efficiency of Parliament' (and with Peel's relationship to the party system) in the year that the first volume of *Memoirs* was published.[66]

A similar sense of dissatisfaction with the state of Peel scholarship was displayed by Jelinger Cookson Symons, in his unduly depreciated study of *Sir Robert Peel as a type of Statesmanship* (1856).[67] As the title somewhat sarcastically suggested, Symons was in anything but universal agreement with the picture which was circulating as a result of the *Memoirs* and the early laudatory studies of Peel:

> Inasmuch, therefore, as public men regard their future more than their present reputation, so should they be influenced rather by the mature opinions passed on those who have gone through their career, than by the immediate censures and praises which attend their own acts, and seldom outlive the impulses or interests which called them forth … on the character of no statesmen of this century, is opinion among reflective men more unsettled and divided. And there is none which patient and calm investigation can more usefully determine.

Symons' objective was to portray 'in a somewhat stronger light than prevails at present, the policy, as well as duty of straightforwardness and unswerving principle in those public men whose ambition extends beyond the tenure of office, to posthumous reputation'.[68] As such, Symons re-opened the controversies surrounding Peel's legacy in the areas which he had selected for praise – notably Emancipation, Repeal and Taxation policy – by subjecting them to critical scrutiny. In many respects, Symons was the forgotten 'comrade-in-arms' of Walter Bagehot, who published his famous response to the publication of the *Memoirs*, 'The Character of Sir Robert Peel' in the same period.[69] Indeed, Symons' castigation of Peel's 'statesmanship' bears a close resemblance to one of Bagehot's more seductive and frequently quoted aphorisms:

> If Sir Robert Peel was deficient as an orator, he was equally so in the creative faculties of Statesmanship. He never originated a single great measure; but no man equalled him in accomplishing them: and he was signally skilled as an administrator. Such is the dispensation of Providence in the division of labour. It is designed that one man should conceive, and another execute: that one should be the man of vision, the other of action. Sir Robert Peel performed the latter function with devoted zeal.[70]

* * *

The *Memoirs* were consciously designed as the prelude to an edition of Peel's Correspondence, 'written with all the unreserve of personal regard or official connexion' – and it was on this basis that the publication of the *Memoirs* was received in some quarters.[71] However, the subsequent history of that enterprise was pursued with anything but Peelite efficiency. Indeed, it did much to perpetuate the troubled limbo-land in which Peel's historic reputation resided for much of the late Victorian and Edwardian period. Whilst Peel 'obtained admission to that rather wide-open temple of fame the *Dictionary of National Biography*',[72] the Conservative Party increasingly abrogated Peel's legacy in preference for a Disraelian orthodoxy enshrined in its mass membership auxiliary, the Primrose League (formed in 1883), and in the cynicism of the 'Hotel Cecil', occupied by the Marquess of Salisbury and his nephew Arthur Balfour. Salisbury declared that Peel was his most hated historical figure. Meanwhile Balfour, who revived a system of Tory nepotism not witnessed for well over half a century (by succeeding his uncle as Prime Minister), famously promised never to 'do another Peel' by splitting his party over the resurgent issue of Protection versus Free Trade.[73] Moreover, apart from Peel's cousin (Lawrence) and his grandson (George), there was no sustained Peel family dynasty devoted to staking out an alternative historical claim on his behalf.[74] As Sir Lawrence Peel concluded, with admirable equanimity, in 1860:

> When a statesman is living, he is judged by samples unfairly picked. After death we deal more justly. We look on his whole life: and we compare the dead with his fellows. We can then allow for the necessary admixtures of evil with all earthly good; and can pass in a spirit of charity and of truth, taught by our own human hearts, a juster judgment on the dead than on the living. Peel is now undergoing this test.[75]

The consequence was that Conservatism came to be defined, almost symbiotically, by reference to the Cecils, the Churchills and the Chamberlains. It was an orthodoxy against which Norman Gash was specifically recoiling when he came to write his biography of Peel.[76]

On the other hand, Peel became the somewhat incongruous begetter and precursor of Gladstonian Liberalism – a line of argument subsequently revived (in reaction against Gash's reading of Peel) by Boyd Hilton.[77] In Gladstone's 'Temple of Peace' at Hawarden Castle in Flintshire, a bust of Disraeli stared down on Gladstone like a standing motivation to vindicate his patron's memory. Historically speaking, Gladstone did so by appropriating Peel for Liberalism. Consequently, by the 1890s:

> Peel no longer looked like a Tory ... but appeared an apprentice Liberal confronting heroically his generation's lack of insight and humanity – a visionary seen in contrast to those around him rather than figuring among their accomplices. For the Tories themselves he had frozen in to memory as the man who tried to make two and two make five.[78]

It was an irony that, in speaking to Lionel Tollemache in 1896, Gladstone considered
'Peel's reputation as a statesman [to be] somewhat too high'.[79] In a pointed reference,
Gladstone observed that 'the great virtue of Peel was that he had such an enormous
conscience. Conscience, they say, is a very expensive thing to keep. Peel certainly
kept one.'[80]

In many respects, Peel remained in the position of the conscientious proto-Liberal
statesman until his papers were opened up to public scrutiny, after being deposited in
the British Museum (subsequently the British Library) in the 1920s. Thereafter,
George Kitson Clark and Norman Gash began the process of trying to 'relocate Peel
in a stream of civilised Conservative values' – a tradition which has lately been revived
by Douglas Hurd who studied under Kitson Clark at Trinity College, Cambridge.[81]
That this process ran against the current of 'received' historical opinion on Peel (both
Liberal and Conservative inspired) may be judged by Michael Bentley's mature
assessment on the subject:

> Peel would spend the first three-quarters of the twentieth century professing
> Liberalism to his bone-headed party and then preferring to put the country's
> interests before theirs or his own. It was a perspective that unified his life in a
> satisfying way, and one that helped to unify also Gladstone's – much the more
> significant achievement historiographically.

To that extent, Kitson Clark and Gash may be considered as 'revisionists', challenging
the accepted (Liberal) envisioning of Peel by attempting to reclaim him for the
Conservative Party.[82] A further (residual) irony may be the fact that so proud a
Lancastrian as Peel owed so much, in historical terms, to the collective labours of
more than one Yorkshire man.[83]

* * *

The attempt to construct a literary monument to Peel compared unfavourably with
Gladstone – whose official biography (by John Morley) was completed within five
years of his death – and Monypenny and Buckle's six-volume *Life* of Disraeli, which
began publication within thirty years of its subject's demise.[84] The consequence was
that Peel's memory and legacy came to be dominated by a series of intermediate
appraisals founded on little more than was already available on public record. These
were, as Peter Ghosh notes, often the outcome of editorial commissions rather than
authorial *pietas* towards Peel.[85] Foreign observers, notably Francois Guizot, also stole
a march on their English counterparts. Guizot's *Memoirs of Sir Robert Peel* (1857)
were dismissed by Macaulay, who felt momentarily impelled to write his own
account of Peel before abandoning the idea just as quickly.[86] Likewise, Gladstone
refused an invitation to review it for *The Quarterly Review*: 'it leads me over tender
ground, & naturally prompts a distribution of praise and blame in accounting for
our present political evils', he observed. 'At the present moment looking upon

dishonour as the great characteristic of Lord Palmerston's government, I would not willingly run the *risk* of wounding Lord Derby or any friend of his.'[87]

Similar sensitivities to the prospect of 'Conservative Reunion' had not dissuaded Disraeli, six years earlier, from inserting a character-sketch of Peel in his biography of *Lord George Bentinck*. It was an integral part of the biography but one which, considering the author's own relation to the subject, cost him a good deal of care and attention:

> He read me passages from a life, or account of the public career of George Bentinck. He said it had occupied many months of his time, especially a character of Peel, which 'had almost turned his hair grey'. He had composed it over and over again, not on paper, but in his memory: and was at last satisfied with the result. He read it out: but I think it was not then complete, or has been since altered.[88]

Disraeli's portrayal of Peel (which both Greville and *The Times* considered fair) has stood the test of time remarkably well.[89] The author was not above 'puffing' his own literary compositions, modestly observing – in the preface to the eighth edition of the biography, published in 1871, at the height of Gladstone's first ministry – that it remained superior to any portrayal of Peel he had subsequently seen.[90]

Meanwhile, Mahon (who inherited his father's title as Earl Stanhope in 1855) and Cardwell continued to agonise over their proposed course of action. 'I am by no means so much impressed as you are with the utility or advantage to us of compiling from various sources a summary of the events in the life of Sir Robert Peel,' Stanhope remarked in February 1856. 'But the question for me is only whether you being desirous through yourself or your kinsman Mr Parker to undertake such a compilation I ought to interpose any obstacle in the way.'[91] The 'kinsman' in question was Charles Stuart Parker, Cardwell's son-in-law and one-time private secretary, who was subsequently (after another interminable delay[92]) to assume responsibility for producing the standard triple-decker edition of Peel's papers.[93] However, Parker proved himself to be 'a mere compiler of documents he did not always understand or accurately transcribe' and his election as Liberal MP for Perthshire and Perth (under Gladstone's patronage) betrayed the political bias he brought to bear in relation to his subject. Indeed, it was Parker (encouraged in his task by Peel's son, Arthur, who became Speaker of the House of Commons) who completed the 'Liberal embalming' of Peel during the 1890s.[94] Little wonder that he enjoyed the active co-operation and assistance of 'The Grand Old Man' himself.[95]

However, for three decades – between 1856 and 1886 – the prospect of an edition of Peel's papers was put to one side whilst the trustees pursued the idea of producing an official biography of Peel, based on the full extent of his surviving papers. The man entrusted with the task was Goldwin Smith, Regius Professor of Modern History at Oxford. Smith combined all the academic credentials of the University establishment with the politics of the 'Manchester School' and a naked aversion to Peel's contemporary critics in the Conservative Party – a telling enough indication of his approach to the subject.[96] The first fruits of his proposed study (an article for the *Encyclopedia Britannica* in 1858) drew the critical attention of Cardwell and Parker. On reviewing the text, they informed Smith that they would like to see three alterations made – a reference to Peel's 'dry, sarcastic humour', more attention to the fact that 'almost every one of the great practical improvements of our days, either originated with him, or obtained its realization from him' and more stress on 'the personal influence of Sir Robert Peel' which, in their view, 'contributed more than any other circumstance to solve the Duke [of Wellington's] enigma 'How is the Queen's Government to be carried on?':

> His policy announced in 1835 has been the policy of all succeeding administrations, & the tone which he gave to the Debates, has been followed by all succeeding ministers, i.e. in the main … If I am right in two of my principal suggestions above tendered … can it be doubted whether, or no, he was a model of Statesmanship for a practical age, and for a Reformed Parliament?

In making these suggestions, Cardwell clearly had in mind a refutation of Thomas Doubleday's study, *The Political Life of the Right Honourable Sir Robert Peel* (2 Volumes, 1856), of which he openly disapproved.[97]

In response, Goldwin Smith remarked that he had drawn Peel:

> no greater than I really believed him to be – He was quite great enough to bear to be painted 'with his wrinkles' as Cromwell said. The inclines which a man gains over his own defects in rising to greatness are quite as hard and quite as interesting as those which he gains over opponents and circumstances. Nothing is more worthless in the age of the next generation than a biography which does not show how these victories were won … I hope the biography of Peel will be written in the strictest spirit of historical truth; and I can only think & believe if it was so written it would not only be a doubly interesting book, but a high lesson of political honor and patriotism at a time when it is much needed.[98]

In spite of these high ideals, Goldwin Smith's prevarication prevented such an account from maturing from his pen.[99] When he accepted an invitation to assume a chair at Cornell University in 1868 the commission was abandoned. 'To speak frankly [Stanhope told Cardwell] I am sorry that we ever allowed that gentleman any access to our papers … within these last two or three years he appears to have come out as the most extreme of the extreme:'

> I think it probable that he would have done great injustice to the memory of our departed chief if he had treated of it at length; & I am glad therefore to conclude from the expression in your letter 'bidding farewell to his connection with us' that he had relinquished or at all events postponed his design & is now intent on American objects. In these he will be more at home.[100]

Stanhope's frustration was understandable. In twelve years, Goldwin Smith had only completed about eighty pages of the biography down to Peel's assumption of the Chief Secretaryship of Ireland (the period at which the mass of Peel's surviving papers commenced). In this he had been assisted by T.J. Blackford who worked on the Duke of Newcastle's Education Commission in the mid-1860s.[101] This association ended in mutual recrimination – whether Blackford had a claim of £100 to £150 on the Peel Trust Fund or whether Goldwin Smith had already settled this in payment for his services. Nevertheless, writing from Toronto thirteen years later, in complaint at John Morley's 'unjust' treatment of Peel in his *Life of Cobden* (1881), Goldwin Smith had the temerity to observe: 'It is about time that a Life of Peel should appear. Misrepresentations gather round his memory. I trust the papers are in safe keeping, and will never drift into Bentinckian or Beaconsfieldian hands.'[102]

* * *

In December 2006 the Conservative Party called for Peel to be included in the schools history curriculum as one of the twelve most influential Britons of all time, together with Saint Columba, Alfred the Great, Henry II, Simon de Montfort, James IV of Scotland, Sir Thomas Gresham, Oliver Cromwell, Robert Clive, Isaac Newton, Dame Millicent Garrett Fawcett and Aneurin Bevan.[103] It was a remarkable transformation in fortunes for a man not normally placed at the service of the party. Unlike Disraeli – who had done as much as Peel to keep the Conservatives out of office in the mid-nineteenth century – the party raised no institutional outworks to its fallen leader. The Primrose League functioned effectively from the mid-1880s to the mid-1930s as a beacon for Beaconsfieldism whilst the invocation of Disraeli's name and example by Stanley Baldwin, Winston Churchill and Edward Heath (to name but three) burnished his posthumous utility to the party. By contrast, Peel found himself more admired than emulated.[104] There was no 'Peel Society' established until 1979 (the sesquicentenary of the foundation of the Metropolitan Police Force). In any case, the society – with its strong foundations in Tamworth, external links to surviving family members and broad political patronage – has not proved to be rooted in, or motivated by, the aim of serving the political ends of the Conservative Party.[105]

At the start of the twenty-first century, we remember Peel for breaking down what he built up (notably his 1842 Corn Law and, more controversially, the Conservative Party itself) or amending what he found (for example, in Ireland and at the Home Office) as well as for the unintended consequences of some of his achievements (not least in respect of the Income Tax and Bank Charter Act). From his youth, Peel was offered up on the altar of Pittite pieties to the future service of the nation.[106] To that extent, he has become part of the heroic genealogy of political leaders stretching thenceforth from the Younger Pitt by way of Canning down to Gladstone and the triumph of a progressive strand of Conservatism and/or conservative strand of Liberalism. To designate him a false 'Tory', a renegade 'Conservative', a 'Liberal Tory', a 'Liberal Conservative' or a proto-Gladstonian Liberal, is to play, semantically, with the career of a shrewd, ambitious and complex political operator and try and give it helpful characterisation within a sometimes limited political vocabulary. Peel's own outlook and views combined a rigid adherence to certain fixed principles – his Protestantism, his executive outlook, his attachment to Bullionist theory and his growing commitment to the tenets of Free Trade – within an overall process of self-education as to the means of furthering them. As Edward Stanley shrewdly observed:

> The high strain of Liberalism which some of those who admired his conduct in 1846 were pleased to attribute to him, was, so far as I can judge from observation and from the testimony of his living friends, entirely the creation of their fancy. I do not believe he would willingly have enlarged the franchise: nor dealt with the Church: nor yet dared to grapple with the question of a non-sectarian education. The whole bent of his mind was Conservative ... and if in his later days he ever held language of a contrary tendency – as in the compliment to Cobden – I conceive such phrases to have been momentary ebullitions of wounded pride than expressions of his real feeling.[107]

Peel's political education in itself reflects some of the contradictions inherent in early nineteenth-century British politics (whether 'Conservative' or 'Liberal'). Unfortunately, the corollary was always that other men must pay the price for Peel's prior 'ignorance' and subsequent 'enlightenment' by conforming to his supposedly superior reading of the political situation. As one critic put it, Peel's 'only discoveries have been, that he had previously been in error'. His justification for this was always framed by reference to a posterity which he felt would ultimately vindicate him.[108] This was particularly necessary, given that Peel's political journey involved the repudiation of previously held viewpoints and an unwillingness (or inability) to dispel the certainties of those who believed him a steadfast advocate of their cause or the doubts of those who feared his fidelity on the issue at hand.

Peel's was a heroic example of political achievement in a context whose structures (or, occasionally, lack of them) still allowed a minister to act the part of a second Sir Robert Walpole – the historical precedent which most appealed to Peel's imagination.[109] It was not an example which could be repeated often without destabilising the very basis of the system he sought to uphold. In conversation with Lord John Russell in 1875, Cardwell:

> understood him to refer to a conversation he had had with Lord Lyndhurst, in which they had agreed that Sir Robert was not to be considered entitled to the epithet 'Great' but that he was entitled to the praise of having been of all party leaders the most entirely devoted to the public good.[110]

Subsequent political leaders have faced the sterner challenge of building upon his success whilst avoiding the long-term political damage which he inflicted. Gladstone, who became Peel's political legatee (by default as well as design), emulated both his example and his methods, damaging the Liberal Party as effectively over 'Home Rule' (in 1886) as Peel had damaged the Conservative Party over the Corn Laws four decades earlier. Nevertheless, in the opinion of one well-placed contemporary diarist, Lewis Harcourt, 'the moral intoxication of present power' outweighed 'all considerations of posthumous fame' insofar as Gladstone was concerned.[111] To that extent, Gladstone's priorities were different from Peel's. Moreover, as Gash himself conceded, 'few party politicians can work within such simple terms of reference' as an appeal to posterity. 'For them the approval of subsequent generations is an insubstantial reward; posterity has no votes at the ballot-box or in the lobbies. It may be observed on the other hand that for a determined and self-willed man the appeal to posterity has one decided advantage; the verdict comes too late to affect his action.'[112] The same sentiment was expressed, with more than usual clarity, by Lord Ashley, whose habitual tendency to self-flagellate himself in words in the privacy of his diary was only redeemed by his genuine concern for the welfare of others. On reviewing reactions to Peel's death, Ashley observed:

> the same minds that have recorded the panegyrics [to Peel] will, as soon as the peculiar shock is over, review his course with critical "justice", and qualify the praise that was uttered in the moment of sympathy. Human applause is very tempting; but woe to the man who confides in it; there is no secure and fruitful honour, but that 'which cometh from God only'.[113]

Given the persistent suspicions to which Peel's political character and methods gave rise, it is not surprising why he was fixated with issues of reputation, consistency, honour and posthumous judgement, for these remained his only hope of future salvation. Peel did not merely hope for his reward in heaven – but in history.[114]

NOTES

Chapter One

1 For accessible short studies of Peel, see Edward G. Power, *Robert Peel, Free Trade and the Corn Laws* (1975); Paul Adelman, *Peel and the Conservative Party, 1830–50* (1989); Eric J. Evans, *Sir Robert Peel: Statesmanship, Power and Party* (1991); Terence A. Jenkins, *Sir Robert Peel* (1999); Graham Goodlad, *Peel* (2005).

2 Douglas Hurd's recent (2007) biography of Peel is the first notable attempt at rehabilitation by a practising Conservative politician. It represents an admiring political memorial.

3 See Richard A. Gaunt, 'Disraeli, Peel and the Corn Laws: the making of a conservative reputation', *The Historian*, 97, 2008, 30–33.

4 The standard biography is by Norman Gash in two volumes: *Mr Secretary Peel: The Life of Sir Robert Peel before 1830*, [originally published in 1961] 2nd Edition (1985) and *Sir Robert Peel: The Life of Sir Robert Peel after 1830*, [originally published in 1972] 2nd Edition (1986). For an abridged version, see his *Peel* (1976).

5 William Thomas, *The Quarrel of Macaulay and Croker. Politics and History in the Age of Reform* (Oxford, 2000), pp.95–7; on Peel's lack of knowledge of the world, see Christopher Hibbert, *Greville's England. Selections from the Diaries of Charles Greville, 1818–1860* (1981), pp.122–3.

6 Something observable in such seemingly trivial incidences as the fact that reviews of Lord Hurd's biography were frequently illustrated by a picture of the third (as opposed to the second) Sir Robert Peel: *The Daily Mail*, 22 June 2007, p.68; *Literary Review*, June 2007, p.5. In his lifetime, the assassin Daniel McNaughtan managed to confuse Peel's private secretary, Edward Drummond, with the Prime Minister – thereby saving the premier's life: see Richard Moran, *Knowing Right From Wrong. The Insanity Defense of Daniel McNaughtan* (New York, 1981).

7 For two cases in point, from the Peel-Croker relationship, see Louis J. Jennings, (editor), *The Correspondence and Diaries of the late Right Honorable John Wilson Croker*, 2-Volume edition (New York, 1884), I, 346; II, 296–7.

8 See below, chapter 8.

9 See Richard Salter, *Peel, Gladstone and Disraeli* (1991), p.5. The 'false Tory' premise is the key motif of *Reflections Suggested by the career of the late Premier* (1847).

10 Arthur Aspinall, 'Extracts from Lord Hatherton's Diary', *Parliamentary Affairs*, XVII/4, 1964, 386; cf. *A Letter on the present state of Ireland to...Sir Robert Peel...By an Irish Catholic* (1846), pp.29–30.

11 See the comments of *The Times*, 21 March 1844, p.4 on Peel's habitual tendency to conceal his intended line of conduct (which went beyond mere political stratagem). For Peel's defence of his policy, see Sandon Hall, Harrowby Manuscripts, XVIII, ff.106–8, Peel to

Lord Sandon, 21 January [1837?]. For later, conflicting, interpretations of Peel's conduct (much influenced by the political context), see *Blackwood's Edinburgh Magazine,* LV, January 1844, 109; LX, August 1846, 252–3.

12 See George Kitson Clark, *Peel* (1936) and Robert Blake *The Conservative Party from Peel to Churchill* (1970) for summations of their viewpoint.

13 For an attempt to reconcile the two viewpoints, see John Morrow, 'The Paradox of Peel as Carlylean Hero', *Historical Journal,* 40, 1997, 107 n.35. Hilton's work, and critiques of it, forms a central focus in subsequent chapters of this study.

14 Jonathan Parry, 'Lord John Russell, First Earl Russell' in Robert Eccleshall and Graham Walker, (editors), *Biographical Dictionary of British Prime Ministers* (1998), pp.151–61; *idem.,* 'Past and future in the later career of Lord John Russell' in T.C.W. Blanning and David Cannadine, (editors), *History and Biography: Essays in Honour of Derek Beales* (Cambridge, 1996), pp.142–72; Paul Scherer, *Lord John Russell* (1999); Angus Hawkins, *The Forgotten Prime Minister, The 14th Earl of Derby, Ascent, 1799–1851* (Oxford, 2007); Neville Thompson, *Wellington after Waterloo* (1986).

15 A theme I will be developing in my *Conservative Politics in the Age of Reform, 1780–1850.*

16 See Anna Gambles, 'Rethinking the Politics of Protection: Conservatism and the Corn Laws, 1830–1852', *English Historical Review,* CXIII, 1998, 928–52; *idem., Protection and Politics. Conservative Economic Discourse, 1815–1852* (Woodbridge, 1999).

17 Norman Gash, *Peel and Posterity* (Tamworth, 2000), p.9. Also see Gash, *Mr Secretary Peel,* pp.viii–xv.

18 Donald Read, *Peel and the Victorians* (Oxford, 1987).

19 Read noted this fact but did not dwell upon it: *ibid.,* p.2. For graphic portrayals associating Peel with these achievements, see *The Illustrated London News,* 13 July 1850, front cover; Power, *Peel, Free Trade and the Corn Laws,* pp.98–9.

20 A full (but by no means complete) bibliography of writings about Peel may be found in Leonard Cowie, *Sir Robert Peel, 1788–1850. A Bibliography* (Westport, Connecticut, 1996).

21 See Charles Richmond and Paul Smith, (editors), *The Self–Fashioning of Disraeli, 1818–1851* (Cambridge, 1998).

22 *Blackwood's Edinburgh Magazine,* LXIV, November 1848, 633.

23 George Henry Francis, *Sir Robert Peel as Statesman and Orator* (1846), pp.16–17.

24 *The Illustrated London News,* 30 September 1843, p.211.

25 A facet noted by two commentators. James Grant, *Random Recollections of the House of Commons* (1836), pp.112, 114; The Seventh Duke of Wellington, (editor), *Wellington and His Friends* (1965), p.129. Also see Dudley W.R. Bahlman, (editor), *The Diary of Sir Edward Walter Hamilton, 1885–1906* (Hull, 1993), p.82.

26 *Blackwood's Edinburgh Magazine,* LXVIII, September 1850, 371; W.M. Torrens, *Memoirs of the Right Honourable William Second Viscount Melbourne,* 2 Volumes (1878), II, 53. For examples of Peel's carefully prepared remarks, see *The Times,* 24 May 1841, p.5; George Otto Trevelyan, *The Life and Letters of Lord Macaulay* (Oxford, 1978), I, 177–8; Magdalen Goffin, (editor), *The Diaries of Absalom Watkin, A Manchester Man, 1787–1861* (Stroud, 1993), p.264.

27 Gash, *Mr Secretary Peel,* p.45.

28 William D. Rubinstein, *Who Were the Rich? A biographical directory of British wealth-holders. Volume One, 1809–1839* (2009), p.319; Roland G. Thorne, (editor), *The History of Parliament. The Commons, 1790–1820,* 5 Volumes (1986), IV, 745.

29 Gash, *Mr Secretary Peel,* chapter 2; James Marshall and Marie-Louise Osborn Collection, Beinecke Rare Book and Manuscript Library, Yale University, 11528, Sir Robert Peel to Richard Davies, 17 December 1808.

30 Sir Lawrence Peel, *A Sketch of the Life and Character of Sir Robert Peel* (1860), pp.48–9; cf. Peter Ghosh, 'Gladstone and Peel' in Peter Ghosh and Lawrence Goldman, (editors),

Politics & Culture in Victorian Britain. Essays in Memory of Colin Matthew (Oxford, 2006), p.47 n.10.

31 Jean Baptiste Honoré Raymond Capefigue, 'Character of Sir Robert Peel' in William Cooke Taylor, *The Life and Times of Sir Robert Peel*, III.2 (1851), pp.534, 542; cf. *The Times*, 13 October 1845, p.6; *Punch*, XII, January–June 1847, 239.

32 Rubinstein, *Who were the rich?*, pp.318–9; *The Times*, 12 June 1830, p.5; *The Economist*, 23 May 1846, 665.

33 *The Economist*, 29 November 1845, 1192. For a satirical attempt to provide an appropriate 'coat of arms' for Peel, see *Punch*, XIII, July–December 1847, 160. Conversely, Hatherton considered Peel's 1841 cabinet too 'lordly' and lacked few members (including Peel) who could strictly be regarded as 'commoners': Aspinall, 'Hatherton', *Parliamentary Affairs*, XVII/3, 263.

34 For Peel as cotton spinner, *The Times*, 11 October 1828, p.3. Drayton Manor was demolished in the 1930s and became a popular theme park and leisure attraction. 'Peel would not have relished the irony': Goodlad, *Peel*, p.40.

35 Thomas, *Quarrel*, pp.95–7. cf. Ghosh, 'Gladstone and Peel', p.49 n.19. For Croker's importance as Peel's unofficial cultural attaché, see *Croker Papers*, II, 73–5, 124–5, 135.

36 Francis Bamford and the Seventh Duke of Wellington, (editors), *The Journal of Mrs Arbuthnot, 1820–1832*, 2 Volumes (1950), II, 187; cf. 235.

37 On Peel's public/private dilemma, see Ghosh, 'Gladstone and Peel', p.48.

38 'I could not help thinking that, after all, Duke and H.R.H., everybody, and everything were, for the moment, under him – he is master, the son of a cotton-spinner': Lady Dorchester, (editor), *Recollections of a long life by Lord Broughton (John Cam Hobhouse). With additional extracts from his private diaries*, 6 Volumes (1910–11), VI, 126–7.

39 Captain Henry Martin, *A Personal Sketch of the late lamented Sir Robert Peel, as a Parliamentary Speaker and Party Leader in the British House of Commons &c* (Hamburg, 1850), pp.17–18 (and see p.22); cf. Grant, *Recollections*, p.112.

40 Edward Pearce, (editor), with Deanna Pearce, *The Diaries of Charles Greville* (2005), p.142; Virginia Surtees, *A Second Self. The Letters of Harriet Granville, 1810–1845* (Wilton, 1990), p.271; *Broughton Diary*, V, 198; VI, 89; Aspinall, 'Hatherton', *Parliamentary Affairs*, XVII/3, 262.

41 Christopher Hibbert, *Queen Victoria in her Letters and Journals* (Stroud, 2000), p.50.

42 Pearce, *Greville*, p.204.

43 The Peels retained a Lancashire estate at Oswaldtwistle, which was yielding £4,000 per annum in 1847: *The Times*, 19 April 1847, p.6.

44 In addition to the entries in H.C.G. Matthew and Brian Harrison, (editors), *The Oxford Dictionary of National Biography*, 60 Volumes (Oxford, 2004), see Thorne, *History of Parliament*, IV, 740–50 and Grant, *Recollections*, p.119.

45 *Two Letters to Sir Robert Peel, on his proposed Banking measures; by an ex-M.P.* (1844), p.5 footnote.

46 Willard Bissell Pope, (editor), *The Diary of Benjamin Robert Haydon*, 5 Volumes (Harvard, 1960–3), III, 498–500; IV, 472; V, 130–1. See Frank Herrmann, 'Peel and Solly. Two nineteenth-century art collectors and their sources of supply', *Journal of the History of Collections*, 3/1, 1991, 89–96; J. Mordaunt Crook, 'Sir Robert Peel. Patron of the Arts', *History Today*, 16, January 1966, 3–11; R. Walker, 'Sir Robert Peel, Patron of the Arts', *Apollo*, 52, 1950, 16–18.

47 Third Lord Colchester, (editor), *Political Diary of Edward Law, Lord Ellenborough, 1828–30*, 2 Volumes (1881), I, 175; James Anthony Froude, *Thomas Carlyle. A History of His Life in London, 1834–1881*, 2 Volumes (1884), II, 44; Hibbert, *Greville's England*, p.116; Northamptonshire Record Office, X1384, Diaries of George Agar Ellis, 3 April 1824.

48 M.R.D. Foot and H.C.G. Matthew, (editors), *The Gladstone Diaries*, 14 Volumes (Oxford, 1968–94), IV, 49.

49 Nottingham University Manuscripts Department, Newcastle of Clumber Collection, Ne C 5289/2–3, Peel to [Newcastle], c.October 1843.

50 *The Times,* 26 April 1847, p.6; *The Economist,* 1 May 1847, 503; 8 May 1847, 531; *Croker Papers,* II, 307.

51 *Punch,* XII, January–June 1847, 44. The National Gallery acquired 77 of the 130 paintings in the Peel Collection (for £75,000) in 1871: see *Gladstone Diaries,* VII, 491.

52 Southampton University Library, Broadlands Papers, Shaftesbury Diaries, SHA/PD/1, f.83, 6 May 1834.

53 The National Archives, Kew, Ellenborough Diaries, PRO 30/12/28/5, p.252, 3 April 1835.

54 *Punch,* VIII, January–June 1845, 267. Joseph Mallord William Turner (1775–1851) was a famous English Romantic landscape and marine artist.

55 *Gladstone Diaries,* X, 443; John Brooke and Mary Sorensen, (editors), *Prime Ministers Papers: W.E. Gladstone,* 4 Volumes (1971–81), II, 89. In 1843, Peel told Gladstone that he judged a speech according to its 'direct influence upon his voting supporters, the good aspect in argument towards the Opposition for debate, and the general relation to public opinion and the character of the Administration out of doors': *ibid.,* 194.

56 Francis, *Peel as Statesman and Orator,* pp.12–13. Lawrence Peel thought his cousin came first in the second rank of orators: *Sketch,* pp.300–1. *Blackwood's Edinburgh Magazine* felt the same: XXV, March 1829, 285. For other contemporary observations on Peel's oratory, see Benjamin Disraeli, *Lord George Bentinck: A Political Biography* (New Brunswick, New Jersey, 1998), pp.205–6; Angus Hawkins and John Powell, (editors), *The Journal of John Wodehouse, First Earl of Kimberley for 1862–1902,* Royal Historical Society, Camden, 5th Series, 9 (1997), p.46.

57 Brian Harrison and Patricia Hollis, (editors), *Robert Lowery. Radical and Chartist* (1979), p.140. For a positive appraisal of Peel as an extra-parliamentary speaker, see Henry Jephson, *The Platform. Its Rise and Progress,* 2 Volumes (New York, 1968), II, 162, 173–86, 307–9, 597 n.1.

58 The misfortunes of other parliamentary speakers could also provoke fits of laughter: M.G. Wiebe *et al,* (editors), *Benjamin Disraeli: Letters,* 7 Volumes to date (Toronto, 1982–2004), IV, 1214 n.8.

59 Grant, *Recollections,* p.115. Gladstone considered that ministers were more concerned with these issues than was generally realised: Brooke and Sorensen, *Gladstone,* II, 131.

60 *Croker Papers,* I, 69–71; Bawa Satinder Singh, (editor), *The Letters of the First Viscount Hardinge of Lahore to Lady Hardinge and Sir Walter and Lady James, 1844–1847,* Royal Historical Society, Camden, 4th Series, 32, (1986), p.88 and n.174; William Cooke Taylor (edited by Patrick Maume), *Reminiscences of Daniel O'Connell During the Agitations of the Veto, Emancipation and Repeal* (Dublin, 2005), pp.42–3; Historical Manuscripts Commission, *Report on the Manuscripts of Earl Bathurst* (1923), pp.385–6. Also see Patrick M. Geoghegan, *King Dan. The Rise of Daniel O'Connell, 1775–1829* (Dublin, 2008), chapter 8.

61 *Broughton Diary,* IV, 110–12. Henry Hardinge made something of a career of being a 'second', having performed that office in the famous encounter between the Duke of Wellington and Lord Winchilsea, at Battersea Fields, in March 1829.

62 Lord Stanley thought Peel was remarkably 'thin skinned' – something Gladstone knew for himself: Brooke and Sorensen, *Gladstone,* I, 74; II, 131.

63 *Croker Papers,* II, 118.

64 The National Archives, Kew, Cardwell MSS, PRO 30/48/53, ff.114–16, Cardwell to Goldwin Smith, 3 March 1864.

65 John Vincent, (editor), *Disraeli, Derby and the Conservative Party: the Political Journals of Lord Stanley, 1849–69* (Hassocks, 1978), p.201. Peel's brother challenged Disraeli to a duel during the same period: *Disraeli Letters,* IV, 1482 and n.2.

66 Brooke and Sorensen, *Gladstone,* II, 219; *Punch,* VI, January–June 1844, 116, 130.

67 *Broughton Diary,* V, 50; cf. 134–5. Peel's occasionally witty anecdotes were repeatedly relayed – an indication of their rarity: see *ibid.,* VI, 87; Earl of Stanhope, (editor), *Conversations with Wellington* (1998), p.190.

68 *Disraeli Letters,* II, 459; cf. Disraeli, *Bentinck,* pp.202–3.

69 Michael Bentley, *Politics without Democracy, 1815–1914,* 2nd edition (1996), p.59.

70 *Mrs Arbuthnot's Journal,* II, 423; cf. 172, 187, 189–90, 196, 200, 311–12, 316, 331, 355–6, 372–4, 377, 381–2, 398, 401, 411, 415–16. For Greville's dissatisfaction with Peel, in the same period, see Pearce, *Greville,* p.74.

71 R.J. Olney and Julia Melvin, (editors), *Prime Ministers Papers: Wellington, Political Correspondence, Volume II: 1834–1835* (1986), p.561.

72 Shaftesbury Diaries, SHA/PD/2, ff.56, 78, 12 July, 22 October 1841; Vincent, *Derby Diaries,* p.3. G.H. Francis observed that Peel's 'cold reserve repels political friendship': *Peel as Statesman and Orator,* p.5 (and the ensuing discussion to p.10).

73 Asa Briggs, (editor), *Gladstone's Boswell. Late Victorian Conversations* (Brighton, 1984), p.117; cf. *Hamilton Diary,* pp.57–8. Gladstone observed at first-hand that Peel was not good in large parties: *Gladstone Diaries,* II, 217.

74 Asa Briggs, 'Sir Robert Peel' in Herbert Van Thal, (editor), *The Prime Ministers. Volume I. From Sir Robert Walpole to Sir Robert Peel* (1974), p.377.

75 Brooke and Sorensen, *Gladstone,* II, 172. Gladstone told Peel, in 1846, that his administration had not been a Cabinet government but a government of 'the heads of departments each in communication with you' (to which Peel assented): *ibid.,* III, 29.

76 *Broughton Diary,* III, 260.

77 Arthur Aspinall, (editor), *The Correspondence of Charles Arbuthnot,* Royal Historical Society, Camden, 3rd Series, LXV, (1941), 237; cf. *Broughton Diary,* VI, 268; Brooke and Sorensen, *Gladstone,* III, 28; John Morley, *The Life of Richard Cobden,* 2 Volumes (1908), I, 427–8.

78 Brooke and Sorensen, *Gladstone,* II, 260, 279; Arthur Christopher Benson and Viscount Esher, (editors), *The Letters of Queen Victoria. A Selection from Her Majesty's Correspondence between the years 1837–1861,* 3 Volumes (Honolulu, 2002), II, 35.

79 And a reputedly 'big head' needed an equally 'big hat': see Christopher Hibbert, *Captain Gronow. His Reminiscences of Regency and Victorian Life, 1810–1860* (1991), p.87.

80 Pearce, *Greville,* p.113; Arthur Aspinall, (editor), *Three Early Nineteenth Century Diaries* (1952), pp.253, 258; cf. *Broughton Diary,* IV, 228.

81 *Punch,* VI, January–June 1844, 260; VII, July–December 1844, 25, 100. For Peel as an actor, see *ibid.,* VIII, January–June 1845, 37; *The Times,* 11 August 1845, p.4.

82 Trevelyan, *Macaulay,* II, 212 n.1; Shaftesbury Diaries, SHA/PD/2, f.61, 28 August 1841.

83 *The Economist,* 16 March 1844, 596.

84 Brooke and Sorensen, *Gladstone,* I, 128; cf. Briggs, *Gladstone's Boswell,* p.59.

85 *The Illustrated London News,* 13 July 1850, p.46; cf. *Letter to the Right Honourable Sir Robert Peel, Bart. On Free Trade and Finance By a Member of the Middle Temple* (1844), pp.4, 25–6.

86 David Bebbington, *The Mind of Gladstone: Religion, Homer, and Politics* (Oxford, 2004); Michael Bentley, *Lord Salisbury's World. Conservative Environments in Late-Victorian Britain* (Cambridge, 2001). For the new turn in Disraelian scholarship, see n.21 above.

87 For one advocate of Peel's 'strong egotistical desire of power and fame', see *Reflections suggested,* p.84; cf. *An Answer to the arguments of the Right Hon. Robert Peel in favour of further concessions to the Catholics* (1829), p.52.

Chapter Two

1 William Cooke Taylor, (edited by Patrick Maume), *Reminiscences of Daniel O'Connell During the Agitations of the Veto, Emancipation and Repeal* (Dublin, 2005), pp.28–9.

2 John Brooke and Mary Sorensen, (editors), *Prime Ministers Papers: W.E. Gladstone,* 4 Volumes (1971–81), III, 77.

3 Arthur Aspinall, *The Later Correspondence of George III,* 5 Volumes (Cambridge, 1962–70), V, 277, letter 3876 n. As a pocket borough, Peel felt no compulsion to visit his constituency.

4 The principal sources for Peel's time as Chief Secretary are: Norman Gash, *Mr Secretary Peel: The Life of Sir Robert Peel before 1830,* 2nd Edition (1985); Robert Carl Shipkey, *Robert Peel's Irish Policy: 1812–1846* (1987); Brian Jenkins, 'The Chief Secretary' in D.G. Boyce and Alan O'Day, (editors), *Defenders of the Union. A Survey of British and Irish Unionism since 1801* (2001), pp.39–64; *idem, Era of Emancipation: British Government of Ireland, 1812–1830* (Kingston and Montreal, 1988).

5 Of the 81 Chief Secretaries between 1566 and 1818, ten served for six years (eight of these before 1680). By contrast, nine Chief Secretaries served in the period from May 1801 to August 1812; Stanley H. Palmer, *Police and Protest in England and Ireland, 1780–1850* (Cambridge, 1988), p.672 n.93. Peel's son and heir, Robert (the third baronet [1822–95]) served as Chief Secretary from 1861–5.

6 Norman Gash, 'Peel and Ireland: A Perennial Problem' in Peter Catterall, (editor), *Britain, 1815–1867* (1994), pp.68–9.

7 Jenkins, 'The Chief Secretary', pp.43–5; K. Theodore Hoppen, 'An Incorporating Union? British Politicians and Ireland 1800–1830', *English Historical Review,* CXXIII, April 2008, 338.

8 Lewis Melville, (editor), *The Huskisson Papers* (1931), p.118; Charles Duke Yonge, *The Life and Administration of Robert Banks, Second Earl of Liverpool, K.G.,* 3 Volumes (1868), I, 425–6. Henry Wellesley regretted that Charles Arbuthnot had not been appointed Chief Secretary: Arthur Aspinall, (editor), *The Correspondence of Charles Arbuthnot,* Royal Historical Society, Camden, 3rd Series, LXV, (1941), p.8.

9 Historical Manuscripts Commission, *Report on the Manuscripts of Earl Bathurst* (1923), p.193; cf. Lord Colchester, (editor), *The Diary and Correspondence of Charles Abbot, Lord Colchester,* 3 Volumes (1861), II, 404.

10 Hoppen, 'An Incorporating Union?', 339, 348.

11 *The Hatherton Diaries. The Diaries of the First Lord Hatherton. Extracts from the personal diary, between the years 1817–1862 of Edward Walhouse Littleton afterwards The First Lord Hatherton, 1791–1863* (Privately printed, n.d.), entry for 15 October 1818; cf. Shipkey, *Peel's Irish Policy,* p.507.

12 *The Times,* 29 July 1818, p.3.

13 Louis J. Jennings, (editor), *The Correspondence and Diaries of the late Right Honorable John Wilson Croker,* 2-Volume edition (New York, 1884), I, 106.

14 *Colchester Diary,* II, 588–9.

15 *Croker Papers,* I, 42; Sandon Hall, Harrowby Papers, XIV, f.104, Bathurst to Harrowby, 25 November 1821; Christopher Hibbert, (editor), *Captain Gronow. His Reminiscences of Regency and Victorian Life, 1810–1860* (1991), p.241.

16 John Prest, 'Sir Robert Peel', in H.C.G. Matthew and Brian Harrison, (editors), *The Oxford Dictionary of National Biography,* 60 Volumes (Oxford, 2004), XLIII, 408.

17 Jenkins, 'The Chief Secretary', p.45; Robert Carl Shipkey, 'Problems of Irish Patronage during the Chief Secretaryship of Robert Peel, 1812–1818', *Historical Journal,* X, 1967, especially 44, 55. Peel's strong control over patronage may explain the persistence of his Irish 'friends' after his departure from office: *The Hatherton Diaries,* entry for 28 June 1820.

18 For Peel and the Irish press, see Yonge, *Liverpool,* I, 445; Arthur Aspinall, *Politics and the Press, c.1780–1850* (1949), especially pp.117, 141; Shipkey, *Peel's Irish Policy,* pp.50–2, 165–8.

19 *ibid.*, pp.97, 102.

20 *ibid.*, pp.3–5; Hoppen, 'An Incorporating Union?', 335. For Peel and Gregory, see Lady Gregory, (editor), *Mr Gregory's Letter-Box* (1898).

21 See Roland G. Thorne, (editor), *The History of Parliament. The Commons, 1790–1820*, 5 Volumes (1986), IV, 745–8.

22 F.C. Mather, (editor), *Chartism and Society* (1980), p.58.

23 Arthur Aspinall, (editor), 'Extracts from Lord Hatherton's Diary', *Parliamentary Affairs*, XVII/4, 1964, 378–9.

24 Jean Baptiste Honoré Raymond Capefigue, 'Character of Sir Robert Peel' in William Cooke Taylor, *The Life and Times of Sir Robert Peel*, III.2 (1851), p.546; Sir J. Prior, *The Remonstrance of a Tory to the Right Hon Robert Peel* (1827), pp.40–1; *A Few Plain Words to Sir Robert Peel* (1836), p.13; *Suggestions on the Best Modes of Employing the Irish Peasantry, as an anti-famine precaution: a letter to Sir Robert Peel, Bart., By Agricola* (1845), p.126.

25 R. Warwick Bond, (editor), *The Marlay Letters, 1778–1820* (1937), p.233.

26 See Peel's Speeches of 23 January 1810 and 18 March 1811: *Speeches delivered in the House of Commons by the late Rt. Hon. Sir Robert Peel*, 4 Volumes (New York, 1972), I, 5–11.

27 Jenkins, 'Chief Secretary', pp.39–42; Hoppen, 'An Incorporating Union?', 346–7.

28 *Colchester Diary*, III, 38–9; cf. Hoppen, 'An Incorporating Union?', 342.

29 Taylor, *Reminiscences of O'Connell*, p.29.

30 See Palmer, *Police and Protest*, p.194 on Peel's lack of legislative intervention.

31 Magdalen Goffin, (editor), *The Diaries of Absalom Watkin, A Manchester Man, 1787–1861* (Stroud, 1993), p.251; for comparable views, see Prest, 'Peel', 407–8.

32 Hoppen, 'An Incorporating Union?', 348.

33 Richard Edgcumbe, (editor), *The Diary of Frances Lady Shelley, 1818–1873*, 2 Volumes (1913), II, 18–20; Shipkey, *Peel's Irish Policy*, p.23; *Croker Papers*, I, 68–9.

34 Hoppen, 'An Incorporating Union?', 345 n.104, 346, 348.

35 Peel would have left in 1816–17, but was persuaded to stay on for Lord Talbot's first year as Viceroy (reputedly on the promise of a Cabinet place): Historical Manuscripts Commission, *Report on the Manuscripts of J.B. Fortescue Esq., Preserved at Dropmore*, X (1927), 430, 443; Earl Stanhope, (editor), *Conversations with Wellington* (1998), p.215.

36 See Michael Wheeler, *The Old Enemies. Catholic and Protestant in Nineteenth-Century English Culture* (Cambridge, 2006).

37 Wendy Hinde, *Catholic Emancipation. A Shake to Men's Minds* (Oxford, 1992); G.I.T. Machin, *The Catholic Question in English Politics, 1820–1830* (Oxford, 1964); Catholic Relief achieved Commons majorities of 9 (1821), 5 (1822), 6 (1823), 21 (1825), 6 (1828) and 188 (1829).

38 Shipkey, *Peel's Irish Policy*, pp.163, 189, 194–6.

39 For the 1825 crisis, see Francis Bamford and the Seventh Duke of Wellington, (editors), *The Journal of Mrs Arbuthnot, 1820–1832*, 2 Volumes (1950), I, 392–4; Arthur Aspinall, (editor), *The Diary of Henry Hobhouse, 1820–1827* (1947), p.115.

40 *Bathurst*, pp.579, 581.

41 Richard Duke of Buckingham and Chandos, *Memoirs of the Court of George IV*, 2 Volumes (1859), I, 326; *Journal of Mrs Arbuthnot*, II, 200–1, 206; Aspinall, *Charles Arbuthnot*, pp.105–6.

42 *A Detailed Report of the Public Meeting at Hereford ... May 25, 1827, with the address to Mr Peel, [on his retirement from office,] adopted on the motion of Sir Edwyn Scudamore Stanhope, Bart., Seconded by the Rev. Arthur Matthews, B.D. Prebendary of Hereford* (1827), p.31. Anicius Manlius Severinus Boethius (475–524) was a Christian philosopher and statesman. Ironically (given the context), he was canonized by the Catholic Church.

43 Reverend Robert Bradley, *A Letter to the Right Honourable Robert Peel ... on Catholic Emancipation* (Manchester, 1824), p.8.

44 Shipkey, *Peel's Irish Policy*, p.193; Gerard O'Brien, 'Robert Peel and the Pursuit of Catholic Emancipation, 1813–1817', *Archivium Hibernicum*, 43, 1988, 137–8. For Peel's justification of acting by proclamation rather than legislation, see *Colchester Diary*, II, 469–72, 498.

45 Shipkey, *Peel's Irish Policy*, p.164. Peel opposed Emancipation in notable speeches on 3 February 1812, 28 February 1821, 6 March 1827, 9 May 1828 and 12 June 1828.

46 George Henry Francis, *The late Sir Robert Peel, Bart. A Critical Biography. Reprinted, with additions, from Fraser's Magazine* (1852), p.58; *Colchester Diary*, II, 576–7.

47 *Croker Papers*, I, 81; *A Letter Addressed to the Right Honorable Sir Robert Peel, Bart., on the Political Aspect of Popery* (1837), p.19 (glossing Peel's sentiments against Burdett's Catholic Relief motion of March 1827).

48 For the key passages, see *Speeches*, I, 78–84; Northamptonshire Record Office, X1384, Diaries of George Agar Ellis, 9 May 1817.

49 Ian Ker, *et al* (editors), *The Letters and Diaries of John Henry Newman*, 32 Volumes to date (Oxford, 1961–2008), I, 37–8; Gredington, Whitchurch, Shropshire, Diaries of Lord Kenyon, 30–31 May 1817, *Colchester Diary*, II, 620; *Bathurst*, p.434.

50 Edward Copleston, *A Letter to the Right Hon Robert Peel ... on the pernicious effects of a variable standard of value especially as it regards the condition of the lower orders and the poor laws* (1819), pp.88–9.

51 Josceline Bagot, (editor), *George Canning and his friends. Containing hitherto unpublished letters, jeux d'esprit, etc*, 2 Volumes (1909), II, 45–6, 50–1.

52 *Blackwood's Edinburgh Magazine*, 25, March 1829, 285. For a fuller discussion of the issue, see chapter 4.

53 For Norman Gash, it represents the former: *Mr Secretary Peel*, pp.545–98.

54 British Library, 731 m.14 [Oxford by-election materials, 1829], *Letter from the Reverend J. Blanco White to a friend in Oxford*, p.2.

55 For Peel as indispensable minister, see *Arbuthnot Journal*, II, 239; Third Lord Colchester, (editor), *Political Diary of Edward Law, Lord Ellenborough, 1828–30*, 2 Volumes (1881), I, 299.

56 Southampton University Library, Broadlands Papers, Palmerston Journal, PP/D2, pp.102–3, December 1828.

57 Shipkey, *Peel's Irish Policy*, pp.248, 511.

58 Boyd Hilton, 'The Ripening of Robert Peel' in Michael Bentley, (editor), *Public and Private Doctrine: Essays in British History Presented to Maurice Cowling* (Cambridge, 1993), pp.63–84.

59 O'Brien, 'Catholic Emancipation', 135. For a contemporary discussion of the timing of Peel's 'revolution of mind', see *Blackwood's Edinburgh Magazine*, 25, March 1829, 296. For *Blackwood's*, the salient point was whether Peel became committed to Emancipation in June or December 1828.

60 Peel supported a bill of 1823 extending this privilege to English Catholics: *Colchester Diary*, III, 280–1, 289.

61 Fergus O'Ferrall, *Catholic Emancipation. Daniel O'Connell and the Birth of Irish Democracy, 1820–1830* (Dublin, 1985).

62 The Protestant population of Ireland was approximately two million (about 1.2m of which was based in the historic – as opposed to modern geographical – province of Ulster).

63 Shipkey, *Peel's Irish Policy*, p.171.

64 *A Letter to the Rt. Hon. Robert Peel, M.P., on the present state of the Catholic Question* (1828), pp.2–3; cf. *Speeches*, I, 612–23.

65 For Peel's role in Repeal, see *Ellenborough Diary*, I, 39; *Colchester Diary*, III, 553, 558; Agar Ellis Diary, 26 February, 18 March 1828.

66 *Mrs Arbuthnot's Journal*, II, 202; Kenneth Bourne, (editor), *The Letters of the Third Viscount Palmerston to Laurence and Elizabeth Sulivan, 1804–1863*, Royal Historical Society, Camden, 4th Series, 23, (1979), p.212; *Ellenborough Diary*, I, 182.

67 Sir Joseph Arnould, *Memoir of Thomas, First Lord Denman, formerly Lord Chief Justice of England*, 2 Volumes (1873), I, 301; *Mrs Arbuthnot's Journal*, II, 226; The Seventh Duke of Wellington, (editor), *Wellington and His Friends* (1965), p.86. On 12 January 1829, Peel agreed to stay in Wellington's ministry and oversee the Relief Bill.

68 *Mrs Arbuthnot's Journal*, II, 243–4; *Colchester Diary*, III, 595; Arthur Aspinall, (editor), *The Letters of George IV*, 3 Volumes (Cambridge, 1938), letter 1556. For criticism of Peel's justification, see *Blackwood's Edinburgh Magazine*, LXVIII, September 1850, 364; Jelinger Cookson Symons, *Sir Robert Peel As a Type of Statesmanship* (1856), pp.65–6.

69 Capefigue, 'Character of Sir Robert Peel', p.548; Durham Record Office, Londonderry Papers, D/Lo/C96 (2), Peel to Londonderry, 24 February 1829.

70 *Croker Papers*, I, 409; John Rylands University Library Manchester, W.H. Clinton Diary, 8 February 1829; *A Letter to the Right Hon. Robert Peel on the danger and impolicy of the measures … proposed to the British Parliament, for the purpose of rendering Roman Catholics eligible to some of the highest offices in the State* (1829), p.4.

71 Lady Dorchester, (editor), *Recollections of a long life by Lord Broughton (John Cam Hobhouse). With additional extracts from his private diaries*, 6 Volumes (1910–11), III, 302; Agar Ellis Diary, 5 February 1829; Nottingham University Manuscripts Department, J.E. Denison Diary, Os 3 D1/132, 5 February 1829; *Ellenborough Diary*, I, 325.

72 *A Letter Addressed to the Right Honorable Sir Robert Peel, Bart., on the Political Aspect of Popery* (1837), p.11; cf. Clinton Diary, 6 March 1829.

73 *Speeches*, I, 724; cf. *Broughton Diary*, III, 308; Agar Ellis Diary, 5 March 1829; *Ellenborough Diary*, I, 380; Kenyon Diaries, 5 March 1829.

74 Palmerston Journal, PP/D2, p.72, 12 June 1828.

75 This paragraph is based on the excellent discussion in O'Ferrall, *Catholic Emancipation*, pp.318–23; cf. *The Times*, 4 April 1835, p.5.

76 Joseph Wood, *Mr Peel's Measures for Catholic Emancipation considered; in a letter to Lord Milton, M.P.*, (1829), p.4.

77 O'Ferrall, *Catholic Emancipation*, pp.319, 323.

78 Aspinall, 'Hatherton', *Parliamentary Affairs*, XVII/1, 1963, 21; Devonshire MSS, Chatsworth, Diary of the 6th Duke of Devonshire, 6 March 1829; Arnould, *Denman*, I, 302; *The Times*, 9 April 1829, p.5; Agar Ellis Diary, 8 April 1829. Coryphaeus was the leader of the Chorus in ancient Greek drama.

79 Willard Bissell Pope, (editor), *The Diary of Benjamin Robert Haydon*, 5 Volumes (Harvard, 1960–3), III, 500; *Croker Papers*, I, 412, II, 357. *Blackwood's Edinburgh Magazine* also complained about the 'equivocation and mental reservation' which Peel demonstrated at Manchester: 25, March 1829, 283.

80 George Henry Francis, *Opinions and Policy of The Right Honourable Viscount Palmerston, G.C.B., M.P., &c, as Minister, Diplomatist, and Statesman, During More than Forty Years of Public Life. With a Memoir* (1852), p.81; Bourne, *Palmerston–Sulivan Letters*, p.235.

81 Northamptonshire Record Office, Finch Hatton Papers, 4650, M.J. Stapleton to Lord Winchilsea, 10 September 1829 (my italics). Also see Captain H. Martin, *A Personal Sketch of the late lamented Sir Robert Peel, as a Parliamentary Speaker and Party Leader in the British House of Commons &c* (Hamburg, 1850), p.11.

82 *Croker Papers*, I, 407.

83 *Blackwood's Edinburgh Magazine*, 25, March 1829, 295.

84 For the Oxford contest, see *Newman Letters and Diaries*, II, 117–18, 120–9, 133, 135, 146; *Colchester*, III, 598; Agar Ellis Diary, 14–26 February 1829; *Broughton Diary*, III, 305; *Ellenborough Diary*, I, 366; *The Times*, 9 April 1845, p.6; *Oratio Demosthenica et Poetica* (1829).

85 For other examples, see Centre for Kentish Studies, Maidstone, Knatchbull Papers, U951, C59/15, Anniversary Ode for the 28th of February 1829 (the date of Inglis' victory at Oxford); Lancashire Record Office, Kenyon Papers, DDKE 7840, Box 67, 'Peeliana' (by John Graham), 20 February 1835.

86 Reverend Charles Girdlestone, *Substance of a Speech for the Convocation House, Oxford* (Oxford, 1829), p.6.

87 Christopher Hibbert, *Greville's England. Selections from the Diaries of Charles Greville, 1818–1860* (1981), pp.44, 47; Henry Reeve, (editor), *The Greville Memoirs. A Journal of the Reigns of King George IV, King William IV and Queen Victoria*, 8 Volumes (1888), VI, 360–1.

88 *An Answer to the arguments of the Right Hon Robert Peel in favour of further concessions to the Catholics* (1829), pp.7, 22.

89 Arthur Aspinall, (editor), *Three Early Nineteenth Century Diaries* (1952), p.172; Hughe Knatchbull-Hugessen, *Kentish Family* (1960), p.224.

90 Richard A. Gaunt, (editor), *Unrepentant Tory. Political Selections from the Diaries of the Fourth Duke of Newcastle-under-Lyne, 1827–38* (Woodbridge, 2006), p.190; National Register of Archives (Scotland), 776, Mansfield Papers, Box 110, Lord Mansfield's Political Notes, September 1833, pp.59–60.

91 Southampton University Library, Broadlands Papers, Shaftesbury Diaries, SHA/PD/4, f.94, 18 May 1846.

92 Shipkey, *Peel's Irish Policy*, pp.159, 505–9.

93 *The Political Aspect of Popery* (1837), p.33.

94 The two sides of the debate are best studied in, respectively, Richard Brent, *Liberal Anglican Politics. Whiggery, Religion, and Reform 1830–1841* (Oxford, 1987) and John Wolffe, *The Protestant Crusade in Great Britain, 1829–60* (Oxford, 1991).

95 For Peel's Irish policy in the 1840s see, pre-eminently, Donal A. Kerr, *Peel, Priests and Politics, Sir Robert Peel's Administration and the Roman Catholic Church in Ireland, 1841–1846* (Oxford, 1982); *idem.*, 'Peel and the Political Involvement of the Priests', *Archivium Hibernicum*, 36, 1981, 16–25; Oliver MacDonagh, *O'Connell. The Life of Daniel O'Connell, 1775–1847*, 1-Volume edition (1991); Peter Gray, *Famine, Land and Politics: British Government and Irish Society, 1843–50* (2001).

96 David Eastwood, '"Recasting Our Lot": Peel, the Nation, and the Politics of Interest' in Laurence Brockliss and David Eastwood, (editors), *A Union of Multiple Identities. The British Isles, c.1750–c.1850* (Manchester, 1997), p.40.

97 David Eastwood, 'Peel and the Tory Party Reconsidered', *History Today*, 42, March 1992, 29–30; cf. 'Recasting our Lot', pp.39–40.

98 E. Jones Parry, (editor), *The Correspondence of Lord Aberdeen and Princess Lieven, 1832–1854*, 2 Volumes, Royal Historical Society, Camden, 3rd Series, LX, LXII (1938–9), I, 241; Shaftesbury Diaries, SHA/PD/4, ff.42, 44, 2 and 10 December 1845.

99 Reverend William Kellock Tatam, *A Letter to the Right Hon. Sir Robert Peel, Bart., on the Endowment of the Papacy,* [originally published in 1844] (1894), pp.5, 9.

100 We await Simon Skinner's forthcoming history of the Maynooth Grant for a renewed understanding of its scope and significance. Hitherto, it has too often been seen through the difficulties it created for Gladstone: Brooke and Sorensen, *Gladstone,* II, 269–79.

101 *The Freeman's Journal*, 29 June 1846.

102 Peel later declared that the Insurrection Act was 'bad in principle, and has the effect of placing the higher classes in hostility against the lower': *Ellenborough Diary*, II, 136 (16 November 1829).

103 Eastwood, 'Recasting Our Lot', pp.39–40.

104 Nottingham University Manuscripts Department, Marlay Papers, My 171/1–2, Peel to Charleville, 18 April [1846?].

105 *Speeches*, IV, 788–804; Edward Pearce, (editor), with Deanna Pearce, *The Diaries of Charles Greville* (2005), p.272.

106 James Marshall and Marie-Louise Osborn Collection, Beinecke Rare Book and Manuscript Library, Yale University, 11557, Peel to Thomas Campbell Foster, 16 April 1849.

107 Jules Seigel, 'Carlyle and Peel: The prophet's search for a heroic politician and an unpublished fragment', *Victorian Studies*, 26, 1983, 187–88; James Anthony Froude, *Thomas Carlyle. A History of His Life in London, 1834–1881*, 2 Volumes (1884), I, 452. Eastwood characterises Peel's policy as an 'activist, ameliorative role for the State': 'Recasting our Lot', p.40.

108 *The Times*, 9 March 1849, p.5; cf. 5 April 1849, p.5.

109 *The Economist*, 14 April 1849, 412; cf. 28 April 1849, 474 and 27 October 1849, 1197; John Vincent, (editor), *Disraeli, Derby and the Conservative Party: the Political Journals of Lord Stanley, 1849–69* (Hassocks, 1978), p.3.

110 For a (not unfounded) rumour that Peel supported a state-paid Catholic priesthood, see Vincent, *Disraeli, Derby*, p.3.

111 Shipkey, *Peel's Irish Policy*, pp.62, 73, 75, 81–2, 85, 90; cf. Gash, *Mr Secretary Peel*, pp.224–6.

112 *Punch*, XVI, January–June 1849, 172. Judas Iscariot betrayed Christ whilst the Roman Emperor Flavius Claudius Julianus (331–63) was known as 'Julian the Apostate' for rejecting Christianity.

113 *A Letter on the present state of Ireland to … Sir Robert Peel … By an Irish Catholic* (1846), p.9.

114 *Quarterly Review*, LXXXI, June 1847, 306; cf. LXXVIII, September 1846, 574; *Blackwood's Edinburgh Magazine*, LXVIII, September 1850, 363–4. Green was the colour most closely associated with Catholic Ireland.

115 Symons, *Sir Robert Peel*, pp.88–90.

116 Walter Bagehot, 'The Character of Sir Robert Peel' [1856] in Norman St-John Stevas, (editor), *The Collected Works of Sir Walter Bagehot, Volume III, The Historical Essays* (1968), p.241.

Chapter Three

1 James Marshall and Marie-Louise Osborn Collection, Beinecke Rare Book and Manuscript Library, Yale University, 11616, Peel to [unknown], 29 December 1835.

2 But see Samuel Turner, *A Letter addressed to the Right Hon. Robert Peel* (1819), pp.4–8 for a critical commentary on Peel's conversion, written a week later.

3 However, see Peel's speech on William Cobbett's motion to remove him from the Privy Council for having proposed the resumption of cash payments, 16 May 1833; *Speeches delivered in the House of Commons by the late Rt. Hon. Sir Robert Peel*, 4 Volumes (New York, 1972), II, 694–704.

4 This argument was first put forward by Hilton in his 'Peel: A Reappraisal', *Historical Journal*, 22, 1979, 585–614; cf. *The Age of Atonement. The Influence of Evangelicalism on Social and Economic Thought, 1785–1865* (Oxford, 1988), pp.218–36, quote at p.224.

5 For the history of the English currency system see, amongst contemporary accounts, Benjamin Massey, *The Money Crisis; Its Causes, Consequences, and Remedy. In a letter to the Right Hon. Sir Robert Peel, Bart.* (1847).

6 It was laid down that the resumption of cash payments was to be achieved six months after definitive peace terms were agreed between Britain and France.

7 See J.H. Clapham, *The Bank of England. A history, Volume 2: 1797–1914* (Cambridge, 1944); Ranald C. Michie, (editor), *The development of London as a financial centre, Volume 1: 1700–1850* (1998) and Lucy A. Newton and Philip L. Cottrell, 'Joint-stock banking in the English provinces, 1826–1857: to branch or not to branch?', *Business and Economic History*, 27/1 (1998), 115–28, each of which have continuing relevance for what follows.

8 One writer estimated the depreciation in the value of the currency during inconvertibility at 25–35 per cent: *Two Letters to Sir Robert Peel, on his proposed Banking measures; by an ex-M.P.* (1844), p.9.

9 The preceding account is based on Edwin Cannan, (editor), *The Paper Pound of 1797–1821. The Bullion Report* [of 1810], 2nd Edition [1925] (New York, 1969), quote at p.xxii.

10 *The Economist,* 13 January 1844, 387; for the wider issues, see Boyd Hilton, *Corn, Cash, Commerce: The Economic Policies of the Tory Governments, 1815–1830* (Oxford, 1977).

11 Sandon Hall, Harrowby Papers, XVI, ff.75–6, Redesdale to Harrowby, 14 October 1810.

12 John Jolliffe, (editor), *Neglected Genius. The Diaries of Benjamin Robert Haydon, 1808–1846* (1990), p.204. Before decimalisation in 1971, there were 12 pence in the shilling and 20 shillings (or 240 pence) in the pound. Haydon's complaint (much echoed by contemporaries) was that 'Peel's Act' had made money scarce by making its value dear. For similar sentiments, see Gregory Claeys, (editor), *The Chartist Movement in Britain, 1838–50,* 6 Volumes (2001), VI, 419, 421.

13 *Two Letters to Sir Robert Peel,* pp.9, 25.

14 George Henry Francis, *The late Sir Robert Peel, Bart. A Critical Biography. Reprinted, with additions, from Fraser's Magazine* (1852), p.40. The partial resumption was suspended on 6 April 1819 whilst the committees of inquiry sat: *Speeches,* I, 114–5.

15 For the committee, *A very short letter to the Right Hon. R. Peel* (1819), p.71; amongst opposition politicians, Lords Grenville, Lansdowne and Althorp were noted Whig 'Bullionists'. For a condemnation of 'Peel's Act' as a Whig measure, see *Fraser's Magazine,* IX, January 1834, 24.

16 Boyd Hilton, 'The Political Arts of Lord Liverpool', *Transactions of the Royal Historical Society,* 5th Series, 38, 1988, 147–70; Louis J. Jennings, (editor), *The Correspondence and Diaries of the late Right Honorable John Wilson Croker,* 2-Volume edition (New York, 1884), I, 135.

17 Compare Gladstone's attitude; 'I admit facts, and abstract principles only in subservience to facts, as the true standard of commercial and financial legislation': Nottingham University Manuscripts Department, Newcastle of Clumber Collection, Ne C 5385, Gladstone's Election Address at Newark, 4 August 1832.

18 Peel was impressed by the arguments of Lloyd's Oxford contemporary, Edward Coplestone, *A Letter to the Right Hon. Robert Peel ... on the pernicious effects of a variable standard of value especially as it regards the condition of the lower orders and the poor laws* (1819); Salim Rashid, 'Edward Copleston, Robert Peel, and cash payments', *History of Political Economy,* 15, 1983, 249–59.

19 Quoted in Boyd Hilton, *Atonement,* p.230 (my additions in square brackets).

20 Harrowby Papers, XVI, f.74, Redesdale to Harrowby, 30 September 1810.

21 For comments on the currency as Peel's 'fixed principle', see J.C. Colquhoun, *The Effects of Sir Robert Peel's Administration on the Political State and Prospects of England* (1847), p.23; George Henry Francis, *Sir Robert Peel as Statesman and Orator* (1846), p.17; Benjamin Disraeli, *Lord George Bentinck: A Political Biography,* (New Brunswick, New Jersey, 1998), p.199; *The Illustrated London News,* 13 July 1850, p.46.

22 *The Economist,* 7 February 1857, 145. However, Croker maintained that Peel would prove himself inconsistent on the currency question if the pressure was strong enough: *The Quarterly Review,* LXXVIII, September 1846, 551; *Croker Papers,* II, 345–6.

23 John Morley, *The Life of Richard Cobden,* 2 Volumes (1908), I, 393; cf. Adam Hodgson, *A Letter to Sir Robert Peel on the Currency* (Liverpool, 1848), p.18; Francis, *The late Sir Robert Peel,* p.50.

24 Earl Stanhope, (editor), *Conversations with Wellington* (1998), p.215; Arthur Aspinall, (editor), *The Correspondence of Charles Arbuthnot,* Royal Historical Society, Camden, 3rd Series, LXV, (1941), pp.16–17.

25 Stanhope, *Wellington,* p.215; Roland G. Thorne, (editor), *The History of Parliament. The Commons, 1790–1820,* 5 Volumes (1986), IV, 748; John Prest, 'Sir Robert Peel', in H.C.G. Matthew and Brian Harrison, (editors), *The Oxford Dictionary of National Biography,* 60 Volumes (Oxford, 2004), XLIII, 408.

26 See William Smart, *Economic Annals of the Nineteenth Century,* 2 Volumes (New York, 1964), I, 674–9; Norman Gash, *Mr Secretary Peel: The Life of Sir Robert Peel before 1830,*

2nd Edition (1985), pp.239–45; Boyd Hilton, *A Mad, Bad, & Dangerous People? England, 1783–1846* (Oxford, 2006), pp.257–64, 278–9, 323–8.

27 Robert Torrens, *The Principles and Practical Operation of Sir Robert Peel's Bill of 1844 Explained, and Defended Against the Objections of Tooke, Fullarton, and Wilson* (1848), p.22. Torrens was an 'Anti-Bullionist' in 1819 although he later supported the Bank Charter Act.

28 *Speeches*, I, 128.

29 In 1844 one writer complained that the younger Peel 'saw nothing to *approve of* in Mr Pitt's measure, and nothing to *regret* in [his] own': John Taylor, *What is a Pound? A letter to the Premier on his new currency measures, in reply to his speech on the Bank Charter Act, May 6, 1844*, 2nd Edition (1844), p.43.

30 *The Times*, 14 April 1826, p.3; *Croker Papers*, II, 346–7.

31 Torrens, *Peel's Bill of 1844*, p.22.

32 *A Letter to the Right Hon. R. Peel upon the necessity of adopting some parliamentary measure to control the issues of Country bankers, and to prevent the recurrence of the late shock to public and private credit, with the heads of a bill for that purpose* (1826), pp.5–13; *The Currency Question freed from mystery, in a letter to Mr Peel shewing how the distress may be relieved without altering the standard* (1830), pp.8–10; *A Plan for regulating the circulation on the principle of Sir R. Peel's celebrated Currency Bill of 1819* (1840), pp.5–9; Lewis Melville, (editor), *The Huskisson Papers* (1931), pp.313–19; Third Lord Colchester, (editor), *Political Diary of Edward Law, Lord Ellenborough, 1828–30*, 2 Volumes (1881), I, 186–7.

33 Jelinger Cookson Symons, *Sir Robert Peel as a type of Statesmanship* (1856), p.123.

34 The situation remained different in Scotland, where small-value notes continued to circulate successfully and where the joint-stock banking system was considered stronger.

35 Charles Stuart Parker, *Sir Robert Peel from his Private Papers*, 3 Volumes (1891–9), I, 383. For Gash on Hilton, see his review of *The Age of Atonement* in *English Historical Review*, CIV, 1989, 136–40.

36 Parker, *Peel*, II, 170–1.

37 Claeys, *Chartist Movement*, VI, 431 (O'Brien was writing in 1849–50). For an Ultra Tory view, Sir Richard Vyvyan, *A Letter from Sir Richard Vyvyan to his constituents upon the commercial and financial policy of Sir Robert Peel's Administration* (1842), pp.27–8.

38 Centre for Kentish Studies, Maidstone, Stanhope MSS, 301, 304, Kenyon to Stanhope, 18 December 1826, 9 February 1828. I am grateful to Bruce Dolphin for providing me with these transcripts.

39 Conversely, Wade hailed Peel's Act for undermining the Bank of England's monopoly and checking its note-issue: John Wade, (editor), *The Black Book* (New York, 1970), pp.559–60; cf. Symons, *Peel*, p.124; *Blackwood's Edinburgh Magazine*, LXVIII, September 1850, 362; Claeys, *Chartist Movement*, IV, 314.

40 *Croker Papers*, II, 8–9. For Vyvyan's insistence (1 May 1833) that an adjustment of the currency question was a pre-requisite to Peel's election as leader of the Conservative Party, see Arthur Aspinall, (editor), *Three Early Nineteenth Century Diaries* (1952), p.324.

41 John Brooke and Julia Gandy, (editors), *Prime Ministers Papers: Wellington, Political Correspondence, Volume I: 1833–1834* (1975), pp.17, 124–6.

42 M.R.D. Foot and H.C.G. Matthew, (editors), *The Gladstone Diaries*, 14 Volumes (Oxford, 1968–94), II, 24; Christopher Morris, (editor), *William Cobbett's Illustrated Rural Rides 1821–1832* (Waltham Abbey, 1984), 43; cf. 138–9.

43 Smart, *Annals*, I, 679 n.2.

44 Willard Bissell Pope, (editor), *The Diary of Benjamin Robert Haydon*, 5 Volumes (Harvard, 1960–3), IV, 78; National Register of Archives (Scotland), 776, Mansfield Papers, Box 110, Lord Mansfield's Political Notes, September 1833, p.3; John Brooke and Mary Sorensen, (editors), *Prime Ministers Papers: W.E. Gladstone*, 4 Volumes (1971–81), I, 55.

45 Hilton, 'Peel: A Reappraisal', 595; *idem.*, 'Robert Peel' in Robert Eccleshall and Graham Walker, (editors), *Biographical Dictionary of British Prime Ministers* (1998), p.148.

46 *Speeches*, IV, 365–6. In November 1847, the Ultra Tory King of Hanover called the Bank Charter Act Peel's 'own bantling' (or plaything): Charles Whibley, (editor), *Letters of the King of Hanover to Viscount Strangford, G.C.B.* (1925), p.125.

47 *Gladstone Diaries*, X, 448 (writing in 1883); cf. III, 373; Brooke and Sorensen, *Gladstone*, II, 227.

48 Hilton, *Mad, Bad*, p.548; *The Times*, 2 September 1846, p.7.

49 Geoffrey G. Riley, 'Peel and the Bank Act, 1844', *Institute of Bankers Journal*, February 1963, 79–86; Norman Gash, *Sir Robert Peel: The Life of Sir Robert Peel after 1830*, 2nd Edition (1986), pp.431–8; Hilton, *Mad, Bad*, pp.548–51.

50 The Bank of England's bullion reserves did increase, subsequently, but this had more to do with unforeseen events (the discovery of new sources of gold) than anything else; *ibid.*, p.551.

51 See, for example, 18 May 1844, 793–6 (on Robert Torrens); 15 June 1844, 889–90 (on Robert Torrens and Thomas Tooke); 8 and 15 March 1845, 5 and 12 April 1845 and 23 October 1847.

52 Hilton, *Mad, Bad*, pp.548–9; Gash, *Peel*, p.433; for *The Economist's* view of the anti-Bullionists, see 9 October 1847, 1158.

53 *The Economist*, 3 May 1845, 405.

54 There was separate legislation for Scotland and Ireland, introduced the following year; *ibid.*, 26 April 1845.

55 Prest, 'Peel', 414; I.C. Wright, *The Evils of the Currency: An Exposition of Sir Robert Peel's Act of 1844*, 6th Edition (1855), p.4.

56 *Speeches*, IV, 351. For criticism, see Taylor, *What is a pound?*, pp.14, 56–7.

57 *The Economist*, 8 June 1844, 884; 15 June 1844, 901–2; *Croker Papers*, II, 347–8.

58 William Leckie, *A Letter to the Rt. Hon. Sir Robert Peel, Bart., M.P., on the Bank Charter Bill: with a view to its modification or repeal* (1847), p.5; M.G. Wiebe *et al*, (editors), *Benjamin Disraeli: Letters*, 7 Volumes to date (Toronto, 1982–2004), VII, letter 2995 n.1; Wright, *Evils of the Currency*, p.5. For humorous representations of the same point, see *Punch*, XII, January–June 1847, 220; XIII, July–December 1847, 115.

59 Thomas Joplin, *An Examination of Sir Robert Peel's Currency Bill of 1844. In a letter to the Bankers of the United Kingdom*, 2nd edition (1845), p.20; *Croker Papers*, II, 352–3.

60 Taylor, *What is a pound?*, pp.70–1; *Two Letters to Sir Robert Peel*, pp.10, 17.

61 For the details, see H.M. Boot, *The Commercial Crisis of 1847* (Hull, 1984).

62 Torrens, *Peel's Bill of 1844*, p.162.

63 Gash, *Peel*, pp.436–7; *The Economist*, 15 June 1844, 901–2.

64 For the end of the crisis, Gash, *Peel*, pp.627–31. For criticism of the Act's operation in 1847, Torrens, *Peel's Bill of 1844*, pp.176–7.

65 Nottingham University Manuscripts Department, Portland of Welbeck Collection, Pw L 417/3, Lord George Bentinck to Lord Henry Bentinck, 18 August 1847.

66 Catherine Molyneux, 'Reform as Process: The Parliamentary Fate of the Bank Charter Act of 1844' in Michael Turner, (editor), *Reform and Reformers in Nineteenth Century Britain* (Sunderland, 2004), pp.63–80.

67 Hilton, *Mad, Bad*, pp.548–51.

68 I am grateful to Chris Wrigley for his advice on this point.

69 *Croker Papers*, II, 345–6; Hodgson, *Letter to Sir Robert Peel*, pp.18–19; cf. *Quarterly Review*, LXXXI, June 1847, 303–4.

70 Southampton University Library, Broadlands Papers, Shaftesbury Diaries, SHA/PD/5, f.15, 27 October 1847.

71 See the sentiments of Bronterre O'Brien's 'National Reform League', March 1850 in F.C. Mather, (editor), *Chartism and Society* (1980), p.94. For more prosaic denunciations, see

Punch, XIII, July–December 1847, 234; Edmund Taunton, *Gross Injustices, and idolatrous sacrifice of millions to a golden idol! The patent sliding slippery currency scale of 1819. The improved patent doubly slippery in 1844, etc.,* 2nd edition (Birmingham, 1847), p.10.

Chapter Four

1 *Speeches delivered in the House of Commons by the late Rt. Hon. Sir Robert Peel,* 4 Volumes (New York, 1972), I, 509.
2 *Blackwood's Edinburgh Magazine,* 27, May 1830, 727–8.
3 See Norman Gash, *Mr Secretary Peel,* 2nd Edition (1985), pp.308–43.
4 For rumours of a Peel-Wellington cabinet in 1819, see Richard Edgcumbe, (editor), *The Diary of Frances Lady Shelley, 1818–1873,* 2 Volumes (1913), II, 34; cf. Historical Manuscripts Commission, *Report on the Manuscripts of J.B. Fortescue Esq., Preserved at Dropmore,* X (1927), 445.
5 Donald Read, *Peterloo. The Massacre and its Background* (Manchester, 1958).
6 E.A. Smith, *A Queen on Trial. The Affair of Queen Caroline* (Stroud, 1993).
7 Louis J. Jennings, (editor), *The Correspondence and Diaries of the late Right Honorable John Wilson Croker,* 2-Volume edition (New York, 1884), I, 155–6. For an interesting comparative account of Peel's views (in 1824), see Arthur Aspinall, (editor), *Three Early Nineteenth Century Diaries* (1952), p.118.
8 *Lady Shelley's Diary,* II, 17, 21. Metternich was the premier continental statesman of the day. He was also a noted reactionary.
9 Francis Bamford and the Seventh Duke of Wellington, (editors), *The Journal of Mrs Arbuthnot, 1820–1832,* 2 Volumes (1950), I, 56.
10 This was the view of Henry Bankes: Second Lord Colchester, (editor), *The Diary and Correspondence of Charles Abbot, Lord Colchester,* 3 Volumes (1861), III, 95.
11 Arthur Aspinall, (editor), *The Letters of George IV,* 3 Volumes (Cambridge, 1938), II, letter 890; *Croker Papers,* I, 162; Historical Manuscripts Commission, *Report on the Manuscripts of Earl Bathurst* (1923), p.490.
12 Bootle Wilbraham to Colchester, 26 January 1821, in *Colchester Diary,* III, 202. Peel had married Julia Floyd on 8 June 1820.
13 *Mrs Arbuthnot's Journal,* I, 90 (cf. 82, 92); Arthur Aspinall, (editor), *The Diary of Henry Hobhouse, 1820–1827* (1947), p.100; *Croker Papers,* I, 172; cf. *Colchester Diary,* III, 242; *Three Diaries,* p.190.
14 *Croker Papers,* I, 172; *Mrs Arbuthnot's Journal,* I, 97.
15 *Mrs Arbuthnot's Journal,* I, 100; cf. *Bathurst,* pp.497–8.
16 *Hobhouse Diary,* p.62; *Croker Papers,* I, 173, 175.
17 Gredington, Whitchurch, Shopshire, Diaries of Lord Kenyon, 6 December 1821; George Pellew, *The Life and Correspondence of the Rt. Hon. Henry Addington, First Viscount Sidmouth,* 3 Volumes (1847), III, 394–5. For other reactions, see *Bathurst,* p.524; *George IV Letters,* II, letter 969; Northamptonshire Record Office, X1384, Diaries of George Agar Ellis, 2 December 1821; *Mrs Arbuthnot's Journal,* I, 130; *Hobhouse Diary,* pp.81, 85; Sandon Hall, Harrowby Manuscripts, XIV, ff.110, 115, Bathurst to Harrowby, 2 December 1821, 18 January 1822; *Colchester Diary,* III, 239; Lady Dorchester, (editor), *Recollections of a long life by Lord Broughton (John Cam Hobhouse). With additional extracts from his private diaries,* 6 Volumes (1910–11), II, 174; *Croker Papers,* I, 200.
18 Norman Gash, *Pillars of Government and Other Essays on State and Society c.1770–c.1880* (1986), p.37.
19 *Croker Papers,* I, 417; W.T. Haly, *The Opinions of Sir R. Peel, expressed in Parliament and in Public,* 2nd edition (1850), p.xiv.
20 The classic account is Leon Radzinowicz, *A History of English Criminal Law and its Administration from 1750,* 3 Volumes (1948).
21 The principal reforms were: *4 Geo. IV, cc.46–48 and 53–4* (1823) which abolished capital punishment for larceny (to the value of £2 in shops and ships) and for the impersonation

of Greenwich pensioners and repealed the Waltham Black Act of 1723; *7 & 8 Geo. IV c.29* (1827) which dealt with larceny; *7 & 8 Geo. IV cc.29–31* (1827) concerning malicious damage (including outrage against the Hundred); *9 Geo. IV c.31* regarding offences against the person (1828); and *11 Geo. IV & Will. IV c.66* (1830) reforming the laws on forgery.

22 *6 Geo. IV c.50* (1825) consolidated 85 laws relating to juries into a single Act, 'set up local rate-paid gaols in every county and major town, and regulated prison disciplines and magistrates' inspection': V.A.C. Gatrell, *The Hanging Tree. Execution and the English People, 1770–1868* (Oxford, 1994), p.578; *The Times,* 12 July 1825, p.2.

23 K.J.M. Smith, 'Anthony Hammond: "Mr Surface" Peel's Persistent Codifier', *Journal of Legal History,* 20, 1999, 25–7.

24 John Prest, 'Sir Robert Peel' in H.C.G. Matthew and Brian Harrison, (editors), *The Oxford Dictionary of National Biography,* 60 Volumes, (Oxford, 2004), XLIII, 409.

25 Richard Rush, *A Residence at the Court of London* (1987 edition), p.234.

26 Richard A. Gaunt, (editor), *Unrepentant Tory. Political Selections from the Diaries of the Fourth Duke of Newcastle-under-Lyne, 1827–38* (Woodbridge, 2006), p.5; *George IV Letters,* III, letter 1231; cf. Arthur Aspinall, (editor), *The Formation of Canning's Ministry,* Royal Historical Society, Camden, 3rd Series, LIX, (1937), p.18.

27 Gaunt, *Unrepentant Tory,* p.5.

28 Desmond H. Brown, 'Abortive attempts to codify English criminal law', *Parliamentary History,* 11, 1992, 14–18.

29 See Philip Schofield, *Utility & Democracy. The Political Thought of Jeremy Bentham* (Oxford, 2006).

30 See *Colchester Diary,* III, 418–20 for Colchester's recommendation to Peel to be more precise in the wording of his legislation.

31 An issue personified in the case of *Jarndyce vs Jarndyce* in Charles Dickens' *Bleak House* (1853).

32 See Michael Lobban, 'Old Wine in New Bottles: The Concept and Practice of Law Reform, 1780–1830' in Joanna Innes and Arthur Burns, (editors), *Rethinking the Age of Reform* (Cambridge, 2003), pp.114–35; Randall McGowen, 'The image of justice and reform of the criminal law in early nineteenth-century England', *Buffalo Law Review,* 32, 1983, 89–125.

33 For a classic exposition of this view, see Douglas Hay *et al., Albion's Fatal Tree: Crime and Society in Eighteenth-Century England* (1975), pp.17–63.

34 Peter King, *Crime, Justice and Discretion in England, 1740–1820* (Oxford, 2000).

35 Luke O'Sullivan and Catherine Fuller, (editors), *The Correspondence of Jeremy Bentham, Volume 12, July 1824 to June 1828* (Oxford, 2006), pp.240–1; Smith, 'Hammond', 26, 38.

36 Charles Duke Yonge, *The Life and Administration of Robert Banks, Second Earl of Liverpool, K.G.,* 3 Volumes (1868), III, 216–17.

37 Prest, 'Peel', 409.

38 *A Short View of the Recent Changes; in which the question – Does Mr Canning's Government merit the Confidence of the Country? is impartially discussed* (1827), p.27; *The Times,* 9 April 1829, p.5; *Blackwood's Edinburgh Magazine,* LXVIII, September 1850, 358; George Kitson Clark, *The Life and Work of Sir Robert Peel* (1950), p.4. The Roman Emperor Justinian (527–565) commissioned the *Codex Justinianus,* the *Institutes* and the *Digest* of Roman jurisprudence.

39 Nottingham University Manuscripts Department, Denison Diary, Os 3 D1/13, 9 March 1826; Arthur Aspinall, *Lord Brougham and the Whig Party* (Stroud, 2005 edition), p.431; cf. Sir Joseph Arnould, *Memoir of Thomas, First Lord Denman, formerly Lord Chief Justice of England,* 2 Volumes (1873), I, 254.

40 James A. Jaffe, (editor), *'The Affairs of Others': The Diaries of Francis Place, 1825–1836,* Royal Historical Society, Camden, 5th Series, 30 (2007), p.236.

41 Aspinall, *Canning's Ministry*, pp.202–5; *Broughton Diary*, III, 170.

42 *Speeches*, I, 410.

43 Sir James Prior, *The Remonstrance of a Tory to the Right Hon. Robert Peel* (1827), pp.1, 9–10; cf. *A Short View of the Recent Changes*, pp.26–7.

44 *Bentham Letters*, p.338; *Three Diaries*, p.210.

45 Arthur Aspinall, 'Extracts from Lord Hatherton's Diary', *Parliamentary Affairs*, XVII/4, 1964, 377; cf. Aspinall, *Canning's Ministry*, p.275; *Broughton Diary*, VI, 164.

46 Bentham was impressed by Peel's 1830 declaration that he wished to tackle the thorny issue of legal fees and patent offices. *Mrs Arbuthnot's Journal*, II, 185, 342, 358–9; Schofield, *Utility and Democracy*, p.332.

47 The principal authorities are Elaine Reynolds, *Before the Bobbies: The Night Watch and Police Reform in Metropolitan London, 1720–1830* (Houndmills, 1998); Ruth Paley, '"An Imperfect, Inadequate & Wretched System?" Policing London before Peel', *Criminal Justice History*, X, 1989, 95–130 and Stanley H. Palmer, *Police and Protest in England and Ireland, 1780–1850* (Cambridge, 1988), pp.277–315.

48 F.C. Mather, (editor), *Chartism and Society* (1980), p.58; Gaunt, *Unrepentant Tory*, pp.120, 127, 130–2, 150, 168–9, 172, 199, 216–17, 227, 240.

49 Palmer, *Police*, pp.288, 291; *Speeches*, I, 556–64; the select committee report is quoted in David Eastwood, *Governing Rural England. Tradition and Transformation in Local Government, 1780–1840* (Oxford, 1994), p.225. For contemporary accounts which stress the primacy of Peel's role see (for example), *The Quarterly Review*, LXXXI, June 1847, 304 and *Blackwood's Edinburgh Magazine*, LXVIII, September 1850, 356–7.

50 *The Times*, 26 December 1828, p.3; 27 December 1828, p.3; 30 December 1828, p.3; 8 January 1829, p.3.

51 *Place Diaries*, p.284.

52 Palmer, *Police*, 277–315; Anthony Brundage, 'Ministers, Magistrates and Reformers: The Genesis of the Rural Constabulary Act of 1839', *Parliamentary History*, 5, 1986, 55–64.

53 H.G. Cocks, *Nameless Offences. Homosexual Desire in the 19th Century* (2003), pp.51–2, citing the work of Paley and Reynolds noted above.

54 Tadhg Ó Ceallaigh, 'Peel and Police Reform in Ireland, 1814–1818', *Studia Hibernica*, 6, 1966, 36.

55 In addition to Ceallaigh, 'Police Reform', see Palmer, *Police*, pp.193–217 and Galen Broeker, 'Robert Peel and the Peace Preservation Force', *Journal of Modern History*, 33, 1961, 363–73.

56 Palmer, *Police*, p.201; *Speeches*, I, 25–30.

57 Peel to Colchester, 30 September 1814, in *Colchester Diary*, II, 517.

58 Kenneth Bourne and William Banks Taylor, (editors), *The Horner Papers. Selections from the Letters and Miscellaneous Writings of Francis Horner, M.P., 1795–1817* (Edinburgh, 1994), p.607. Horner later withdrew his opposition; *ibid.*, p.805.

59 Ceallaigh, 'Police Reform', 32, 42.

60 Robert Carl Shipkey, *Robert Peel's Irish Policy: 1812–1846* (1987), pp.129, 138–40.

61 See *Ellenborough Diary*, II, 79–80.

62 Ceallaigh, 'Police Reform', 39.

63 Palmer, *Police*, p.217; Broeker, 'Peace Preservation Force', 363; Ceallaigh, 'Police Reform', 41.

64 This was a reference to Wellington's perceived ability, as Prime Minister, to railroad George IV into unpopular measures. See my 'Wellington in petticoats: the duke as caricature' in C.M. Woolgar, (editor), *Wellington Studies IV* (Southampton, 2008), pp.148–50.

65 Derek Beales, 'Peel, Russell and Reform', *Historical Journal*, XVII, 1974, 873–82. Gash remained unmoved by the argument: see his *Aristocracy and People. Britain, 1815–1865* (1979), p.118.

66 Gatrell, *Hanging Tree*, pp.568–9, 571, 585.

67 Third Lord Colchester, (editor), *Political Diary of Edward Law, Lord Ellenborough, 1828–30,* 2 Volumes (1881), I, 154–5.

68 *Hobhouse Diary,* pp.87, 104; *Colchester Diary,* III, 297; *George IV Letters,* III, letters 1208, 1550; *Ellenborough Diary,* II, 225.

69 Gatrell, *Hanging Tree,* pp.558, 566.

70 Boyd Hilton, *A Mad, Bad, & Dangerous People? England, 1783–1846* (Oxford, 2006), pp.318–20; cf. his 'The Gallows and Mr Peel' in T.C.W. Blanning and David Cannadine, (editors), *History and Biography: Essays in Honour of Derek Beales* (Cambridge, 1996), pp.88–112.

71 W.G. Brock, *Lord Liverpool and Liberal Toryism, 1820–1827* [1941], 2nd Edition (1967).

72 Hilton, *Mad, Bad,* pp.315–16, 320–1; for the stages by which Hilton worked out this argument, see his *Corn, Cash, Commerce: The Economic Policies of the Tory Governments, 1815–1830* (Oxford, 1977); *The Age of Atonement: The Influence of Evangelicalism on social and economic thought, 1795–1865* (Oxford, 1988), pp.218–36 and 'The Political Arts of Lord Liverpool', *Transactions of the Royal Historical Society,* 5th Series, 38, 1988, 147–70.

73 For critiques of Hilton, see Norman Gash's review of *Age of Atonement* in the *English Historical Review,* CIV, 1989, 136–40 and Stephen M. Lee, *George Canning and Liberal Toryism, 1801–1827* (Woodbridge, 2008), pp.135–51.

74 Simon Devereaux, 'Peel, Pardon and Punishment: The Recorder's Report Revisited' in Simon Devereaux and Paul Griffiths, (editors), *Punishing the English. Penal Practice and Culture, 1500–1900* (2004), pp.258–84: quotations at 259, 261, 265, 267–8, 279.

75 *Speeches,* I, 509. David Craig is currently working on a history of the terms 'liberal' and 'liberalism' during this period which is likely to reveal more about the changing context (and application) of them.

76 *Mrs Arbuthnot's Journal,* II, 103.

77 Palmerston is a case in point. See Stephen M. Lee, 'Palmerston and Canning' in David Brown and Miles Taylor, (editors), *Palmerston Studies I* (Southampton, 2007), pp.1–18.

78 John Gore, (editor), *The Creevey Papers* (1970), p.206; cf. Centre for Kentish Studies, Maidstone, Camden Papers, U840/C528/1, Hardinge to Camden, 20 October 1822; *Croker Papers,* I, 206, for conflicting reports of their rivalry.

79 The National Archives, Kew, WORK 20/31, Documents relating to the erection of Peel's statue in Parliament Square.

80 *Punch,* I, July–December 1841, 111; cf. *Blackwood's Edinburgh Magazine,* L, September 1841, 403; October 1841, 544. In 1827, Lord Ashley recorded a hostile appreciation of Canning's political character, declaring a preference for Peel's 'honesty and truth': Southampton University Library, Broadlands Papers, Shaftesbury Diaries, SHA/PD/1, 17 April, 20 May 1827.

81 Arthur Aspinall, (editor), *The Later Correspondence of George III,* 5 Volumes (Cambridge, 1962–70), V, letter 4126 n; *Croker Papers,* I, 41.

82 See *Mrs Arbuthnot's Journal,* I, 213; II, 69–70 for a retrospective view of their importance.

83 See Arthur Aspinall, 'Canning's return to office in September 1822', *English Historical Review,* LXXVIII, 1963, 531–45.

84 Kenneth Bourne, (editor), *The Letters of the Third Viscount Palmerston to Laurence and Elizabeth Sulivan, 1804–1863,* Royal Historical Society, Camden, 4th Series, 23, (1979), p.152; cf. Richard, Duke of Buckingham and Chandos, *Memoirs of the Court of George IV,* 2 Volumes (1859), I, 353.

85 *Croker Papers,* I, 209–10, 214.

86 *Hobhouse Diary,* pp.95–6; cf. *Memoirs of the Court of George IV,* I, 371.

87 Sandon Hall, Harrowby Manuscripts, XIV, f.119, Bathurst to Harrowby, 23 August 1822; The Seventh Duke of Wellington, (editor), *Wellington and His Friends* (1965), p.28.

88 *The Illustrated London News,* 6 July 1850, p.9.

89 *Hobhouse Diary*, pp.101–2; *Memoirs of the Court of George IV*, I, 475, 481; II, 105, 126; *Mrs Arbuthnot's Journal*, I, 271; II, 29, 69; *Bathurst*, p.543; Rachel Weigall, (editor), *Correspondence of Lord Burghersh afterwards Eleventh Earl of Westmorland, 1808–1840* (1912), p.255.

90 The definitive account of these proceedings is Aspinall, *Formation of Canning's Ministry*.

91 See Peel's letters to Canning and Eldon in Augustus Granville Stapleton, *George Canning and His Times* (1859), pp.590–6 and Horace Twiss, (editor), *The Public and Private Life of Lord Chancellor Eldon, with Selections from his Correspondence*, 3 Volumes (1844), II, 589–90.

92 For conflicting reports of Peel's intentions, see *Mrs Arbuthnot's Journal*, II, 79; *Creevey Papers*, p.257; Aspinall, *Formation of Canning's Ministry*, pp.22–4, 43; *Bathurst*, p.630; *Colchester Diary*, III, 469, 476; *Hobhouse Diary*, p.128.

93 *Mrs Arbuthnot's Journal*, II, 99; Aspinall, *Formation of Canning's Ministry*, pp.63–4, 67, 123; Agar Ellis Diary, 1 May 1827; John Brooke and Mary Sorensen, (editors), *Prime Ministers Papers: W.E. Gladstone*, 4 Volumes (1971–81), I, 190; cf. *Memoirs of the Court of George IV*, II, 348.

94 Devonshire MSS, Chatsworth, Diary of the 6th Duke of Devonshire, 11 April 1827; on Wellington's emergence as a candidate for the premiership, see Norman Gash, 'The Duke of Wellington and the Prime Ministership, 1824–30' in Norman Gash, (editor), *Wellington. Studies in the military and political career of the first Duke of Wellington* (Manchester, 1990), pp.117–38.

95 See my 'The Fourth Duke of Newcastle, the Ultra Tories and the Opposition to Canning's Administration', *History*, 88, 2003, 568–86.

96 Not least, by suspecting Croker's motivations (the result of his support for Canning): *Croker Papers*, I, 346; William Thomas, *The Quarrel of Macaulay and Croker. Politics and History in the Age of Reform* (Oxford, 2000), pp.97–8.

97 *George IV Letters*, III, letter 1323; Agar Ellis Diary, 3 May 1827; Denison Diary, Os 3 D1/68–9, 98, 3–4 May, 12 August 1827. The same point was later made by *Blackwood's Edinburgh Magazine*, 26, August 1829, 232; cf. *Lady Shelley's Diary*, II, 156.

98 Prior, *Remonstrance*, pp.10–11, 27, 40–1. Like Denison, Prior also referred to Peel's 'self-martyrdom' (p.42).

99 *Creevey Papers*, p.264.

100 Palmerston habitually acknowledged Peel as the Canningites' main supporter in Wellington's cabinet: Southampton University Library, Broadlands Papers, Palmerston Journal, PP/D2 (1828), pp.4–5, 23, 28–9, 35–6.

101 Thomas, *Quarrel*, p.98; William J. Baker, *Beyond Port and Prejudice. Charles Lloyd of Oxford, 1784–1829* (Maine, 1981), pp.173–4.

102 *Ellenborough Diary*, II, 195, 198–9, 270–1, 274, 316, 413; *Mrs Arbuthnot's Journal*, II, 342, 358–9.

103 For Toryism as 'constitutional conservatism', see Bruce Coleman, '1841–6', in Anthony Seldon, (editor), *How Tory Governments Fall: The Tory Party in power since 1783* (1996), p.111; for 'Tory' as synonymous with 'anti-catholic', Lee, *George Canning*, p.173.

104 *Croker Papers*, II, 62.

105 David Eastwood, '"Recasting Our Lot": Peel, the Nation, and the Politics of Interest' in Laurence Brockliss and David Eastwood, (editors), *A Union of Multiple Identities. The British Isles, c.1750–c.1850* (Manchester, 1997), pp.38–9.

106 Lee, *George Canning*, p.174.

107 John Vincent, (editor), *Disraeli, Derby and the Conservative Party: the Political Journals of Lord Stanley, 1849–69* (Hassocks, 1978), p.240; Lee, *George Canning, passim*.

108 *The Times*, 10 January 1829, p.2; *Ellenborough Diary*, I, 293.

109 George Otto Trevelyan, *The Life and Letters of Lord Macaulay* (Oxford, 1978), I, 214.

110 *Broughton Diary*, VI, 176–8; M.G. Wiebe *et al*, (editors), *Benjamin Disraeli: Letters*, 7 Volumes to date (Toronto, 1982–2004), IV, letter 1499 n.2; Arthur Christopher Benson

and Viscount Esher, (editors), *The Letters of Queen Victoria. A Selection from Her Majesty's Correspondence between the years 1837–1861*, 3 Volumes (Honolulu, 2002), II, 79–80.

111 Christopher Hibbert, *Greville's England. Selections from the Diaries of Charles Greville, 1818–1860* (1981), pp.209–10; cf. Shaftesbury Diaries, SHA/PD/4, 9 June 1846; *The Economist*, 20 June 1846, 794–6; *The Preston Chronicle*, 27 June 1846; Bawa Satinder Singh, (editor), *The Letters of the First Viscount Hardinge of Lahore to Lady Hardinge and Sir Walter and Lady James, 1844–1847,* Royal Historical Society, Camden, 4th Series, 32, (1986), p.186.

112 On the 'vehemence' of the Peelites, see Vincent, *Disraeli, Derby*, p.25.

Chapter Five

1 Lord Mahon and Edward Cardwell, (editors), *Memoirs of Sir Robert Peel* (New York, 1969), II, 59, 62.

2 Norman Gash, 'The Founder of Modern Conservatism' [1970], reprinted in his *Pillars of Government and other essays on state and society, c.1770–c.1880* (1986), pp.153–61. This was the period of Edward Heath's 'One Nation' leadership of the Conservative Party (1965–75); the party's acknowledged historian was the noted Disraeli scholar and Oxford academic, Robert Blake: *Disraeli* (1966); *The Conservative Party from Peel to Churchill* (1970).

3 Gash, *Pillars*, p.153; cf. *idem, Sir Robert Peel: The Life of Sir Robert Peel after 1830*, 2nd Edition (1986), pp.708–15. For a contemporary commentary on Peel as the party's 'founder', see *Blackwood's Edinburgh Magazine*, LV, January 1844, 104, 108.

4 Robert Blake, (editor), *The Sayings of Disraeli* (1992), p.47; M.G. Wiebe *et al*, (editors), *Benjamin Disraeli: Letters,* 7 Volumes to date (Toronto, 1982–2004), VII, letter 3385, c.June 1859.

5 Compare Gash's 'Peel and the Party System, 1830–1850', *Transactions of the Royal Historical Society,* 5th series, 1, 1951, 47–69 with his *Reaction and Reconstruction in English Politics, 1832–1852* (Oxford, 1965), pp.119–56.

6 Peter Ghosh, 'Gladstone and Peel' in Peter Ghosh and Lawrence Goldman, (editors), *Politics & Culture in Victorian Britain. Essays in Memory of Colin Matthew* (Oxford, 2006), p.45. For an endorsement of Gash's views, see J.T. Ward, 'Derby and Disraeli' in Donald Southgate, (editor), *The Conservative Leadership, 1832–1932* (1974), pp.91–2.

7 John Ramsden, *An Appetite for Power. A History of the Conservative Party since 1830* (1998), p.10. See Norman Gash, *Politics in the Age of Peel,* 2nd Edition (Hassocks, 1977); *idem,* 'Wellington and Peel' in Southgate, *Conservative Leadership,* pp.35–57; *idem,* 'From the Origins to Sir Robert Peel' in Lord Butler, (editor), *The Conservatives: A History from their Origins to 1965* (1977), pp.21–108; *idem,* 'The Organization of the Conservative Party, 1832–1846, Part I: The Parliamentary Organization', 'Part II: The Electoral Organization', *Parliamentary History,* 1–2, 1982–3, 137–59, 131–52; *idem,* Review of Robert Stewart, *The Foundation of the Conservative Party, 1830–1867* (1978), *English Historical Review,* XCIV, 1979, 870–7.

8 Paul Adelman, *Peel and the Conservative Party, 1830–50* (1989), p.93; Norman Gash, *The Radical Element in the History of the Conservative Party* (1989).

9 Robert Blake, 'In the top half dozen of history', *The Times,* 30 November 1990; cf. Stephen Evans, 'Thatcher and the Victorians: A Suitable Case for Comparison?', *History,* 82, 1997, 602 and Boyd Hilton, 'Robert Peel' in Robert Eccleshall and Graham Walker, (editors), *Biographical Dictionary of British Prime Ministers* (1998), pp.142–51.

10 Norman Gash, *Peel and Posterity* (Tamworth, 2000), p.8. For a nuanced study of this theme, see Michael Bentley, *Lord Salisbury's World. Conservative Environments in Late-Victorian Britain* (Cambridge, 2001), pp.295–321.

11 Also see William O. Aydelotte, 'Parties and Issues in Early Victorian England', *Journal of British Studies,* V, 1966, 95–114; David Close, 'The Formation of a two-party alignment

in the House of Commons between 1832 and 1841', *English Historical Review,* LXXXIV, 1969, 257–77 and 'The Rise of the Conservatives in the Age of Reform', *Bulletin of the Institute of Historical Research,* XLV, 1972, 89–103.

12 R.H. Cameron, 'Parties and Policies in Early Victorian Britain: A Suggestion for Revision', *Canadian Journal of History,* 13, 1979, 375–93; I.D.C. Newbould, 'The Emergence of a Two-Party System in England from 1830 to 1841: Roll call and Reconsideration', *Parliaments, Estates and Representation,* 5, 1985, 25–31.

13 I.D.C. Newbould, *Whiggery and Reform, 1830–41: The Politics of Government* (1990); Richard Brent, *Liberal Anglican Politics. Whiggery, Religion, and Reform 1830–1841* (Oxford, 1987); Peter Mandler, *Aristocratic Government in the Age of Reform. Whigs and Liberals, 1830–1852* (Oxford, 1990). Gash's response to this work appeared in *English Historical Review,* CV, 1990, 748; CIX, 1994, 490–1, 757–8. He had earlier regretted the comparative lack of attention devoted to the Whigs and Liberals in this period; *Sir Robert Peel,* p.vii.

14 Norman Gash, *The Historical Significance of the Tamworth Manifesto* (Tamworth, 1984) [also reprinted in *Pillars,* chapter 9]; Richard W. Davis, 'From Toryism to Tamworth: The Triumph of Reform, 1827–35', *Albion,* 12, 1980, 132–46; Betty Kemp, 'The General Election of 1841', *History,* XXXVII, 1952, 146–57; Robert Stewart, 'The Ten Hours and Sugar Crises of 1844: Government and the House of Commons in the Age of Reform', *Historical Journal,* XII, 1969, 35.

15 Edwin Jaggard, 'The 1841 British General Election: A Reconsideration', *Australian Journal of Politics and History,* 30, 1984, 99–114; Gilbert A. Cahill, 'Irish Catholicism and English Toryism', *Review of Politics,* 19, 1957, 62–76; John Wolffe, *The Protestant Crusade in Great Britain, 1829–60* (Oxford, 1991), chapter 3.

16 Jonathan Parry, *The Age of Peel* (1996), p.7. I am grateful to Jon Parry for providing me with a copy of this lecture (delivered to the Conservative Political Centre), which stresses Peel's traditional – rather than aggressively progressive – leadership of the Conservative Party.

17 Travis L. Crosby, *Sir Robert Peel's Administration, 1841–1846* (Newton Abbot, 1976); Bruce Coleman, '1841–6', in Anthony Seldon, (editor), *How Tory Governments Fall: The Tory Party in power since 1783* (1996), pp.104–57; D.R. Fisher, *The Opposition to Sir Robert Peel in the Conservative Party, 1841–1846* (PhD Thesis, University of Cambridge, 1970); *idem,* 'Peel and the Conservative Party: The Sugar Crisis of 1844 Reconsidered', *Historical Journal,* XVIII, 1975, 279–302; W.O. Aydelotte, 'The Disintegration of the Conservative Party in the 1840s: A Study of Political Attitudes' in William O. Aydelotte, A.G. Bogue and R. Fogel, (editors), *The Dimension of Quantitative Research in History* (Princeton, 1972), pp.319–46; *idem,* 'Voting Patterns in the British House of Commons in the 1840s', *Comparative Studies in Society and History,* 5, 1963, 134–63.

18 David Eastwood, 'Peel and the Tory Party Reconsidered', *History Today,* 42, March 1992, 32.

19 David Large, 'The House of Lords and Ireland in the Age of Peel, c.1832–50' in Clyve Jones and David Lewis Jones, (editors), *Peers, Politics and Power* (1986), pp.373–405; J.M. Sweeney, *The House of Lords in British Politics, 1830–1841* (DPhil Thesis, University of Oxford, 1973).

20 The National Archives, Kew, Ellenborough Papers, PRO 30/12/6/6, f.22, Peel to Ellenborough, 28 July 1835.

21 See A.D. Kriegel, (editor), *The Holland House Diaries, 1831–1840* (1977), p.327; Spencer Walpole, *The Life of Lord John Russell,* 2 Volumes (Honolulu, 2005), I, 245.

22 Sheffield Archives, Wharncliffe Papers, Wh M 516/43, Peel to Wharncliffe, 4 September 1835.

23 Richard W. Davis, *A Political History of the House of Lords, 1811–1846* (Stanford, 2008), p.258. Also see, F.C. Mather, 'Wellington and Peel: Conservative Statesmen of the 1830s,'

Transactions of the Peel Society, 5, 1985–6, 7–23; *idem,* '"Nestor or Achilles?", The Duke of Wellington in British Politics, 1832–46' in Norman Gash, (editor), *Wellington. Studies in the military and political career of the first Duke of Wellington* (Manchester, 1990), pp.170–95.

24 I.D.C. Newbould, 'Sir Robert Peel and the Conservative Party, 1832–1841: A study in failure?', *English Historical Review,* XCVIII, 1983, 529–57.

25 See Coleman, '1841–6', pp.107–10 for detailed figures.

26 Philip Salmon, *Electoral Reform at Work. Local Politics and National Parties, 1832–1841* (Woodbridge, 2002).

27 William Thomas, *The Quarrel of Macaulay and Croker. Politics and History in the Age of Reform* (Oxford, 2000), p.94; Coleman, '1841–6', p.152. For a contemporary argument that the Conservative revival was not all about Peel, see *Corn and Consistency. A Few Remarks in reply to a pamphlet entitled "Sir Robert Peel and the Corn Law Crisis"* (1846), pp.23–5.

28 Thomas, *Quarrel,* p.94 n.2. Kitson Clark never completed his proposed book on Peel and the Corn Laws which might have addressed the issue: Norman Gash, 'George Kitson Clark' in H.C.G. Matthew and Brian Harrison, (editors), *The Oxford Dictionary of National Biography,* 60 Volumes (Oxford, 2004), XI, 802. In its absence, see George Kitson Clark, 'The Electorate and the Repeal of the Corn Laws', *Transactions of the Royal Historical Society,* 5th Series, 1, 1951, 109–26 and 'The Repeal of the Corn Laws and the Politics of the Forties', *Economic History Review,* 2nd Series, IV, 1951, 1–13.

29 See Robert Stewart, *The Foundation of the Conservative Party, 1830–1867* (1978) and Gash's review, cited above in n.7.

30 Sandon Hall, Harrowby Papers, XIX, ff.126–7, Peel to Harrowby, 5 February 1832.

31 Thomas, *Quarrel,* p.107.

32 *Blackwood's Edinburgh Magazine,* LV, January 1844, 103; Thomas, *Quarrel,* p.100; for the Merchant Taylor's Hall speech, see Kenneth Baker, (editor), *The Faber Book of Conservatism* (1993), p.26.

33 Gash, 'Peel and the party system', 56.

34 *Speeches delivered in the House of Commons by the late Rt. Hon. Sir Robert Peel,* 4 Volumes (New York, 1972), III, 802; cf. *ibid.,* 703, 810–11; Louis J. Jennings, (editor), *The Correspondence and Diaries of the late Right Honorable John Wilson Croker,* 2–Volume edition (New York, 1884), II, 179.

35 Edward Pearce, (editor), with Deanna Pearce, *The Diaries of Charles Greville* (2005), p.186

36 Third Lord Colchester, (editor), *Political Diary of Edward Law, Lord Ellenborough, 1828–30,* 2 Volumes (1881), II, 315, 433; Arthur Aspinall, (editor), *Three Early Nineteenth Century Diaries* (1952), p.27.

37 Carola Oman, *The Gascoyne heiress: the life and diaries of Frances Mary Gascoyne-Cecil, 1802-39* (1968), p.204; Donald Read, *Peel and the Victorians* (Oxford, 1987), p.7.

38 Ghosh, 'Gladstone and Peel', p.54 and n.45.

39 Michael Brock, *The Great Reform Act* (1973) remains the standard account of the Bill's subsequent history and passage.

40 Aspinall, *Three Diaries,* pp.13–15; Pearce, *Greville,* pp.70, 121; E.A. Smith, *Reform or Revolution? A Diary of Reform in England, 1830–32* (Stroud, 1992), p.51; John Brooke and Mary Sorensen, (editors), *Prime Ministers Papers: W.E. Gladstone,* 4 Volumes (1971–81), II, 52.

41 *Blackwood's Edinburgh Magazine,* LXVIII, September 1850, 358; Henry Reeve, (editor), *The Greville Memoirs. A Journal of the Reigns of King George IV, King William IV and Queen Victoria,* 8 Volumes (1888), VI, 361–2.

42 Greville thought Peel had 'eminently distinguished himself' in March 1831: Pearce, *Greville,* p.96; Ghosh, 'Peel and Gladstone', p.54.

43 Pearce, *Greville,* p.90; *Speeches,* II, 424–33.

44 *Holland House Diaries*, p.178; Brooke and Sorensen, *Gladstone*, II, 24.

45 Notably, in his speech at the opening of the Reformed Parliament on 7 February 1833: *Speeches*, II, 604–13.

46 Thomas, *Quarrel*, p.100. Although he distances himself from Gash, Thomas's stress on Peel's 'executive' ethic is very much in the same tradition: *ibid.*, p.94.

47 Philip Harling, *The Waning of 'Old Corruption': The Politics of Economical Reform in Britain, 1779–1846* (Oxford, 1996); Angus Hawkins, '"Parliamentary Government" and Victorian Political Parties, c.1830–1880', *English Historical Review*, CIV, 1989, 638–69.

48 Coleman, '1841–6', p.469 n.6 (commenting on Newbould's work, cited above in n.24).

49 From Peel's speech at a dinner to his Tamworth constituents: *The Times*, 26 January 1835, p.1; cf. 22 January 1835, p.2.

50 Margaret Thatcher, *The Downing Street Years* (1993), p.281; Arthur Aspinall, *Politics and the Press, c.1780–1850* (1949), p.192.

51 The National Archives, Ellenborough Diaries, PRO 30/12/28/5, p.67, 13 December 1834; Pearce, *Greville*, p.135.

52 I.D.C. Newbould, 'William IV and the Dismissal of the Whigs, 1834', *Canadian Journal of History*, XI, 1976, 311–30.

53 Robert Blake, 'Foreword' in (editor), *Oxford Illustrated Encyclopedia. Volume 4. World History From 1800 to the Present Day* (Oxford, 1988).

54 See the letter addressed to Peel in *The Times*, 26 December 1834, p.3. Out of office, Peel declared that he 'had not undertaken to govern on ultra principles': *The Times*, 5 September 1835, p.4.

55 *The Times*, 22 December 1834, p.3; Angus Hawkins, *The Forgotten Prime Minister, The 14th Earl of Derby, Ascent, 1799–1851* (Oxford, 2007), chapter 3.

56 *The Times*, 25 December 1834, p.2; Southampton University Library, Broadlands Papers, Shaftesbury Diaries, SHA/PD/1, f.109, 26 December 1834; Harrowby Papers, XVI, f.210, Wharncliffe to Harrowby, 25 December 1834; Ellenborough Diaries, p.98, 23 December 1834.

57 This element in Stanley's character is well brought out in Jon Parry's review of Hawkins' biography: *Parliamentary History*, 27, 2008, 299–302.

58 See John Vincent, (editor), *Disraeli, Derby and the Conservative Party: the Political Journals of Lord Stanley, 1849–69* (Hassocks, 1978), p.26. It was Stanley (and not, as is so often maintained, Peel) whom O'Connell had in view when he compared his smile to 'the silver plate on a coffin'. However, it says everything about Peel's character and temperament that he could stand proxy for Stanley, in the jibe, without raising much dissent: Norman Gash, *Mr Secretary Peel: The Life of Sir Robert Peel before 1830,* 2nd Edition (1985), pp.x–xi; Roy Jenkins, *The Chancellors* (1998), pp.182–3.

59 John Brooke and Julia Gandy, (editors), *Prime Ministers Papers: Wellington, Political Correspondence, Volume I: 1833–1834* (1975), p.228.

60 *Croker Papers*, II, 56–7. The same point was made in a long appeal from Lord Harrowby's heir (Lord Sandon) to Stanley: Harrowby Papers, XVII, ff.197–9, 10 December 1834.

61 Ruscombe Foster, 'Peel and his Party: "The Age of Peel" Reassessed' in Peter Catterall, (editor), *Britain, 1815–1867* (1994), p.79. Boyd Hilton calls the Manifesto's sentiments 'vacuous': 'Robert Peel', p.147.

62 Ellenborough Diaries, p.29, 28 November 1834; Lloyd C. Sanders, (editor), *Lord Melbourne's Papers* (1889), p.240; *Wellington, Political Correspondence,* p.130.

63 Lord Rosebery, 'Sir Robert Peel', *Anglo-Saxon Review*, I, 1899, 100; cf. British Library, Peel Papers, 40418, ff.133, 158, Buckingham and Chandos to Peel, Kenyon to Peel, 26 March 1835.

64 For accounts which stress the decline of the Ultra Tories at this period, see B.T. Bradfield, 'Sir Richard Vyvyan and the Country Gentlemen, 1830–34', *English Historical Review*, LXXXIII, 1968, 729–43; D.G.S. Simes, *The Ultra Tories in British Politics, 1824–1834*

(DPhil Thesis, University of Oxford, 1974); Stewart, *Foundation of the Conservative Party*, p.104.

65 *Holland House Diaries*, p.279.

66 Ellice to Durham, 19 March 1835 in Arthur Aspinall, *Lord Brougham and the Whig Party* (Stroud, 2005), pp.449–50.

67 George Henry Francis, *The late Sir Robert Peel, Bart. A Critical Biography. Reprinted, with additions, from Fraser's Magazine* (1852), p.73.

68 *The Times*, 19 December 1834, p.2; Pearce, *Greville*, p.137; Ellenborough Diaries, p.91, 20 December 1834.

69 John Morrow, (editor), *Young England. The New Generation. A Selection of Primary Texts* (Leicester, 1999), p.142. For a counter-view, see John Phillips and Charles Wetherell, 'The Great Reform Act of 1832 and the political modernization of England', *American Historical Review*, C, 1995, 433–4.

70 British Library, Peel Papers, 40418, f.264, Clarendon to Peel, 29 March 1835 (for Peel's reply of 30 March see f.265); Michael Ledger-Lomas, 'The Character of Pitt the Younger and Party Politics, 1830–1860', *Historical Journal*, 47, 2004, 652; cf. Gregory Claeys, (editor), *The Chartist Movement in Britain, 1838–50*, 6 Volumes (2001), II, 409.

71 *Croker Papers*, II, 67; British Library, Peel Papers, 40418, f.188, Peel to Haddington, 26 March 1835; *Holland House Diaries*, p.283; cf. Ellenborough Diaries, p.242, 28 March 1835.

72 Gredington, Whitchurch, Shropshire, Diaries of Lord Kenyon, 18 February 1835; Shaftesbury Diaries, SHA/PD/1, f.98, 15 December 1834.

73 Ellenborough Diary, pp.231–2, 235, 25–6 March 1835; cf. *Wellington, Political Correspondence*, pp.557–8, 589–90; Hughe Knatchbull-Hugessen, *Kentish Family* (1960), pp.222–5.

74 *A Letter to Sir Robert Peel on the present crisis* (1835), pp.4–5.

75 Pearce, *Greville*, p.144.

76 Thomas, *Quarrel*, pp.103–4; cf. *The Quarterly Review*, LIII, February 1835, 261–87.

77 Gash, *Pillars*, chapter 9; Patrick C. Lipscomb, 'Party Politics, 1801–1802: George Canning and the Trinidad Question', *Historical Journal*, 12, 1969, 466.

78 Numerous attempts had been made to offer Peel the party leadership after 1830: for one (which dispirited Hardinge), see *Ellenborough Diary*, II, 441.

79 Thomas, *Quarrel*, pp.100, 106.

80 Lady Rose Weigall, (editor), *Correspondence of Lady Burghersh with the Duke of Wellington* (1903), pp.76–7; cf. *Wellington, Political Correspondence*, p.255; E. Jones Parry, (editor), *The Correspondence of Lord Aberdeen and Princess Lieven, 1832–1854*, 2 Volumes, Royal Historical Society, Camden, 3rd Series, LX, LXII (1938–9), I, 99, 138; Brooke and Sorensen, *Gladstone*, II, 92–3, 97–8.

81 Thomas, *Quarrel*, p.111.

82 Grant attributed this dominance to Peel's independent fortune and 'great talents': James Grant, *Random Recollections of the House of Commons* (1836), pp.116, 119; cf. *The Times*, 7 January 1836, p.4. By contrast, another critic said that Peel's superiority was magnified by the deficiency of the alternatives: *A Few Plain Words to Sir Robert Peel* (1836), p.11.

83 Wharncliffe Papers, Wh M 516/69, Wellington to Wharncliffe, 26 January 1836; Francis, *Peel*, pp.77–8.

84 National Register of Archives Scotland, 901, Hamilton Papers, Newcastle to the Duke of Hamilton, 29 June 1835.

85 Blake, *Sayings*, p.49; Benjamin Disraeli, *Lord George Bentinck: A Political Biography* (New Brunswick, New Jersey, 1998), p.201.

86 *Disraeli Letters*, II, letter 557. Disraeli was more charitable towards Peel in his public letter (under the pseudonym 'Runnymede') in *The Times*, 27 January 1836, p.2.

87 Arthur Christopher Benson and Viscount Esher, (editors), *The Letters of Queen Victoria. A Selection from Her Majesty's Correspondence between the years 1837–1861*, 3 Volumes

(Honolulu, 2002), I, 58; Nottingham University Manuscripts Department, Newcastle of Clumber Collection, Ne C 5778, Hamilton to Newcastle, 1 February 1837.

88 After hearing Peel's speech to 300 Conservative MPs at the Merchant Taylor's Hall (in May 1838), Gladstone noted that Peel 'is not best after dinner': M.R.D. Foot and H.C.G. Matthew, (editors), *The Gladstone Diaries*, 14 Volumes (Oxford, 1968–94), II, 370.

89 *Authentic Report of the Glasgow Festival, with biography and essay on Sir Robert Peel's personal and political character* (5th edition, 1837), p.32; *The Times*, 13–16 January 1837; *Gladstone Diaries*, II, 274.

90 *Holland House Diaries*, p.355.

91 *Croker Papers*, II, 101; Arthur Aspinall, 'Extracts from Lord Hatherton's Diary', *Parliamentary Affairs*, XVII/2, 1963, 135; Thomas, *Quarrel*, p.113.

92 *The Times*, 30 April 1839, p.4.

93 Christopher Hibbert, *Queen Victoria in her Letters and Journals* (Stroud, 2000), p.48; cf. pp.49, 62. William IV's consort, Queen Adelaide, was widely believed to be a Tory partisan at the time of the Reform Bill.

94 See Read, *Peel and the Victorians*, pp.63–96.

95 Ellenborough Diaries, pp.270–1, 8 April 1835.

96 *Blackwood's Edinburgh Magazine*, LXVIII, September 1850, 359; Reeve, *Greville Memoirs*, 362–3.

97 Christopher Hibbert, *Greville's England. Selections from the Diaries of Charles Greville, 1818–1860* (1981), pp.124–5.

98 See the reports in *The Times*, 17, 27–30 April, 1, 16 and 21 May 1835.

99 Charles Vincent Graham, *Heads or Tails: A Poetical Epistle* (1835), p.7; cf. *The Times*, 15 August 1837, p.6; 17 August 1837, p.5.

100 From Peel's response to the address of the City of London: *The Times*, 7 April 1835, p.5.

101 George Kitson Clark, *The Life and Work of Sir Robert Peel* (1950), p.4; cf. Arthur Burns, 'English Church Reform Revisited, 1780–1840' in Joanna Innes and Arthur Burns, (editors), *Rethinking the Age of Reform* (Cambridge, 2003), pp.136–62.

102 Harrowby Papers, XVI, ff.50–1, Peel to Harrowby, 12 January 1835.

103 P.J. Welch, 'Blomfield and Peel: a Study in Co-operation between Church and State, 1841–46', *Journal of Ecclesiastical History*, 12, 1961, 71–84; for the equivalent of an Ultra Tory cleric, see G.C.B. Davies, *Henry Phillpotts, Bishop of Exeter, 1778–1869* (1954).

104 *Croker Papers*, II, 63–5; Richard A. Gaunt, (editor), *Unrepentant Tory. Political Selections from the Diaries of the Fourth Duke of Newcastle-under-Lyne, 1827–38* (Woodbridge, 2006), p.262; cf. Ellenborough Diaries, pp.140–1, 173, 19 January, 5 February 1835; Brooke and Sorensen, *Gladstone*, II, 189.

105 David Eastwood, '"Recasting Our Lot": Peel, the Nation, and the Politics of Interest' in Laurence Brockliss and David Eastwood, (editors), *A Union of Multiple Identities. The British Isles, c.1750–c.1850* (Manchester, 1997), p.39.

106 The event was advertised in *The Times*, 30 April 1835, p.4 and 1 May 1835, p.2.

107 *Gladstone Diaries*, II, 169; *Blackwood's Edinburgh Magazine*, XXXVIII, July 1835, 2.

108 In fact, Wellington was reported to be upset at both the dinner and Peel's reference to the Reform Act as unalterable: Ellenborough Diaries, p.282, 12 May 1835.

109 *On Sir Robert Peel's Speech delivered at a dinner at Merchant Tailor's Hall, Monday, May 11th, 1835* (Bath, 1835); cf. *The Times*, 12 May 1835, p.5.

110 *The Hatherton Diaries. The Diaries of the First Lord Hatherton. Extracts from the personal diary, between the years 1817–1862 of Edward Walhouse Littleton afterwards The First Lord Hatherton, 1791–1863* (Privately printed, n.d.), entry for 14 December 1845; *The Times*, 13 December 1845, p.4. For a similar argument, see Charles Cavendish Fulke Greville, *Sir Robert Peel and the Corn Law Crisis*, 3rd Edition (1846), pp.4–9.

111 Gash, *Sir Robert Peel*, pp.ix–x. For David Eastwood, the lessons of Lord Liverpool's ministry had taught Peel 'that a broadly Liberal Tory leadership could reasonably expect the loyalty of more obviously high Tory back-benchers': 'Peel and the Tory Party', 28.

112 *Memoirs of Sir Robert Peel*, II, 322.
113 For a corrected version of Peel's speech and Newman's letters, see Ian Ker, *et al* (editors), *The Letters and Diaries of John Henry Newman*, 32 Volumes to date (Oxford, 1961–2008), VIII, 525–61.
114 See the comments of *The Morning Chronicle*, 12 February 1841 and Walter's letter to Newman, 10 February 1841 [the letter is misdated 1840]; *ibid.*, 30, 40 n.4.
115 See Walter to Newman, 12 February 1841, *ibid.*, 31; *The Times*, 12 February 1841, p.4; for external criticism of the letters, see *The Times*, 10 March 1841, p.4. For the whole dispute, see Wendell V. Harris, 'Newman, Peel, Tamworth, and the Concurrence of Historical Forces', *Victorian Studies*, 32 (1989), 189–208.
116 R.H. Cameron, 'The Melbourne Administration, the Liberals and the Crisis of 1841', *Durham University Journal*, 38, 1976, 83–102.
117 Nottingham University Manuscripts Department, Ne C 5577, Lincoln to Newcastle, 1 May 1841.
118 The most direct historical parallel for these events also resulted in a Conservative administration. James Callaghan's Labour government was defeated (by one vote) on a vote of no-confidence, in March 1979. Margaret Thatcher was elected Prime Minister at the subsequent General Election in May: Thatcher, *The Downing Street Years*, pp.3–19.
119 *The Illustrated London News*, 13 July 1850, p.46.
120 *Speeches*, III, 757 (18 May 1841).
121 See Vincent, *Disraeli, Derby*, p.53; Hibbert, *Greville*, pp.186–8 (especially 6 September 1841); *Punch*, I, July–December 1841, 90.
122 Thomas, *Quarrel*, p.114.
123 For a modern example, see Douglas Hurd, 'Sir Robert Peel. The Making of a Party', *History Today*, 57, July 2007, 11–17, which concentrates on 1832–41, rather than the aftermath. It is hardly surprising that the Conservative Party's current (at 2009) leader, David Cameron, has likened his mission in opposition to that of Sir Robert Peel. This has been the habitual resort of the party in opposition. For example, R.A. Butler likened the party's *Industrial Charter* (1947) to the Tamworth Manifesto.
124 Disraeli set a new historical precedent by resigning as Prime Minister in November 1868 on the basis of the General Election results, without testing his voting strength in the House of Commons: Blake, *Disraeli*, p.514.

Chapter Six
1 *Speeches delivered in the House of Commons by the late Rt. Hon. Sir Robert Peel*, 4 Volumes (New York, 1972), IV, 716–17.
2 Walter L. Burn, *The Age of Equipoise* (1964); George Peel, (editor), *The Private Letters of Sir Robert Peel* (1920), p.282.
3 George Kitson Clark, *The Making of Victorian England* (1962); Norman Gash, *The Historical Importance of the Repeal of the Corn Laws* (Tamworth, 1996).
4 In spite of contentions to the contrary (notably, some purple passages in Disraeli's biography of *Lord George Bentinck*), there was no discernible difference in the social and economic backgrounds of Protectionist and Peelite MPs: William O. Aydelotte, 'The Country Gentlemen and the Repeal of the Corn Laws', *English Historical Review*, LXXXII, 1967, 47–60.
5 *The Economist*, 20 December 1845, 1286. For accounts which are 'revisionist' in different ways, see Robert Stewart, *The Politics of Protection: Lord Derby and the Protectionist Party, 1841–1852* (Cambridge, 1971); Angus MacIntyre, 'Lord George Bentinck and the Protectionists: A lost cause?', *Transactions of the Royal Historical Society*, 5th Series, 39, 1989, 141–65; Bruce Coleman, '1841–6', in Anthony Seldon, (editor), *How Tory Governments Fall: The Tory Party in power since 1783* (1996), pp.104–57; Anna Gambles, 'Rethinking the Politics of Protection: Conservatism and the Corn Laws, 1830–1852',

English Historical Review, CXIII, 1998, 928–52; *idem, Protection and Politics. Conservative Economic Discourse, 1815–1852* (Woodbridge, 1999); William Thomas, *The Quarrel of Macaulay and Croker. Politics and History in the Age of Reform* (Oxford, 2000), pp.128–34; Richard A. Gaunt, 'Disraeli, Peel and the Corn Laws: the making of a conservative reputation', *The Historian,* 97, 2008, 30–33.

6 Boyd Hilton, *A Mad, Bad, & Dangerous People? England, 1783–1846* (Oxford, 2006), p.558; for an alternative view, see David Eastwood, '"Recasting Our Lot": Peel, the Nation, and the Politics of Interest' in Laurence Brockliss and David Eastwood, (editors), *A Union of Multiple Identities. The British Isles, c.1750–c.1850* (Manchester, 1997), p.42 n.25.

7 Boyd Hilton, *The Age of Atonement: The Influence of Evangelicalism on social and economic thought, 1795–1865* (Oxford, 1988), pp.248–51; *idem,* 'Peel, Potatoes, and Providence', *Political Studies,* 49, 2001, 106–9; *Speeches,* IV, 626.

8 Hilton, *Mad, Bad,* p.551.

9 Norman Gash, *Mr Secretary Peel: The Life of Sir Robert Peel before 1830,* 2nd Edition (1985), pp.xii–xiii. For Peel as a second Huskisson, see *The Times,* 11 February 1842, p.5.

10 *The Quarterly Review,* LXXXI, September 1847, 556 (and see 577); cf. *ibid.,* June 1847, 313–14 and LXXVIII, September 1846, 553, 557. For one example of the speech's posthumous purchase, see Joseph Arnould, *Memorial Lines on Sir Robert Peel* (1850), p.7.

11 Boyd Hilton, 'Robert Peel' in Robert Eccleshall and Graham Walker, (editors), *Biographical Dictionary of British Prime Ministers* (1998), p.150. Richard Cobden maintained that it was the 'unsparing hostility' of Peel's opponents in 1846 which 'inflicted martyrdom upon him': Jean Scott Rogers, *Cobden and his Kate, the story of a marriage* (1990), p.94.

12 Eastwood, 'Recasting Our Lot', p.30. This was Croker's complaint: Louis J. Jennings, (editor), *The Correspondence and Diaries of the late Right Honorable John Wilson Croker,* 2-Volume edition (New York, 1884), II, 274–5.

13 David Eastwood, 'Peel and the Tory Party Reconsidered', *History Today,* 42, March 1992, 27–8, 30, 33, 37.

14 Arthur Christopher Benson and Viscount Esher, (editors), *The Letters of Queen Victoria. A Selection from Her Majesty's Correspondence between the years 1837–1861,* (Honolulu, 2002), II, 82; Lady Rose Weigall, (editor), *Correspondence of Lady Burghersh with the Duke of Wellington* (1903), p.174; Christopher Hibbert, *Greville's England. Selections from the Diaries of Charles Greville, 1818–1860* (1981), p.210. Also see Norman Gash, (editor), *The Age of Peel* (1968), p.180.

15 For positive appraisals (including international comment), see *The Times,* 9 July 1846, p.3; *The Economist,* 4 July 1846, 857; *Punch,* X, January–June 1846, 164; XI, July–December 1846, 14–15, 25; Donald Read, *Peel and the Victorians* (Oxford, 1987), pp.230–41.

16 *Reflections Suggested by the career of the late Premier* (1847), p.37.

17 Lady Dorchester, (editor), *Recollections of a long life by Lord Broughton (John Cam Hobhouse). With additional extracts from his private diaries,* 6 Volumes (1910–11), VI, 180–1. Hobhouse was consistently unmoved by Peel's parliamentary speeches as Prime Minister; cf. 57–8, 136–7.

18 *Letters of Queen Victoria,* II, 82–3.

19 Disraeli called Peel's peroration 'elaborate, but rather clumsily expressed': *Lord George Bentinck: A Political Biography* (New Brunswick, New Jersey, 1998), p.197; Anthony Howe, (editor), *The Letters of Richard Cobden. Volume One, 1815–1847* (Oxford, 2007), p.448. George Henry Francis admitted 'something very much like arrogance' in Peel's speech: *The late Sir Robert Peel, Bart. A Critical Biography. Reprinted, with additions, from Fraser's Magazine* (1852), pp.91–2.

20 *Letters of Queen Victoria,* II, 85, 87.

21　*The Northern Star,* 4 July 1846, p.4, cols.3–6; for complaints that Peel had kicked at the aristocracy which had raised him to power, see *Blackwood's Edinburgh Magazine,* LXI, January 1847, 98–9, 107 and *Reflections Suggested by the career of the late Premier,* p.49.

22　Southampton University Library, Broadlands Papers, Shaftesbury Diaries, SHA/PD/4, ff.108–9, 3 July 1846 (cf. 6 July 1846).

23　M.R.D. Foot and H.C.G. Matthew, (editors), *The Gladstone Diaries,* 14 Volumes (Oxford, 1968–94), III, 547; John Brooke and Mary Sorensen, (editors), *Prime Ministers Papers: W.E. Gladstone,* 4 Volumes (1971–81), III, 19–25 (also see II, 279); cf. Bawa Satinder Singh, (editor), *The Letters of the First Viscount Hardinge of Lahore to Lady Hardinge and Sir Walter and Lady James, 1844–1847,* Royal Historical Society, Camden, 4th Series, 32, (1986), p.190.

24　*The Economist,* 17 July 1847, 808. For an earlier declaration in the same vein see Shaftesbury Diaries, SHA/PD/4, f.33, 27 October 1845.

25　*The Economist,* 24 July 1847, 834; cf. *ibid.,* 31 July 1847, 864–5. For the letter and its aftermath, see *The Times,* 17 July 1847, p.6; *Punch,* XIII, July–December 1847, 4, 29, 44; *The Quarterly Review,* LXXXI, September 1847, 541–78.

26　John Morley, *The Life of Richard Cobden,* 2 Volumes (1908), I, 374. Cobden was writing in 1856.

27　*The Economist,* 27 June 1846, 825–8.

28　*Speeches,* III, 591; cf. Brooke and Sorensen, *Gladstone,* II, 229; *Croker Papers,* II, 24–5 and Joshua Proctor Brown Westhead, *A Letter to the Rt. Hon. Sir Robert Peel Bart on the Corn Laws* (Manchester, 1839).

29　See Richard A. Gaunt, (editor), *'The Last of the Tories'. Political Selections from the Diaries of the Fourth Duke of Newcastle-under-Lyne, 1839–50* (forthcoming).

30　For the letter, dated 6 August 1846, see *The Times,* 2 September 1846, p.7; *The Quarterly Review,* LXXVIII, September 1846, 562–3, LXXXI, June 1847, 314; *The Economist,* 9 January 1847, 32–3; 23 January 1847, 96.

31　The seriousness of the social and economic situation is brought out in George Kitson Clark, 'Hunger and Politics in 1842', *Journal of Modern History,* 25, 1953, 355–74.

32　Francis Bamford and the Seventh Duke of Wellington, (editors), *The Journal of Mrs Arbuthnot, 1820–1832,* 2 Volumes (1950), II, 343, 345; Third Lord Colchester, (editor), *Political Diary of Edward Law, Lord Ellenborough, 1828–30,* 2 Volumes (1881), II, 213, 216; Jelinger Cookson Symons, *Sir Robert Peel as a type of Statesmanship* (1856), pp.128–44.

33　Martin Daunton, *Trusting Leviathan. The Politics of Taxation in Britain, 1799–1914* (Cambridge, 2001), p.80.

34　Brooke and Sorensen, *Gladstone,* III, 270; *The Times,* 26 April 1842, p.4.

35　*Croker Papers,* II, 173; *Punch,* II, January–June 1842, 118, 128, 138–9. Income Tax was not introduced into Ireland until 1853 although Peel imposed it on absentee landlords and equalised the duties on spirits between England and Ireland: Eastwood, 'Recasting Our Lot', p.36.

36　*Croker Papers,* II, 175, 178.

37　*ibid.,* 177, 183; *The Quarterly Review,* LXX, September 1842, 489–94, 511–13; Daunton, *Trusting Leviathan,* p.86; cf. *The Times,* 13 May 1842, p.6.

38　Nottingham University Manuscripts Department, Newcastle of Clumber Collection, Ne C 7834, John Parkinson to Lord Lincoln, 18 March 1842; cf. John Jolliffe, (editor), *Neglected Genius. The Diaries of Benjamin Robert Haydon, 1808–1846* (1990), p.204.

39　Brooke and Sorensen, *Gladstone,* III, 270. For reactions to the 1845 budget, see Edward Pearce, (editor), with Deanna Pearce, *The Diaries of Charles Greville* (2005), p.231; *The Economist,* 15 February 1845, 142; Valerie Sanders, (editor), *Harriet Martineau. Selected Letters* (Oxford, 1990), p.109.

40　*Punch,* VIII, January–June 1845, 115; cf. 76, 102–3, 118, 129.

41 See Goulburn's deferential tone towards Peel even whilst dissenting from the necessity for the Repeal of the Corn Laws in 1845: Gash, *Age of Peel*, p.128.

42 Brooke and Sorensen, *Gladstone*, II, 221.

43 For example, see Lancashire Record Office, Kenyon Papers, DDKE 7840, Box 73, Guilford to Kenyon, 12 February 1843. John Henry Newman also thought the Income Tax a 'swing[e]ing concern': Ian Ker, *et al* (editors), *The Letters and Diaries of John Henry Newman*, 32 Volumes to date (Oxford, 1961–2008), IX, 50.

44 *Hardinge Letters*, p.47 n.100.

45 The former was indirect in the sense that the income derived was dependent on the quantity consumed (bought and sold), which was at the discretion of the purchaser. The latter was 'direct' because the individual taxed had no choice in the matter.

46 *Speeches*, IV, 696.

47 Eastwood, 'Recasting our Lot', p.33; cf. Daunton, *Trusting Leviathan*, p.78; Philip Harling, *The Waning of 'Old Corruption': The Politics of Economical Reform in Britain, 1779–1846* (Oxford, 1996), pp.228–54.

48 Gregory Claeys, (editor), *The Chartist Movement in Britain, 1838–50*, 6 Volumes (2001), IV, 188 (cf. 94); cf. *The Economist*, 3 November 1849, 1214–15.

49 The two views may be compared in, respectively, Gareth Stedman Jones, 'Rethinking Chartism' in his *Languages of Class: Studies in English Working Class History, 1832–1982* (Oxford, 1983), pp.90–178 and Tony Dickson and Tony Clarke, 'Social concern and social control in nineteenth century Scotland: Paisley, 1841–1843', *Scottish Historical Review*, LXV, 1986, 48–60.

50 *The Economist*, 22 January 1848, 85–7; M.G. Wiebe *et al*, (editors), *Benjamin Disraeli: Letters*, 7 Volumes to date (Toronto, 1982–2004), V, 1636 n.2.

51 Nottinghamshire Archives, Craven Smith Milnes of Hockerton Manor MSS, DD/CW/7/19 (bundle), John Evelyn Denison to E.P. Burnell, 20 February [1848].

52 Daunton, *Trusting Leviathan*, p.83.

53 *The Quarterly Review*, LXXXI, September 1847, 570, 576–7.

54 Hughe Knatchbull-Hugessen, (editor), *Kentish Family* (1960), pp.257–8; *Croker Papers*, II, 282; *The Times*, 15 July 1846, p.4. In 1842, Knatchbull thought that the Income Tax would help to 'overset the Government': *Kentish Family*, p.239.

55 *The Times*, 8 March 1848, p.4.

56 Brooke and Sorensen, *Gladstone*, I, 46.

57 *The Quarterly Review*, LXX, September 1842, 519.

58 Gredington, Whitchurch, Shropshire, Diaries of Lord Kenyon, 11 March 1842; Hibbert, *Greville's England*, p.192; cf. The Seventh Duke of Wellington, (editor), *Wellington and His Friends* (1965), p.181; E. Jones Parry, (editor), *The Correspondence of Lord Aberdeen and Princess Lieven, 1832–1854*, 2 Volumes, Royal Historical Society, Camden, 3rd Series, LX, LXII (1938–9), I, 203.

59 *The Times*, 13 April 1842, p.13.

60 Morley, *Cobden*, I, 255, 259–60; *Cobden Letters*, pp.265, 271. Cobden constantly drew an analogy between Peel's stance on the Corn Laws and his role in Catholic Emancipation; *ibid.*, pp.210, 250.

61 Sir Richard Vyvyan, *A Letter from Sir Richard Vyvyan to his constituents upon the commercial and financial policy of Sir Robert Peel's Administration* (1842), p.17; cf. Kenyon Diaries, 19 February 1842; Brooke and Sorensen, *Gladstone*, II, 176; *Speeches*, IV, 60–78.

62 On Sugar, the issue centred on the relative margin between the duties paid by colonial and foreign (free-grown) sugar. Peel's 1844 reforms reduced the margin to about 10 shillings (25 shillings 3 pence for colonial, 34 shillings for foreign). Previously, the duty on foreign (slave-grown) sugar had been 63 shillings.

63 For competing interpretations of the consequences, see Robert Stewart, 'The Ten Hours and Sugar Crises of 1844: Government and the House of Commons in the Age of

Reform', *Historical Journal,* XII, 1969, 35–57; D.R. Fisher, 'Peel and the Conservative Party: The Sugar Crisis of 1844 Reconsidered', *Historical Journal,* XVIII, 1975, 279–302.

64 For Stanley's gradual retirement from the seat of political action, see Angus Hawkins, *The Forgotten Prime Minister, The 14th Earl of Derby, Ascent, 1799–1851* (Oxford, 2007), chapter 5; Brooke and Sorensen, *Gladstone,* I, 61–2.

65 *The Times,* 28 December 1849, p.4; *The Economist,* 29 December 1849, 1441–2.

66 Cobden's initiative is discussed in G.R. Searle, *Entrepreneurial Politics in Mid-Victorian Britain* (Oxford, 1993), chapter 2.

67 For subsequent comments on Peel's letter, see *The Economist,* 5 January 1850, 7; 12 January 1850, 30.

68 *Disraeli Letters,* V, Letter 1943; cf. 1944, 1949.

69 For the argument that the Corn Laws were repealed in conformity with this logic, see D.C. Moore, 'The Corn Laws and High Farming', *Economic History Review,* 2nd series, XVIII, 1965, 544–61.

70 *Newman Letters and Diaries,* VIII, 528.

71 *The Economist,* 30 September 1843, 71; Gaunt, *Last of the Tories,* 3 October 1843.

72 *The Economist,* 28 October 1843, 143–4; Gaunt, *Last of the Tories,* 27 October 1843.

73 On Peel's habitual display of egotism at the event, see *Punch,* V, July–December 1843, 196; cf. 230.

74 *Peel, Partridges and Potatoes; or leash, leases and lashes. Dedicated by permission to the Tamworth Farmer's Club* (1843), pp.5, 18–19.

75 *The Economist,* 21 December 1844, 1547; 1 November 1845, 1065; 16 October 1847, 1190. Protectionist wits might have been moved to observe that Peel was apt 'to talk Bull' at Drayton Manor.

76 Alexander Somerville, *The Whistler at the Plough* (1969 edition), pp.424–32, especially p.429; cf. *The Economist,* 28 October 1848, 1225.

77 Durham Record Office, Londonderry Papers, D/Lo/C96 (69), Peel to Londonderry, 2 December 1846; *The Economist,* 19 January 1850, 68–9.

78 *The Quarterly Review,* LXXII, September 1843, 557.

79 Nottingham University Manuscripts Department, Portland of Welbeck Collection, Pw H 178/2, 198/1, Lord George Bentinck to Portland, 7 January 1845, 17 January 1846.

80 Brooke and Sorensen, *Gladstone,* I, 60.

81 *Speeches,* III, 822–38.

82 Morley, *Cobden,* I, 233.

83 David Eastwood, 'The Corn laws and their Repeal 1815–1846. Realities behind the Myths', *History Review,* 25, 1996, 7; David Spring and Travis L. Crosby, 'George Webb Hall and the Agricultural Association', *Journal of British Studies,* II, 1962, 115–31; Travis L. Crosby, *English Farmers and the Politics of Protection, 1815–1852* (Hassocks, 1977).

84 *Kentish Family,* pp.237–8; David Spring, 'Lord Chandos and the Farmers, 1818–1846', *Huntingdon Library Quarterly,* XXXIII, 1969–70, 257–81. Lord Kenyon also thought it 'too low a scale': Kenyon Diary, 9 February 1842.

85 Brooke and Sorensen, *Gladstone,* II, 172. Lord Ripon was the former Frederick John Robinson, who had been responsible for introducing the 1815 Corn Law in the House of Commons. He afterwards served as Chancellor of the Exchequer (1823–7) and (as Viscount Goderich) Prime Minister (1827–8).

86 *Croker Papers,* II, 178; *The Times,* 10 February 1842, p.4.

87 Pearce, *Greville,* p.208; Shaftesbury Diaries, SHA/PD/2, f.97, 11 March 1842.

88 *Blackwood's Edinburgh Magazine,* LI, April 1842, 539–43, 550.

89 *The Quarterly Review,* LXXVII, December 1845, 320; cf. 304–5, 317; *Blackwood's Edinburgh Magazine,* LV, January 1844, 118; LIX, March 1846, 378.

90 Eastwood, 'Corn Laws', 9.

91 See Anthony Howe, *Free Trade and Liberal England, 1846–1946* (Oxford, 1997), chapter 1.
92 *Broughton Diary*, VI, 164.
93 Symons, *Sir Robert Peel*, p.148.
94 The classic account of events, from Peel's perspective, is Gash, *Sir Robert Peel*, chapter 16. For the Whigs, see F.A. Dreyer, 'The Whigs and the Political Crisis of 1845', *English Historical Review*, LXXX, 1965, 514–37. For one of the better poetic renditions of the Repeal drama, see *Punch*, X, January–June 1846, 76.
95 *Kentish Family*, p.253.
96 *The Quarterly Review*, LXXXI, June 1847, 298.
97 *Blackwood's Edinburgh Magazine*, LIX, March 1846, 382–3; LX, August 1846, 249; *The Quarterly Review*, LXXVII, December 1845, 311–12; LXXXI, June 1847, 294–5. On the wider issues, see Susan Fairlie, 'The Nineteenth Century Corn Law Reconsidered', *Economic History Review*, 18, 1965, 562–75.
98 Kenyon Papers, Box 73, Lord Combermere to Kenyon, 28 December 1845; cf. Kenyon Diaries, 29 December 1845.
99 To embarrass matters further, Peel mistook Wellington's description as a compliment: Pearce, *Greville*, p.241; *Kentish Family*, p.256; *Wellington and his Friends*, p.203; cf. Brooke and Sorensen, *Gladstone*, III, 15.
100 Portland Papers, Pw H 206/2, Lord George Bentinck to Portland, 14 February 1846.
101 Henry Reeve, (editor), *The Greville Memoirs. A Journal of the Reigns of King George IV, King William IV and Queen Victoria*, 8 Volumes (1888), VI, 363–4.
102 *Cobden Letters*, p.391.
103 *Broughton Diary*, VI, 159.
104 Both David Eastwood and Boyd Hilton agree that Repeal actually worsened the situation in Ireland: 'Recasting Our Lot', p.35.
105 Arthur Aspinall, (editor), *The Correspondence of Charles Arbuthnot*, Royal Historical Society, Camden, 3rd Series, LXV, (1941), p.240.
106 Eastwood, 'The Corn Laws', 9.
107 Symons, *Sir Robert Peel*, pp.161–2.
108 Brooke and Sorensen, *Gladstone*, III, 16.
109 Spencer Walpole, *The Life of Lord John Russell*, 2 Volumes (Honolulu, 2005), I, 406–9.
110 *Letters of Queen Victoria*, II, 49.
111 *The Monarch Mart*, quoted in *The Economist*, 13 December 1845, 1281. See Read, *Peel and the Victorians*, chapter 4, for press coverage during the crucial period.
112 *The Times*, 6 November 1845, p.5; cf. Pearce, *Greville*, p.238.
113 Shaftesbury Diaries, SHA/PD/4, f.46, 12 December 1845.
114 *The Quarterly Review*, LXXVII, December 1845, 304; Richard Edgcumbe, (editor), *The Diary of Frances Lady Shelley, 1818–1873*, 2 Volumes (1913), II, 268–9, 271.
115 *Cobden Letters*, p.409.
116 F.C. Mather, (editor), *Chartism and Society* (1980), p.228.
117 *Punch*, X, January–June 1846, 25, 49, 52, 104.
118 Mather, *Chartism*, p.230.
119 John Prest, *Politics in the Age of Cobden* (1977), especially p.133, stresses Peel's 'surrender' in the face of the League's electoral activities.
120 *The Quarterly Review*, LXXVIII, September 1846, 551.
121 Coleman, '1841–6', p.471 n.29.
122 *Letters of Queen Victoria*, II, 50, 66.
123 The trial of the assassin, Daniel McNaughtan, revealed that he had mistaken Drummond for Peel; his trial led to the 'McNaughtan' rules on insanity (measured by the ability to know the difference between right and wrong): see Richard Moran, *Knowing Right From Wrong. The Insanity Defense of Daniel McNaughtan* (New York, 1981).

124 For the dispute (on 17 February 1843) and its eventual resolution, see *Speeches*, IV, 149; *Letters of Queen Victoria*, I, 466; Morley, *Cobden*, I, 276–85, 379–80; *Cobden Letters*, pp.312–14, 410–11; Sanders, *Harriet Martineau*, pp.112–15; *The Economist*, 28 February 1846, 262.

125 Portland Papers, Pw H 221/2, Lord George Bentinck to Portland, 28 September 1846. On the depth of partisan animosity against Peel, see Hibbert, *Greville's England*, pp.208–9; *Broughton Diary*, VI, 173; Shaftesbury Diaries, SHA/PD/4, ff.82–3, 30 March 1846.

126 Pearce, *Greville*, p.241; *Blackwood's Edinburgh Magazine*, LIX, March 1846, 374–5; LXVIII, September 1850, 364–8. *The Economist* had also discussed the connections between Repeal and 'Peel's Act': 13 January 1844, 387.

127 Searle, *Entrepreneurial Politics*, chapter 1.

128 Brooke and Sorensen, *Gladstone*, I, 75; *Hardinge Letters*, p.148; *Letters of Queen Victoria*, II, 64; cf. *The Economist*, 29 August 1846, 1121–2.

129 *The Economist*, 14 March 1846, 327; Shaftesbury Diaries, SHA/PD/4, f.95, 22 May 1846.

130 Thomas, *Quarrel*, p.130.

131 This may help to explain Peel's opposition to those Conservatives who decided to resign their seats and seek a new electoral mandate on the basis of their changed opinions. On this subject, see Betty Kemp, 'Reflections on the Repeal of the Corn Laws', *Victorian Studies*, VI, 1962, 189–204.

132 The National Archives, Kew, Cardwell MSS, PRO 30/48/53, f.85, Cardwell to Goldwin Smith, 4 October 1858.

133 *Corn and Consistency. A few remarks in reply to a pamphlet entitled, 'Sir Robert Peel and the Corn Law Crisis'* (1846), pp.48–9.

134 *Gladstone Diaries*, III, 506–7. A modern parallel would be the American President Richard Nixon asking his Secretary of State (Henry Kissinger) to pray with him during the Watergate crisis.

135 *Letters of Queen Victoria*, II, 62–3.

136 Richard W. Davis, *A Political History of the House of Lords, 1811–1846* (Stanford, 2008), chapter 23; Richard F. Mullen, *The House of Lords and the Repeal of the Corn Laws* (DPhil Thesis, University of Oxford, 1974).

137 Brooke and Sorensen, *Gladstone*, III, 78–9.

138 Aspinall, *Charles Arbuthnot*, p.244. This view was widely shared: John Vincent, (editor), *Disraeli, Derby and the Conservative Party: the Political Journals of Lord Stanley, 1849–69* (Hassocks, 1978), pp.24, 26.

139 Gash, *Age of Peel*, p.132.

140 Hobhouse, *Recollections*, VI, 159–60; cf. Hibbert, *Greville's England*, p.206; *Speeches*, IV, 567–81 (especially 580–1).

141 Shaftesbury Diaries, SHA/PD/4, ff.60–2, 23 January 1846.

142 Lord Mahon and Edward Cardwell, (editors), *Memoirs of Sir Robert Peel* (New York, 1969), II, 251–2.

143 *Disraeli Letters*, IV, Letter 1455.

144 Hence Greville's famous aphorism, 'Everybody expects that [Peel] means to go on, and in the end to knock the Corn Laws on the head, and endow the Roman Catholic Church; but nobody knows how or when he will do these things': Hibbert, *Greville's England*, p.202.

145 James Anthony Froude, *Thomas Carlyle. A History of His Life in London, 1834–1881*, 2 Volumes (1884), I, 375–7; Jules Seigel, 'Carlyle and Peel: The prophet's search for a heroic politician and an unpublished fragment', *Victorian Studies*, 26, 1983, 192–5.

146 *Letter to Sir R. Peel on the mode of meeting the present crisis. From M.P., a supporter hitherto of the League* (1846), pp.31–2.

147 Morley, *Cobden*, I, 418–30. For a similar sentiment, see George Henry Francis, *Sir Robert Peel as Statesman and Orator* (1846), p.18.

148 John Morrow, 'The Paradox of Peel as Carlylean Hero', *Historical Journal*, 40, 1997, 108–9.

149 *Cobden Letters*, pp.391, 418.

Chapter Seven

1 *A Sketch of the Life and Character of Sir Robert Peel* (1860), p.306.

2 J.R. Thursfield, *Peel* (1891), pp.238–46, quote at p.238; cf. Justin McCarthy, *Sir Robert Peel* (1891), pp.162–72.

3 *Speeches delivered in the House of Commons by the late Rt. Hon Sir Robert Peel*, 4 Volumes (New York, 1972), IV, 804–5.

4 See *Punch*, XI, July–December 1846, 142. Sir Roger de Coverley was the archetypal English country gentleman (of simplistic Tory politics) portrayed in *The Spectator* (1711).

5 See my 'Gladstone and Peel's Mantle' in Roger Swift and David Bebbington, (editors), *Gladstone Bicentenary Essays* (forthcoming).

6 This provided a useful (and ample) supply of revenue until Robert Lowe abolished it, as Chancellor of the Exchequer, in 1869: John Prest, 'A Large amount or a Small? Revenue and the Nineteenth-Century Corn Laws', *Historical Journal*, XXXIX, 1996, 467–78.

7 See *The Times*, 28 June 1849, p.5; 29 June 1849, p.5.

8 Hon. Evelyn Ashley, *The Life of Henry John Temple, Viscount Palmerston, 1846–1865. With Selections from His Speeches and Correspondence*, Volume I (1876), 118–9.

9 Benjamin Disraeli, *Lord George Bentinck: A Political Biography* (New Brunswick, New Jersey, 1998), p.207.

10 *The Economist*, 4 September 1847, 1025; 11 September 1847, 1056; 16 October 1847, 1195–6; 23 October 1847, 1224.

11 *The Times*, 15 October 1849, p.8; *The Economist*, 20 October 1849, 1169.

12 This was a view that was also aired by Cardwell: Nottingham University Manuscripts Department, Newcastle of Clumber Collection, Ne C 12424/1, Edward Cardwell to Lord Lincoln, 15 October 1849.

13 *Punch*, XIII, July–December 1847, 110. Ferdinand Magellan (1480–1521) was the noted Portuguese navigator.

14 For its peroration, see *Speeches*, IV, 856.

15 Norman Gash, *Sir Robert Peel: The Life of Sir Robert Peel after 1830*, 2nd Edition, (1986), pp.655, 657. It was this which led Gladstone to conclude that Peel died at peace with all mankind – 'even with Disraeli': Helen M. and Marvin Swartz, (editors), *Disraeli's Reminiscences* (1975), pp.33, 40.

16 For the immediate circumstances of Peel's death and funeral, see *The Times*, 1–4, 10, 13 July 1850; *The Economist*, 6 July 1850; *The Illustrated London News*, 6, 13 July 1850; Richard Edgcumbe, (editor), *The Diary of Frances Lady Shelley, 1818–1873*, 2 Volumes (1913), II, 291–2.

17 W.T. Haly, *The Opinions of Sir R Peel, expressed in Parliament and in Public*, 2nd Edition (1850), p.xi; cf. p.xxvii.

18 There seems little foundation for Ellenborough's comment to Lord Clare, 'I really do not think that the sensation produced in the world here by this terrible event is as great as might have been expected': The National Archives, Kew, Ellenborough Papers, PRO 30/12/21/1, ff.491–2, 5 July 1850.

19 Ne C 11941, Sidney Herbert to Lincoln, 6 July 1850; E. Jones Parry, (editor), *The Correspondence of Lord Aberdeen and Princess Lieven, 1832–1854*, 2 Volumes, Royal Historical Society, Camden, 3rd Series, LX, LXII (1938–9), II, 500. However, Herbert was led into exaggeration by suggesting that Peel 'represented to the nation that System of Parliamentary Government which he had himself established more than any man alive.' See Angus Hawkins, '"Parliamentary Government" and Victorian Political Parties, c.1830–1880', *English Historical Review*, CIV, 1989, 638–69.

194   Sir Robert Peel

20 James Anthony Froude, *Thomas Carlyle. A History of His Life in London, 1834–1881*, 2 Volumes (1884), II, 48.
21 Durham Record Office, Londonderry Papers, D/Lo/Acc.451(D)34/1, Rutland to Lady Londonderry, [?] July 1850.
22 Henry Reeve, (editor), *The Greville Memoirs. A Journal of the Reigns of King George IV, King William IV and Queen Victoria*, 8 Volumes (1888), VI, 366; cf. Michael Bentley, *Politics without Democracy, 1815–1914*, 2nd Edition (1996), pp.137–8; *idem*, 'Victorian Prime Ministers: Changing Patterns of Commemoration' in Miles Taylor and Michael Wolff, (editors), *The Victorians since 1901. Histories, Representations and Revisions* (Manchester, 2004), pp.45–6.
23 Lady Dorchester, (editor), *Recollections of a long life by Lord Broughton (John Cam Hobhouse). With additional extracts from his private diaries*, 6 Volumes (1910–11), VI, 261; Ne C 11696/1, Lincoln to Gladstone, 16 July 1850.
24 John Vincent, (editor), *Disraeli, Derby and the Conservative Party: the Political Journals of Lord Stanley, 1849–69* (Hassocks, 1978), pp.23, 25.
25 Boyd Hilton, 'Robert Peel' in Robert Eccleshall and Graham Walker, (editors), *Biographical Dictionary of British Prime Ministers* (1998), p.150; *idem*, 'Moral Disciplines' in Peter Mandler, (editor), *Liberty and Authority in Victorian Britain* (Oxford, 2006), pp.231–2.
26 Donald Read, *Peel and the Victorians* (Oxford, 1987), pp.287–304; Stanley H. Palmer, *Police and Protest in England and Ireland, 1780–1850* (Cambridge, 1988), p.664 n.1.
27 A point made by Greville: Reeve, *Greville*, VI, 357.
28 George Otto Trevelyan, *The Life and Letters of Lord Macaulay* (Oxford, 1978), II, 212–3; Louis J. Jennings, (editor), *The Correspondence and Diaries of the late Right Honorable John Wilson Croker*, 2-Volume edition (New York, 1884), II, 297. Unlike Croker, Macaulay had the consolation of having made his peace with Peel over past political disagreements.
29 See Peter W. Sinnema, *The Wake of Wellington: Englishness in 1852*, (Ohio, 2006).
30 Terry Wyke, with Harry Cocks, *Public Sculpture of Greater Manchester* (Liverpool, 2004), p.252.
31 *The Times*, 21 July 1852, p.4. Also see Norman Gash, 'The Peelites after Peel' in Peter Catterall, (editor), *Britain, 1815–1867* (1994), pp.83–90.
32 Bulwer Lytton told Disraeli that 'there was nothing left for him to do': M.G. Wiebe *et al*, (editors), *Benjamin Disraeli: Letters*, 7 Volumes to date (Toronto, 1982–2004), V, Appendix V [e].
33 Lady Rose Weigall, (editor), *Correspondence of Lady Burghersh with the Duke of Wellington* (1903), p.178; Arthur Aspinall, (editor), *The Correspondence of Charles Arbuthnot*, Royal Historical Society, Camden, 3rd Series, LXV, (1941), p.241; cf. *Blackwood's Edinburgh Magazine*, LXIV, November 1848, 632–40.
34 *The Northern Star*, 13 July 1850, p.5.
35 *Disraeli Letters*, V, Appendix V [f]; Vincent, *Disraeli, Derby*, pp.23–4.
36 Reeve, *Greville*, VI, 357; Vincent, *Disraeli, Derby*, p.25. However, this sentiment was not merely the product of political opportunism. Disraeli encouraged Herries (a former colleague of Peel) to make a parliamentary tribute on behalf of the Protectionists, rather than allowing the party to sit there in 'sullen silence': *Disraeli Letters*, V, 2014.
37 Londonderry Papers, D/Lo/C96 (69), Peel to Londonderry, 2 December 1846.
38 Flintshire Record Office, Glynne-Gladstone MSS, 2960, F.R. Bonham to Lincoln, 8 October 1849. For Bonham, see Norman Gash, *Pillars of Government and other essays on state and society, c.1770–c.1880* (1986), pp.108–35.
39 Aspinall, *Charles Arbuthnot*, pp.240–1.
40 See *Punch*, XII, January–June 1847, 50 and *The Economist*, 16 January 1847, 67.
41 Christopher Hibbert, *Greville's England. Selections from the Diaries of Charles Greville, 1818–1860* (1981), p.219.

42 *Croker Papers*, II, 308; Glamorgan Record Office, Cardiff, Lyndhurst Papers, DLY 19/58, Croker to Brougham, 24 July 1846.

43 James Anthony Froude, *Thomas Carlyle. A History of His Life in London, 1834–1881*, 2 Volumes (1884), II, 47; cf. *Latter Day Pamphlets* (1850), pamphlets 3 and 4.

44 *Blackwood's Edinburgh Magazine*, LXI, January 1847, 114, 127. The article was later published as *Reflections suggested by the career of the late premier* (1847).

45 Gregory Claeys, (editor), *The Chartist Movement in Britain, 1838–50*, 6 Volumes (2001), V, 297; Southampton University Library, Broadlands Papers, Shaftesbury Diaries, SHA/PD/5, f.162, 17 April 1847; cf. *Punch*, XV, July–December 1848, 10 for Peel as an advanced political reformer.

46 Jones Parry, *Aberdeen-Lieven*, I, 271, 282; Bawa Satinder Singh, (editor), *The Letters of the First Viscount Hardinge of Lahore to Lady Hardinge and Sir Walter and Lady James, 1844–1847*, Royal Historical Society, Camden, 4th Series, 32, (1986), p.223.

47 Hibbert, *Greville's England*, p.212; cf. The Seventh Duke of Wellington, (editor), *Wellington and His Friends* (1965), p.206.

48 John Brooke and Mary Sorensen, (editors), *Prime Ministers Papers: W.E. Gladstone*, 4 Volumes (1971–81), III, 19–20, 23, 28–30.

49 Reeve, *Greville Memoirs*, 368–9.

50 Hughe Knatchbull-Hugessen, (editor), *Kentish Family* (1960), p.256; *Punch*, XIX, July–December 1850, 3; cf. *Aberdeen-Lieven*, II, 303 for Peel as a 'spectator' of events.

51 *Physiology of the Peel Party; or an inquiry into the nature of the new neutral policy* (1847), pp.24–5.

52 Notably, over the publication of *The Commercial Policy of Pitt and Peel, 1783–1846* (1847) which argued for a line of continuity (and consistency) in the commercial policy of the two statesmen: Aspinall, *Arbuthnot*, p.244; *The Quarterly Review*, LXXXI, June 1847, 274–316; *Croker Papers*, II, 310–16.

53 *The Quarterly Review*, LXXVIII, September 1846, 570–1; cf. LXXXI, September 1847, 578. For the 'well-informed quarters', see *Croker Papers*, II, 288.

54 Brooke and Sorensen, *Gladstone*, III, 46.

55 As discussed in Hawkins, 'Parliamentary Government'.

56 The relative position of the two men gave rise to the famous doggerel couplet, 'As Pitt is to Addington / So London is to Paddington'. For Greville's charge that Peel emulated Pitt's tactics during the 'Days of May' in 1832, see Edward Pearce, (editor), with Deanna Pearce, *The Diaries of Charles Greville* (2005), pp.108–9.

57 Liverpool Record Office, Derby Papers, 920 DER (14) 178/1, p.195, Stanley to Disraeli, 6 January 1849.

58 Hibbert, *Greville's England*, p.219; Ellenborough Papers, 30/12/21/1, ff.399–400, Ellenborough to Clare, 24 December 1847.

59 See J.B. Conacher, *The Peelites and the Party System, 1846–52* (Newton Abbot, 1972) and A.B. Erickson and W.D. Jones, *The Peelites, 1846–1857* (Ohio, 1972).

60 Brooke and Sorensen, *Gladstone*, I, 71; cf. 67, 76.

61 *The Hatherton Diaries. The Diaries of the First Lord Hatherton. Extracts from the personal diary, between the years 1817–1862 of Edward Walhouse Littleton afterwards The First Lord Hatherton, 1791–1863* (Privately printed, n.d.), entry for 11 January 1862.

62 Agatha Ramm, (editor), *The Gladstone-Granville Correspondence* (Cambridge, 1998), p.360.

63 Ne C 11995/1–2, Peel to Lincoln, 11 April 1847 (in making this comment, Peel had Goulburn in mind); Centre for Kentish Studies, Maidstone, Stanhope MSS, U1590/C330/3 (bundle), F.R. Bonham to Lord Mahon, 9 October 1848; cf. Brooke and Sorensen, *Gladstone*, III, 32–41, 47–8.

64 Brooke and Sorensen, *Gladstone*, III, 37, 75–6, 267–8.

65 M.R.D. Foot and H.C.G. Matthew, (editors), *The Gladstone Diaries*, 14 Volumes (Oxford, 1968–94), IV, 13.

66 Vincent, *Disraeli, Derby,* pp.13, 22.

67 Brooke and Sorensen, *Gladstone,* III, 38–9.

68 Ellenborough Papers, PRO 30/12/21/1, f.35, Ellenborough to Clare, 9 August 1846; cf. *Croker Papers,* II, 290–1 for Peel's behind-the-scenes canvassing on the measure.

69 *The Times,* 29 July 1846, p.5. Paul Potter (1625–54) was a Dutch painter noted for his pictures of animals.

70 *Blackwood's Edinburgh Magazine,* LX, August 1846, 257. For earlier ruminations on a political future without Peel, see A.D. Kriegel, (editor), *The Holland House Diaries, 1831–1840* (1977), p.371; *The Times,* 13 November 1845, p.6.

71 The extent of equine culpability for Peel's death was a matter of contemporary dispute and comment. The most charitable interpretation was that the accident was preventable, had Peel exercised more care and discretion. The alternative view was that Peel was a poor rider. Few argued that Peel's horse had done him a disservice. The argument may be regarded as a metaphor for Peel's relationship with his political followers: Arthur Christopher Benson and Viscount Esher, (editors), *The Letters of Queen Victoria. A Selection from Her Majesty's Correspondence between the years 1837–1861,* 3 Volumes (Honolulu, 2002), II, 254–5; Ashley, *Palmerston,* 226.

Chapter Eight

1 *The Times,* 30 August 1855, p.6.

2 Both Thomas Carlyle and the King of Hanover – who occupied different sympathetic positions with respect to Peel – stated that his death had affected them like no other event in their lifetime: Edwin W. Marrs, (editor), *The Letters of Thomas Carlyle to His Brother Alexander with related family letters* (Cambridge, Massachusetts, 1968), pp.678–9; Charles Whibley, (editor), *Letters of the King of Hanover to Viscount Strangford, G.C.B.* (1925), p.xv.

3 *The Economist,* 27 July 1850, 817.

4 Asa Briggs, *Victorian Things* (1988), p.149. The Staffordshire figure of Peel astride a horse was influenced by a contemporary portrait in *The Illustrated London News* whilst another Peel figure was a pair for one of Cobden. I am grateful to Lord Briggs for information on this point.

5 Norman Gash, (editor), *The Age of Peel* (1968), p.180.

6 For some excruciating poetic verse in this tradition, see *The Death of the Right Honourable Sir Robert Peel* (1850): 'Sad, sad was the day when misfortune that way / From health, strength, and vigour had tossed him / Upon the hard ground to receive his death wound / Oh mourn!! mourn! Britannia, we've lost him'. cf. Joseph Arnould, *Memorial Lines on Sir Robert Peel* (1850).

7 Elisabeth Darby and Nicola Smith, *The Cult of the Prince Consort* (New Haven and London, 1983); John Wolffe, *Great Deaths. Grieving, Religion, and Nationhood in Victorian and Edwardian Britain* (Oxford, 2000).

8 Arthur Aspinall, (editor), *Three Early Nineteenth Century Diaries* (1952), p.157; George Henry Francis, *Sir Robert Peel as Statesman and Orator* (1846), p.17. At the opening of the new London Bridge, in 1831, Lord Holland noted that Peel occupied a barge adorned with his name in large letters: A.D. Kriegel, (editor), *The Holland House Diaries, 1831–1840* (1977), p.21.

9 George Henry Francis, *The late Sir Robert Peel, Bart. A Critical Biography. Reprinted, with additions, from Fraser's Magazine* (1852), p.119; cf. W.T. Haly, *The Opinions of Sir R Peel, expressed in Parliament and in Public,* 2nd Edition (1850), pp.xxvi–xxvii.

10 Donald Read, *Peel and the Victorians* (Oxford, 1987), pp.287–312.

11 *Blackwood's Edinburgh Magazine,* LXVIII, September 1850, 354.

12 *The Times,* 4 July 1850, p.4.

13 However, over the long term, Peter Ghosh maintains that 'significant reference to Peel largely vanished from considered reflection by later Victorians on their immediate

predecessors': Peter Ghosh, 'Gladstone and Peel' in Peter Ghosh and Lawrence Goldman, (editors), *Politics & Culture in Victorian Britain. Essays in Memory of Colin Matthew* (Oxford, 2006), pp.46–7.

14 Bawa Satinder Singh, (editor), *The Letters of the First Viscount Hardinge of Lahore to Lady Hardinge and Sir Walter and Lady James, 1844–1847,* Royal Historical Society, Camden, 4th Series, 32, (1986), p.183; *Punch,* XIX, July–December 1850, 157; John Morley, *The Life of Richard Cobden,* 2 Volumes (1908), II, 232. For Peel as a fixed point in comparing subsequent political success, see Michael Bentley, *Lord Salisbury's World. Conservative Environments in Late-Victorian Britain* (Cambridge, 2001), p.311.

15 Melanie Stafford, 'Peel's Statue in Leeds – a first for town and country', *Leeds Art Calendar,* 90, 1982, 9.

16 Read, *Peel and the Victorians,* pp.294–301.

17 The foundry of Messrs Robinson and Cottam, Pimlico did extremely well out of the business, casting the large bronze statues of Peel for Leeds, Bury and Manchester. The foundry was remarkable for its ability to cast them in one piece: Stafford, 'Peel's Statue in Leeds', 7; Terry Wyke, with Harry Cocks, *Public Sculpture of Greater Manchester* (Liverpool, 2004), pp.113, 252.

18 For Disraeli's cynicism on this movement, see M.G. Wiebe *et al,* (editors), *Benjamin Disraeli: Letters,* 7 Volumes to date (Toronto, 1982–2004), VI, 2599 n.2.

19 Boyd Hilton, 'Moral Disciplines' in Peter Mandler, (editor), *Liberty and Authority in Victorian Britain* (Oxford, 2006), pp.231–2.

20 Wyke and Cocks, *Public Sculpture,* p.252.

21 See *The Times,* 24 July 1850, p.8; E. Jones Parry, (editor), *The Correspondence of Lord Aberdeen and Princess Lieven, 1832–1854,* 2 Volumes, Royal Historical Society, Camden, 3rd Series, LX, LXII (1938–9), II, 503.

22 Sir Lawrence Peel, *A Sketch of the Life and Character of Sir Robert Peel* (1860), p.306.

23 Southampton University Library, Broadlands Papers, Shaftesbury Diaries, SHA/PD/5, ff.187–8, 6, 11 July 1850.

24 See Read, *Peel and the Victorians,* pp.288–94; *The Times,* 6 July 1850, p.8; 13 July 1850, p.8; 18 July 1850, p.4; 5 September 1850, p.3.

25 *The Illustrated London News,* 13 July 1850, p.42. Unlike its co-habitants in the Abbey, the Peel statue lacks any form of memorial inscription.

26 For Peel's will, see *The Times,* 17 August 1850, p.7; 31 August 1850, p.6.

27 Lady Dorchester, (editor), *Recollections of a long life by Lord Broughton (John Cam Hobhouse). With additional extracts from his private diaries,* 6 Volumes (1910–11), VI, 261–2.

28 John Vincent, (editor), *Disraeli, Derby and the Conservative Party: the Political Journals of Lord Stanley, 1849–69* (Hassocks, 1978), p.25; cf. M.R.D. Foot and H.C.G. Matthew, (editors), *The Gladstone Diaries,* 14 Volumes (Oxford, 1968–94), IV, 223.

29 Shaftesbury Diaries, SHA/PD/5, f.189, 16 July 1850; cf. Earl of Stanhope, (editor), *Conversations with Wellington* (1998), pp.247–8

30 Wyke and Cocks, *Public Sculpture,* pp.335, 351–2. I am particularly grateful to Harry Cocks for drawing my attention to this work.

31 Stafford claims the honour for Leeds, but William Behnes' statue (originally sited at the Court House) was not inaugurated until 20 August 1852. The statue was moved to the Town Hall after 1896 and in the mid-1930s transferred to Woodhouse Moor: Stafford 'Peel's Statue in Leeds', *passim.*

32 For Tamworth, see *The Times,* 23 July 1850, p.8. The statue was unveiled on 23 July 1852.

33 The statue was removed from Peel Park in 1954 and ended up in private hands after 1969: Wyke and Cocks, *Public Sculpture,* pp.167–9, 195.

34 *The Economist,* 14 September 1844, 1206; John Morrow, (editor), *Young England. The New Generation. A Selection of Primary Texts* (Leicester, 1999), p.182; Shaftesbury Diaries,

SHA/PD/3, f.129, 12 September 1844. At this period, the government was opposing Ashley's 'Ten Hours Bill', which proposed a reduction in the maximum working day for factory operatives.

35 *The Times,* 13 July 1850, p.4; Wyke and Cocks, *Public Sculpture,* pp.111, 195, 251; Stafford, 'Peel's Statue in Leeds', 7.

36 Wyke and Cocks, *Public Sculpture,* p.258. Wyke and Cocks do not note the misdating of Peel's resignation speech (27 January 1846 instead of 29 June 1846). However, errors in memorialising Peel were not uncommon. John G. Mossman's statue of Peel (1853), in Glasgow's George Square, managed to get Peel's principal dates wrong; in this, it followed the iconic and influential front cover of *The Illustrated London News,* 13 July 1850.

37 Wyke and Cocks, *Public Sculpture,* p.288; *Gladstone Diaries,* IV, 597.

38 *Gladstone Diaries,* IV, 562. For the history of the statue, see *The Times,* 9 July 1850, p.5; *The Illustrated London News,* 13 July 1850, p.47; *The Economist,* 13 July 1850, 760; 20 July 1850, 796; 17 August 1850, 906.

39 Magdalen Goffin, (editor), *The Diaries of Absalom Watkin, A Manchester Man, 1787–1861* (Stroud, 1993), pp.300–2; cf. Wyke and Cocks, *Public Sculpture,* pp.111–13.

40 See Richard A. Gaunt, 'Wellington in petticoats: the duke as caricature' in C.M. Woolgar, (editor), *Wellington Studies IV* (Southampton, 2008), pp.140–72.

41 The committee members were Ashburton, Colonel Wilson Patten (survivors from the original committee), Newcastle (the former Lord Lincoln), Buccleuch, Stanhope (the former Mahon), Hardinge, Gladstone (in lieu of Aberdeen), Canning, Hardinge, Herbert and Cardwell (Chairman).

42 This account is based on the documents contained in The National Archives, Kew, Ministry of Works Papers, WORK 20/31. The abstract has proved especially useful. For Molesworth's views, see his memorandum of December 1853 and his subsequent letter to Cardwell of 6 January 1854.

43 *Gladstone Diaries,* VII, 457; VIII, 98.

44 WORK 20/31, Documents relating to the erection of Peel's statue in Parliament Square, abstract and W 2503/75.

45 See Ghosh, 'Gladstone and Peel', p.47.

46 For an example of the former which is nevertheless conscious of the latter, see Norman Gash, *Peel and Posterity* (Tamworth, 2000). For an early and accomplished forerunner of this tradition, which embraces the 'golden idol' image of Peel (quite literally), see Lord Rosebery, 'Sir Robert Peel', *Anglo-Saxon Review,* I, 1899, 97–123.

47 Norman Gash, *Mr Secretary Peel: The Life of Sir Robert Peel before 1830,* 2nd Edition (1985), p.viii.

48 Morley, *Cobden,* I, 419 n.1; Ghosh, 'Gladstone and Peel', p.48 n.15.

49 Which Llewellyn Woodward, who drew attention to it, certainly did. See Gash, *Mr Secretary Peel,* pp.663–4; Sir Llewellyn Woodward, *The Age of Reform, 1815–1870,* 2nd Edition (Oxford, 1962).

50 Arthur Christopher Benson and Viscount Esher, (editors), *The Letters of Queen Victoria. A Selection from Her Majesty's Correspondence between the years 1837–1861,* 3 Volumes (Honolulu, 2002), II, 76–7.

51 The National Archives, Kew, Cardwell Papers, PRO 30/48/53, ff.3–6, Peel's preface to his papers.

52 A fear also shared (in a more humorous vein) by Disraeli: see Robert Blake, *Disraeli* (1966), p.747.

53 Cardwell Papers, PRO 30/48/53, ff.3–6, Peel's preface to his papers.

54 George Kitson Clark, *The Life and Work of Sir Robert Peel* (1950), p.3.

55 *The Times,* 17 August 1850, p.7; 31 August 1850, p.6.

56 Cardwell Papers, PRO 30/48/53, f.2, Mahon and Cardwell's agreement, 11 December 1850.

57 *ibid.*, f.62 [*sic*] (mistakenly foliated and in fact f.68), Mahon to Cardwell, 11 October 1851; Stanhope, *Conversations with Wellington*, p.247. Admittedly, Stanhope was the recorder of this piece of self-praise but there seems little reason to doubt its accuracy.

58 Cardwell Papers, PRO 30/48/53, f.61 [*sic*] (mistakenly foliated and in fact f.67), Mahon to Cardwell, 11 October 1851.

59 For example, in 1876, Cardwell refused his assistance to W.M. Torrens, who was at work on a biography of Lord Melbourne, even though Torrens was disposed to show 'how far an honourable confidence existed between Melbourne and Peel on matters of higher moment than those of party'. See Cardwell Papers, PRO 30/48/53, ff.165–73, Torrens to Cardwell, 31 December 1875; Cardwell to Lord Cowper, 2 January 1876; Cardwell to Torrens, 6 January 1876. cf. W.M. Torrens, *Memoirs of the Right Honourable William Second Viscount Melbourne*, 2 Volumes (1878).

60 Cardwell Papers, PRO 30/48/53, ff.64–6, Mahon to Cardwell, 11 October 1851.

61 *Gladstone Diaries*, IV, 361. It took Gladstone 9 ½ hours to read them.

62 John Brooke and Mary Sorensen, (editors), *Prime Ministers Papers: W.E. Gladstone*, 4 Volumes (1971–81), III, 77.

63 George Otto Trevelyan, *The Life and Letters of Lord Macaulay* (Oxford, 1978), II, 378–9.

64 *The Economist*, 7 June 1856, 618; cf. *Notes and Queries*, 2nd Series, No. 21, 24 May 1856, 423. cf. Gash, *Mr Secretary Peel*, p.664.

65 *The Economist*, 14 March 1857, 283.

66 See Ghosh, 'Gladstone and Peel', pp.55–70. It would be well not to exaggerate this mood of Gladstonian introspection. In 1876, Gladstone was still to be found lamenting the great loss of 'moral force' in the House of Commons, in consequence of Peel's death: Brooke and Sorensen, *Gladstone*, III, 268. Also see Richard Shannon, 'Peel, Gladstone and Party', *Parliamentary History*, 18, 1999, 317–52.

67 E.g. Bentley, *Lord Salisbury's World*, p.308.

68 Jelinger Cookson Symons, *Sir Robert Peel as a type of Statesmanship* (1856), pp.2–3, 5, 88.

69 Norman St-John Stevas, (editor), *The Collected Works of Sir Walter Bagehot, Volume III, The Historical Essays* (1968), pp.238–71.

70 Symons, *Sir Robert Peel*, p.194; cf. Read, *Peel and the Victorians*, pp.307–8.

71 *Notes and Queries*, 2nd Series, No. 63, 14 March 1857, 219.

72 Edwin Cannan, (editor), *The Paper Pound of 1797–1821. The Bullion Report* [of 1810], 2nd Edition [1925] (New York, 1969), p.xlii. See below n.79.

73 See Richard A. Gaunt, 'Disraeli, Peel and the Corn Laws: the making of a conservative reputation', *The Historian*, 97, 2008, 30–33.

74 Bentley, *Lord Salisbury's World*, pp.308–9; George Peel, (editor), *The Private Letters of Sir Robert Peel* (1920). George Peel also wrote the entry on Sir Robert Peel in the *Dictionary of National Biography* and contributed a summary of his life to Parker's edition of the Peel papers (III, 561–623). See below n.91, 93.

75 Sir Lawrence Peel, *A Sketch of the Life and Character of Sir Robert Peel* (1860), pp.301–2.

76 Gash's challenge was clear from his very first line: *Mr Secretary Peel*, p.1.

77 Boyd Hilton, 'Peel: A Reappraisal', *Historical Journal*, XXII, 1979, 585–614; *idem*, 'Robert Peel' in Robert Eccleshall and Graham Walker, (editors), *Biographical Dictionary of British Prime Ministers* (1998), pp.142–51.

78 Bentley, *Lord Salisbury's World*, p.310; cf. Michael Bentley, 'Victorian Prime Ministers: Changing Patterns of Commemoration' in Miles Taylor and Michael Wolff, (editors), *The Victorians since 1901. Histories, Representations and Revisions* (Manchester, 2004), pp.45–6.

79 At the same time, Gladstone observed (with a mixture of regret and humour) that whilst fifteen pages were devoted to Peel in the *Dictionary of National Biography*, the Irish politician Charles Stewart Parnell (1846–91) gained twenty: Asa Briggs, (editor), *Gladstone's Boswell. Late Victorian Conversations* (Brighton, 1984), pp.126–7.

80 *ibid.* cf. *Gladstone Diaries*, IV, 223; Hilton, 'Robert Peel', p.143 states 'no politician ever referred more profligately to the dictates of "his conscience"'.

81 Boyd Hilton is also a Trinity man. See Bentley, *Lord Salisbury's World*, pp.314–15; Douglas Hurd, *Robert Peel* (2007), pp.1, 402; Ghosh, 'Gladstone and Peel', p.46 n.3.

82 Bentley, 'Victorian Prime Ministers', p.46. Gash may also be considered a revisionist in his *Politics in the Age of Peel* (1953). This challenged the prevailing 'Whig' conception of the 'Great' Reform Act of 1832 as ending the outmoded, out-dated forms of electoral behaviour prevalent before then. See Walter L. Arnstein, 'Norman Gash: Peelite' in his *Recent Historians of Great Britain* (Iowa, 1991), pp.147–72. It is to be hoped that the death of Norman Gash (1 May 2009) may give rise to a more considered appraisal of his contribution to nineteenth-century British history.

83 Two of Peel's more ardent twentieth-century admirers (Kitson Clark and Asa Briggs) are Yorkshire men. Gash briefly held a chair at the University of Leeds (1953–55) before emulating his hero's holiday preferences by going north of the border to the University of St Andrews (1955–80). For another admiring Yorkshire man, see Harold Wilson, *A Prime Minister on Prime Ministers* (1977). For a Lancastrian's (generally positive) perspective, see A.J.P. Taylor, (edited by Chris Wrigley), *From Napoleon to the Second International: Essays on Nineteenth-Century Europe* (1993), pp.120–8.

84 Michael Partridge and Richard A. Gaunt, (editors), *Lives of Victorian Political Figures I*, 4 Volumes (2006), II, ix–xix; Bentley, *Lord Salisbury's World*, pp.312–13.

85 Ghosh, 'Glastone and Peel', pp.45–7. A poorly-printed edition of Peel's speeches (which remains the only so far attempted) was published in 1853: *Speeches delivered in the House of Commons by the late Rt. Hon. Sir Robert Peel*, 4 Volumes (New York, 1972).

86 Trevelyan, *Macaulay*, II, 379 n.1; cf. *The Economist*, 7 February 1857, 144–5. Hobhouse also declared an intention 'one day or the other … to put on paper what I think of this much-lamented man': *Broughton Diary*, VI, 261.

87 *Gladstone Diaries*, V, 207 n.4. Gladstone later refused a request to review J.R. Thursfield's *Sir Robert Peel* (1891) for the *English Historical Review*: *Gladstone Diaries*, XII, 379 n.11.

88 Vincent, *Disraeli, Derby*, p.34; cf. p.25.

89 *Disraeli Letters*, V, 2204 n.2; 2216 n.1. For similar estimates (from across the political spectrum), see *ibid.*, VI, 2221 n.6; 2227 n.6.

90 Benjamin Disraeli, *Lord George Bentinck: A Political Biography* (New Brunswick, New Jersey, 1998), chapter XVII.

91 Cardwell Papers, PRO 30/48/53, f.71, Stanhope to Cardwell, 3 February 1856. Stanhope did impose four restrictions on Parker: only one tin box of manuscripts to be in his possession at any one time; the present order of the papers to be preserved; the letters of the Queen and Prince Albert to be withheld and no copies to be taken without the consent of the trustees. In the event, George Peel completed this commission (see above n.74).

92 Which spanned the deaths of Stanhope (1875) and Cardwell (1886).

93 Charles Stuart Parker, *Sir Robert Peel from his Private Papers*, 3 Volumes (1891–9); cf. Rosebery's review of the edition with its famous (and over-sanguine) conclusion that 'the historical monument to Sir Robert Peel is now almost complete': 'Sir Robert Peel', 97.

94 William Thomas, *The Quarrel of Macaulay and Croker. Politics and History in the Age of Reform* (Oxford, 2000), p.128; Bentley, *Lord Salisbury's World*, pp.309–10; *idem*, 'Victorian Prime Ministers', pp.45–6. Also see Gash, *Mr Secretary Peel*, pp.viii–ix.

95 *Gladstone Diaries*, XI, 635; XII, 194, 325, 381–2.

96 E.g. 'So Derby has closed his shallow, vain, selfish, rattling, and profoundly vulgar career, and Dizzy is Prime Minister of England. Who can be proud of such a country or leave it with unmixed regret?': Cardwell Papers, PRO 30/48/53, f.128, Goldwin Smith to Cardwell, 27 February 1868.

97 *ibid.*, ff.84–5, Cardwell to Goldwin Smith, 4 October 1858. For a later attempt to shape Smith's account, see ff.114–16, Cardwell to Goldwin Smith, 3 March 1864.

98 *ibid.,* ff.92–3, Goldwin Smith to Cardwell, 6 October 1858.

99 The nearest he came was in his *Reminiscences,* edited by Theodore Arnold Haultain, (New York, 1910), in the chapter on 'Cobden and Bright'.

100 Cardwell Papers, PRO 30/48/53, ff.129–30, Stanhope to Cardwell, 27 October [1868].

101 This Duke of Newcastle was the 5th Duke (formerly Lord Lincoln), an ardent Peelite.

102 Cardwell Papers, PRO 30/48/53, f.184, Goldwin Smith to Cardwell, 28 February 1881.

103 One cannot help thinking that Thomas Carlyle would have approved of Peel's company: *The Daily Mail,* 26 December 2006, p.25.

104 To adapt a phrase of Lord Briggs: 'Sir Robert Peel, 1788–1850. A Statesman Much-Attacked but More-Admired', *The Historian,* 17, 1987/8, 3–6. However, Edward Stanley wondered whether Peel's conduct in 1829 and 1846 was not 'rather excused, or at most vindicated as necessary, than held up to admiration': Vincent, *Disraeli, Derby,* p.26. Elsewhere, he had publicly proclaimed Peel's 'application, industry, and energy, and devotion to his purpose' to be 'most worthy of imitation and respect': *Disraeli Letters,* VI, 2018XA n.3.

105 See the society's website (correct, as of September 2009): http://www.thepeelsociety.org.uk/.

106 See Spencer Walpole, *The Life of the Rt. Hon Spencer Perceval Including His Correspondence With Numerous Distinguished Persons,* 2 Volumes (1874), II, 58.

107 Vincent, *Disraeli, Derby,* p.25. For a contrary view, see Morley, *Cobden,* II, 45.

108 *Reflections suggested by the career of the late premier* (1847), p.93; cf. *Blackwood's Edinburgh Magazine,* LX, August 1846, 256; Bentley, *Lord Salisbury's World,* p.309.

109 Ghosh, 'Gladstone and Peel', pp.49, 52. The analogy was also favoured by Peel's critics: see *Disraeli Letters,* IV, 1391 and n.4.

110 Cardwell Papers, PRO 30/48/53, f.164, Note of a conversation with Lord John Russell, 30 July 1875.

111 Patrick Jackson, (editor), *Loulou: Selected Extracts from the Journals of Lewis Harcourt, 1880–1895* (Madison, New Jersey, 2006), p.74.

112 Norman Gash, *Sir Robert Peel: The Life of Sir Robert Peel after 1830,* 2nd Edition (1986), pp.541–2.

113 Shaftesbury Diaries, SHA/PD/5, f.187, 5 July 1850.

114 In this respect, Peel's nearest (twentieth century) competitor is Winston Churchill: David Reynolds, *In Command of History. Churchill Fighting and Writing the Second World War* (2004). The jury is still out on Tony Blair.

BIBLIOGRAPHY

Manuscript Collections

Beinecke Rare Book and Manuscript Library, Yale University
  James Marshall and Marie-Louise Osborn Collection

The British Library, London
  Peel MSS

Chatsworth House, Derbyshire
  Devonshire MSS

Durham Record Office
  Londonderry MSS

Flintshire Record Office, Hawarden
  Glynne-Gladstone MSS

Glamorgan Record Office, Cardiff
  Lyndhurst MSS

Gredington, Whitchurch, Shropshire
  Kenyon Diaries

The Centre for Kentish Studies, Maidstone
  Camden MSS
  Knatchbull MSS
  Stanhope MSS

Lancashire Record Office, Preston
  Kenyon MSS

Liverpool Record Office
  Derby MSS

John Rylands University Library, Manchester
  Clinton MSS

The National Archives, Kew (Public Record Office)
    Cardwell MSS
    Colchester MSS
    Ellenborough MSS
    Ministry of Works MSS

The National Register of Archives (Scotland), Edinburgh
    Mansfield MSS

Northamptonshire Record Office, Northampton
    Finch Hatton (Winchilsea) MSS
    Holdenby (Agar Ellis) MSS

Nottingham University Manuscripts Department
    Denison MSS
    Marlay MSS
    Newcastle MSS
    Portland MSS

Nottinghamshire Archives
    Craven Smith Milnes of Hockerton Manor MSS

Sandon Hall, Staffordshire
    Harrowby MSS

Sheffield Archives
    Wharncliffe MSS

Hartley Library, Southampton University
    Broadlands MSS

Newspapers and Periodicals
Blackwood's Edinburgh Magazine (est. 1817)

The Economist (est. 1843)

Fraser's Magazine for Town and Country (est. 1830)

The Illustrated London News (est. 1842)

The Northern Star (est. 1838)

Punch (est. 1841)

The Quarterly Review (est. 1809)

The Times (est. 1785)

Printed Primary Sources

(Place of publication is London unless otherwise stated)

Arnould, Sir Joseph, *Memoir of Thomas, First Lord Denman, formerly Lord Chief Justice of England,* 2 Volumes (1873)

Arnould, Sir Joseph, *Memorial Lines on Sir Robert Peel* (1850)

Ashley, the Hon. Evelyn, *The Life of Henry John Temple, Viscount Palmerston, 1846–1865. With Selections from His Speeches and Correspondence,* Volume I (1876)

Aspinall, Arthur, (editor), *The Correspondence of Charles Arbuthnot,* Royal Historical Society, Camden, 3rd Series, LXV, (1941)

Aspinall, Arthur, (editor), *The Correspondence of George, Prince of Wales, 1770–1812,* 8 Volumes (1963–71)

Aspinall, Arthur, (editor), *The Diary of Henry Hobhouse, 1820–1827* (1947)

Aspinall, Arthur, (editor), *The Formation of Canning's Ministry,* Royal Historical Society, Camden, 3rd Series, LIX, (1937)

Aspinall, Arthur, (editor), *The Later Correspondence of George III,* 5 Volumes (Cambridge, 1962–70)

Aspinall, Arthur, (editor), *The Letters of George IV,* 3 Volumes (Cambridge, 1938)

Aspinall, Arthur, (editor), *Three Early Nineteenth Century Diaries* (1952)

Aspinall, Arthur, 'Extracts from Lord Hatherton's Diary', Parts 1–4, *Parliamentary Affairs,* XVII, 1963–4

Aspinall, Arthur and E.A. Smith, (editors), *English Historical Documents, 1783–1832* (1959)

Bagot, Josceline, (editor), *George Canning and his friends. Containing hitherto unpublished letters, jeux d'esprit, etc,* 2 Volumes (1909)

Bahlman, Dudley W.R., (editor), *The Diary of Sir Edward Walter Hamilton, 1885–1906* (Hull, 1993)

Bamford, Francis and the Seventh Duke of Wellington, (editors), *The Journal of Mrs Arbuthnot, 1820–1832,* 2 Volumes (1950)

Benson, Arthur Christopher and Viscount Esher, (editors), *The Letters of Queen Victoria. A Selection from Her Majesty's Correspondence between the years 1837–1861,* 3 Volumes [1908], (Honolulu, 2002)

Bond, R. Warwick, (editor), *The Marlay Letters, 1778–1820* (1937)

Bourne, Kenneth, (editor), *The Letters of the Third Viscount Palmerston to Laurence and Elizabeth Sulivan, 1804–1863,* Royal Historical Society, Camden, 4th Series, 23, (1979)

Bourne, Kenneth and William Banks Taylor, (editors), *The Horner Papers. Selections from the Letters and Miscellaneous Writings of Francis Horner, M.P., 1795–1817* (Edinburgh, 1994)

Bradley, Reverend Robert, *A Letter to the Right Honourable Robert Peel ... on Catholic Emancipation* (Manchester, 1824)

Briggs, Asa, (editor), *Gladstone's Boswell. Late Victorian Conversations* (Brighton, 1984)

Brooke, John and Julia Gandy, (editors), *Prime Ministers Papers: Wellington, Political Correspondence, Volume I: 1833–1834* (1975)

Brooke, John and Mary Sorensen, (editors), *Prime Ministers Papers: W.E. Gladstone,* 4 Volumes (1971–81)

Buckingham and Chandos, Richard Duke of, *Memoirs of the Court of George IV,* 2 Volumes (1859)

Cannan, Edwin, (editor), *The Paper Pound of 1797–1821. The Bullion Report* [of 1810], 2nd Edition [1925], (New York, 1969)

[Canning, George], *A Short View of the Recent Changes; in which the question – Does Mr Canning's Government merit the Confidence of the Country? is impartially discussed* (1827)

Capefigue, Jean Baptiste Honoré Raymond, 'Character of Sir Robert Peel' in William Cooke Taylor, *The Life and Times of Sir Robert Peel,* III.2 (1851)

Carlyle, Thomas, *Latter Day Pamphlets* (1850)

Claeys, Gregory, (editor), *The Chartist Movement in Britain, 1838–50*, 6 Volumes (2001)

Colchester, Second Lord, (editor), *The Diary and Correspondence of Charles Abbot, Lord Colchester*, 3 Volumes (1861)

Colchester, Third Lord, (editor), *Political Diary of Edward Law, Lord Ellenborough, 1828–30*, 2 Volumes (1881)

Colquhoun, J.C., *The Effects of Sir Robert Peel's Administration on the Political State and Prospects of England* (1847)

Copleston, Edward, *A Letter to the Right Hon Robert Peel ... on the pernicious effects of a variable standard of value especially as it regards the condition of the lower orders and the poor laws* (1819)

Court, Major M. Henry, *An Analysis of the Natural Price of Corn; with observations on the speech of Sir Robert Peel ... to his constituents at Tamworth, in illustration of the impolicy of existing corn laws by inducing the evil effects of artificial prices of corn* (1841)

Crutwell, Richard, *English finance. With reference to the resumption of cash-payments at the Bank, etc.* (1818)

[Currency Bill of 1819], *A Plan for regulating the circulation on the principle of Sir R. Peel's celebrated Currency Bill of 1819* (1840)

[Currency Bill of 1819] *The Currency Question freed from mystery, in a letter to Mr Peel shewing how the distress may be relieved without altering the standard* (1830)

Disraeli, Benjamin, *Lord George Bentinck: A Political Biography* [1851], (New Brunswick, New Jersey, 1998)

Dorchester, Lady, (editor), *Recollections of a long life by Lord Broughton (John Cam Hobhouse). With additional extracts from his private diaries*, 6 Volumes (1910–11)

Edgcumbe, Richard, (editor), *The Diary of Frances Lady Shelley, 1818–1873*, 2 Volumes (1913)

Fitzgerald, Maurice, *A Letter to Sir Robert Peel on the Endowment of the Roman Catholic Church of Ireland* (1845)

Foot, M.R.D and H.C.G. Matthew, (editors), *The Gladstone Diaries*, 14 Volumes (Oxford, 1968–94)

Francis, George Henry, *Opinions and Policy of The Right Honourable Viscount Palmerston, G.C.B., M.P., &c, as Minister, Diplomatist, and Statesman, During More than Forty Years of Public Life. With a Memoir* (1852)

Francis, George Henry, *Sir Robert Peel as Statesman and Orator* (1846)

Francis, George Henry, *The late Sir Robert Peel, Bart. A Critical Biography. Reprinted, with additions, from Fraser's Magazine* (1852)

Froude, James Anthony, *Thomas Carlyle. A History of His Life in London, 1834–1881*, 2 Volumes (1884)

Gash, Norman, (editor), *The Age of Peel* (1968)

Gaunt, Richard A., (editor), *Unrepentant Tory. Political Selections from the Diaries of the Fourth Duke of Newcastle-under-Lyne, 1827–38* (Woodbridge, 2006)

Gaunt, Richard A., (editor), *'The Last of the Tories'. Political Selections from the Diaries of the Fourth Duke of Newcastle-under-Lyne, 1839–50* (forthcoming)

Girdlestone, Reverend Charles, *Substance of a Speech for the Convocation House, Oxford, 26 February 1829* (Oxford, 1829)

[Glasgow Festival], *Authentic Report of the Glasgow Festival, with biography and essay on Sir Robert Peel's personal and political character*, 5th Edition (1837)

Goffin, Magdalen, (editor), *The Diaries of Absalom Watkin, A Manchester Man, 1787–1861* (Stroud, 1993)

Gore, John, (editor), *The Creevey Papers* (1970)

Graham, Charles Vincent, *Heads or Tails: A Poetical Epistle ... to Sir Robert Peel, on the reappearance of a Whig Administration* (1835)

Grant, James, *Random Recollections of the House of Commons* (1836)

Gregory, Lady, (editor), *Mr Gregory's Letter-Box* (1898)

Gresley, Sir Roger, *A Letter to the Right Honorable Robert Peel on Catholic emancipation. To which is added an account of the apparition of a cross at Migné, on the 17th December 1826*, translated from the Italian (1827)

Greville, Charles Cavendish Fulke, *Sir Robert Peel and the Corn Law Crisis*, 3rd Edition (1846)

Corn and Consistency. A few remarks in reply to a pamphlet entitled, 'Sir Robert Peel and the Corn Law Crisis' (1846)

Guizot, Francois, *Memoirs of Sir Robert Peel* (1857)

Haly, W.T., *The Opinions of Sir R. Peel, expressed in Parliament and in Public*, 2nd Edition (1850)

Harrison, Brian and Patricia Hollis, (editors), *Robert Lowery. Radical and Chartist* (1979)

The Hatherton Diaries. The Diaries of the First Lord Hatherton. Extracts from the personal diary, between the years 1817–1862 of Edward Walhouse Littleton afterwards The First Lord Hatherton, 1791–1863 (Privately printed, n.d.)

Hawkins, Angus and John Powell, (editors), *The Journal of John Wodehouse, First Earl of Kimberley for 1862–1902*, Royal Historical Society, Camden, 5th Series, 9, (1997)

Hibbert, Christopher, *Captain Gronow. His Reminiscences of Regency and Victorian Life, 1810–1860* (1991)

Hibbert, Christopher, *Greville's England. Selections from the Diaries of Charles Greville, 1818–1860* (1981)

Hibbert, Christopher, *Queen Victoria in her Letters and Journals* [1984] (Stroud, 2000)

Historical Manuscripts Commission, *Report on the Manuscripts of Earl Bathurst* (1923)

Historical Manuscripts Commission, *Report on the Manuscripts of J.B. Fortescue Esq., Preserved at Dropmore*, X (1927)

Hodgson, Adam, *A Letter to Sir Robert Peel on the Currency* (Liverpool, 1848)

Howe, Anthony, (editor), *The Letters of Richard Cobden. Volume One, 1815–1847* (Oxford, 2007)

Jackson, Patrick, (editor), *Loulou: Selected Extracts from the Journals of Lewis Harcourt, 1880–1895* (Madison, New Jersey, 2006)

Jaffe, James A., (editor), *'The Affairs of Others': The Diaries of Francis Place, 1825–1836*, Royal Historical Society, Camden, 5th Series, 30, (2007)

Jennings, Louis J., (editor), *The Correspondence and Diaries of the late Right Honorable John Wilson Croker*, 2-Volume Edition (New York, 1884)

Jolliffe, John, (editor), *Neglected Genius. The Diaries of Benjamin Robert Haydon, 1808–1846* (1990)

Jones Parry, E., (editor), *The Correspondence of Lord Aberdeen and Princess Lieven, 1832–1854*, 2 Volumes, Royal Historical Society, Camden, 3rd Series, LX, LXII, (1938–9)

Joplin, Thomas, *An Examination of Sir Robert Peel's Currency Bill of 1844. In a letter to the Bankers of the United Kingdom*, 2nd Edition (1845)

Ker, Ian, *et al* (editors), *The Letters and Diaries of John Henry Newman*, 32 Volumes to date (Oxford, 1961–2008)

Kriegel, A.D., (editor), *The Holland House Diaries, 1831–1840* (1977)

Leckie, William, *A Letter to the Rt. Hon. Sir Robert Peel, Bart., M.P., on the Bank Charter Bill: with a view to its modification or repeal* (1847)

Marrs, Edwin W., (editor), *The Letters of Thomas Carlyle to His Brother Alexander with related family letters* (Cambridge, Massachusetts, 1968)

Martin, Captain Henry, *A Personal Sketch of the late lamented Sir Robert Peel, as a Parliamentary Speaker and Party Leader in the British House of Commons &c* (Hamburg, 1850)

Martin, Sir Theodore, *A Life of Lord Lyndhurst*, 2nd Edition (1884)

Martineau, John, *The Life of Henry Pelham, Fifth Duke of Newcastle, 1811–1864* (1908)

Massey, Benjamin, *The Money Crisis; its Causes, Consequences, and Remedy. In a Letter to the Right Hon. Sir Robert Peel, Bart.* (1847)

Mather, F.C., (editor), *Chartism and Society* (1980)

Melville, Lewis, (editor), *The Huskisson Papers* (1931)

Morley, John, *The Life of Richard Cobden,* 2 Volumes [1881] (1908)

Morris, Christopher, (editor), *William Cobbett's Illustrated Rural Rides 1821–1832* (Waltham Abbey, 1984)

Morrow, John, (editor), *Young England. The New Generation. A Selection of Primary Texts* (Leicester, 1999)

Nattrass, Leonora, (editor), *William Cobbett: Selected Writings,* 6 Volumes (1998)

Nicolson, Reverend William, *A Warning to the Rulers of this Land, specially addressed to the Right Hon. Sir Robert Peel, with reference to the proposed endowment of Popery* (1845)

O'Sullivan, Luke and Catherine Fuller, (editors), *The Correspondence of Jeremy Bentham, Volume 12, July 1824 to June 1828* (Oxford, 2006)

Olney, R.J. and Julia Melvin, (editors), *Prime Ministers Papers: Wellington, Political Correspondence, Volume II: 1834–1835* (1986)

[Oxford By-Election, 1829], *A List of the committee for the re-election of Mr Peel as representative of the University of Oxford; with two circular letters* (1829)

[Oxford By-Election, 1829], *Oratio Demosthenica et Poetica* (1829)

Parker, Charles Stuart, *Sir Robert Peel from his Private Papers,* 3 Volumes (1891–9)

Partridge, Michael and Richard A. Gaunt, (editors), *Lives of Victorian Political Figures I,* 4 Volumes (2006)

Pearce, Edward, (editor), with Deanna Pearce, *The Diaries of Charles Greville* (2005)

Peel, George, (editor), *The Private Letters of Sir Robert Peel* (1920)

Peel, Sir Lawrence, *A Sketch of the Life and Character of Sir Robert Peel* (1860)

Peel, Sir Robert, edited by Lord Mahon and Edward Cardwell, *Memoirs of Sir Robert Peel* [2 Volumes, 1856–7], 1-Volume Edition (New York, 1969)

Peel, Sir Robert, *Speeches delivered in the House of Commons by the late Rt. Hon. Sir Robert Peel,* 4 Volumes [1853], (New York, 1972)

[Peel, Sir Robert], *A very short Letter to the Right Hon. R. Peel [on prices as affected by the bank notes in circulation]* (1819)

[Peel, Sir Robert], *A Letter to the Right Hon. R. Peel on the danger of the Protestant Church of Ireland, from any further concession to the Roman Catholics* (1821)

[Peel, Sir Robert], *A Letter to the Right Hon. R. Peel upon the necessity of adopting some parliamentary measure to control the issues of Country bankers, and to prevent the recurrence of the late shock to public and private credit, with the heads of a bill for that purpose* (1826)

[Peel, Sir Robert], *A Detailed Report of the Public Meeting at Hereford ... May 25, 1827, with the address to Mr Peel, [on his retirement from office,] adopted on the motion of Sir Edwyn Scudamore Stanhope, Bart., Seconded by the Reverend Arthur Matthews, B.D. Prebendary of Hereford* (1827)

[Peel, Sir Robert], *A Letter to the Right Hon. R. Peel, M.P., on the present state of the Catholic Question* (1828)

[Peel, Sir Robert], *A Letter to the Right Hon. Robert Peel on the danger and impolicy of the measures ... proposed to the British Parliament, for the purpose of rendering Roman Catholics eligible to some of the highest offices in the State* (1829)

[Peel, Sir Robert], *An Answer to the arguments of the Right Hon. Robert Peel in favour of further concessions to the Catholics* (1829)

[Peel, Sir Robert], *What can be done? A Letter to Sir Robert Peel on the Reform Question* (1831)

[Peel, Sir Robert], *A Letter to the Rt. Hon. Sir Robert Peel, Bart., M.P., on the present condition and prospects of the Established Church* (1832)

[Peel, Sir Robert], *On Sir Robert Peel's Speech, delivered at a dinner at Merchant Tailor's Hall, Monday, May 11th, 1835* (1835)

[Peel, Sir Robert], *Hints to the Conservatives, in a letter addressed to Sir Robert Peel, Bart., M.P.* (1835)

[Peel, Sir Robert], *A Letter to Sir Robert Peel on the present crisis* (1835)

[Peel, Sir Robert], *A Few Plain Words to Sir Robert Peel* (1836)

[Peel, Sir Robert], *A Letter Addressed to the Right Honorable Sir Robert Peel, Bart., on the Political Aspect of Popery* (1837)

[Peel, Sir Robert], *Peel and the Premier: or, Power without Place, and Place without Power. Russeliana; or, Craft and Corn Laws* (1841)

[Peel, Sir Robert], *Peel, Partridges and Potatoes; or leash, leases and lashes. Dedicated by permission to the Tamworth Farmer's Club* (1843)

[Peel, Sir Robert], *Reflections Suggested by the career of the late Premier* (1847)

[Peel, Sir Robert], *Some of the Difficulties of Ireland, in the way of an improving government, stated, in a letter to Sir R. Peel* (1843)

[Peel, Sir Robert], *Letter to the Right Honourable Sir Robert Peel, Bart., on Free Trade and Finance* (1844)

[Peel, Sir Robert], *Two Letters to Sir Robert Peel, on his proposed Banking measures; by an ex-M.P.* (1844)

[Peel, Sir Robert], *Sir Robert Peel The Greatest Radical of the Age, and the best friend of O'Connell* (1845)

[Peel, Sir Robert], *Suggestions on the Best Modes of Employing the Irish Peasantry, as an anti-famine precaution: a letter to Sir Robert Peel, Bart., By Agricola* (1845)

[Peel, Sir Robert], *Letter to Sir R. Peel on the mode of meeting the present crisis. From M.P., a supporter hitherto of the League* (1846)

[Peel, Sir Robert], *A Letter on the present state of Ireland to ... Sir Robert Peel ... By an Irish Catholic* (1846)

[Peel, Sir Robert], *Physiology of the Peel Party; or an inquiry into the nature of the new neutral policy* (1847)

[Peel, Sir Robert], *The Death of the Right Honourable Sir Robert Peel. A Song* (1850)

Pellew, George, *The Life and Correspondence of the Rt. Hon. Henry Addington, First Viscount Sidmouth,* 3 Volumes (1847)

Pope, Willard Bissell, (editor), *The Diary of Benjamin Robert Haydon,* 5 Volumes (Harvard, 1960–3)

Prior, Sir James, *The Remonstrance of a Tory to the Right Hon. Robert Peel* (1827)

Ramm, Agatha, (editor), *The Gladstone-Granville Correspondence* [2 Volumes, 1952], 1-Volume Edition (Cambridge, 1998)

Reeve, Henry, (editor), *The Greville Memoirs. A Journal of the Reigns of King George IV, King William IV and Queen Victoria,* 8 Volumes (1888)

Rush, Richard, *A Residence at the Court of London* [1833] (1987)

Ryan, John, *Personal Narrative. Sir Robert Peel's claims to the confidence of Protestant Conservatives* (1841)

Sanders, Lloyd C., (editor), *Lord Melbourne's Papers* (1889)

Sanders, Valerie, (editor), *Harriet Martineau. Selected Letters* (Oxford, 1990)

Singh, Bawa Satinder, (editor), *The Letters of the First Viscount Hardinge of Lahore to Lady Hardinge and Sir Walter and Lady James, 1844–1847,* Royal Historical Society, Camden, 4th Series, 32, (1986)

Somerville, Alexander (edited by K.D.M. Snell), *The Whistler at the Plough* [1852] (1969)

Smith, E.A., *Reform or Revolution? A Diary of Reform in England, 1830–32* (Stroud, 1992)

Smith, Goldwin, (edited by Theodore Arnold Haultain), *Reminiscences* (New York, 1910)

St-John Stevas, Norman, (editor), *The Collected Works of Sir Walter Bagehot, Volume III, The Historical Essays* (1968)

Stanhope, Earl of, (editor), *Conversations with Wellington* [1888] (1998)

Stapleton, Augustus Granville, *George Canning and His Times* (1859)

Surtees, Virginia, *A Second Self. The Letters of Harriet Granville, 1810–1845* (Wilton, 1990)

Swartz, Helen M. and Marvin, (editors), *Disraeli's Reminiscences* (1975)

Symons, Jelinger Cookson, *Sir Robert Peel as a type of Statesmanship* (1856)

Tatam, Reverend William Kellock, *A Letter to the Right Hon. Sir Robert Peel, Bart., on the Endowment of the Papacy* [1844] (1894)

Taunton, Edmund, *Gross Injustices, and idolatrous sacrifice of millions to a golden idol! The patent sliding slippery currency scale of 1819. The improved patent doubly slippery in 1844, etc.,* 2nd Edition (Birmingham, 1847)

Taylor, Ernest, *The Taylor Papers. Being a Record of Certain Reminiscences, Letters, and Journals in the Life of Lieut-Gen. Sir Herbert Taylor G.C.B., G.C.H.* (1913)

Taylor, John, *What is a Pound? A letter to the Premier on his new currency measures, in reply to his speech on the Bank Charter Act, May 6, 1844,* 2nd Edition (1844)

Taylor, William Cooke, (edited by Patrick Maume), *Reminiscences of Daniel O'Connell During the Agitations of the Veto, Emancipation and Repeal* [1847], (Dublin, 2005)

Torrens, Robert, *A Letter to the Right Honourable Sir Robert Peel, Bart., M.P., on the condition of England and on the means of removing the causes of distress,* 2nd Edition (1849)

Torrens, Robert, *The Principles and Practical Operation of Sir Robert Peel's Bill of 1844 Explained, and Defended Against the Objections of Tooke, Fullarton, and Wilson* (1848)

Torrens, W.M., *Memoirs of the Right Honourable William Second Viscount Melbourne,* 2 Volumes (1878)

Trevelyan, George Otto, *The Life and Letters of Lord Macaulay* [2 Volumes, 1876], 1-Volume Edition (Oxford, 1978)

Turner, Samuel, *A Letter addressed to the Right Hon. Robert Peel ... with reference to the expediency of the resumption of cash payments at the period fixed by law ...,* 3rd Edition (1819)

Twiss, Horace, (editor), *The Public and Private Life of Lord Chancellor Eldon, with Selections from his Correspondence,* 3 Volumes (1844); 2-Volume Edition (Philadelphia, 1844)

Vincent, John, (editor), *Disraeli, Derby and the Conservative Party: the Political Journals of Lord Stanley, 1849–69* (Hassocks, 1978)

Vyvyan, Sir Richard, *A Letter from Sir Richard Vyvyan to his constituents upon the commercial and financial policy of Sir Robert Peel's Administration* (1842)

Wade, John, (editor), *The Black Book* [1832 Edition], (New York, 1970)

Walpole, Spencer, *The Life of Lord John Russell,* 2 Volumes [1889], (Honolulu, 2005)

Walpole, Spencer, *The Life of the Rt. Hon. Spencer Perceval Including His Correspondence With Numerous Distinguished Persons,* 2 Volumes (1874)

Weigall, Rachel, (editor), *Correspondence of Lord Burghersh afterwards Eleventh Earl of Westmorland, 1808–1840* (1912)

Weigall, Lady Rose, (editor), *Correspondence of Lady Burghersh with the Duke of Wellington* (1903)

Wellington, The Seventh Duke of, (editor), *Wellington and His Friends* (1965)

Westhead, Joshua Proctor Brown, *A Letter to the Rt. Hon. Sir Robert Peel, Bart., on the Corn Laws* (Manchester, 1839)

Whibley, Charles, (editor), *Letters of the King of Hanover to Viscount Strangford, G.C.B.* (1925)

Wiebe, M.G. *et al,* (editors), *Benjamin Disraeli: Letters,* 7 Volumes to date (Toronto, 1982–2004)

Wood, Joseph, *Mr Peel's Measures for Catholic Emancipation considered; in a letter to Lord Milton, M.P.,* (1829)

Wright, I.C., *The Evils of the Currency: An Exposition of Sir Robert Peel's Act of 1844,* 6th Edition (1855)

Yonge, Charles Duke, *The Life and Administration of Robert Banks, Second Earl of Liverpool, K.G.,* 3 Volumes (1868)

Printed Secondary Sources

Adelman, Paul, *Peel and the Conservative Party, 1830–50* (1989)

Arnstein, Walter L., 'Norman Gash: Peelite' in Walter L. Arnstein, (editor), *Recent Historians of Great Britain* (Iowa, 1991), pp.147–72

Aspinall, Arthur, *Lord Brougham and the Whig Party* [1927], (Stroud, 2005)

Aspinall, Arthur, *Politics and the Press, c.1780–1850* (1949)

Aydelotte, William O., 'Constituency Influence on the British House of Commons, 1841–7' in William O. Aydelotte, (editor), *The History of Parliamentary Behavior* (Princeton, 1977), pp.225–46

Aydelotte, William O., 'The Disintegration of the Conservative Party in the 1840s: A Study of Political Attitudes' in William O. Aydelotte, A.G. Bogue and R. Fogel, (editors), *The Dimension of Quantitative Research in History* (Princeton, 1972), pp.319–46

Baker, Kenneth, (editor), *The Faber Book of Conservatism* (1993)

Baker, William J., *Beyond Port and Prejudice. Charles Lloyd of Oxford, 1784–1829* (Maine, 1981)

Bebbington, David, *The Mind of Gladstone: Religion, Homer, and Politics* (Oxford, 2004)

Bentley, Michael, *Politics without Democracy, 1815–1914*, 2nd Edition (1996)

Bentley, Michael, *Lord Salisbury's World. Conservative Environments in Late-Victorian Britain* (Cambridge, 2001)

Bentley, Michael, 'Victorian Prime Ministers: Changing Patterns of Commemoration' in Miles Taylor and Michael Wolff, (editors), *The Victorians since 1901. Histories, Representations and Revisions* (Manchester, 2004), pp.44–58

Blake, Robert, *Disraeli* (1966)

Blake, Robert, *The Conservative Party from Peel to Churchill* (1970)

Blake, Robert, *The Sayings of Disraeli* (1992)

Blake, Robert, (editor), *Oxford Illustrated Encyclopedia. Volume 4. World History From 1800 to the Present Day* (Oxford, 1988)

Boot, H.M., *The Commercial Crisis of 1847* (Hull, 1984)

Brent, Richard, *Liberal Anglican Politics. Whiggery, Religion, and Reform 1830–1841* (Oxford, 1987)

Briggs, Asa, 'Sir Robert Peel' in Herbert Van Thal, (editor), *The Prime Ministers. Volume I. From Sir Robert Walpole to Sir Robert Peel* (1974), pp.371–85

Briggs, Asa, *Victorian Things* (1988)

Brock, Michael, *The Great Reform Act* (1973)

Brock, W.G., *Lord Liverpool and Liberal Toryism, 1820–1827*, 2nd Edition (1967)

Burn, Walter L, *The Age of Equipoise* (1964)

Burns, Arthur, 'English Church Reform Revisited, 1780–1840' in Joanna Innes and Arthur Burns, (editors), *Rethinking the Age of Reform* (Cambridge, 2003), pp.136–62

Clapham, J.H., *The Bank of England. A history, Volume 2: 1797–1914* (Cambridge, 1944)

Clark, Jonathan C.D., *English Society, 1688–1832* (Cambridge, 1985)

Clark, Jonathan C.D., *English Society, 1660–1832* (Cambridge, 2000)

Cocks, H.G., *Nameless Offences. Homosexual Desire in the 19th Century* (2003)

Coleman, Bruce, '1841–6', in Anthony Seldon, (editor), *How Tory Governments Fall: The Tory Party in power since 1783* (1996), pp.104–57

Coleman, Bruce, *Conservatism and the Conservative Party in Nineteenth Century Britain* (1988)

Conacher, J.B., *The Peelites and the Party System, 1846–52* (Newton Abbot, 1972)

Cowie, Leonard, *Sir Robert Peel, 1788–1850. A Bibliography* (Westport, Connecticut, 1996)

Crosby, Travis L., *English Farmers and the Politics of Protection, 1815–1852* (Hassocks, 1977)

Crosby, Travis L., *Sir Robert Peel's Administration, 1841–1846* (Newton Abbot, 1976)

Dalling, Lord and George Bentley, *Sir Robert Peel: An Historical Sketch* (1874)

Darby, Elisabeth and Nicola Smith, *The Cult of the Prince Consort* (New Haven and London, 1983)

Daunton, Martin, *Trusting Leviathan. The Politics of Taxation in Britain, 1799–1914* (Cambridge, 2001)

Davies, G.C.B., *Henry Phillpotts, Bishop of Exeter, 1778–1869* (1954)

Davis, Richard W., *A Political History of the House of Lords, 1811–1846* (Stanford, 2008)

Devereaux, Simon, 'Peel, Pardon and Punishment: The Recorder's Report Revisited' in Simon Devereaux and Paul Griffiths, (editors), *Punishing the English. Penal Practice and Culture, 1500–1900* (2004), pp.258–84

Doubleday, Thomas, *The Political Life of the Right Honourable Sir Robert Peel*, 2 Volumes (1856)

Eastwood, David, *Governing Rural England. Tradition and Transformation in Local Government, 1780–1840* (Oxford, 1994)

Eastwood, David, '"Recasting Our Lot": Peel, the Nation, and the Politics of Interest' in Laurence Brockliss and David Eastwood, (editors), *A Union of Multiple Identities. The British Isles, c.1750–c.1850* (Manchester, 1997), pp.29–43

Erickson, A.B. and W.D. Jones, *The Peelites, 1846–1857* (Ohio, 1972)

Evans, Eric J., *Sir Robert Peel: Statesmanship, Power and Party* (1991)

Foster, Ruscombe, 'Peel and his Party: "The Age of Peel" Reassessed' in Peter Catterall, (editor), *Britain, 1815–1867* (1994), pp.76–82

Gambles, Anna, *Protection and Politics. Conservative Economic Discourse, 1815–1852* (Woodbridge, 1999)

Gash, Norman, *Aristocracy and People. Britain, 1815–1865* (1979)

Gash, Norman, 'From the Origins to Sir Robert Peel' in Lord Butler, (editor), *The Conservatives: A History from their Origins to 1965* (1977), pp.21–108

Gash, Norman, *Mr Secretary Peel: The Life of Sir Robert Peel before 1830*, 2nd Edition (1985)

Gash, Norman, *Peel* (1976)

Gash, Norman, 'Peel and Ireland: A Perennial Problem' in Peter Catterall, (editor), *Britain, 1815–1867* (1994), pp.68–75

Gash, Norman, *Peel and Posterity* (Tamworth, 2000)

Gash, Norman, *Pillars of Government and other essays on state and society, c.1770–c.1880* (1986)

Gash, Norman, *Politics in the Age of Peel*, 2nd Edition (Hassocks, 1977)

Gash, Norman, *Reaction and Reconstruction in English Politics, 1832–1852* (Oxford, 1965)

Gash, Norman, *Sir Robert Peel: The Life of Sir Robert Peel after 1830*, 2nd Edition (1986)

Gash, Norman, *The Historical Significance of the Tamworth Manifesto* (Tamworth, 1984)

Gash, Norman, *The Historical Importance of the Repeal of the Corn Laws* (Tamworth, 1996)

Gash, Norman, 'The Peelites after Peel' in Peter Catterall, (editor), *Britain, 1815–1867* (1994), pp.83–90

Gash, Norman, *The Radical Element in the History of the Conservative Party* (1989)

Gash, Norman, 'Wellington and Peel' in Donald Southgate, (editor), *The Conservative Leadership, 1832–1932* (1974), pp.35–57

Gash, Norman, 'The Duke of Wellington and the Prime Ministership, 1824–30' in Norman Gash, (editor), *Wellington. Studies in the military and political career of the first Duke of Wellington* (Manchester, 1990), pp.117–38

Gaunt, Richard A., 'Gladstone and Peel's Mantle' in Roger Swift and David Bebbington, (editors), *Gladstone Bicentenary Essays* (forthcoming).

Gaunt, Richard A., 'Wellington in petticoats: the duke as caricature' in C.M. Woolgar, (editor), *Wellington Studies IV* (Southampton, 2008), pp.140–72

Gatrell, V.A.C., *The Hanging Tree. Execution and the English People, 1770–1868* (Oxford, 1994)

Geoghegan, Patrick M., *King Dan. The Rise of Daniel O'Connell, 1775–1829* (Dublin, 2008)

Ghosh, Peter, 'Gladstone and Peel' in Peter Ghosh and Lawrence Goldman, (editors), *Politics & Culture in Victorian Britain. Essays in Memory of Colin Matthew* (Oxford, 2006), pp.45–73

Goodlad, Graham, *Peel* (2005)

Gray, Peter, *Famine, Land and Politics: British Government and Irish Society, 1843–50* (2001)

Harling, Philip, *The Waning of 'Old Corruption': The Politics of Economical Reform in Britain, 1779–1846* (Oxford, 1996)

Hawkins, Angus, *The Forgotten Prime Minister, The 14th Earl of Derby, Ascent, 1799–1851* (Oxford, 2007)

Hay, Douglas, *et al.*, *Albion's Fatal Tree: Crime and Society in Eighteenth-Century England* (1975)

Hilton, Boyd, *The Age of Atonement: The Influence of Evangelicalism on social and economic thought, 1795–1865* (Oxford, 1988)

Hilton, Boyd, *Corn, Cash, Commerce: The Economic Policies of the Tory Governments, 1815–1830* (Oxford, 1977)

Hilton, Boyd, 'The Gallows and Mr Peel' in T.C.W. Blanning and David Cannadine, (editors), *History and Biography: Essays in Honour of Derek Beales* (Cambridge, 1996), pp.88–112

Hilton, Boyd, *A Mad, Bad, & Dangerous People? England, 1783–1846* (Oxford, 2006)

Hilton, Boyd, 'Moral Disciplines' in Peter Mandler, (editor), *Liberty and Authority in Victorian Britain* (Oxford, 2006), pp.224–46

Hilton, Boyd, 'The Ripening of Robert Peel' in Michael Bentley, (editor), *Public and Private Doctrine: Essays in British History Presented to Maurice Cowling* (Cambridge, 1993), pp.63–84

Hilton, Boyd, 'Robert Peel' in Robert Eccleshall and Graham Walker, (editors), *Biographical Dictionary of British Prime Ministers* (1998), pp.142–51

Hinde, Wendy, *Catholic Emancipation. A Shake to Men's Minds* (Oxford, 1992)

Howe, Anthony, *Free Trade and Liberal England, 1846–1946* (Oxford, 1997)

Hurd, Douglas, *Robert Peel* (2007)

Jenkins, Brian, 'The Chief Secretary' in D.G. Boyce and Alan O'Day, (editors), *Defenders of the Union. A Survey of British and Irish Unionism since 1801* (2001), pp.39–64

Jenkins, Brian, *Era of Emancipation: British Government of Ireland, 1812–1830* (Kingston and Montreal, 1988)

Jenkins, Roy, *The Chancellors* (1998)

Jenkins, Terence A., *Sir Robert Peel* (1999)

Jephson, Henry, *The Platform. Its Rise and Progress,* 2 Volumes [1892], (New York, 1968)

Jones, Gareth Stedman, 'Rethinking Chartism' in his *Languages of Class: Studies in English Working Class History, 1832–1982* (Oxford, 1983), pp.90–178

Kerr, Donal A., *Peel, Priests and Politics, Sir Robert Peel's Administration and the Roman Catholic Church in Ireland, 1841–1846* (Oxford, 1982)

King, Peter, *Crime, Justice and Discretion in England, 1740–1820* (Oxford, 2000)

Kitson Clark, George, *The Life and Work of Sir Robert Peel* (1950)

Kitson Clark, George, *Peel* (1936)

Kitson Clark, George, *Peel and the Conservative Party, 1832–1841: A Study in Party Politics,* 2nd Edition (1964)

Kitson Clark, George, *The Making of Victorian England* (1962)

Knatchbull-Hugessen, Hughe, *Kentish Family* (1960)

Large, David, 'The House of Lords and Ireland in the Age of Peel, c.1832–50' in Clyve Jones and David Lewis Jones, (editors), *Peers, Politics and Power* (1986), pp.373–405

Lee, Stephen M., *George Canning and Liberal Toryism, 1801–1827* (Woodbridge, 2008)

Lee, Stephen M., 'Palmerston and Canning' in David Brown and Miles Taylor, (editors), *Palmerston Studies I* (Southampton, 2007), pp.1–18

Lever, Sir Tresham, *The Life and Times of Sir Robert Peel* (1942)

Lobban, Michael, 'Old Wine in New Bottles: The Concept and Practice of Law Reform, 1780–1830' in Joanna Innes and Arthur Burns, (editors), *Rethinking the Age of Reform* (Cambridge, 2003), pp.114–35

Machin, G.I.T., *The Catholic Question in English Politics, 1820–1830* (Oxford, 1964)

MacDonagh, Oliver, *O'Connell. The Life of Daniel O'Connell, 1775–1847*, 1-Volume Edition (1991)

Mandler, Peter, *Aristocratic Government in the Age of Reform. Whigs and Liberals, 1830–1852*

Mather, F.C., '"Nestor or Achilles?", The Duke of Wellington in British Politics, 1832–1846' in Norman Gash, (editor), *Wellington: Studies in the military and political career of the First Duke of Wellington* (Manchester, 1990), pp.170–95

Matthew, H.C.G. and Brian Harrison, (editors), *The Oxford Dictionary of National Biography*, 60 Volumes (Oxford, 2004)

McCarthy, Justin, *Sir Robert Peel* (New York, 1891)

Michie, Ranald C., (editor), *The development of London as a financial centre, Volume 1: 1700–1850* (1998)

Molyneux, Catherine, 'Reform as Process: The Parliamentary Fate of the Bank Charter Act of 1844' in Michael Turner, (editor), *Reform and Reformers in Nineteenth Century Britain* (Sunderland, 2004), pp.63–80

Moran, Richard, *Knowing Right From Wrong. The Insanity Defense of Daniel McNaughtan* (New York, 1981)

Newbould, I.D.C., *Whiggery and Reform, 1830–41: The Politics of Government* (1990)

Noyce, Karen A., 'The Duke of Wellington and the Catholic Question' in Norman Gash, (editor), *Wellington: Studies in the military and political career of the First Duke of Wellington* (Manchester, 1990), pp.139–58

O'Ferrall, Fergus, *Catholic Emancipation. Daniel O'Connell and the Birth of Irish Democracy, 1820–1830* (Dublin, 1985)

Office of 'The Times', *History of 'The Times': Volume I: 'The Thunderer' in the Making, 1785–1841* (1935)

Oman, Carola, *The Gascoyne heiress: the life and diaries of Frances Mary Gascoyne-Cecil, 1802–39* (1968)

Palmer, Stanley H., *Police and Protest in England and Ireland, 1780–1850* (Cambridge, 1988)

Parry, Jonathan, *The Age of Peel* (1996)

Parry, Jonathan, 'Lord John Russell, First Earl Russell' in Robert Eccleshall and Graham Walker, (editors), *Biographical Dictionary of British Prime Ministers* (1998), pp.151–61

Parry, Jonathan, 'Past and future in the later career of Lord John Russell' in T.C.W. Blanning and David Cannadine, (editors), *History and Biography: Essays in Honour of Derek Beales* (Cambridge, 1996), pp.142–72

Parry, Jonathan, *The Rise and Fall of Liberal Government in Victorian Britain* (New Haven, 1993)

Prest, John, *Politics in the Age of Cobden* (1977)

Power, Edward G., *Robert Peel, Free Trade and the Corn Laws* (1975)

Radzinowicz, Leon, *A History of English Criminal Law and its Administration from 1750*, 3 Volumes (1948)

Ramsden, John, *An Appetite for Power. A History of the Conservative Party since 1830* (1998)

Read, Donald, *Peel and the Victorians* (Oxford, 1987)

Read, Donald, *Peterloo. The Massacre and its Background* (Manchester, 1958)

Reynolds, David, *In Command of History. Churchill Fighting and Writing the Second World War* (2004)

Reynolds, Elaine, *Before the Bobbies: The Night Watch and Police Reform in Metropolitan London, 1720–1830* (Houndmills, 1998)

Richmond, Charles and Paul Smith, (editors), *The Self-Fashioning of Disraeli, 1818–1851* (Cambridge, 1998)

Rogers, Jean Scott, *Cobden and his Kate, the story of a marriage* (1990)

Rubinstein, William D., *Who Were the Rich? A biographical directory of British wealth-holders. Volume One, 1809–1839* (2009)

Salter, Richard, *Peel, Gladstone and Disraeli* (1991)

Salmon, Philip, *Electoral Reform at Work. Local Politics and National Parties, 1832–1841* (Woodbridge, 2002)

Scherer, Paul, *Lord John Russell* (1999)

Schofield, Philip, *Utility & Democracy. The Political Thought of Jeremy Bentham* (Oxford, 2006)

Searle, Geoffrey R., *Entrepreneurial Politics in Mid-Victorian Britain* (Oxford, 1993)

Shipkey, Robert Carl, *Robert Peel's Irish Policy: 1812–1846* [1962] (1987)

Sinnema, Peter W., *The Wake of Wellington: Englishness in 1852*, (Ohio, 2006)
Smart, William, *Economic Annals of the Nineteenth Century*, 2 Volumes [1915], (New York, 1964)
Smith, E.A., *A Queen on Trial: The Affair of Queen Caroline* (Stroud, 1993)
Stephen, Leslie and Sidney Lee, (editors), *The Dictionary of National Biography*, 63 Volumes (1885–1901)
Stewart, Robert, *The Foundation of the Conservative Party, 1830–1867* (1978)
Stewart, Robert, *The Politics of Protection: Lord Derby and the Protectionist Party, 1841–1852* (Cambridge, 1971)
Taylor, A.J.P., (edited by Chris Wrigley), *From Napoleon to the Second International: Essays on Nineteenth-Century Europe* (1993)
Thatcher, Margaret, *The Downing Street Years* (1993)
Thomas, William, *The Quarrel of Macaulay and Croker. Politics and History in the Age of Reform* (Oxford, 2000)
Thompson, Neville, *Wellington after Waterloo* (1986)
Thorne, Roland G., (editor), *The History of Parliament. The Commons, 1790–1820*, 5 Volumes (1986)
Thursfield, J.R., *Peel* (1891)
Ward, J.T., 'Derby and Disraeli' in Donald Southgate, (editor), *The Conservative Leadership, 1832–1932* (1974), pp.58–100
Wheeler, Michael, *The Old Enemies. Catholic and Protestant in Nineteenth-Century English Culture* (Cambridge, 2006)
Wilson, Harold, *A Prime Minister on Prime Ministers* (1977)
Woodward, Sir Llewellyn, *The Age of Reform, 1815–1870*, 2nd Edition (Oxford, 1962)
Wolffe, John, *Great Deaths. Grieving, Religion, and Nationhood in Victorian and Edwardian Britain* (Oxford, 2000).
Wolffe, John, *The Protestant Crusade in Great Britain, 1829–60* (Oxford, 1991)
Wyke, Terry, with Harry Cocks, *Public Sculpture of Greater Manchester* (Liverpool, 2004)

Journal Articles
Aspinall, Arthur, 'Canning's return to office in September 1822', *English Historical Review*, LXXVIII, 1963, 531–45
Aydelotte, William O., 'Parties and Issues in Early Victorian England', *Journal of British Studies*, V, 1966, 95–114
Aydelotte, William O., 'The Country Gentlemen and the Repeal of the Corn Laws', *English Historical Review*, LXXXII, 1967, 47–60
Aydelotte, William O., 'Voting Patterns in the British House of Commons in the 1840s', *Comparative Studies in Society and History*, 5, 1963, 134–63
Beales, Derek, 'Peel, Russell and Reform', *Historical Journal*, XVII, 1974, 873–82
Bradfield, B.T., 'Sir Richard Vyvyan and the Country Gentlemen, 1830–34', *English Historical Review*, LXXXIII, 1968, 729–43
Bradfield, B.T., 'Sir Richard Vyvyan and the fall of Wellington's Government', *University of Birmingham Historical Journal*, XI, 1968, 141–56
Briggs, Asa, 'Sir Robert Peel, 1788–1850. A Statesman Much-Attacked but More-Admired', *The Historian*, 17, 1987/8, 3–6
Broeker, Galen, 'Robert Peel and the Peace Preservation Force', *Journal of Modern History*, 33, 1961, 363–73
Brown, Desmond H., 'Abortive attempts to codify English criminal law', *Parliamentary History*, 11, 1992, 1–39
Brundage, Anthony, 'Ministers, Magistrates and Reformers: The Genesis of the Rural Constabulary Act of 1839', *Parliamentary History*, 5, 1986, 55–64
Cameron, R.H., 'Parties and Policies in Early Victorian Britain: A Suggestion for Revision', *Canadian Journal of History*, 13, 1979, 375–93

Cameron, R.H., 'The Melbourne Administration, the Liberals and the Crisis of 1841', *Durham University Journal,* 38, 1976, 83–102

Ceallaigh, Tadhg Ó., 'Peel and Police Reform in Ireland, 1814–1818', *Studia Hibernica,* 6, 1966, 25–48

Close, David, 'The Formation of a two-party alignment in the House of Commons between 1832 and 1841', *English Historical Review,* LXXXIV, 1969, 257–77

Close, David, 'The Rise of the Conservatives in the Age of Reform', *Bulletin of the Institute of Historical Research,* XLV, 1972, 89–103

Conacher, J.B., 'The Peelites and Peel, 1846–50', *English Historical Review,* LXXIII, 1958, 431–52

Crook, J. Mordaunt, 'Sir Robert Peel. Patron of the Arts', *History Today,* 16, January 1966, 3–11

Davis, Richard W., 'From Toryism to Tamworth: The Triumph of Reform, 1827–1835', *Albion,* 12, 1980, 132–46

Dickson, Tony and Clarke, Tony, 'Social concern and social control in nineteenth-century Scotland: Paisley, 1841–1843', *Scottish Historical Review,* LXV, 1986, 48–60

Dreyer, F.A., 'The Whigs and the Political Crisis of 1845', *English Historical Review,* LXXX, 1965, 514–37

Eastwood, David, 'Peel and the Tory Party Reconsidered', *History Today,* 42, March 1992, 27–33

Eastwood, David, 'The Corn laws and their Repeal 1815–1846. Realities behind the Myths', *History Review,* 25, 1996, 6–10

Evans, Eric, 'Sir Robert Peel: A Suitable Case for Reassessment?', *History Review,* 18, 1994, 25–30

Evans, Stephen, 'Thatcher and the Victorians: A Suitable Case for Comparison?', *History,* 82, 1997, 601–20

Fairlie, Susan, 'The Nineteenth-Century Corn Law Reconsidered', *Economic History Review,* 18, 1965, 562–75

Fisher, D.R., 'Peel and the Conservative Party: The Sugar Crisis of 1844 Reconsidered', *Historical Journal,* XVIII, 1975, 279–302

Gambles, Anna, 'Rethinking the Politics of Protection: Conservatism and the Corn Laws, 1830–1852', *English Historical Review,* CXIII, 1998, 928–52

Gash, Norman, 'Peel and the Party System, 1830–1850', *Transactions of the Royal Historical Society,* 5th series, 1, 1951, 47–69

Gash, Norman, 'The Organization of the Conservative Party, 1832–1846, Part I: The Parliamentary Organization', *Parliamentary History,* 1, 1982, 137–59

Gash, Norman, 'The Organization of the Conservative Party, 1832–1846, Part II: The Electoral Organization', *Parliamentary History,* 2, 1983, 131–52

Gaunt, Richard A., 'The Fourth Duke of Newcastle, the Ultra Tories and the Opposition to Canning's Administration', *History,* 88, 2003, 568–86

Gaunt, Richard A., 'Disraeli, Peel and the Corn Laws: the making of a conservative reputation', *The Historian,* 97, 2008, 30–33

Harris, Wendell V., 'Newman, Peel, Tamworth, and the Concurrence of Historical Forces', *Victorian Studies,* 32 (1989), 189–208

Hawkins, Angus, '"Parliamentary Government" and Victorian Political Parties, c.1830–1880', *English Historical Review,* CIV, 1989, 638–69

Herrmann, Frank, 'Peel and Solly. Two nineteenth-century art collectors and their sources of supply', *Journal of the History of Collections,* 3/1, 1991, 89–96

Hilton, Boyd, 'Peel: A Reappraisal', *Historical Journal,* XXII, 1979, 585–614

Hilton, Boyd, 'Peel, Potatoes, and Providence', *Political Studies,* 49, 2001, 106–9

Hilton, Boyd, 'The Political Arts of Lord Liverpool', *Transactions of the Royal Historical Society,* 5th Series, 38, 1988, 147–70

Hoppen, K. Theodore, 'An Incorporating Union? British Politicians and Ireland 1800–1830', *English Historical Review,* CXXIII, April 2008, 328–50

Hurd, Douglas, 'Sir Robert Peel. The Making of a Party', *History Today,* 57, July 2007, 11–17

Jaggard, Edwin, 'The 1841 British General Election: A Reconsideration', *Australian Journal of Politics and History,* 30, 1984, 99–114

Kemp, Betty, 'Reflections on the Repeal of the Corn Laws', *Victorian Studies,* VI, 1962, 189–204

Kemp, Betty, 'The General Election of 1841', *History,* XXXVII, 1952, 146–57

Kerr, Donal, 'Peel and the Political Involvement of the Priests', *Archivium Hibernicum,* 36, 1981, 16–25

Kitson Clark, George, 'Hunger and Politics in 1842', *Journal of Modern History,* 25, 1953, 355–74

Kitson Clark, George, 'The Electorate and the Repeal of the Corn Laws', *Transactions of the Royal Historical Society,* 5th Series, 1, 1951, 109–26

Kitson Clark, George, 'The Repeal of the Corn Laws and the Politics of the Forties', *Economic History Review,* 2nd Series, IV, 1951, 1–13

Ledger-Lomas, Michael, 'The Character of Pitt the Younger and Party Politics, 1830–1860', *Historical Journal,* 47, 2004, 641–61

Lipscomb, Patrick C., 'Party Politics, 1801–1802: George Canning and the Trinidad Question', *Historical Journal,* 12, 1969, 442–66

Machin, G.I.T., 'The Catholic Emancipation Crisis of 1825', *English Historical Review,* LXXVIII, 1963, 458–82

MacIntyre, Angus, 'Lord George Bentinck and the Protectionists: A lost cause?', *Transactions of the Royal Historical Society,* 5th Series, 39, 1989, 141–65

Mather, F.C., 'Wellington and Peel: Conservative Statesmen of the 1830s', *Transactions of the Peel Society,* 5, 1985/6, 7–23

McGowen, Randall, 'The image of justice and reform of the criminal law in early nineteenth-century England', *Buffalo Law Review,* 32, 1983, 89–125

Moore, D.C., 'The Corn Laws and High Farming', *Economic History Review,* 2nd series, XVIII, 1965, 544–61

Morrow, John, 'The Paradox of Peel as Carlylean Hero', *Historical Journal,* 40, 1997, 97–110

Newbould, Ian D.C., 'Sir Robert Peel and the Conservative Party, 1832–1841: A study in failure?', *English Historical Review,* XCVIII, 1983, 529–57

Newbould, Ian D.C., 'The Emergence of a Two-Party System in England from 1830 to 1841: Roll call and Reconsideration', *Parliaments, Estates and Representation,* 5, 1985, 25–31

Newbould, Ian D.C., 'William IV and the Dismissal of the Whigs, 1834', *Canadian Journal of History,* XI, 1976, 311–30

Newton, Lucy A. and Philip L. Cottrell, 'Joint-stock banking in the English provinces, 1826–1857: to branch or not to branch?', *Business and Economic History,* 27/1 (1998), 115–28

O'Brien, Gerard, 'Robert Peel and the Pursuit of Catholic Emancipation, 1813–1817', *Archivium Hibernicum,* 43, 1988, 135–41

Paley, Ruth, '"An Imperfect, Inadequate & Wretched System?" Policing London before Peel', *Criminal Justice History,* X, 1989, 95–130

Phillips, John and Charles Wetherell, 'The Great Reform Act of 1832 and the political modernization of England', *American Historical Review,* C, 1995, 411–36

Prest, John, 'A Large amount or a Small? Revenue and the Nineteenth-Century Corn Laws', *Historical Journal,* XXXIX, 1996, 467–78

Rashid, Salim, 'Edward Copleston, Robert Peel, and cash payments', *History of Political Economy,* 15, 1983, 249–59.

Riley, Geoffrey G., 'Peel and the Bank Act, 1844', *Institute Bankers Journal,* February 1963, 79–86

Rosebery, Lord, 'Sir Robert Peel', *Anglo-Saxon Review*, I, 1899, 97–123

Seigel, Jules, 'Carlyle and Peel: The prophet's search for a heroic politician and an unpublished fragment', *Victorian Studies*, 26, 1983, 181–95

Shannon, Richard, 'Peel, Gladstone and Party', *Parliamentary History*, 18, 1999, 317–52

Shipkey, Robert, 'Problems of Irish Patronage during the Chief Secretaryship of Robert Peel, 1812–1818', *Historical Journal*, X, 1967, 41–56

Smith, K.J.M., 'Anthony Hammond: "Mr Surface" Peel's Persistent Codifier', *Journal of Legal History*, 20, 1999, 24–44

Spring, David, 'Lord Chandos and the Farmers, 1818–1846', *Huntingdon Library Quarterly*, XXXIII, 1969–70, 257–81

Spring, David and Travis L. Crosby, 'George Webb Hall and the Agricultural Association', *Journal of British Studies*, II, 1962, 115–31

Stafford, Melanie, 'Peel's Statue in Leeds – a first for town and country', *Leeds Art Calendar*, 90, 1982, 4–11

Stewart, Robert, 'The Ten Hours and Sugar Crises of 1844: Government and the House of Commons in the Age of Reform', *Historical Journal*, XII, 1969, 35–57

Walker, R., 'Sir Robert Peel, Patron of the Arts', *Apollo*, 52, 1950, 16–18

Welch, P.J., 'Blomfield and Peel: a Study in Co-operation between Church and State, 1841–46', *Journal of Ecclesiastical History*, 12, 1961, 71–84

Unpublished Dissertations and Theses

Fisher, D.R., *The Opposition to Sir Robert Peel in the Conservative Party, 1841–1846* (PhD Thesis, University of Cambridge, 1970)

Gaunt, R.A., *The Political Activities and Opinions of the Fourth Duke of Newcastle (1785–1851)* (PhD Thesis, University of Nottingham, 2000)

Mullen, R.F., *The House of Lords and the Repeal of the Corn Laws* (DPhil. Thesis, University of Oxford, 1974)

Simes, D.G.S., *The Ultra Tories in British Politics, 1824–1834* (DPhil. Thesis, University of Oxford, 1974)

Sweeney, J.M., *The House of Lords in British Politics, 1830–1841* (DPhil. Thesis, University of Oxford, 1973)

INDEX